CHURCHILL DOWNS
100th
KENTUCKY DERBY

·

First Centennial

·

Compiled under the Auspices
of
Churchill Downs

1875 – 1974

Edited By Bob Gorham

CONTENTS

FOREWORD

The Board of Directors of Churchill Downs determined it would be in the public interest to compile and publish a book containing information about each of the past winners of the Kentucky Derby.

This book is the result of that project and is presented as part of the One Hundredth Anniversary running of the Derby in 1974.

Churchill Downs is indebted to the Sponsors who have so graciously contributed to this project, and is pleased to provide this acknowledgment of these contributions.

The Sponsors' concern for the public interest is sincerely appreciated.

In addition to the records, statistics, and general information about the Derby, we have attempted to provide an interesting and informative book for the enjoyment of everyone.

Every effort was made to present a written and pictorial review of this great event that will do justice to the people and horses that make the Kentucky Derby the "Greatest Two Minutes in Sports".

LYNN STONE
President, CHURCHILL DOWNS

History of Churchill Downs

Of necessity, history recites facts and facts tend to be cold. They are informing but not necessarily exciting.

For instance, the fact the first Kentucky Derby was run on May 17, 1875 is well known. But how do you capture the excitement of that moment when the dreams and planning of Col. M. Lewis Clark came to fruition before a crowd of 10,000?

Do you believe Col. Clark could envision the race lasting without interruption to this time when we are celebrating its centennial?

Racing was at a low ebb in Kentucky, and in fact in America, when Clark organized the Louisville Jockey Club in June, 1874. There were only a half dozen tracks of any consequence in the country—Monmouth, Jerome and Saratoga in the East and North, and New Orleans, Nashville and Lexington in the South. Kentucky breeders were seriously considering closing their stock farms because yearlings were selling for a mere hundred dollars or so.

It was necessary to create a demand for the thoroughbred and the formation of a Jockey Club was thought to be the remedy. With it would come the establishment of a system of stakes that would demonstrate the superiority of certain classes and ages and by reason of the value of such stakes, create a demand for the race horse.

The land on which the Jockey Club was located was secured from John and Henry Churchill. John Churchill owned a few thoroughbreds, but the Churchill family as such was not a racing family although John Churchill became treasurer of the Jockey Club in 1878.

John Churchill was the great-great-great grandfather of both Warner Jones and Thruston Morton. Jones, a widely known breeder, has been on Churchill Downs' board of directors since 1941 and Morton, a former senator from Kentucky, now is chairman of the board.

In 1894, the Louisville Jockey Club, although solvent at the time, made an assignment so the property could be legally conveyed to a new organization, incorporated as the New Louisville Jockey Club.

Col. Clark no longer was president, but continued as presiding judge. Nearly $100,000 was spent for improvements—a new twin-spired grandstand, betting shed, paddock and stables—and the entire layout of the plant was changed.

All the old stakes were remodeled and the Derby distance was reduced from a mile and a half to a mile and a quarter.

Col. Clark had visited Europe in 1872 to study the systems of stakes, the rules for racing and other facets of the sport. He was the guest of Admiral Rous, the Nestor of English racing and the "Father of Handicappers".

Originally, Clark set up the Kentucky Derby as the great event for three-year-olds at one mile and a half. The Kentucky Oaks for fillies only was set at a mile and a quarter. The Clark Stakes, run a week later than the Derby, was to accentuate the Derby form of the three-year-olds at a distance of two miles.

The St. Leger, run in the fall, also was for three-year-olds at two miles and designed to enhance the prestige of the winner of the Derby or Clark Stakes or both . . . or some other horse, could he beat them.

The Derby was an important race from its inception and the May 22 Spirit of the Times of 1875 reported it as a race "which has created deep interest throughout the country".

It is difficult trying to imagine what was in Clark's mind on April 22, 1899 when he shot himself in Nashville, Tennessee. That was just twelve days before the 25th anniversary of the Derby. Supposedly, he was despondent over poor health and financial reverses.

In any case, the next three years were difficult ones for the track, now called Churchill Downs because an unidentified newspaperman so dubbed it.

It was at this time that a rather amazing transformation began. A Louisville tailor named Matt Winn was convinced to give up his shop and take over the running of a race track. Quite a change, even though Winn was familiar with the Downs and the Derby. After all, he had seen every Derby, the first at age 13 from his father's wagon in the infield.

How did a tailor run a race track? Quite successfully, thank you.

When Winn was 80 in 1941, Damon Runyon wrote of him:

"The State of Kentucky and the City of Louisville each owes Colonel Matt J. Winn a monument, the former for the fame he has added to its fair name, the latter for both the renown and the millions of dollars he has brought to the community.

"The Sport of Kings—horse racing—owes him still another monument for contributing its greatest and most spectacular event, and for his untiring efforts down through the years to preserve and enhance the stability and honor of the game. . .

"But I suppose we can just let the Kentucky Derby stand as the living symbol of Colonel Winn and his works. No man could want more. . ."

There have been other presidents of Churchill Downs but none with the flair for promotion that Winn exhibited in making the Derby the No. 1 race in the world. He became a giant in racing circles with affiliations throughout the country, but his heart was with the Derby.

The Derby has survived for 100 runnings but not without its problems.

In 1886, bookmakers did not operate at the track because of failure to reach a license agreement with management.

In 1892 and 1905, only three horses went to the post.

In 1929, 1.19 inches of rain fell to make this the wettest Derby of all time.

In 1932, the field of 20 milled around the starting gate for 15½ minutes before the start. A horse called Tick On, the favorite, which finished sixth, created most of the disturbance which caused the delay.

It was in 1932 also that more than 5,000 fans crashed over a backside fence and poured into the centerfield. Police tried to stop the surge at the start, but then stood helplessly by.

In 1945, it appeared that the uninterrupted runnings of the Derby would halt. War-time restrictions banned all racing on January 3, but on May 8 after VE day, racing was resumed and the Derby was run on June 9.

In 1965, fire broke out in the clubhouse near the first turn. Fans refused to leave their seats, however, and there was little damage—more smoke than fire— as a national television audience watched.

In 1967, a civil disturbance Derby week during which teenagers ran across the track in front of horses brought headaches to the track management.

In 1968, the purse was taken from the first place finisher, Dancer's Image, because post-race testing revealed an illegal medication.

But the Derby has survived—and grown!

Daniel E. O'Sullivan, a newspaper man who became resident manager of the Downs, wrote the following in 1924 just before Black Gold won the 50th Derby:

"The golden anniversary of Churchill Downs! Sacred and priceless its memories; beyond all price its half century of high ideals and honorable endeavor! What thoughts of departed friends, and old favorites stir the heart and throng the portals of the mind eager for utterance! Aristides, Vagrant, Baden-Baden, Day Star, Lord Murphy, Fonso, Ben Brush, Old Rosebud, and their fellows, all under the turf which they do so much to ennoble.

"Gone are the countless gay companies where youth and beauty and high estate made the vanished days resplendent. Gone beyond recall are those who lived the historic scenes we now celebrate: M. Lewis Clark, the fearless, peerless Judge; Frank Harper, the quaint owner of Ten Broeck; Gen. Abe Buford, who confidently expected to meet his thoroughbreds on the bluegrass fields of the new Jerusalem; the Churchills, the Clays, the Breckinridges, the Blackburns, the Johnsons, Grinstead, Ten Broeck, Woodford, and the lamented Charles F. Grainger, all gone out into the shadows.

But their spirits revisit the Downs, keep green its fields and bright its paths, hover above it in kindly council, inspire its managers and pass judgment on their decisions.

"The month of May, caparisoned in her garments of gladness, violets blooming where she walks, always claims Derby Day as her own. It is a name to conjure with, at once an inspiration and a delight. The bluegrass curtsies a welcome. An infinite, cloudless sky spreads the benison of its silken tent over the scene. The brown ribbon of the course is unfolded as from a golden reel. Thoroughbreds pick their way daintily across the field, or arch their prideful necks in preliminary gallops. Myriads of American flags swim in the sun-kissed air. Glad thousands occupy every coign of vantage, their faces radiant with joy and their hearts free from care. The stands are vibrant with unconcealed emotion. The air is electrical with expectation. A carnival spirit is everywhere. It is Kentucky's annual tribute to the Thoroughbred, in which all America joins."

O'Sullivan listed the greats of the first half century. For the second half could be added the names of such as Gallant Fox, War Admiral, Whirlaway, Citation, Tim Tam, Northern Dancer, Secretariat, Calumet Farm, Ben Jones, A. B. Hancock, Jr., Horatio Luro, Wathen Knebelkamp and many others.

It was under the regime of Knebelkamp, who took over as president in 1960, that the track made its biggest physical improvements.

Knebelkamp hired Lynn Stone, a former baseball executive, to be his resident manager. Together they fashioned a building program which cost nearly $5,000,000 in the next ten years. Included was the present Fourth Floor Skye Terrace, or "Millionaires Row"; a new press box; a new jockey quarters; hundreds of thousands of dollars in new restroom facilities; vast improvements in the barn area; the Kentucky Derby Museum, and a multitude of other improvements.

Stone succeeded Knebelkamp as president in 1970. He has more than carried on the Winn tradition of promotion and the improvements started by Knebelkamp.

Under Stone's regime, the Derby has set betting and attendance records each of his three years and the 1973 Derby marked the first time more than $3,000,000 had been bet on a single race—$3,284,962.

Everything about the Kentucky Derby is magnified —the good and the bad. The tiniest hair out of place on one of the contestants is cause for columns of newspaper copy. It takes a staff of more than 10,000 people to service the crowds of more than 130,000 who now annually throng this historic site the first Saturday of May.

God bless them all. It has been a great century.

JOE HIRSCH

JOE HIRSCH, *a columnist and member of the Editorial Board of Daily Racing Form, has been with that paper for 25 years. For the past 17 years, he's specialized in detailed coverage of the Triple Crown races, with particular emphasis on the Kentucky Derby through his Derby Doings, a daily account of pre-Derby activity during the month preceding the Run for the Roses. He was elected first President of the National Turf Writers Association upon its founding in 1959 and has been active in the affairs of that organization ever since.*

Outstanding Training Achievements

He came out of Argentina: a tall, stately man with a deft turn of phrase and a keen knowledge of the thoroughbred and his ways. His horse came out of Canada: an engaging, little bay son of Nearctic with four white stockings, muscles in his forearms and gaskins, and the determination of a bulldog. Together they made history at Churchill Downs in the spring of 1964, Horatio Luro and his fleet Northern Dancer, owned by E. P. Taylor.

To achieve the pinnacle in any field of human endeavor is a difficult task, and winning a Kentucky Derby is the premier accomplishment for any trainer in the United States. In that sense, every man who has trained a winner of the Run for the Roses has performed an outstanding feat, from Andy Anderson, who saddled Henry Price McGrath's Aristides to win the inaugural Derby on May 17, 1875, to Lucien Laurin, who sent out Meadow Stable's Secretariat to win the 99th Derby so sensationally on May 5, 1973.

Yet some training achievements leading to victory in America's greatest horse race are justifiably more celebrated than others. A man who starts with the best horse and brings him up to the Derby in the peak of form has done a fine job. But can his work compare to that of a man who wins the Derby with a horse who is not best, or one whose horse is at a disadvantage because of injury or physical handicap or disposition or pedigree or conformation?

For these reasons, and others, Max Hirsch's feat of bringing off the 1946 Kentucky Derby with King Ranch's club-footed Assault has long enjoyed the critical acclaim of his colleagues. No man worked more patiently with a difficut horse than Ben Jones did with the talented, willful Whirlaway. The Missourian spent hours and days and weeks and months under a hot sun, coaching and equipping Mr. Longtail to run straight and true. The result was a brilliant Derby performance, an eight-length victory and a new track record.

So many others merit salutes. Guy Bedwell, winning the 1919 Derby with a maiden, J.K.L. Ross' Sir Barton; Roy Waldron, preparing the 35-1 Gallahadion so skillfully to upset Bimelech and others in a fine field that contested the 1940 Derby; Jimmy Jones' deft hand with the moody Iron Liege to beat perhaps the finest Derby field of all in 1957; Jimmy Conway's careful handling of Chateaugay that led the Darby Dan colt to victory in 1963.

No man ever had a horse looking in more resplendent condition for a Kentucky Derby than Johnny Longden, who polished Majestic Prince like some rare jewel, prior to the 1969 running which he won from as fine a competitor as Arts and Letters. And no man ever brought a horse to a Derby under more personal pressure than Lucien Laurin with the $6,080,000 Secretariat last spring. His carefully planned campaign foreshortened by syndication developments, his every move closely scrutinized by the national media, Laurin had to work quickly and with a flair for improvisation in order for Secretariat to be so right he set a record of 1:59⅖ that may stand for decades.

But in a century of Derby it is questionable if any trainer contributed more of himself to victory in the Run for the Roses than Senor Luro did in Northern Dancer's year.

As Northern Dancer turned 3 he developed a quarter-crack that would have kept the average horse sidelined for several months, and in most cases forcing him to miss the Derby altogether. Luro, however, brought blacksmith Bill Bane from California to Florida to patch the colt's foot with Bane's unique process.

Then there was the matter of developing Northern Dancer to stay a distance. He was a horse of brilliant speed, and in another man's hands might have become one of the outstanding milers of our time. But Luro, early on, realized the tremendous depth of class in this agile, combative colt and called upon all the experience at his command, plus a great respect for the classics, in an attempt to harness Northern Dancer's zip.

Morning and afternoon, Luro spent hours with this little (15.2 hands) horse that had so caught his fancy. The turning point was a work at Keeneland, shortly before the Blue Grass Stakes. With Bill Hartack in the saddle, Northern Dancer went his first half-mile in :50, and that told Luro he would rate. That was what he wanted to know.

Hill Rise might have been best in that 1964 Derby. Certainly he was the favorite, at 7-5, and Bill Shoemaker had taken off Northern Dancer to ride him. But Luro enjoyed Hartack's confidence and the greatest Derby rider of them all turned in another superb performance to assist Northern Dancer in beating Hill Rise by a neck. The day, however, and the horse were Luro's handiwork, the craftsmanship of a consummate artist. This was the brightest hour on the Downs in 100 years of training for a Kentucky Derby.

FRED RUSSELL, *vice president and sports director of the Nashville Banner, has covered 40 consecutive Kentucky Derbies. Three books of sports humor by Russell were followed in 1957 by his semi-autobiographical "Bury Me In An Old Press Box." Russell from 1949 through 1962 wrote the annual "Pigskin Preview" for The Saturday Evening Post. He is chairman of the Honors Court of the National Football Hall of Fame and was winner of the first Grantland Rice Memorial Award by the Sportsmanship Brotherhood.*

FRED RUSSELL

No Dream Is Impossible

Those magic moments of the Kentucky Derby, glorious spectacle that is our country's oldest continuous sporting event, and perhaps the brightest, belong to the world. It's the race almost everyone in thoroughbred racing and breeding most wants to win.

Yet 76 of these 99 Derbies have been won by Kentucky-breds. Up to 1956, the record was 66 out of 81, the other 15 being from Tennessee (3), New Jersey (2), Texas (2), California (2), Montana, Missouri, Ohio, Kansas, Virginia — and England.

Most conspicuous absentee, or nonfulfillment, was Florida.

Thoroughbreds were being bred, foaled and raised at farms on the limestone ridge around Ocala, extending northwest to Tallahassee. But none had come close to the winner's circle in the "Run for the Roses" at Churchill Downs.

In the early 1950s, Bonnie Heath, a young geologist from Tulsa, and his oil partner, Jackson Dudley, formed the D. & H. Stable on a 613-acre farm near Ocala. This pair of successful Oklahomans, ardent fishermen, kept a pleasure cruiser at a Fort Lauderdale marina. Docked next to them, living on a houseboat, was horse trainer Hugh Fontaine, 60, an adventurous character whose experiences ranged from pre-medical courses at Washington and Lee University, a stay at Rush School of Medicine in Chicago, to World War I as an aviator in France with the U.S. 49th Pursuit Group, followed by a fling at polo.

"My disposition was indisposed toward medicine," said Fontaine, whose father had been a prominent New Orleans surgeon. "Racing fascinated me. I had enjoyed some 'ups' but I was in the 'downs' when I met and made friends with Bonnie Heath and Jack Dudley."

Fontaine first tried, unsuccessfully, to get Heath and Dudley to buy the colts Abbe Sting and Brown Booter. "Both did well," Heath recalls. "So we figured Hugh knew something about horses. At his urging, in January, 1955, we bought a two-year-old named Needles for $20,000."

This son of 1949 Kentucky Derby winner Ponder, out of a rather obscure mare, Noodle Soup, had pneumonia as a yearling, was shot full of penicillin, thus the name Needles.

Conceived in Kentucky, with W. E. Leach the breeder,

Needles officially became a Florida-bred when foaled at the Dickey Farm adjacent to the Heath-Dudley 620 acres southwest of Ocala. The farm manager there, Elmo Shropshire, became just as high on the colt as was Hugh Fontaine.

"We also felt better about our $20,000 investment after Menolene, a half-sister to Needles, won the $25,000 Jasmine Stakes at Hialeah in 1955," Heath recalled.

But in those days all Florida-breds had their detractors. Even later, after Needles as a three-year old singed one-fifth of a second off the Gulfstream Park track record for a mile and an eighth winning the Florida Derby, one could hear the disparaging comment: "Wait 'til he has to carry 126 pounds and go a mile and a quarter."

On May 5, 1956, at the end of the first half-mile of the 82nd Kentucky Derby, slowly moving Needles was 25½ lengths off the pace, ahead of only one horse in the field of 17 starters. In the next quarter-mile he picked up four lengths on the leader, Terrang, but was still running 16th. Then jockey Dave Erb turned it on. Needles passed eight horses, zoomed on to catch front running Fabious at the head of the stretch and won going away, the first Florida-bred ever to capture a Kentucky Derby.

Hugh Fontaine, sporting a blackthorn cane on the presentation stand with Needles' jubilant owners, was too happy to be embarrassed by a U.S. marshal serving an attachment on his winnings for about $2,000 in back income tax. He and Needles had made history.

Five years later, Jack and Katherine Price's captivating colt Carry Back, not royally bred, brought Florida its second Kentucky Derby winner.

The South rose again last May, so dramatically that Secretariat, the first Virginia-bred since unforgettable Reigh Count in 1928, represented triumphantly in the record-breaking time of 1:59⅖ the first combination of owner-trainer-jockey — Mrs. John B. Tweedy, Lucien Laurin and Ron Turcotte — ever to win consecutive Kentucky Derbies.

No dream is impossible on the first Saturday of May, in Louisville, in what has been described picturesquely yet succinctly as a "tugging, tingling, tense, thin slice of time carved out of eternity."

RED SMITH

RED SMITH *is one of America's foremost sportswriters. The following is his own self-portrait in words: "... a former order clerk for the Morley-Murphy Co., a wholesale hardware firm in Green Bay Wis., a former soda jerk, waiter, apprentice dry cleaner and cherry picker. I also served as elevator operator in the Northland Hotel in Green Bay, where I was replaced by a button. Failing to gain distinction in these fields, I entered the newspaper business and over a 40-year span contributed to the demise of some of the most distinguished papers in America—The St. Louis Star, Philadelphia Record, New York Herald Tribune, New York World-Journal-Tribune, etc. I am now hacking away at the New York Times."*

Derby Cup Means More Than Money

In the days when men could travel by rail as comfortably as hogs, Conn McCreary and Jack Amiel shared a bedroom on a train from Louisville to New York. It was the night of May 5, 1951. A few hours earlier, McCreary had sailed past the finish post in the 77th Derby aboard Count Turf, a son of Count Fleet and grandson of Reigh Count, both Derby winners in their time.

Amiel, McCreary and Count Turf were neither the first nor the last team from the East to score in America's most famous race. As early as 1876 when the Derby was one year old, New York's William Astor won the $2,950 purse with Vagrant, and ever since then Yankee invaders have come in waves—Phil and Mike Dwyer, the Brooklyn butcher boys who won with Hindoo in 1881 and Ben Brush in 1896; William Woodward, the New York banker whose Belair Stud won with Gallant Fox in 1930, Omaha in 1935 and Johnstown in 1939; Samuel D. Riddle with War Admiral, Harry Sinclair with Zev, and the Whitneys of Greentree Stable to mention a few.

None of these, however, was so emphatically representative of the sidewalks of New York as the delegation that descended on Churchill Downs 33 years ago. Jack Amiel was and is a plump, smiling Broadway restaurateur known as the softest touch for a hardluck story within a mile and a quarter of Times Square. A comparative newcomer to racing, he had paid $3,700 for Count Turf at the Saratoga yearling sales and turned him over to Sol Rutchick, a trainer who had started as a candy peddler on Fourteenth Street.

The colt had won the Dover Stakes at Delaware as a two-year-old but that was the closest he had come to running back to his breeding. Rutchick didn't regard him as Derby material and when Amiel insisted on shipping to Louisville the trainer refused to go along.

Rutchick further disapproved of Amiel's riding choice, McCreary. In this he was supported by just about every trainer in America, for Conn had fallen into such a slump they all had quit on him. Indeed, McCreary had quit on himself halfway through 1950, stowed his tack and remained away from the track until the winter season in Florida. There he had gotten a few mounts and ridden them with minimal success.

With twenty horses ready to start, Count Turf was relegated to the mutuel field. He got so lost in the crowd that his blacksmith couldn't find the right barn to re-shoe him for the race. Slim Sully, Rutchick's assistant, hoisted McCreary into the saddle and helped to adjust the stole of roses over the colt's withers after Count Turf won by four widening lengths. A legitimate 100-to-1 chance, the winner paid only $31.20 because he was coupled in the betting with four other field horses.

That night in their bedroom on the train, Amiel and McCreary opened a mahogany box and drew the Derby Gold Cup from its swaddling of flannel. Gingerly, cradling it between outstretched palms, they placed it on a folding chair before them. They sat and worshipped it like an idol.

"It seems like a dream," Amiel said, "but the best part of this dream, when I wake up this'll still be here."

"The money, too," a visitor said.

"Oh, the money!" Amiel said. "Anybody can make $98,000, but how many men have one of these?"

McCreary's gaze had not wavered from the cup. "I wish they'd have a little one for the jockey," he said. "I'd rather have it than the money."

When that remark got back to Bill Corum, president of Churchill Downs, he said, "Conn will get his cup." Conn did, at the Derby of 1952 when they began the custom of giving a trophy to the winning rider.

Count Turf wasn't McCreary's first Derby winner. Conn had scored with Pensive in 1944 when he was young and lately arrived in the big leagues. That had been a high spot on a joyride that promised to go on forever. Then the ride ended but Count Turf brought a reprieve and an existence that had seemed finished began all over again. Conn sailed along at the top of his game for another decade.

"You know what the Derby means to me?" he said years later. "Say I went on the bum, say I was the worst bum on the Bowery and I put the arm on a couple of guys and one of them handed me a buck. 'What do you want to do that for?' his friend might say. 'That little creep is no good.' 'Why,' the other guy would say, 'he win the Derby!'"

NELSON FISHER, *who has covered the Kentucky Derby since 1947 for the San Diego Union, was the fourth president of the National Turf Writers Association.*

Turf editor, handicapper and general sports columnist, Fisher twice won the Thoroughbred Racing Association's Bill Corum Award for best columns on racing. His stories on Venetian Way's Kentucky Derby, Royal Orbit's Preakness and a farewell-to-racing column on Swaps were reproduced in E. P. Dutton's annual anthology of best sports stories.

NELSON FISHER

Some California Horses Make Good

Morvich, first of three California-bred winners of the Kentucky Derby, was a storied horse from birth. He was born and died in California but never raced in his native state.

Morvich (pronounced Mor-vick) grew up with knobby fore-knees, a crooked foreleg and overlengthy hind legs. He was destined to be a castoff as the ugly duckling of his sire Runnymede's crop that year at the Napa Stock Farm of Adolph B. Spreckels, heir to a sugar fortune.

For all his malformation and loneliness in the shadow of his flossy half-brother in blood, Runstar, the blocky Morvich was blessed with intense speed, once he reached the racetrack. More important, he possessed an indomitable spirit to win, come mud or whatever adversity. He won all his 11 races as a 2-year-old.

Morvich was offered to Baron Long of San Diego, Spreckel's friend, for $5,000. Long, soon to become a top echelon breeder-owner, declined because of the lumpy knees.

Taken East by boxcar, Morvich made his debut in the Suffolk Selling Stakes at Jamaica May 6, 1921, at a $3,000 tag. Jockey Metcalfe was up, the odds closed at 50-1 and Morvich streaked back by 10.

Two days later Max Hirsch bought Morvich for $4,500. Hardly had the colt been moved to his new barn at Jamaica before he was sold by Hirsch to Fred Burlew for $7,500. Ten days after the first race Burlew risked Morvich in a selling race for the last time and he won by six.

The next month, after Morvich scampered by six in an Aqueduct allowance race, Ben Block of Wall Street bought half-interest in him for $25,000, with Burlew continuing the training. They took three more sprints at Empire City and Aqueduct.

By now winner of six straight, Morvich was entered in the United Hotel Stakes at Saratoga. He opened at 8 to 5. Block bet $10,000. The price crept to 2-1 and Block bet another $10,000. Morvich outgamed Harry Sinclair's Kai-Sang, who had Earle Sande up, a neck and Block bought Burlew's interest for $35,000. Burlew was retained as trainer.

Through the Saratoga Special and the Hopeful Stakes they continued the winning wave.

The Eastern Shore Handicap at Havre de Grace and the one-mile Pimlico Futurity Nov. 5 extended Morvich's perfect juvenile year through 11 races and $11,235 in purses.

Skeptics hooted when Morvich, for his first race at 3, was sent into the Kentucky Derby May 13, 1922, on speed drills and one nine-furlong gallop of 1:59 in New York before shipping to Louisville. Three days before the Derby Morvich breezed 1¼ miles in 2:08⅕.

Criticism didn't deter bettors and Morvich closed the 6-to-5 favorite. He shaded 11 seconds for the first furlong, killing his field, continued under a hand-ride by Albert Johnson to a length and one-half margin over Colonel Ed Bradley's Bet Mosie, whose stablemate Busy American broke down. The time 2:04⅗, was respectable under the conditions of the era.

Morvich never won another race. After four losing efforts he was retired to stud. Eleven of his foals won stakes and in December of 1939 Miss Elizabeth Daingerfield, who managed his affairs at her Haylands Farm near Lexington, arranged with Miss Justine Mosse to return Morvich to California. It was a long trip in a trailer behind a light car, over roads frequently icy.

Arizona cowboys Rex Ellsworth and Meshach Tenney became the talk of the 1955 renewal when they brought Swaps, son of Khaled, to Churchill Downs. The Santa Anita Derby champion, though bet to second favoritism, stunned the East when Bill Shoemaker sent him into an early lead and they upset favored Nashua a length and a half with Summer Tan a spent and remote third.

At Hollywood Park the next month Swaps set a world record for 1-1/16 miles and, Horse of the Year in 1956, he established four more world records.

George Pope, Jr.'s, Decidedly became the third California-bred Derby champion. The son of Determine (Kentucky-bred 1954 Derby king) erased Whirlaway's track record with a full second faster trip of 2:00⅖ for Bill Hartack.

Swaps and Determine were two of five Santa Anita Derby winners repeating in the Kentucky Derby. Others were Hill Gail (1952), Lucky Debonair (1965) and the beautiful Majestic Prince (1969).

Derby champions Swaps, Decidedly and Determine were California-owned. Determine was the property of Andrew Crevolin.

JOHN P. CARMICHAEL *retired from the Chicago Daily News in October of 1972 after 49 years in the newspaper business. The last 41 were with the News where he served as conductor of the Barber Shop column for 36 years and also sports editor for 25 years. The Derby he likes to remember best was Whirlaway's sweeping triumph in 1941. He presently is connected with the Chicago White Sox baseball team in the public relations department.*

JOHN P. CARMICHAEL

The Story of "The Chicago Splurge"

The largest field ever to break from the starting gate in the Kentucky Derby numbered 22 almost a half-century ago. Out of it came a strapping chestnut colt named Reigh Count to win by three lengths and return the favorite's mutuels of $6.12 under a well-guided ride by Chick Lang.

The popular triumph was remarkable in three ways for the purposes of this recollection. They were, not necessarily in the order of importance:

The first Derby of 44 in a row that I saw.

Reigh Count was owned by two prominent Chicagoans, John Hertz, the taxicab magnate, and Otto Lehmann, department store merchant prince.

He was the first victor ever to sire a son (Count Fleet in 1943) and through him, a grandson, (Count Turf in 1951) who carried the bloodlines to subsequent Derby triumphs. Only one other horse, Pensive in '44, could boast of a similar lineage achievement in his old age.

The purpose of this recapitulation serves to emphasize the fact that, on the eve of the Derby's 100th running, the green and white facades at historic Churchill Downs aren't emblazoned with the names of many winners born into the midwest area dominated by Chicago racing.

For instance: there has been only one Derby champion foaled in Illinois and he was Dust Commander in 1970, so lightly regarded that he paid $32.60 while carrying jockey Mike Manganello to his big victory. Even if you include Kansas and Ohio, only two other winners were foaled in this regional map, Wintergreen (1909) in Ohio and Lawrin (1938) on the Woolford farm, sprawled among the wheat fields of Kansas.

This is understandable because in those days (and even now) the midwest doesn't have the lavish breeding farms as in Kentucky, where 76 Derby kings have been foaled.

But because ownership of Derby starters, let alone winners, can be a matter of sale as well as birthplace, Chicago has held title to such valuable horseflesh as far back as 1888 when the Chicago stable, a loosely-knitted group, sent McBeth II into action at Louisville and saw him win. Then there was Ed Corrigan, a swashbuckling Windy City sportsman, who bought Riley in 1890 just in time to see him capture the Run for the

Roses with the legendary black rider, Isaac Murphy, aboard.

Then on down the line through Hertz and his Reigh Count and into 1940 when Mrs. Ethel Mars, the Chicago candy-bar tycooness, was pleasantly shocked when her Gallahadion, at 35-1, upset the favored Bimelech under the training aegis of Roy Waldron. One year later the first Calumet colt, Whirlaway, launched a parade of champions from this same stable.

Owned by Warren Wright, the Calumet baking-powder magnate from Chicago, eight of his equine progeny have carried the devil-red silks to Derby immortality. Whirlaway, who set a record of 2:01⅖ which stood for 25 years, was followed by Pensive, Citation, Ponder, Hill Gail, Iron Liege, Tim Tam and Forward Pass as Wright's widow (now Mrs. Gene Markey) carried on the winning tradition which also catipulted the Jones boys (Ben and Jimmy) and jockey Eddie Arcaro into unprecedented success in the book of records.

Those were the days of the big 'Chicago splurge', but there aren't too many owners (and trainers) anywhere who had even one-third of those triumphs to report in the most prestigious of all three-year-old races. But in 1960 a sprightly colt named Venetian Way, trained by Vic Sovinski, raced home in front under the colors of the Sunny Blue Farm, owned by Isaac Blumberg, a machine-tool builder cast in the Chicago mold.

In 1965 Mrs. Ada Rice, wife of the Chicago grain broker (Dan) watched her Lucky Debonair beat Dapper Dan and Tom Rolfe as the post-time choice, Bold Lad, was 10th in an 11-horse race.

That about wraps up the achievements of the midwest.

But it isn't a bad summation of success, thanks largely to the original Calumet ownership, even if its breeding grounds are, like so many other such farms, nestled in the rolling blue grass of Kentucky.

And only a year ago two Chicago Derby starters, My Gallant and Shecky Greene, tried to team up on the field, the one owned by Arthur Appleton of Northbrook and the other by Joe Kellman. They ran out of the money as an entry trained by Lou Goldfine . . . but even Chicago, capitol of the midwest empire, can't win 'em all.

NTH RACE
CD
Y 5, 1973

1¼ MILES. (2:00). Ninety-ninth running KENTUCKY DERBY. $125,000 added. 3-year-olds. By subscription of $100 each in cash, wh tion for both the Kentucky Derby and Derby Trial. All nomination fe $2,500 to pass the entry box, Thursday, May 3, $1,500 additional to st of which $25,000 to second, $12,500 to third, $6,250 to fourth, $100 winner (to be divided equally in event of a dead-heat). Weight, 120 winner to receive a gold trophy. Closed with 218 nominations.

lue of race, $198,800. Value to winner $155,050; second, $25,000; third, $12,500; fourth, $6,250 tuel Pool, $3,284,962.

Last Raced	Horse	EqtAWt	PP	¼	½	¾	1	Str	Fin	Jockeys	Owne
-21-73⁷ Aqu³	Secretariat	b3 126	10	11ʰ	6½	5¹	2¹¹	1¹	1²¹	RTurcotte	Meado
-21-73⁷ Aqu²	Sham	b3 126	4	5¹	3²	2¹	1¹	2⁶	2⁸	LPincayJr	S Som
-26-73⁶ Kee²	Our Native	b3 126	7	6½	8¹¹	8¹	5ʰ	3ʰ	3½	DBrumfield	Pr'ch'
-26-73⁶ Kee⁵	Forego	3 126	9	9¹₂10¹	6½	6²	4½	4²¹₂	PAnderson	Lazy
-28-73⁷ CD²	Restless Jet	3 126	1	7¹¹7ʰ	10¹½	7¹½	6¹¹	5²¹₄	MHole	J Kel'
-28-73⁷ CD¹	Shecky Greene	b3 126	11	1¹¹ 1³	1¹¹	3³	5¹	6¹½	LAdams	J Ste
-26-73⁶ Kee⁶	Navajo	b3 126	5	10¹¹10¹11⁴	8¹¹	8²	7ⁿᵒ	WSoirez	Aisco
-26-73⁶ Kee⁷	Royal and Regal	3 126	8	3¹ 4³	4³	4¹	7¹¹	8³¹	WBlum	A I A
-26-73⁶ Kee¹	My Gallant	b3 126	12	8ʰ11¹¹12³	11²	10½	9ʰ	BBaeza	E Wh
-21-73⁷ Aqu¹	Angle Light	3 126	2	4ʰ 5¹½	7¹	10¹½	9¹¹10¹³	JLeBlanc	R Se
5- 1-73⁸ CD⁵	Gold Bag	b3 126	13	2ʰ 2ʰ	3½	9¹	11¹	11ⁿᵒ	EFires	Elme
-28-73⁷ CD⁶	Twice a Prince	b3 126	6	13 13	13	13	12²	12¹½	ASantiago	E E
-26-73⁶ Kee³	Warbucks	3 126	3	12¹ 12³	9ʰ	12¹½ 13	13	WHartack	

a-Coupled, Secretariat and Angle Light; b-Shecky Greene and My Gallant.
Time, :23⅖, :47⅖, 1:11⅘, 1:36⅕, 1:59⅖ (new track record). Track fas

$2 Mutuel Prices:

1A-SECRETARIAT (a-Entry)	5.00
5-SHAM	
8-OUR NATIVE	

Ch. c, by Bold Ruler—Somethingroyal, by Princequillo. Trainer, L. Laurin. Bred by Me
IN GATE—5:37. OFF AT 5:37 EASTERN DAYLIGHT TIME. Start good. Won handily

SECRETARIAT relaxed nicely and dropped back last leaving the gate as the field moved between horses to begin improving position entering the first turn, but passed thereafter. Turcotte roused him smartly with the whip in his right hand leaving the far t strongly raced to the leaders, lost a little momentum racing into the stretch where T again, but then switched it to his left hand and merely flashed it as the winner willing breaking time. SHAM, snugly reserved within striking distance after brushing with NAV around rivals to the front without... of rousing and drew clear between calls er under a stro... after being displaced in the last furlong... re... remainder of the field. OUR NATIVE, reserved... well for his placing FOREGO,... to the turn, came wide in the drive and... entering the far turn, swung wide... th slightly from a fl... the rail entering the far turn... effort. SHECKY OUR NATIVE... the drive. RESTLESS JET saved ground... NAVAJO was outrun. RO pace under light rating for nearly seven furlongs and faltered. MY GALLANT was not a factor. well for a mile and had nothing left in the drive... check when crowded by GOLD BAG on the steadily in a du... forced to... TWICE A PRINCE retired... the gate bri had good s... dropped... WAR... S was dull. then showed nothing in the running.

May 17, 1875

Owner — H. P. McGrath

Jockey — Oliver Lewis

Ulysses S. Grant was President of the United States when the first Derby was run on May 17, 1875.

One of Kentucky's premier soldiers and politician's, John C. Breckinridge, died that day.

FIRST RUNNING

ARISTIDES

$1,000 added. Net to winner $2,850; second $200. 42 nominations.

	Horses	Wt.	Fin.	Jockeys	Owners
	Aristides	100	1	O. Lewis	H. P. McGrath
	Volcano	100	2	Chambers	George H. Rice
	Verdigris	100	3	Williams	C. A. Lewis
	Ten Broeck	—	—	Kelso	F. P. Harper
	Searcher	—	—	Colston	J. B. Rodes
	Enlister	—	—	Halloway	Springfield and Clay
	Warsaw	—	—	Masterson	Springfield and Clay
	McCreery	—	—	D. Jones	Gen. Abe Buford
Also ran	Bill Bruce	—	—	Jones	S. J. Salyer
	Gold Mine	—	—	Stradford	J. A. Grinstead
	Grenoble	—	—	Carter	Gen. Abe Buford
	Bob Wooley	—	—	Walker	Robinson, Morgan & Co.
	Vagabond	—	—	Houston	A. B. Lewis & Co.
	Ascension	—	—	W. Lakeland	W. C. Hull
	Chesapeake	—	—	Henry	H. P. McGrath

Time: 2:37¾. Track fast.

Winner—Ch.c. by *Leamington—Sarong, by Lexington; trained by Andy Anderson; bred in Kentucky by H. P. McGrath.

Auction pools: McGrath entry (Aristides and Chesapeake) $105; Searcher $65; Ascension $55; field $270.

The field was away on the first attempt. VOLCANO went to the front, followed closely by VERDIGRIS, ARISTIDES, and McCREERY. CHESAPEAKE was away poorly. On the backside, ARISTIDES moved into second place, was lapped on VOLCANO at the end of the mile, went to the front shortly thereafter. The field was strung out for a hundred yards in his wake. ARISTIDES continued to increase his lead as VOLCANO was steadied for the final drive. At the head of the stretch, Owner McGrath, who had expected to win with CHESAPEAKE, waved Jockey Lewis on. Immediately, ARISTIDES moved out to win by a length. VOLCANO came strongly through the stretch, but could not reach the winner.

THE WINNER'S PEDIGREE AND CAREER HIGHLIGHTS

ARISTIDES (Chestnut Colt)			
	*Leamington	Faugh-a-Ballagh	Sir Hercules / Guiccioli
		Mare by Pantaloon	Pantaloon / Daphne
	Sarong	Lexington	Boston / Alice Carneal
		Greek Slave	*Glencoe / Margaret Hunter

Year	Age	Sts	1st	2nd	3rd	Won
1874	2	9	3	3	0	$ 1,525
1875	3	9	4	2	1	15,700
1876	4	2	2	0	0	1,100
1878	6	1	0	0	0	—
Totals		21	9	5	1	$18,325

At 2 Years	2ND	Thespian Stakes
	UNP	Saratoga Stakes

At 3 Years	WON	Kentucky Derby, Withers Stakes, Jerome Stakes, Breckinridge Stakes
	2ND	Belmont Stakes, Ocean Hotel Stakes
	3RD	Travers Stakes

The first clubhouse at the Louisville Jockey Club was located in the area now occupied by the barns. It eventually was removed from the premises and re-located on the street now known as Southern Parkway.

The inaugural Kentucky Derby was the second race on the first day of racing. The program pictured here is on display in the Kentucky Derby Museum.

This was the original grandstand. The clubhouse (above) is at the left. Note the twin "towers" similar to those which were featured on the new stands built in 1895 and which are the trademark of the track today.

15

May 15, 1876

Owner — William Astor

Louisville was a city of great importance in 1876. An important factor in its development was the falls in the Ohio River; hence, its nickname "Falls City." A big port city, it was in Louisville that the National Baseball League was formed in 1876.

This was the year, too, of Custer's Last Stand and the birth of the telephone.

Two forms of wagering, the Paris Mutual system and the auction pool, were offered to the patrons of Churchill Downs in its early meetings. It was several years before the "mutual" system caught on. Bookmaking also was once the form of wagering used at Churchill Downs, but the only system permitted in Kentucky since 1908 has been pari-mutuels.

SECOND RUNNING

VAGRANT

$1,500 added.   Net to winner $2,950; second $200.   34 nominations.

Horses	Wt.	Fin.	Jockeys	Owners
Vagrant	97	1	R. Swim	William Astor
Creedmore	100	2	W. Williams	Williams & Owings
Harry Hill	100	3	J. Miller	John Funk
Parole	97	—	Sparling	P. Lorillard
Germantown	100	—	Graham	F. B. Harper
Black colt by Enquirer	97	—	James	F. B. Harper
Marie Michon	97	—	Stratford	J. A. Grinstead
Leamingtonian	100	—	Colston	H. F. Vissman '
Bombay	100	—	Walker	D. Swigert
Red Coat	100	—	Hughes	Green Clay
Bullion	100	—	Kelso	A. Keene Richards

Also ran

Time: 2:38¼.   Weather clear, track fast.

Winner—Br. g. by Virgil—Lazy, by *Scythian; trained by James Williams; bred in Kentucky by M. H. Sanford.

Auction Pools: Vagrant, $525; Parole, $400; Creedmore, $275; Red Coat, $150; Field $135.

PAROLE went to front, immediately after the break, but VAGRANT came up on the outside, took the lead at the mile, and increased it through the stretch, to win by two lengths.

THE WINNER'S PEDIGREE AND CAREER HIGHLIGHTS

VAGRANT (Brown Gelding)	Virgil	Vandal	*Glencoe
			Mare by *Tranby
		Hymenia	*Yorkshire
			Little Peggy
	Lazy	*Scythian	Orlando
			Scythia
		Lindora	Lexington
			Picayune

Year	Age	Sts	1st	2nd	3rd	Won
1875	2	6	5	0	1	$ 3,800
1876	3	4	3	1	0	6,450
1877	4	0	0	0	0	—
1878	5	12	0	0	4	—
1879	6	14	3	2	2	1,175
1880	7	23	7	3	3	1,500
1881	8	21	2	5	2	875
1882	9	7	0	1	0	75
1883	10	1	0	0	0	—
Totals		88	20	12	12	$13,875

At 2 Years	WON	Alexander Stakes, Belle Meade Stakes, Sanford Stakes, Colt Stakes and Colt and Filly Stakes (both at Lexington)
	3RD	Tennessee Stakes
At 3 Years	WON	Kentucky Derby, Phoenix Hotel Stakes, Grand Exposition Stakes
	2ND	Clark Stakes

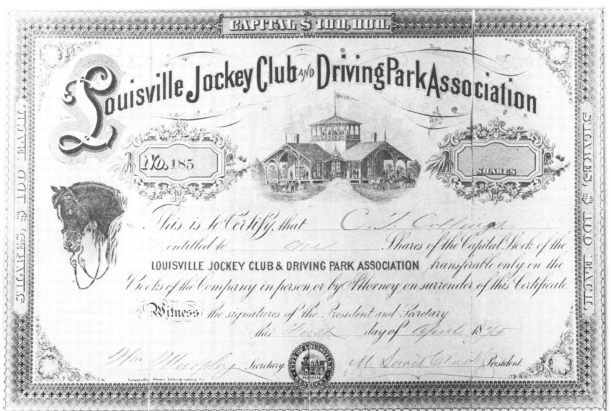

M. Lewis Clark (left) formed the Louisville Jockey Club and Driving Park Association. Each share of stock (above) sold for $100. This share was issued to C. T. Collings. Clark killed himself in Memphis, Tenn. in 1899 and is buried in Cave Hill Cemetery in Louisville on the Churchill family plot. He was a nephew of John Churchill, on whose land the track was built.

May 22, 1877

Owner — Daniel Swigert

Trainer — Ed Brown

Jockey — William Walker

THIRD RUNNING

BADEN-BADEN

$1,500 added. Net to winner $3,000; second $200. 41 nominations.

	Horses	Wt.	Fin.	Jockeys	Owners
	Baden-Baden	100	1	W. Walker	D. Swigert
	Leonard	100	2	Swim	H. P. McGrath
	King William	100	3	Bailey	Smallwood & Co.
	Vera Cruz	97	—	Murphy	J. T. Williams
	Odd Fellow	100	—	Williams	J. J. Merrill
	McWhirter	100	—	H. Moore	Gen. Abe Buford
Also	Malvern	100	—	S. Jones	George H. Rice
ran	Early Light	97	—	W. James	F. B. Harper
	Dan K.	97	—	McGrath	Johnson & Mills
	Lisbon	100	—	Douglass	D. Swigert
	Headlight	100	—	Shelton	L. B. Fields

Time: 2:38. Weather clear, track fast.

Winner—Ch.c. by *Australian—Lavender, by Wagner; trained by Ed Brown; bred in Kentucky by A. J. Alexander.

Auction Pools: Leonard, $150; Vera Cruz, $100; McWhirter, $50; Swigert, $50; Field, (with Baden-Baden included) $45.

LEONARD, the favorite, broke in front. BADEN-BADEN moved steadily from fifth place, to take second position going into the stretch, with KING WILLIAM, third, and VERA CRUZ, fourth. Under slight pressure, BADEN-BADEN, ridden by BILLY WALKER, Negro jockey, passed LEONARD, and won by two lengths.

THE WINNER'S PEDIGREE AND CAREER HIGHLIGHTS

BADEN-BADEN (Chestnut Colt)	*Australian	West Australian	Melbourne / Mowerina
		*Emilia	Young Emilius / Persian
	Lavender	Wagner	Sir Charles / Maria West
		Alice Carneal	*Sarpedon / Rowena

Year	Age	Sts	1st	2nd	3rd	Won
1876	2	4	1	3	0	$ 475
1877	3	6	3	0	1	‡11,950
Totals		10	4	3	1	$ 12,425

‡Including $500 in plate

At 2 Years	WON	Young America Stakes
	2ND	Belle Meade Stakes, Sanford Stakes
At 3 Years	WON	Kentucky Derby, Jersey Derby, Travers Stakes
	3RD	Belmont Stakes
	UNP	Clark Stakes, Kenner Stakes

18

The Southern Baptist Theological Seminary is a Louisville landmark. It was transferred here from Greenville, S. C. in 1877. Its support was uncertain for three years before a private gift of $50,000 saved the school. It was housed at Fifth & Broadway beginning in 1888 and moved to its present site on Lexington Road in 1926.

May 21, 1878

Owner — T. J. Nichols

The centerfield always has been a favorite place to be at the Kentucky Derby. There was free admission to this area in 1878 and nearly 6,000 were in the area.

More than 75,000 jam the space now for every running even though vision of the horses is extremely limited.

Many of the traditions of the Kentucky Derby were established early in its history. For instance, a band annually keys the program with the playing of "My Old Kentucky Home" to announce the horses' entrance onto the track.

A band entertained the 1878 Derby crowd, too, and bands have been part of the annual Derby scene through the years.

F O U R T H   R U N N I N G

DAY STAR

$1,500 added. Net to winner $4,050; second $200. 56 nominations.

Horses		Wt.	Fin.	Jockeys	Owners
Day Star		100	1	J. Carter	T. J. Nichols
Himyar		100	2	Robinson	B. G. Thomas
Leveler		100	3	Swim	R. H. Owens
	Solicitor	100	—	Edward	L. P. Tarlton
	McHenry	100	—	James	Gen. Abe Buford
Also ran	Respond	100	—	Ramey	Rodes & Carr
	Burgundy	100	—	L. Jones	J. M. Wooding
	Earl of Beaconfield	100	—	Mahoney	A. Straus & Co.
	Charlie Bush	100	—	Miller	Jennings & Hunt

Time: 2:37¼ (new Derby record). Weather clear, track good.

Winner—Ch.c. by Star Davis—Squeeze-'Em, by Lexington; trained by Lee Paul; bred in Kentucky by J. M. Clay.

Auction Pools: Himyar, $305; Field, $110. With Himyar out, Day Star, Burgundy and Leveler sold about even.

Mutuel wagering introduced in 1878, with four machines operating, but no prices available.

DAY STAR led from start to finish, winning by two lengths.

THE WINNER'S PEDIGREE AND CAREER HIGHLIGHTS

DAY STAR (Chestnut Colt)
- Star Davis
  - *Glencoe
    - Sultan
    - Trampoline
  - Margaret Wood
    - Priam
    - Maria West
- Squeeze-'Em
  - Lexington
    - Boston
    - Alice Carneal
  - Skedaddle
    - *Yorkshire
    - Magnolia

Year	Age	Sts	1st	2nd	3rd	Won
1877	2	2	0	1	0	$ 100
1878	3	6	2	1	1	7,050
1879	4	8	0	1	0	125
1880	5	9	3	1	2	1,205
1881	6	10	5	3	1	2,450
1882	7	7	1	0	1	450
Totals		42	11	7	5	$11,380

At 2 Years	2ND	Sanford Stakes
At 3 Years	WON	Kentucky Derby, Blue Ribbon Stakes
	2ND	Clark Stakes
At 4 Years	2ND	Merchants' Stakes

Louisville was 100 years old in 1878 and the Courier-Journal, which had moved into this building two years before, reported on the yellow fever epidemic which swept the city; the first Handel & Haydn concert in Louisville; the introduction of electric lights into Kelly's Ax Factory, and many other important events. Charles D. Jacob (inset) was completing his last year as mayor.

Day Star, winner of the 1878 Kentucky Derby, symbolizes the spirit of Louisville's 1978 Centennial. Louisville, the moving-ahead city, with a new skyline, a new Riverfront, the new River City Mall, a city of renewed cultural and economic enterprise. Louisville Centennial 1978.

May 20, 1879

FIFTH RUNNING

†LORD MURPHY

$1,500 added. Net to winner $3,550; second $200. 46 nominations.

	Horses	Wt.	Fin.	Jockeys	Owners
	Lord Murphy	100	1	C. Shauer	Geo. W. Darden & Co.
	Falsetto	100	2	I. Murphy	J. W. H. Reynolds
	Strathmore	100	3	Hightower	George Cadwillader
	Trinidad	100	—	Allen	D. Swigert
	One Dime	100	—	Jones	G. W. Bowen & Co.
Also ran	General Pike	100	—	Stoval	Gen. Abe Buford
	Buckner	100	—	Edwards	H. W. Farris
	Wissahicken	97	—	Hawkins	H. P. McGrath
	Ada Glen	97	—	Ramie	G. D. Wilson

Time: 2:37 (new Derby record). Weather clear, track fast.

Winner—B.c. by Pat Malloy—Wenonah, by Capt. Elgee; trained by George Rice; bred in Tennessee by J. T. Carter.

Auction Pools: Lord Murphy, $175; Strathmore and Falsetto, $60 each; Trinidad, $45; Ada Glen, $25; Field $30. Mutuel tickets sold, but no payoff prices available.

GENERAL PIKE and TRINIDAD broke together, and ran head and head to the first turn, with STRATHMORE, third; FALSETTO, fourth; BUCKNER, fifth. Trying to move up at the turn, LORD MURPHY was bumped by a swerving horse, almost knocked to his knees, recovered, and then, from far back, charged at the field, gained the lead on the back stretch, and won by a length, under a hard drive.

THE WINNER'S PEDIGREE AND CAREER HIGHLIGHTS

†LORD MURPHY (Bay Colt)
- Pat Malloy
  - Lexington
    - Boston
    - Alice Carneal
  - Gloriana
    - American Eclipse
    - Trifle
- Wenonah
  - Capt. Elgee
    - Leviathan
    - Reel
  - Mare by *Albion
    - *Albion
    - Mare by Pacific

Year	Age	Sts	1st	2nd	3rd	Won
1878	2	4	1	2	0	$ 350
1879	3	8	5	3	0	11,050
1880	4	1	0	0	0	—
1881	5	1	0	0	0	—
	Totals	14	6	5	0	$11,400

At 2 Years	2ND	Young America Stakes, Nashville Sweepstakes
	UNP	Flash Stakes
At 3 Years	WON	Kentucky Derby, St. Leger Stakes, January Stakes, Bellemeade Stakes
	2ND	Dixie Stakes, Trial Stakes, Illinois Derby
At 4 Years	UNP	Chatsworth Plate (England)
At 5 Years	4TH	Newmarket Visitor's Plate (England)

†Lord Murphy originally named Patmus.

In the spring of 1879, the Edison Telephone Company was organized. This photo is the earliest one known of a Louisville telephone exchange. At first all the operators were young boys (insert) but they were soon replaced by young women.

May 18, 1880

The first football game ever played west of the Allegheny Mountains was played in Lexington, Ky. in 1880. The teams were from Transylvania and Central (now Centre) universities.

This was the year of the birth of Helen Keller, one of America's most famous blind natives. She became famous as a writer-lecturer and raised millions for the American Foundation for the Blind.

"This Kentucky Derby, whatever it is — a race, an emotion, a turbulence, an explosion — is one of the most beautiful and violent and satisfying things I have ever experienced."

John Steinbeck

SIXTH RUNNING

FONSO

$1,500 added. Net to winner $3,800; second $200. 47 nominations.

Horses	Wt.	Fin.	Jockeys	Owners
Fonso	105	1	G. Lewis	J. S. Shawhan
Kimball	105	2	Lakeland	W. Cottrill
Bancroft	105	3	I. Murphy	M. Young
Also ran Boulevard	105	—	Allen	W. C. McGavock & Co.
Quito	105	—	McLaughlin	Dwyer Bros.

Time: 2:37½. Weather clear, track fast.

Winner—Ch.c. by King Alfonso—*Weatherwitch, by Weatherbit; trained by Tice Hutsell; bred in Kentucky by A. J. Alexander.

Auction Pools: Kimball, $700; Quito, $362; Fonso, $222; Bancroft, $50; Boulevard was not sold because he was not announced as a starter until after the weighing-in bell was rung.

Mutuel tickets sold, but no payoff prices available.

This Derby was run in dust many inches deep, and dust kicked up by leading horse practically obscured the nearest pursuers. FONSO broke in front and stayed there, winning by a length; KIMBALL was always second, and BANCROFT always third. Foul claimed lodged by KIMBALL's jockey against FONSO, not allowed.

THE WINNER'S PEDIGREE AND CAREER HIGHLIGHTS

FONSO (Chestnut Colt)
- King Alfonso
  - *Phaeton
    - King Tom
    - Merry Sunshine
  - Capitola
    - Vandal
    - Mare by *Margrave
- *Weatherwitch
  - Weatherbit
    - Sheet Anchor
    - Miss Letty
  - Mare by Birdcatcher
    - Birdcatcher
    - Colocynth

Year	Age	Sts	1st	2nd	3rd	Won
1879	2	9	3	2	2	$ 2,125
1880	3	3	2	1	0	6,050
Totals		12	5	3	2	$ 8,175

At 2 Years
- WON Maiden Stakes, Colt Stakes
- 2ND Tennessee Stakes
- 3RD Belle Meade Stakes, Colt and Filly Stakes

At 3 Years
- WON Kentucky Derby, Phoenix Stakes
- 2ND Viley Stakes

The Haymarket in Louisville originated in an abandoned railroad yard on Jefferson Street between Floyd and Brook. The Haymarket, though not as large, still exists in the city.

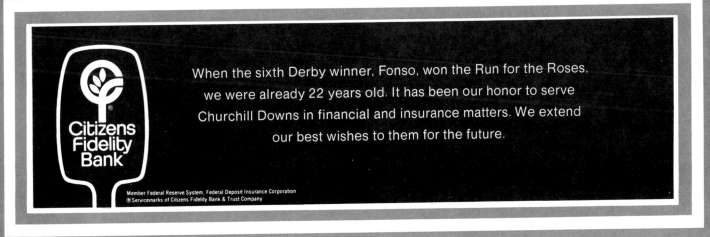

May 17, 1881

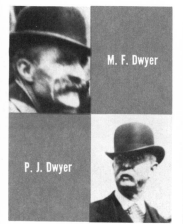

M. F. Dwyer

P. J. Dwyer

Owner — Dwyer Bros.

Trainer — James Rowe, Sr.

Jockey — James McLaughlin

HINDOO

$1,500 added. Net to winner $4,410; second $200. 62 nominations.

Horses	Wt.	Fin.	Jockeys	Owners
Hindoo	105	1	J. McLaughlin	Dwyer Bros.
Lelex	105	2	A. Allen	B. G. Thomas
Alfambra	105	3	G. Evans	G. W. Bowen & Co.
Also ran — Sligo	105	—	Donohue	H. P. McGrath
Getaway	105	—	Fisher	M. Young
Calycanthus	105	—	G. Smith	H. P. McGrath

Time: 2:40. Weather clear, track fast.

Winner—B.c. by Virgil—Florence, by Lexington; trained by James Rowe, Sr.; bred in Kentucky by Daniel Swigert.

Auction Pools: Hindoo, $600; Lelex, $75; McGrath Entry (Sligo and Calycanthus), $70; Alfambra, $40; Getaway, $25.

Mutuel tickets sold, but no payoff prices available.

HINDOO went to the front with the break. At one time or another, every horse came up to challenge him, but HINDOO shook them off, almost without effort, merely galloped through the stretch, and won by four lengths, eased up.

THE WINNER'S PEDIGREE AND CAREER HIGHLIGHTS

HINDOO (Bay Colt)
- Virgil
  - Vandal
    - *Glencoe
    - Mare by *Tranby
  - Hymenia
    - *Yorkshire
    - Little Peggy
- Florence
  - Lexington
    - Boston
    - Alice Carneal
  - *Weatherwitch
    - Weatherbit
    - Mare by Birdcatcher

Year	Age	Sts	1st	2nd	3rd	Won
1880	2	9	7	1	1	$ 9,800
1881	3	20	18	1	1	$49,100
1882	4	6	5	1	0	12,975
Totals		35	30	3	2	$71,875

At 2 Years
- WON Colt and Filly Stakes, Alexander Stakes, Tennessee Stakes, Juvenile Stakes, Jockey Club Stakes, Criterion Stakes, Tremont Stakes
- 2ND Day Boat Line Stakes
- 3RD Windsor Hotel Stakes

At 3 Years
- WON Blue Ribbon Stakes, Kentucky Derby, Clark Stakes, Tidal Stakes, Coney Stakes, Ocean Stakes, Lorillard Stakes, Monmouth Sweepstakes, Travers Stakes, Sequel Stakes, U. S. Hotel Stakes, Kenner Stakes, Champion Stakes, New Jersey St. Leger Stakes
- 2ND Brighton Beach Handicap
- 3RD September Handicap

At 4 Years
- WON Louisville Cup, Merchants' Stakes, Turf Handicap, Coney Island Handicap, Coney Island Cup
- 2ND Dixiana Stakes

Louisville's wharf area was a busy place for mail boats and ferrys between 1880 and 1900. The Columbia was the Jeffersonville ferry.

THE KENTUCKY DERBY PLATE
by
REED & BARTON

A Limited Edition of serially numbered 11″ plates in elegant Reed & Barton Damascene silverplate — rich silver, copper and bronze. Annual plate depicts previous year's Derby winner, and 10 other famous winners. $75 each at finer stores. Reed & Barton, Taunton, Mass. 02780.

May 16, 1882

Green B. Morris
Co-owner and Trainer

J. Patton
Co-owner

Apollo was one of the "winningest" horses ever to win the Derby. He was first 24 times in 55 starts, including nine victories in a row at four.

The seating capacity of Churchill Downs was nearly doubled for the running of the eighth Derby in 1880. The track now has over 42,000 seats, the largest seating capacity of any track in North America.

E I G H T H   R U N N I N G

APOLLO

$1,500 added. Net to winner $4,560; second $200. 64 nominations.

Horses		Wt.	Fin.	Jockeys	Owners
Apollo		102	1	B. Hurd	Morris & Patton
Runnymede		105	2	J. McLaughlin	Dwyer Bros.
Bengal		105	3	S. Fisher	Bowen & Co.
Also ran	Wendover	105	—	Hovey	J. B. Sellers & Co.
	Harry Gilmore	105	—	Gibbs	W. Cottrill
	Ch. c. by Pat Malloy	105	—	Henderson	P. C. Fox
	Robt. Bruce	105	—	L. Jones	A. Jackson
	Babcock	102	—	Kelso	W. Lakeland
	Newsboy	105	—	Quantrell	T. J. Megibben
	Wallensee	107	—	Parker	Rodes & Carr
	Mistral	105	—	Stoval	L. P. Tarlton
	Lost Cause	102	—	Taylor	M. Young
	Highflyer	105	—	Brown	G. Kuhns & Co.

Time: 2:40¼. Weather clear, Track good.

Winner—Ch. g. by *Ashstead or Lever—Rebecca T. Price, by The Colonel; trained by Green B. Morris; bred in Kentucky by Daniel Swigert.

(Three forms of betting in operation, bookmaking, odds being quoted for first time.)

Auction Pools: Runnymede, $250; Mistral, $50; Lost Cause, $40; Robert Bruce, $30; Bengal, $75; Field (with Apollo included), $75.

Bookmaking odds: Runnymeade, 4 to 5, favorite; Apollo, 10 to 1.

Mutuels: $5 win tickets on Apollo paid $169. No place tickets sold.

HARRY GILMORE broke in front, followed by BABCOCK, the PAT MALLOY COLT and ROBERT BRUCE. At the mile, HARRY GILMORE was still on top, with RUNNYMEDE moving on the outside to take third place. As they were well into the stretch, RUNNYMEDE took command, and looked like the winner until APOLLO started a cyclonic rush an eighth of a mile from home. APOLLO caught RUNNYMEDE a few jumps from the wire, and won by a half length.

THE WINNER'S PEDIGREE AND CAREER HIGHLIGHTS

APOLLO
(Chestnut Gelding)

- †Lever
  - Lexington
    - Boston
    - Alice Carneal
  - Levity
    - *Trustee
    - Mare by *Tranby
- Rebecca T. Price
  - The Colonel
    - Albion
    - Lalla Rookh
  - Mare by *Margrave
    - *Margrave
    - Rosalie Somers

†by *Ashstead or Lever

Year		Age	Sts	1st	2nd	3rd	Won
1881		2	0	0	0	0	$ —
1882		3	21	10	7	3	14,030
1883		4	30	14	7	6	7,600
1884		5	4	0	1	0	50
	Totals		55	24	15	9	$21,680

At 3 Years	WON	Kentucky Derby, Cottrill Stakes, Coal Stakes, St. Leger Stakes, Drummers Stakes, Montgomery Stakes
	2ND	Kenner Stakes, U. S. Hotel Stakes, Glass Stakes, Pickwick Stakes
	3RD	Clark Stakes
At 4 Years	WON	Merchants Stakes and 13 other Purses and handicap sweepstakes. Seven of the 14 wins were consecutive in September
	2ND	Cotton Stakes, Howard Cup
	3RD	Excelsior Stakes, Tennessee Club Post Stakes
	4TH	Champion Stakes
At 5 Years	UNP	Wheeler Stakes

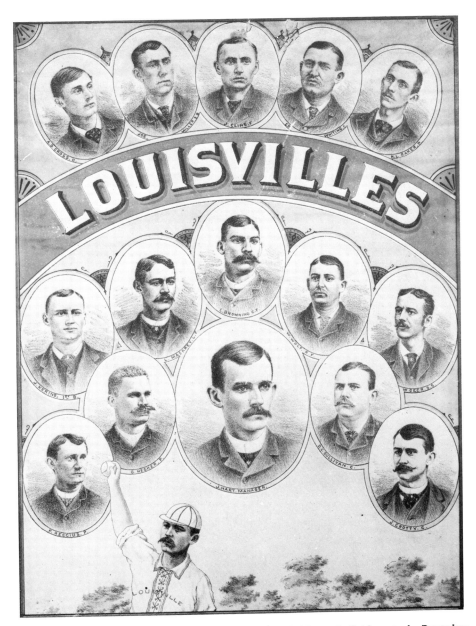

Baseball was organized in Louisville in 1865. This club's centerfielder was L. Browning (top center). It was for Browning that the first Louisville Slugger bat was made in 1884.

May 23, 1883

Owner — Jack Chinn

Owner — G. W. Morgan

Jockey — Billy Donohue

NINTH RUNNING

LEONATUS

$1,500 added. Net to winner $3,760; second $200. 50 nominations.

Horses	Wt.	Fin.	Jockeys	Owners
Leonatus	105	1	W. Donohue	Chinn & Morgan
Drake Carter	102	2	Spellman	Morris & Patton
Lord Ragland	105	3	Quantrell	N. Armstrong
Ascender	102	—	Stoval	R. C. Pate
Also Pike's Pride	102	—	Evans	George Evans
ran Chatter	105	—	Henderson	W. C. McCurdy
Standiford Keller	105	—	Blaylock	J. R. Watts

Time: 2:43. Weather drizzling, track heavy.

Winner—B.c. by Longfellow—Semper Felix, by *Phaeton; trained by Raleigh Colston; bred in Kentucky by John Henry Miller.

Auction Pools: Leonatus, $800; Ascender, $500; Drake Carter, $450; Field $500.

Bookmaking Odds: Bookmakers operated, but prices not available.

Mutuels: $5 win ticket on Leonatus paid $14.80—odds of 1.96 to 1.

DRAKE CARTER was away first, but LEONATUS caught him during the first quarter, and never was headed, winning by three lengths.

THE WINNER'S PEDIGREE AND CAREER HIGHLIGHTS

LEONATUS (Bay Colt)
- Longfellow
  - *Leamington
    - Faugh-a-Ballagh
    - Mare by Pantaloon
  - Nantura
    - Brawner's Eclipse
    - Queen Mary
- Semper Felix
  - *Phaeton
    - King Tom
    - Merry Sunshine
  - Crucifix
    - Lexington
    - Lightsome

Year	Age	Sts	1st	2nd	3rd	Won
1882	2	1	0	1	0	$ 100
1883	3	10	10	0	0	21,335
Totals		11	10	1	0	$21,435

At 2 Years — 2ND Maiden Stakes

At 3 Years — WON Kentucky Derby, Blue Ribbon Stakes, Tobacco Stakes, Woodburn Stakes, Hindoo Stakes, Ripple Stakes, Himyar Stakes, Dearborn Stakes, Green Stakes, Illinois Derby

The Courier-Journal Lithographing Co. began as the Courier-Journal Job Printing Co. on Green Street in 1883. This book was produced by Courier-Journal Lithographing Co.

Courier-Journal Lithographing Company

Fine Lithographing Since *1883*

May 16, 1884

Jockey — Isaac Murphy

When Grover Cleveland was elected President of the United States in 1884, he was the first Democrat in the White House in 28 years.

The Washington Monument was completed in the nation's capital the same year.

Buchanan was the first of three Derby winners ridden by the great Negro jockey, Isaac Murphy. But Murphy had to be forced to accept the mount. He had ridden the colt at Nashville and the horse bolted and ran off. The stewards threatened to set him down if he refused the mount in the Derby. He took it and won and also won the Clark Stakes on Buchanan.

TENTH RUNNING

BUCHANAN

$1,500 added. Net to winner $3,990; second $200. 51 nominations.

Horses	Wt.	Fin.	Jockeys	Owners
Buchanan	110	1	I. Murphy	W. Cottrill
Loftin	110	2	Sayres	A. Johnson & Co.
Audrain	110	3	Fishburn	T. J. Megibben
Bob Miles	110	—	McLaughlin	J. T. Williams
Admiral	110	—	C. Taylor	Clay & Woodford
Also Powhattan III	110	—	D. Williams	R. A. Johnson & Co.
ran Exploit	110	—	Conkling	Wooding & Puryear
Boreas	110	—	O'Brien	R. M. McClelland
Bob Cook	110	—	Gorham	R. M. McClelland

Time: 2:40¼. Weather clear, track good.

Winner—Ch.c. by *Buckden—Mrs. Grigsby, by Wagner; trained by William Bird; bred in Kentucky by Cottrill & Guest.

Auction Pools: Audrain, $700; Bob Miles, $600; Buchanan, $530; Loftin (coupled with Powhattan III as R. A. Johnson & Co.'s entry), $270; Admiral, $125; Field $90.

Bookmaking Odds: Bookmakers did not operate on opening day.

Mutuels: $5 win tickets on Buchanan paid $20.60.

BOB MILES beat the flag, and jumped into a two-length lead, followed by POWHATTAN III, AUDRAIN, the favorite and ADMIRAL. BUCHANAN fractious at the post, was away poorly, but Isaac Murphy, his Negro jockey, saved ground for three-quarters of a mile, and then Murphy called upon him for his best effort. BUCHANAN moved to the front quickly, with gigantic strides, was eased up through the final eighth, and won by two lengths.

THE WINNER'S PEDIGREE AND CAREER HIGHLIGHTS

BUCHANAN (Chestnut Colt)	*Buckden	Lord Clifden	Newminster
			The Slave
		Consequence	Bay Middleton
			Result
	Mrs. Grigsby	Wagner	Sir Charles
			Maria West
		Folly	*Yorkshire
			*Fury

Year	Age	Sts	1st	2nd	3rd	Won
1883	2	6	0	5	1	$ 500
1884	3	5	3	0	2	9,385
1885	4	13	3	5	2	2,100
1886	5	11	2	4	5	1,125
Totals		35	8	14	10	$13,110

At 2 Years	2ND	Maiden Stakes, Criterion Stakes, St. James Hotel Stakes, Alexander Stakes, Jackson Stakes
	3RD	Barrett Stakes, Belle Meade Stakes
At 3 Years	WON	Kentucky Derby, Ripple Stakes, Clark Stakes
	3RD	Hindoo Stakes
At 4 Years	2ND	Brewers' Stakes
At 5 Years	3RD	Granite Mountain Stakes

It was in this turning room at Hillerich & Bradsby that the first Louisville Slugger baseball bat was made in 1884.

Louisville has been plagued with floods through the years. This was Broadway east of Shelby in February, 1884.

May 14, 1885

Owner — J. T. Williams

A. J. Alexander of Woodford County bred five Kentucky Derby winners. Joe Cotton was the third of these. Oddly, Alexander never owned a starter in the Derby.

Tip-sheets are common sights at almost every race track these days. They first appeared at Churchill Downs in 1885 when a group of young boys offered the first selection cards for sale. They proved amazingly accurate.

ELEVENTH RUNNING

JOE COTTON

$1,500 added. Net to winner $4,630; second $200. 69 nominations.

Horses	Wt.	Fin.	Jockeys	Owners
Joe Cotton	110	1	E. Henderson	J. T. Williams
Berson	110	2	West	Morris & Patton
Ten Booker	110	3	Stoval	M. Young
Favor	110	4	Thompkins	Morris & Patton
Irish Pat	110	5	Murphy	E. Corrigan
Keokuk	110	6	Fishbourne	W. P. Hunt
Clay Pete	110	7	Withers	R. C. Pate
Thistle	110	8	Blaylock	P. G. Speth
Playfair	107	9	Conkling	G. W. Darden & Co.
Lord Coleridge	107	10	Hughes	W. Cottrill

Time: 2:37¼. Weather clear, track good.

Winner—Ch.c. by King Alfonso—*Inverness, by Macaroni; trained by Alex Perry; bred in Kentucky by A. J. Alexander.

Auction Pools: Joe Cotton, $500; Bersan and Favor $215 (coupled as Morris & Patton entry); Ten Booker, $75; Irish Pat, $40; Playfair and Thistle, $35 each; Lord Coleridge, $25; Field $30.
Bookmaking Odds: Joe Cotton, even money; Berson, 2 to 1; Ten Booker, 10 to 1.
Mutuels: ($5 win and place betting only): Joe Cotton, $9.30 straight, $8.80 place; Berson, $7.40 place.

Within the first eighth, FAVOR took the lead, KEOKUK, second, the others strung out. They ran that way into the backstretch, where JOE COTTON, in seventh position, started to move. JOE COTTON worked his way to the front, going into the stretch, but had to be ridden to his ultimate effort to stave off the rush of BERSON and TEN BOOKER, who came like whirlwinds in the final eighth.

THE WINNER'S PEDIGREE AND CAREER HIGHLIGHTS

JOE COTTON (Chestnut Colt)	King Alfonso	*Phaeton	King Tom		
			Merry Sunshine		
		Capitola	Vandal		
			Mare by *Margrave		
	*Inverness	Macaroni	Sweetmeat		
			Jocose		
		Elfrida	Faugh-a-Ballagh		
			Espoir		

Year	Age	Sts	1st	2nd	3rd	Won
1884	2	12	2	3	1	$ 725
1885	3	11	8	0	1	21,560
1886	4	8	3	0	2	2,455
1887	5	11	3	2	3	3,925
1888	6	10	1	0	0	700
1889	7	2	0	1	0	—
Totals		54	17	6	7	$29,365

At 2 Years	2ND	Nursery Stakes, Post Stakes
	3RD	Hyde Park Stakes
	UNP	Walnut Hill Stakes, Optional Stakes, Kenwood Stakes
At 3 Years	WON	Kentucky Derby, Great Western Handicap, Coney Island Derby, Tidal Stakes, Himyar Stakes, Louis and Gus Straus Stakes, Tennessee Derby, Cottrill Stakes
	3RD	Clark Stakes
	UNP	Travers Stakes, Oakwood Handicap
At 4 Years	WON	Farewell Stakes
	3RD	Fourth of July Handicap
	UNP	Excelsior Handicap, Suburban Handicap
At 5 Years	WON	Average Stakes, Twin City Handicap, Welter Stakes
At 6 Years	UNP	Suburban Handicap

William Schulte became the second president of Churchill Downs in 1885.

These programs from early Churchill Downs meets are on display in the Kentucky Derby Museum.

May 14, 1886

Owner — J. B. Haggin

All starters in the Derby carried 118 pounds in 1886. It was the first time this heavy a weight had been assigned any horse in the race. All starters now carry 126 pounds with a five pound sex allowance for fillies.

As Kentucky crowned its 1886 Derby king, New York City received a queen — the Statue of Liberty. The huge edifice located in New York's harbor was a gift from France.

BEN ALI

$1,500 added. Net to winner $4,890; second $300; third $150. 107 nominations.

Horses	Wt.	Fin.	Jockeys	Owners
Ben Ali	118	1	P. Duffy	J. B. Haggin
Blue Wing	118	2	Garrison	Melbourne Stable
Free Knight	118	3	W. Fitzpatrick	P. Corrigan
Lijero	118	4	I. Murphy	E. J. Baldwin
Jim Gray	118	5	Withers	Gray & Co.
Grimaldi	118	6	I. Lewis	J. & J. Swigert
Sir Joseph	118	7	Conkling	R. A. Swigert
Harrodsburg	118	8	J. Riley	Chinn & Morgan
Lafitte	118	9	Stovall	J. G. Greener & Co.
Masterpiece	118	10	West	S. S. Brown

Time: 2:36½ (new Derby record). Weather clear, track fast.
Winner—Br.c. by Virgil—Ulrica, by Lexington; trained by Jim Murphy; bred in Kentucky by Daniel Swigert.
Auction Pools: Ben Ali, $500; Free Knight, $385; Blue Wing, $150; Jim Gray, $65; Lijero, $50; Field, $70.
Bookmaking Odds: Bookmakers did not operate because of failure to reach license agreement with management.
Mutuels: $5 win tickets on Ben Ali paid $13.60; $5 place paid $12; $5 place tickets on Blue Wing, $10.

    MASTERPIECE broke in front, and was followed to the first turn by HARRODSBURG and SIR JOSEPH. At the three quarters, FREE KNIGHT took command, followed by BLUE WING and BEN ALI. Down through the stretch it was a furious, whipping finish between BEN ALI and BLUE WING, with BEN ALI the winner by half a length.

THE WINNER'S PEDIGREE AND CAREER HIGHLIGHTS

BEN ALI
(Brown Coit)

- Virgil
  - Vandal
    - *Glencoe
    - Mare by *Tranby
  - Hymenia
    - *Yorkshire
    - Little Peggy
- Ulrica
  - Lexington
    - Boston
    - Alice Carneal
  - *Emilia
    - Young Emilius
    - Persian

Year	Age	Sts	1st	2nd	3rd	Won
1885	2	5	1	0	0	$ 3,340
1886	3	12	7	2	2	18,550
1887	4	17	4	1	0	2,850
1888	5	6	0	0	3	350
Totals		40	12	3	5	$25,090

At 2 Years	WON	Hopeful Stakes
	UNP	Flatbush Stakes, Autumn Stakes, Champion Stallion Stakes, Goodbye Stakes
At 3 Years	WON	Kentucky Derby, Charles Green Stakes, St. Louis Derby, Ocean Stakes, Spirit of the Times Stakes, Winters Stakes
	2ND	First Special Sweepstakes, Champion Stakes
	3RD	Choice Stakes, Omnius Stakes
	UNP	American Derby
At 4 Years	WON	Free Handicap, Fourth of July Handicap
	UNP	Woodlawn Handicap, Suburban Handicap
At 5 Years	3RD	Westchester Handicap
	4TH	Equality Stakes

36

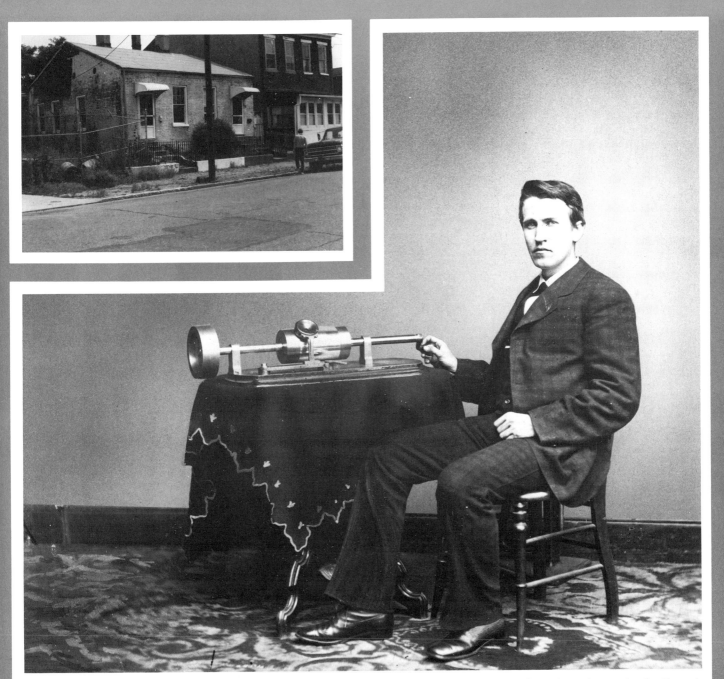

Thomas A. Edison called Louisville home in 1866, but he left when he was fired as a Western Union telegraph operator for "experimenting." He returned in 1883 to install his new electric lamps in the Southern Exposition. Edison lived in the house pictured in the inset, 729 East Washington.

May 11, 1887

Owner — Alexander Labold
(Labold Bros.)

All thoroughbred horses today descend from three male lines — Matchem, Herod and Eclipse. There have been nine Kentucky Derby winners from the Matchem line; nine from the Herod and 81 from the Eclipse.

"Once you have seen the light and learned to be in Louisville on the first Saturday in May, you become a part of the Derby and the Derby becomes a part of you."

Bill Corum
New York Journal

MONTROSE

$1,500 added. Net to winner $4,200; second $300; third $150. 119 nominations.

Horse	Wt.	Fin.	Jockeys	Owners
Montrose	118	1	I. Lewis	Labold Bros.
Jim Gore	118	2	W. Fitzpatrick	A. G. McCampbell
Jacobin	118	3	J. Stoval	R. Lisle
Banburg	115	4	Blaylock	J. D. Morrisey
Clarion	118	5	Arnold	Fleetwood Stable
Ban Yan	118	6	Godfrey	W. O. Scully
Pendennis	118	7	Murphy	Santa Anita Stable

Time: 2:39¼. Track fast.
Winner—B.c. by Duke of Montrose—Patti, by *Billet; trained by John McGinty; bred in Kentucky by Milton Young.
Auction Pools: 8 to 5 against Banburg; 2 to 1, Jim Gore; 4 to 1, Pendennis; 5 to 1, Jacobin; 6 to 1, Ban Yan; 10 to 1 each, Montrose and Clarion.
Bookmaking Odds: Montrose, 10 to 1; Jim Gore, 3 to 1; Jacobin, 6 to 1; Banburg, 7 to 5; Clarion, 10 to 1; Ban Yan, 5 to 1; Pendennis, 4 to 1.
Mutuels: Pay-off figures not available.

THE WINNER'S PEDIGREE AND CAREER HIGHLIGHTS

MONTROSE (Bay Colt)	Duke of Montrose	Waverly	*Australian / Cicily Jopson
		Kelpie	*Bonnie Scotland / Mare by Sovereign
	Patti	*Billet	Voltigeur / Calcutta
		Dora	Pat Malloy / Etta Jr.

Year	Age	Sts	1st	2nd	3rd	Won
1886	2	13	2	2	2	$ 2,690
1887	3	10	3	2	4	10,200
1888	4	12	5	3	0	7,555
1889	5	16	4	4	3	6,876
	Totals	51	14	11	9	$27,321

At 2 Years	WON	Free Handicap, Cotton Exchange Stakes
	2ND	Mechanics Stakes
	3RD	Prospect Stakes, Moet and Chandon Stakes
	UNP	Autumn Stakes, Optional Stakes, Camden Stakes, Red Bank Stakes, St. Louis Hotel Stakes
At 3 Years	WON	Kentucky Derby, St. Leger Stakes, Blue Ribbon Stakes
	2ND	Sheridan Stakes, Phoenix Stakes
	3RD	Latonia Stakes
	UNP	American Derby
At 4 Years	WON	Morrissey Stakes, Kearney Stakes, Great Western Handicap, Distillers and Brewers' Stakes
	2ND	Grand Prize of Saratoga, Boulevard Stakes, Merchants Stakes
At 5 Years	WON	Kearney Stakes, Cincinnati Hotel Handicap
	2ND	Boulevard Stakes, Kentucky Handicap
	3RD	Excelsior Handicap, Free Handicap, Distillers' and Brewers' Stakes
	UNP	Merchants' Stakes

Mule cars were Louisville's main mode of transportation just before the turn of the century. Cartoonist Fontaine Fox made the Brook Street car famous as the "Toonerville Trolley" after it was electrified.

It was a familiar site in 1886 to see the police marching in downtown Louisville. Horse-drawn buggies and trolley cars wait patiently as the officers go to work.

May 14, 1888

Jockey — G. Covington

Everyone makes mistakes: On this Derby Day, the first race on the program was a five-furlong affair for two-year-olds. But, they started the race from the four-furlong pole instead. The correction was simple — they ran the race over from the proper starting point.

The Kentucky Derby was 14 years old when golf was introduced into the United States in 1888. John Reid designed the course in Yonkers, N. Y. and played with equipment imported from Scotland.

FOURTEENTH RUNNING

MACBETH II

$2,500 added. Net to winner $4,740; second $500; third $200. 95 nominations.

Horses	Wt.	Fin.	Jockeys	Owners
Macbeth II	115	1	G. Covington	Chicago Stable
Gallifet	118	2	A. McCarthy	Melbourne Stable
White	118	3	Withers	W. O. Scully
Alexandria	118	4	Jones	Melbourne Stable
The Chevalier	118	5	Lewis	T. J. Clay
Autocrat	118	6	Hamilton	D. Gibson
Col. Zeb Ward	118	7	Blaylock	G. M. Rye

Time: 2:38¼. Weather clear, track fast.
Winner—Br.g. by Macduff—Agnes, by Gilroy; trained by John Campbell; bred in Kentucky by Rufus Lisle.
Auction Pools: Prices not available.
Bookmaking Odds: Gallifet and Alexandria (Melbourne Stable entry), even money; The Chevalier, 3½ to 1; White, 4 to 1; Macbeth II, 6 to 1; Col. Zeb Ward, 12 to 1; Autocrat, 12 to 1.
Mutuels: Pay-off prices not available.

The CHEVALIER took lead, closely followed by AUTOCRAT and COL. ZEB WARD. GALLIFET raced to the front around the first turn, and remained there until an eighth of a mile from the wire, when MACBETH II came with a rush, and won by a length.

THE WINNER'S PEDIGREE AND CAREER HIGHLIGHTS

		*Macaroon	Macaroni / Songstress
	Macduff	Jersey Lass	*King Ernest / Jersey Belle
MACBETH II (Brown Gelding)		Gilroy	Lexington / Magnolia
	Agnes	Laura Bruce	Star Davis / Alida

Year	Age	Sts	1st	2nd	3rd	Won
1887	2	8	1	1	0	$ 1,340
1888	3	25	7	5	5	11,745
1889	4	16	3	1	2	1,600
1890	5	35	10	9	5	4,990
1891	6	9	3	3	1	2,195
1892	7	1	0	0	0	—
1893	8	12	1	2	1	300
Totals		106	25	21	14	$22,170

At 2 Years	WON	Kimball Stakes
	UNP	Maiden Stakes, Belle Meade Stakes, Blue Grass Stakes
At 3 Years	WON	Kentucky Derby, Kansas City Derby, Gayoso Hotel Stakes, Peabody Hotel Stakes
	2ND	Phoenix Stakes, Distillers' Stakes, Merchants' Stakes, Cottrill Stakes
	UNP	Boulevard Stakes
At 4 Years	3RD	Welter Handicap
At 5 Years	WON	Green Stakes, Highweight Handicap
	UNP	Welter Stakes
At 6 Years	WON	Clifton, N. J., New Year's Handicap

The Galt House has been a familiar name in Louisville since 1835. No. 1 was built in 1835. No. 2 is the remodeled version before it burned in 1865. No. 3 is as it appeared in 1880. No. 4 is the eye-catching 1970s version at Fourth and River.

May 9, 1889

Jockey — Thomas Kiley

This was the last year auction pools were sold until the method was revived by Col. Matt Winn in 1908. The auction pools were ruled out following a protest by bookmakers that their business was being handicapped.

Transportation to the Derby got a boost in 1889 when Louisville got its first electric street car. They eventually replaced all the mule - and - horse drawn street cars; the last of which was used in 1901 after being introduced in 1864.

F I F T E E N T H   R U N N I N G

SPOKANE

$2,500 added. Net to winner $4,880; second 300; third $150. 94 nominations.

Horses	Wt.	Fin.	Jockeys	Owners
Spokane	118	1	T. Kiley	N. Armstrong
Proctor Knott	115	2	S. Barnes	Scoggan & Bryant
Once Again	118	3	I. Murphy	M. Young
Hindoocraft	118	4	Armstrong	Scoggan Bros.
Cassius	118	5	Taral	Beverwyck Stable
Sportsman	118	6	I. Lewis	J. K. Megibben & Co.
Outbound	118	7	Hollis	Fleetwood Stable
Bootmaker	118	8	Warwick	Wilson & Young

Time: :24, :48½, 1:14½, 1:41½, 2:09½, 2:34½ (new Derby record). Weather clear, track fast.

Winner—Ch.c. by Hyder Ali—Interpose, by *Intruder; trained by John Rodegap; bred in Montana by Noah Armstrong.

Bookmaking Odds: Proctor Knott, 1 to 2; Spokane, 10 to 1; Once Again and Bootmaker (Young entry), 3 to 1; Hindoocraft, 10 to 1; Cassius, 15 to 1; Outbound, 15 to 1; Sportsman, 15 to 1.

Mutuels: ($2 tickets sold for first time this year.) $2 tickets on Spokane paid $34.80 win, $6.30 place; Proctor Knott, $2.90 place. No show tickets sold.

PROCTOR KNOTT, a wild horse at the barrier, broke away twice, to gallop more than an eighth of a mile, and almost unseated his rider during several spectacular lunges. But he broke along with his field.

HINDOOCRAFT was the early leader, with BOOTMAKER, second, SPOKANE, third. Near the first turn, PROCTOR KNOTT was rushed to the front, and led by three lengths entering the backstretch, with SPORTSMAN, second; HINDOOCRAFT, third; and SPOKANE, fifth, under a careful ride.

All through the backstretch, PROCTOR KNOTT was fighting for his head. Leaving the backstretch, PROCTOR KNOTT was five lengths in front, with HINDOOCRAFT, second; SPOKANE had moved into third place, and gradually was increasing speed.

Taking the turn for home, Barnes was unable to control PROCTOR KNOTT, and the colt lost many lengths by racing to the outer rail, where Barnes succeeded in getting him straightened. Barnes chose to ride the outer rail, rather than lose ground by steering his horse back toward the inside fence.

SPOKANE skimmed the inner rail, and ran through the stretch on the inside rail, with PROCTOR KNOTT on the outside rail. PROCTOR KNOTT had about a half-length advantage an eighth from the wire, but it was obvious that he was a tired horse, while SPOKANE seemed fresh and strong. As the finish wire was crossed, opinion of spectators was divided as to the outcome. One faction was certain that SPOKANE, on the inside, had nosed out PROCTOR KNOTT on the outer rail; another took the opposite viewpoint. The judges Col. Lewis Clark, Gen. Robinson and J. K. Megibben — deliberated quite a while then awarded to SPOKANE by a nose.

THE WINNER'S PEDIGREE AND CAREER HIGHLIGHTS

SPOKANE (Chestnut Colt)	Hyder Ali	*Leamington	Faugh-a-Ballagh / Mare by Pantaloon
		Lady Duke	Lexington / Magdalen
	Interpose	*Intruder	Crater / Lady Bountiful
		Lilac	Lightning / Dolly Carter

Year	Age	Sts	1st	2nd	3rd	Won
1888	2	5	2	0	0	$ 1,535
1889	3	8	3	2	1	24,970
1890	4	4	0	2	1	300
Totals		17	5	4	2	$26,805

At 2 Years
- WON Maiden Stakes
- 4TH Hyde Park Stakes

At 3 Years
- WON Kentucky Derby, American Derby, Clark Stakes
- 2ND Sheridan Stakes, Peabody Hotel Handicap
- 3RD Pelham Bay Handicap
- UNP Twin City Handicap, Drexel Stakes

Mary Bruce Sharon was born in 1878 and grew up in Kentucky. Her early life was filled with beautiful things — huge family gatherings with tables of good food; a May-Day party; fishing with her grandfather; frilly dresses made in New York by a French dressmaker. Then, at the age of 74 in 1952, she began to put those memories on canvas. She was "discovered" through the efforts of her son-in-law and her works achieved importance in the primitive field. She had her paintings exhibited in New York, Cannes, France and in many important galleries.

One of her favorite places was Churchill Downs and the painting on this page is titled "My First Visit to the Kentucky Derby." It was done in 1956 and is to be included in a Smithsonian Institute traveling exhibition as a highlight of America's Bicentennial.

Of the painting, she wrote:

"I was about eight years old when I first attended the Kentucky Derby. I went with Mama and Grandpa in a cousin's tally-ho. I remember the excitement, the gaily dressed crowds, the beautiful horses, the delicious picnic lunch we had, and the band playing "My Old Kentucky Home." Most of all, I remember the horse, owned by one of our Bruce relatives, which sat down at the beginning of the race and refused to budge and how I broke down and cried."

May 14, 1890

Owner-Trainer — Edward Corrigan

Jockey — Isaac Murphy

It rained on this Derby Day, marking the first time since the race's inauguration that the weather was uncooperative. The field of six which went to the post was the smallest in history to that date.

SIXTEENTH RUNNING

†RILEY

$2,500 added. Net to winner $5,460; second $300; third $150. 115 nominations.

Horses	Wt.	Fin.	Jockeys	Owners
Riley	118	1	I. Murphy	E. Corrigan
Bill Letcher	118	2	Allen	W. R. Letcher
Robespierre	118	3	Francis	G. V. Hankins
Palisade	118	4	Britton	S. Williams
Outlook	118	5	Breckinridge	B. J. Treacy
Prince Fonso	118	6	Overton	J. C. Twymann & Co.

Time: 2:45. Track heavy.

Winner—Bay colt by Longfellow—Geneva, by War Dance; trained by Edward Corrigan; bred in Kentucky by C. H. Durkee.

Bookmaking Odds; Robespierre, even money; Riley, 4 to 1; Bill Letcher, 5 to 1; Prince Fonso, 5 to 1; Palisade, 8 to 1; Outlook, 10 to 1.

No auction pools or mutuels sold at track after 1889 until 1908. However, auction pools sold in 1890, 1891 and for years thereafter in downtown Louisville, on night before, and morning of Derby.

BILL LETCHER was away first, and PALISADE, second. ROBESPIERRE, the favorite, took the lead nearing the first turn; OUTLOOK, second. RILEY came from last place, going into the backstretch, and took command, winning easily by two lengths.

THE WINNER'S PEDIGREE AND CAREER HIGHLIGHTS

†RILEY (Bay Colt)			
	Longfellow	*Leamington	Faugh-a-Ballagh Mare by Pantaloon
		Nantura	Brawner's Eclipse Queen Mary
	Geneva	War Dance	Lexington Reel
		La Gitana	Uncle Vic Georgia Wood

Year	Age	Sts	1st	2nd	3rd	Won
1889	2	12	6	3	0	$ 4,505
1890	3	21	11	6	2	21,065
1891	4	15	8	3	1	14,360
1892	5	3	2	1	0	1,050
1893	6	10	2	4	1	2,150
1894	7	3	1	0	0	300
Totals		64	30	17	4	$43,430

At 2 Years	WON	Railway Stakes, Trial Stakes, Merchants' Stakes
	2ND	Kimball Stakes, Gaston Hotel Stakes
	UNP	Westside Stakes
At 3 Years	WON	Kentucky Derby, Clark Stakes, Speculation Handicap, Fairview Lightweight Handicap, Pelham Bay Handicap
	2ND	St. Leger Stakes, Latonia Derby, Himyar Stakes
	3RD	Runnymede Handicap, Brookwood Handicap
At 4 Years	WON	Monmouth Cup, Shrewsbury Handicap, Coney Island Cup, Bay Ridge Handicap, Free Handicap, Brooklyn Cup, Montgomery Stakes
	2ND	Monmouth Champion Stakes, Long Branch Handicap
	3RD	Distillers' Stakes
	UNP	Suburban, Metropolitan Handicap, Brooklyn Jockey Club Handicap
At 6 Years	2ND	Boulevard Stakes

†Riley was originally named Shortfellow.

A devastating tornado cut a swath through the heart of Louisville along the Ohio River on March 27, 1890. There were 76 fatalities.

sullivan & cozart
general contractors
louisville, kentucky

Kinzea Stone
Co-owner of Jacobin Stable

Jockey — Isaac Murphy

"I am as proud of my calling as I am of my record, and I believe my life will be recorded as a success, though the reputation I enjoy was earned in the stable and saddle."

Isaac Murphy
First Jockey to Ride
Three Derby Winners

KINGMAN

$2,500 added. Net to winner $4,550; second $300; third $150. 83 nominations.

Horses	Wt.	Fin.	Jockeys	Owners
Kingman 122		1	I. Murphy	Jacobin Stable
Balgowan 122		2	Overton	T. J. Clay
High Tariff 122		3	R. Williams	Easton & Larabie
Hart Wallace 122		4	Kiley	Bashford Manor

Time: 1:05½ (half), 1:35¾ (six furlongs), 2:01 (mile), 2:52¼. Track slow.

Winner—B.c. by *Glengarry—Patricia, by Vauxhall; trained by Dud Allen; bred in Tennessee by A. C. Franklin.

Bookmaking Odds: Kingman, 1 to 2; Balgowan, 3 to 1; High Tariff, 10 to 1; Hart Wallace, 6 to 1.

This was the slowest of all Derbies. HART WALLACE broke on top; HIGH TARIFF, second; BALGOWAN, third; KINGMAN, fourth. Within a quarter of a mile they all were traveling like a cavalry, side by side, nose and nose, each jockey waiting for the other to set the pace, and none doing it. Each rider had orders to stay back for about a mile and whenever one horse moved a little to the front, his rider restrained him, and the others restrained theirs, too. The mile was covered in 2:01, and the mile and a quarter in 2:26¾. At that point, Murphy started his move with KINGMAN, and Overton let BALGOWAN have his head, but KINGMAN won the race by a length.

THE WINNER'S PEDIGREE AND CAREER HIGHLIGHTS

KINGMAN (Bay Colt)	*Glengarry	Thormanby	‡Windhound
			Alice Hawthorn
		Carbine	Rifleman
			Troica
	Patricia	Vauxhall	Lexington
			Verona
		Minnie Mc	Planet
			Edina

‡Melbourne or Windhound

Year	Age	Sts	1st	2nd	3rd	Won
1890	2	16	4	6	2	$ 3,900
1891	3	12	6	0	4	15,465
Totals		28	10	6	6	$19,365

At 2 Years	2ND	Edgewater Handicap, Railway Stakes, Hyde Park Stakes
	3RD	Monmouth Free Handicap
At 3 Years	WON	Kentucky Derby, Phoenix Stakes, Latonia Derby, St. Paul Free Handicap
	3RD	American Derby
	4TH	Sheridan Stakes

Union Station was completed in 1891 at a cost of $400,000. It was started in 1882 and the architect was F. W. Mowbray.

A Touch Of The Old And The New

The Lincoln Tower is the first tower in the world built with a large bridge-like truss near its top from which the lower floors are suspended. It was designed by Taliesin Associates, founded by the late Frank Lloyd Wright. Very popular with visitors is the outside observation elevator looking out over a beautiful race horse farm and the City of Louisville.

May 11, 1892

Owner — George J. Long

Trainer — John H. Morris

Jockey — Alonzo Clayton

AZRA

$2,500 added. Net to winner $4,230; second $300; third $150. 68 nominations.

Horses	Wt.	Fin.	Jockeys	Owners
Azra	122	1	A. Clayton	Bashford Manor
Huron	122	2	Britton	Ed Corrigan
Phil Dwyer	122	3	Overton	Ed Corrigan

Time: 2:41½. Track heavy.

Winner—B.c. by Reform—Albia, by Alarm; trained by John H. Morris; bred in Kentucky by George J. Long.

Bookmaking Odds: Azra, 3 to 2; Huron and Phil Dwyer (coupled as Corrigan entry), 11 to 20.

HURON broke in front and had a six-length lead well along the backstretch. Then Clayton, aboard AZRA, made his move, caught HURON near the wire, and won by a nose.

THE WINNER'S PEDIGREE AND CAREER HIGHLIGHTS

AZRA (Bay Colt)
- Reform
  - *Leamington
    - Faugh-a-Ballagh
    - Mare by Pantaloon
  - *Stolen Kisses
    - The Knight of Kars
    - Defamation
- Albia
  - Alarm
    - *Eclipse
    - *Maud
  - Elastic
    - Kentucky
    - Blue Ribbon

Year	Age	Sts	1st	2nd	3rd	Won
1891	2	13	2	2	3	$ 5,690
1892	3	10	3	1	4	15,020
Totals		23	5	3	7	$20,710

At 2 Years
- WON Champagne Stakes
- 2ND Essex Stakes
- 3RD Nursery Stakes, Dunmow Stakes, Partridge Stakes
- UNP Select Stakes, Carteret Handicap, White Plains Handicap, Sapphire Stakes

At 3 Years
- WON Kentucky Derby, Travers Stakes
- 2ND Choice Stakes
- 3RD Jerome Stakes, Bridge Handicap, Lorillard Stakes, Garfield Park Derby
- 4TH American Derby

Bashford Manor was the beautiful home of George J. Long, who bred the Derby winners Azra, Manuel and Sir Huon. Long is pictured (below, right) with his trainer, Pete Coyne.

May 10, 1893

Owner — Cushing & Orth

Jockey — E. Kunze

The rule that horses of different ownership being trained by the same man must run as an entry was first invoked by Col. M. Lewis Clark, founder of Churchill Downs, in the year 1893.

LOOKOUT

$3,000 added. Net to winner $3,840; second $400; third $150; fourth $100. 60 nominations.

Horses	Wt.	Fin.	Jockeys	Owners
Lookout	122	1	E. Kunze	Cushing & Orth
Plutus	122	2	A. Clayton	Bashford Manor
Boundless	122	3	R. Williams	Cushing & Orth
Buck McCann	122	4	Thorpe	Scoggan Bros.
Mirage	122	5	I. Murphy	James E. Pepper
Linger	122	6	Flynn	C. E. Railey

Time: 2:39¼. Weather clear.

Winner—Ch.c. by Troubadour—Christina, by King Alfonso; trained by William McDaniel; bred in Kentucky by Scoggan Brothers.

Bookmaking Odds: 7 to 10 (Cushing & Orth's entry), Lookout, Boundless; 3 to 1, Plutus.

Within the first eighth, LOOKOUT, coupled with BOUNDLESS, took the lead, held it throughout, and won by five lengths.

THE WINNER'S PEDIGREE AND CAREER HIGHLIGHTS

LOOKOUT (Chestnut Colt)
- Troubadour
  - Lisbon
    - *Phaeton
    - *Lady Love
  - Glenluine
    - *Glenelg
    - Lute
- Christina
  - King Alfonso
    - *Phaeton
    - Capitola
  - Luileme
    - Lexington
    - Rosette

Year	Age	Sts	1st	2nd	3rd	Won
1892	2	20	9	4	2	$ 5,585
1893	3	8	3	0	0	8,730
1894	4	18	2	2	0	1,000
1895	5	18	3	5	3	1,910
1896	6	2	0	1	0	125
Totals		66	17	12	5	$17,350

At 2 Years
- WON Minneapolis Stakes
- 2ND Turf Exchange Stakes
- 3RD Merchant's Hotel Handicap

At 3 Years
- WON Kentucky Derby, Gibson Stakes, Annual Stakes
- UNP American Derby

At 5 Years
- WON Coney Island Highweight Handicap
- 3RD Toronto Cup
- UNP Royal Canadian Hurdle Handicap

The Jefferson County courthouse looked like this in 1893.

Recognize this fellow? It's Matt Winn. The left photo shows him at the age of 21 in 1882 and the photo at the right was taken in the "gay nineties". He took over the operation of Churchill Downs in 1902.

May 15, 1894

Owner — Leigh & Rose

If you think the crowds at the Derby are tremendous today, read this:

"The crowd was so great that locomotion was almost impossible. The inner field presented one mass of humanity from the head of the stretch . . . the crowd was large enough that it was necessary to provide a police escort to get the starter to his position . . ."

This was written in 1891.

Jockey Frank Goodale, who rode Chant to victory, was killed several days after the Derby when a horse he was riding stumbled and fell in a race.

TWENTIETH RUNNING

CHANT

$2,500 added. Net to winner $4,020; second $300; third $150; fourth $100. 55 nominations.

Horses	Wt.	Fin.	Jockey	Owners
Chant	122	1	F. Goodale	Leigh & Rose
Pearl Song	122	2	R. Williams	C. H. Smith
Sigurd	122	3	Overton	Bashford Manor
Al Boyer	122	4	Ray	Anderson & Gooding
Tom Elmore	122	5	Irving	S. K. Hughes & Co.

Time: 2:41. Weather clear.

Winner—B.c. by Falsetto—Addie C., by Voltigeur; trained by Eugene Leigh; bred in Kentucky by A. J. Alexander.

Bookmaking Odds: Chant, 1 to 2; Pearl Song, 3 to 1; Sigurd, 12 to 1.

SIGURD broke first, followed by CHANT, which took the lead at the half and won by two lengths.

THE WINNER'S PEDIGREE AND CAREER HIGHLIGHTS

CHANT (Bay Colt)
- Falsetto
  - Enquirer
    - *Leamington
    - Lida
  - Farfaletta
    - *Australian
    - Elkhorna
- Addie C.
  - Voltigeur
    - Vandal
    - Duet
  - Aerolite
    - Lexington
    - Florine

Year	Age	Sts	1st	2nd	3rd	Won
1893	2	25	8	5	3	$ 3,900
1894	3	33	13	7	3	13,835
1895	4	4	1	3	0	545
1896	5	1	0	0	0	—
Totals		63	22	15	6	$18,280

At 2 Years	UNP	Sensation Stakes, Harold Stakes
At 3 Years	WON	Kentucky Derby, Clark Stakes, Phoenix Stakes
At 4 Years	2ND	Country Club Stakes

Joseph D. Baldez, a 24-year-old draftsman and native Louisvillian, designed the new stands and twin spires which were built at Churchill Downs in 1894 and first used in 1895. Baldez is shown (inset) at his drawing board. What probably is his most famous work is pictured with a front and back view.

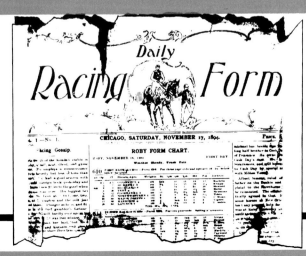

May 6, 1895

Owner-Trainer — Byron McClelland

Jockey — James Perkins

The new grandstand with its twin spires was completed in 1895. The spires have since become the trademark of Churchill Downs and are synonymous with the Kentucky Derby.

TWENTY FIRST RUNNING

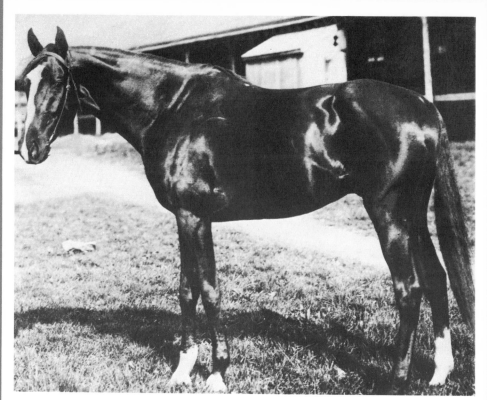

HALMA

$2,500 added. Net to winner $2,970; second $300; third $150; fourth $100. 57 nominations.

Horses	Wt.	Fin.	Jockeys	Owners
Halma	122	1	J. Perkins	B. McClelland
Basso	122	2	W. Martin	C. H. Smith
Laureate	122	3	A. Clayton	Pastime Stable
Curator	122	4	Overton	Bashford Manor

Time: 2:37½. Weather clear.

Winner—Blk.c. by Hanover—Julia L., by Longfellow; trained by Byron McClelland; bred in Kentucky by Eastin & Larrabie.

Bookmaking Odds: Halma, 1 to 3; Basso, 9 to 2; Laureate, 5 to 1; Curator, 20 to 1.

HALMA led from start to finish, only galloping through the stretch, to win by three lengths.

THE WINNER'S PEDIGREE AND CAREER HIGHLIGHTS

HALMA (Black Colt)
- Hanover
  - Hindoo
    - Virgil
    - Florence
  - Bourbon Belle
    - *Bonnie Scotland
    - Ella D.
- Julia L.
  - Longfellow
    - *Leamington
    - Nantura
  - Christine
    - *Australian
    - La Grande Duchesse

Year	Age	Sts	1st	2nd	3rd	Won
1894	2	9	2	1	2	$ 1,785
1895	3	5	4	1	0	13,635
1896	4	0	0	0	0	—
1897	5	2	1	0	1	465
Totals		16	7	2	3	$15,885

At 2 Years
- 2ND Nursery Stakes
- 3RD Dunmow Stakes
- UNP White Plains Handicap, Matron Stakes, Seashore Stakes, Autumn Stakes

At 3 Years
- WON Kentucky Derby, Latonia Derby, Clark Stakes, Phoenix Stakes
- 2ND Himyar Stakes

The Confederate Monument on Third Street was completed in 1895.

Everyone was standing (though everyone was not paying attention) as the field swept past the new grandstand in 1895. The new stands faced away from the afternoon sun, an improvement over the original stands.

May 6, 1896

Owner — M. F. Dwyer

Trainer — Hardy Campbell

Jockey — Willie Simms

BEN BRUSH

Value $6,000. Net to winner $4,850; second $700; third $300. 171 nominations.

Horses	Wt.	Fin.	Jockeys	Owners
Ben Brush 117	1	W. Simms	M. F. Dwyer
Ben Eder 117	2	Tabor	Hot Springs Stable
Semper Ego 117	3	Perkins	L. B. Ringgold
First Mate 117	4	Thorpe	Eastin & Larabie
The Dragon 117	5	Overton	James E. Pepper
Parson 117	6	Britton	Himyar Stable
The Winner 117	7	Walker	William Wallace
Ulysses 117	8	R. Williams	Ed Brown

Time: 2:07¾. Weather clear, track good.

Winner—B.c. by Bramble—Roseville, by Reform; trained by Hardy Campbell; bred in Kentucky by Clay & Woodford.

Bookmaking Odds: Ben Brush, 1 to 2; Ben Eder, 2 to 1; Semper Ego, 9 to 1.

At post 20 minutes, SEMPER EGO took an immediate lead, followed by THE WINNER and FIRST MATE. On the first turn, FIRST MATE was in command, and led to the three-quarter pole. BEN BRUSH, who had stumbled at the start, nearly unseated his rider, and seemed hopelessly out of it, began to move on the backstretch, together with BEN EDER. This pair caught the tired pacemakers going into the stretch, fought it out for almost a quarter of a mile, and BEN BRUSH won by a nose.

THE WINNER'S PEDIGREE AND CAREER HIGHLIGHTS

BEN BRUSH (Bay Colt)	Bramble	*Bonnie Scotland	Iago / Queen Mary
		Ivy Leaf	*Australian / Bay Flower
	Roseville	Reform	*Leamington / *Stolen Kisses
		Albia	Alarm / Elastic

Year	Age	Sts	1st	2nd	3rd	Won
1895	2	16	13	1	1	$22,517
1896	3	8	4	1	1	27,340
1897	4	16	8	3	3	17,045
Totals		40	25	5	5	$66,902

At 2 Years	WON	Champagne Stakes, Albany Stakes, Nursery Stakes, Heavy Handicap (all ages), Prospect Handicap, Holly Handicap, Diamond Stakes, Emerald Stakes, Harold Stakes, Cadet Stakes
	2ND	Flatbush Stakes
	UNP	Great Eastern Handicap
At 3 Years	WON	Kentucky Derby, Latonia Derby, Buckeye Stakes, Schulte Stakes
	2ND	National Derby
	3RD	Oakley Derby
	UNP	Fall Handicap
At 4 Years	WON	Second Special, First Special, Omnium Handicap, The Citizens Handicap, Brighton Handicap, Suburban Handicap
	2ND	Oriental Handicap
	3RD	Brighton Cup, Midsummer Handicap
	UNP	Long Island Handicap, Sheepshead Bay Handicap

The Louisville Bicycle Club members rode out Grand Boulevard (Southern Parkway) to Iroquois Park. A waystop was at the building at the right — it was the original clubhouse at Churchill Downs before being moved off the property in 1894.

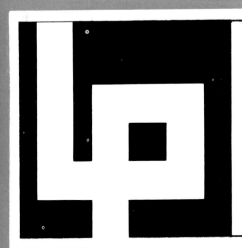

May 12, 1897

Owner — J. C. Cahn

While Typhoon II was rushing to victory in the Derby on a heavy track, thousands of Americans rushed to Alaska for the Klondike gold rush in 1897.

In the next eight years it was estimated that $8,000,000 in gold was taken from the territory.

" 'See America First' is a ringing slogan, but the first thing to see in America is the Kentucky Derby."

Keats Speed
New York Sun

TYPHOON II

Value $6,000. Net to winner $4,850; second $700; third $300. 159 nominations.

Horses	Wt.	Fin.	Jockey	Owners
Typhoon II 117	117	1	F. Garner	J. C. Cahn
Ornament 117	117	2	A. Clayton	C. T. Patterson & Co.
Dr. Catlett 117	117	3	R. Williams	Turney Bros.
Dr. Shepard 117	117	4	J. Hill	Foster Bros.
Goshen 117	117	5	Willhite	J. Rodegap
Ben Brown 117	117	6	Ballard	C. Fleischmann

Time: 2:12½. Track heavy.

Winner—Ch.c. by *Top Gallant—Dolly Varden, by *Glenleg; trained by J. C. Cahn; bred in Tennessee by John B. Ewing.

Bookmaking Odds: Typhoon II, 3 to 1; Ornament, even; Dr. Catlett, 4 to 1.

TYPHOON II led from the start to finish, to win by a head. ORNAMENT, the favorite, was off poorly, and in deep going all the way.

THE WINNER'S PEDIGREE AND CAREER HIGHLIGHTS

TYPHOON II (Chestnut Colt)
- *Top Gallant
  - Sterling
    - Oxford
    - Whisper
  - Sea Mark
    - Adventurer
    - Sea Gull
- Dolly Varden
  - *Glenleg
    - Citadel
    - *Babta
  - Nannie Black
    - Virgil
    - Nannie Butler

Year		Age	Sts	1st	2nd	3rd	Won
1896		2	18	8	6	1	$ 7,565
1897		3	11	8	2	1	12,420
1898		4	10	3	1	1	2,340
	Totals		39	19	9	3	$22,325

At 2 Years		
	WON	Westchester Highweight Handicap, Golden Rod Stakes, Brewers' Stakes
	2ND	Nursery Stakes, Great Eastern Stakes, Two-Year-Old Champion Stakes
	3RD	Kindergarten Stakes
	UNP	White Plains Handicap, Rancocas Stakes, Champagne Stakes

At 3 Years		
	WON	Kentucky Derby, St. Louis Club Members Handicap, Memorial Handicap, Peabody Hotel Handicap, Luehrmann Hotel Stakes, Chickasaw Club Handicap
	2ND	Tennessee Derby
	3RD	St. Louis Derby

At 4 Years		
	WON	Highweight Handicap
	3RD	Coney Island Handicap
	UNP	Fall Handicap, Toboggan Handicap, Metropolitan Handicap

The Louisville Boat Club was organized in 1879 and was located at the end of the public wharf on the Ohio River in 1897.

May 4, 1898

Owner — J. E. Madden

Jockey — Willie Simms

Plaudit won the Derby in 1898 but Andrew Green earned the plaudits of the world when he came up with the plan that year to combine the boroughs of Bronx, Queens, Brooklyn, Manhattan and Richmond into New York City.

PLAUDIT

Value $6,000. Net to winner $4,850; second $700; third $300. 179 nominations.

Horses	Wt.	Fin.	Jockeys	Owners
Plaudit	117	1	W. Simms	J. E. Madden
Lieber Karl	122	2	T. Burns	J. W. Schorr
Isabey	117	3	A. Knapp	Stanton & Tucker
Han d'Or	117	4	J. Conley	G. A. Singerly

Time: 2:09. Weather clear.

Winner—Br.c. by Himyar—*Cinderella, by Tomahawk or Blue Ruin; trained by John E. Madden; bred in Kentucky by Dr. J. D. Neet.

Bookmaking Odds: Plaudit, 3 to 1; Lieber Karl, 1 to 3; Isabey, 12 to 1; Han d'Or, 25 to 1.

LIEBER KARL, the favorite, broke in front and made a runaway race of it until nearing the turn for home, when PLAUDIT came with a terrific rush, and won by a neck.

THE WINNER'S PEDIGREE AND CAREER HIGHLIGHTS

PLAUDIT (Brown Colt)
- Himyar
  - Alarm
    - *Eclipse
    - *Maud
  - Hira
    - Lexington
    - Hegira
- *Cinderella
  - ‡Tomahawk
    - Blue Mantle
    - Raffle
  - Manna
    - Brown Bread
    - Tartlet

‡ by Tomahawk or Blue Ruin.

Year	Age	Sts	1st	2nd	3rd	Won
1897	2	12	4	1	0	$ 8,345
1898	3	8	4	4	0	23,720
Totals		20	8	5	0	$32,065

At 2 Years
- WON Champagne Stakes, Nursery Stakes, Emerald Stakes
- 2ND Dash Stakes
- UNP Great Plains Handicap, Futurity, Diamond Stakes

At 3 Years
- WON Kentucky Derby, Buckeye Stakes, Oakley Derby, Clark Stakes
- 2ND Realization, St. Louis Derby, Latonia Derby

Churchill Downs had a band shell (right) which served the community for night concerts by such musical greats as John Phillip Sousa.

This was Louisville B.P. (before paving) and the water wagons were kept busy sprinkling in the summer months to keep down dust.

May 4, 1899

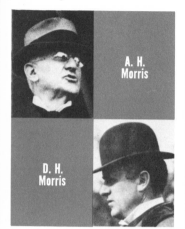

A. H. Morris

D. H. Morris

Owners

Trainer — Robert J. Walden

Jockey — Fred Taral

MANUEL

Value $6,000. Net to winner $4,850; second $700; third $300. 151 nominations.

Horses	Wt.	Fin.	Jockeys	Owners
Manuel	117	1	F. Taral	A. H. & D. H. Morris
Corsini	122	2	T. Burns	E. Corrigan
Mazo	117	3	J. Conley	J. E. Madden
His Lordship	110	4	Turner	J. D. Smith
Fontainebleu	117	5	Overton	J. M. Forsythe

Time: 2:12. Weather clear.

Winner—B.c. by Bob Miles—Espanita, by Alarm; trained by Robert J. Walden; bred in Kentucky by George J. Long.

Bookmaking Odds: Manuel 11 to 20; Corsini, 3 to 1; Mazo, 8 to 1.

MANUEL broke in front, was taken back, and HIS LORDSHIP led to the half-mile. Then the wraps were taken off MANUEL, he was permitted to open, won by two lengths, and never was extended.

THE WINNER'S PEDIGREE AND CAREER HIGHLIGHTS

MANUEL (Bay Colt)

- Bob Miles
  - Pat Malloy
    - Lexington
    - Gloriana
  - Dolly Morgan
    - Revenue
    - Sally Morgan
- Espanita
  - Alarm
    - *Eclipse
    - *Maud
  - Outstep
    - Blue Eyes
    - Etna

Year		Age	Sts	1st	2nd	3rd	Won
1898		2	17	3	4	4	$ 4,540
1899		3	4	1	1	0	5,200
	Totals		21	4	5	4	$ 9,740

At 2 Years
- WON Prospect Stakes
- 2ND White Plains Handicap, Surf Stakes
- 3RD Champagne Stakes, Algeria Stakes, Wenonah Stakes
- UNP Nursery Stakes, Great Eastern Stakes, Autumn Maiden Stakes, Flatbush Stakes

At 3 Years
- WON Kentucky Derby
- 2ND Montgomery Handicap
- UNP Twin City Handicap

62

The Seelbach European Hotel was a landmark in Louisville at the turn of the century. It was located at Sixth and Main. A new Seelbach, with its famed Roof Garden, opened in 1905. The waiters — and some interested spectators — pose at the door of the original hotel.

May 3, 1900

Owner — Charles H. Smith

Trainer — Charles H. Hughes

Jockey — Jimmy Boland

LIEUT. GIBSON

Value $6,000. Net value to winner $4,850; second $700; third $300. 131 nominations.

Horses	Wt.	Fin.	Jockey	Owners
Lieut. Gibson	117	1	J. Boland	Charles H. Smith
Florizar	122	2	Van Dusen	H. J. Scoggan
Thrive	122	3	J. Winkfield	J. C. Cahn
Highland Lad	—	4	Crowhurst	H. J. Scoggan
His Excellency	—	5	Gilmore	T. C. McDowell
Kentucky Farmer	—	6	Overton	Woodford & Buckner
Hindus	—	7	Vititoe	George J. Long

Time: 2:06¼ (new Derby record). Weather clear.

Winner—B.c. by G. W. Johnson—Sophia Hardy, by *Glengarry; trained by Charles H. Hughes; bred in Kentucky by Baker & Gentry.

Bookmaking Odds: Lieut. Gibson, 7 to 10; Florizar, 5 to 1; Thrive, 7 to 1.

HINDUS broke first; KENTUCKY FARMER, second; LIEUT. GIBSON, third. Going around the first turn, LIEUT. GIBSON moved into leadership and merely breezed the rest of the way, to win by four lengths, never extended.

THE WINNER'S PEDIGREE AND CAREER HIGHLIGHTS

LIEUT. GIBSON (Bay Colt)	G. W. Johnson	Iroquois	*Leamington Maggie B. B.
		Brunette	*Bonnie Scotland Variella
	Sophia Hardy	*Glengarry	Thormanby Carbine
		Unaka	Enquirer Wampee

Year	Age	Sts	1st	2nd	3rd	Won
1899	2	18	7	4	2	$ 8,475
1900	3	6	3	1	1	13,015
Totals		24	10	5	3	$21,490

At 2 Years	WON	Kentucky Central Stakes, Kimball Stakes, Flatbush Stakes, Sensation Stakes
	2ND	Westchester Highweight Handicap
	3RD	Harold Stakes
At 3 Years	WON	Kentucky Derby, Clark Stakes, Latonia Derby
	3RD	American Derby
	UNP	Great Western Handicap

You probably won't recognize this street. It was called Grand Boulevard when the photo was taken about 1900, but it is known as Southern Parkway today.

CONGRATULATIONS
on your 100th birthday.

April 29, 1901

Owner — F. B. VanMeter

Jockey — Jimmy Winkfield

The Derby traditionally is a May race, but twice it has been run in another month. The year 1901 was one of these years; the other was in 1945 when it was run on June 9 because of a wartime ban on racing in the early months of the year. The Derby has been run every day of the week except Sunday.

HIS EMINENCE

Value $6,000. Net to winner $4,850; second $700; third $300. 113 nominations.

Horses	Wt.	Fin.	Jockeys	Owners
His Eminence	117	1	J. Winkfield	F. B. Van Meter
Sannazarro	117	2	O'Connor	William Hayes
Driscoll	110	3	J. Boland	Woodford Clay
Amur	110	4	Dupree	George J. Long
Alard Scheck	117	5	J. Woods	J. W. Schorr

Time: 2:07¾. Weather clear.

Winner—B.c. by Falsetto—Patroness, by Pat Malloy; trained by F. B. VanMeter; bred in Kentucky by A. J. Alexander.

Bookmaking Odds: His Eminence, 3 to 1; Sannazarro, 4 to 1; Driscoll, 20 to 1; Amur, 25 to 1; Alard Scheck, 7 to 10.

HIS EMINENCE broke in front and stayed there, winning easily by two lengths.

THE WINNER'S PEDIGREE AND CAREER HIGHLIGHTS

HIS EMINENCE (Bay Colt)
- Falsetto
  - Enquirer
    - *Leamington
    - Lida
  - Farfaletta
    - *Australian
    - Elkhorna
- Patroness
  - Pat Malloy
    - Lexington
    - Gloriana
  - *Inverness
    - Macaroni
    - Elfrida

Year	Age	Sts	1st	2nd	3rd	Won
1900	2	17	6	1	2	$ 1,925
1901	3	7	2	1	1	8,370
1902	4	12	2	2	0	2,740
1903	5	12	1	1	3	3,110
1904	6	5	0	2	2	150
Total		53	11	7	8	$16,295

At 2 Years	3RD	Wenonah Stakes
At 3 Years	WON	Kentucky Derby, Clark Stakes
	UNP	American Derby, Sheridan Stakes
At 4 Years	2ND	Russet Handicap
At 5 Years	2ND	Russet Handicap
	3RD	Twin City Handicap
	UNP	Turf Handicap, Advance Handicap, Sheepshead Bay Handicap, Suburban Handicap

Samuel Culbertson, the fifth president of Churchill Downs, prepares to leave his residence on South Third to attend the Derby.

May 3, 1902

Owner — T. C. McDowell

Jockey — Jimmy Winkfield

Only two men ever have bred, owned and trained a Derby winner. The first was Maj. Thomas C. Mc-Dowell, who had Alan-a-Dale. The other was T. P. Hayes, who had Donerail in 1913. McDowell was the great-grandson of Henry Clay. Alan-a-Dale is the only winner whose only start at three was in the Derby.

ALAN-A-DALE

Value $6,000. Net to winner $4,850; second $700; third $300. 112 nominations.

Horses	Wt.	Fin.	Jockeys	Owners
Alan-a-Dale	117	1	J. Winkfield	T. C. McDowell
Inventor	117	2	R. Williams	T. W. Moore
The Rival	117	3	N. Turner	T. C. McDowell
Abe Frank	122	4	Coburn	G. C. Bennett & Co.

Time: 2:08¾. Weather clear.

Winner—Ch.c. by Halma—Sudie McNairy, by Enquirer; trained by T. C. McDowell; bred in Kentucky by T. C. McDowell.

Bookmaking Odds: Alan-a-Dale (Coupled with The Rival), 3 to 2; Inventor, 11 to 1; Abe Frank, 3 to 5.

THE RIVAL was first to show, but ALAN-A-DALE caught him in the first eighth, opened a four-length lead going into homestretch, went lame in the final eighth, carried on with flawless courage, and won by a nose.

THE WINNER'S PEDIGREE AND CAREER HIGHLIGHTS

ALAN-A-DALE (Chestnut Colt)
- Halma
  - Hanover
    - Hindoo
    - Bourbon Belle
  - Julia L.
    - Longfellow
    - Christine
- Sudie McNairy
  - Enquirer
    - *Leamington
    - Lida
  - Nannie McNairy
    - Jeff Davis
    - Elizabeth McNairy

Year	Age	Sts	1st	2nd	3rd	Won
1901	2	4	3	0	0	$ 8,570
1902	3	1	1	0	0	4,850
1903	4	9	5	3	0	3,940
1904	5	10	5	3	0	5,170
1905	6	13	3	1	1	2,665
Totals		37	17	7	1	$25,195

At 2 Years	WON	Brighton Junior Stakes
	UNP	Foxland Stakes
At 3 Years	WON	Kentucky Derby
At 4 Years	WON	Oakwood Handicap
	UNP	Harlem National Handicap
At 5 Years	2ND	Fall Handicap, The Ocean Handicap, The Flight Handicap
At 6 Years	UNP	Omnium Handicap, Ocean Handicap, Saratoga Handicap, Test Handicap

The new owners of Becker & Durski Harness Shop proudly pose in the doorway of their shop which opened in 1902 on Market Street. The firm still is in business, but now is located adjacent to Churchill Downs and supplies horsemen their needs.

The Eclipse ball park opened at 7th and Kentucky in 1902. The team is pictured along with an overflow crowd at a game.

May 2, 1903

Owner — C. R. Ellison

Trainer — J. P. Mayberry

Jockey — Hal Booker

JUDGE HIMES

Value $6,000. Net to winner $4,850; second $700; third $300. 140 Nominations.

Horses	Eqt Wt	PP	St	½	¾	1	Str	Fin	Jockeys	Owners	Odds $1 Str't
Judge Himes	w 117	4	3	3½	3½	4³	2²	1¾	Booker	Ellison	10.00
Early	w 117	2	4	4⁶	4⁶	1½	1½	2⁶	Winkfield	Tich'r & Co	.60
Bourbon	w 110	5	5	5²	5½½	5½	4³	3½	Crowhurst	McDowell	4.00
Bad News	w 114	1	2	2½	2nk	3¹	3½	4³	Davis	Woodford & Buckner	5.00
Woodlake	wb 117	3	1	1¹	1¹	2nk	5¹	5⁵	Helg'sen	McDowell	4.00
Treacy	w 110	6	6	6	6	6	6	6	Landry	Stevens	15.00

Time: :25½, :51, 1:16½, 1:42, 2:09. Track fast.
†Coupled in betting as T. C. McDowell entry.
Winner—Ch.c. by *Esher—Lullaby, by Longfellow; trained by J. P. Mayberry; bred in Kentucky by Johnson N. Camden.

Start poor. Won driving; second easily. Jockey Booker waited with JUDGE HIMES until in the last quarter before making a move, came through on the inside at the turn into the homestretch, caught EARLY tiring and, after a sharp struggle, was going away at the finish. Winkfield made his run too soon with EARLY, made up a lot of ground while rounding the far turn, but had nothing left when JUDGE HIMES challenged. BOURBON finished well and outgamed BAD NEWS. WOODLAKE quit badly after going a good half-mile. TREACY was never a contender.

THE WINNER'S PEDIGREE AND CAREER HIGHLIGHTS

```
                              ⎧           ⎧ Claremont  ⎧ Blair Athol
                      ⎧ *Esher⎨           ⎨ { Coimbra
                      ⎪       ⎩           ⎩ ‡Dusk
JUDGE HIMES           ⎨           ⎧ Una   ⎧ Conjecture
(Chestnut Colt)       ⎪                   ⎩ *Leamington
                      ⎪       ⎧ Longfellow⎧ Nanura
                      ⎩ Lullaby⎨           ⎩ War Dance
                              ⎩ Lady Richards ⎧ Lucretia
```

‡by Ellington or Dusk.

Year	Age	Sts	1st	2nd	3rd	Won
1902	2	10	1	1	2	$ 400
1903	3	28	7	1	9	19,865
1904	4	32	5	5	3	3,500
1905	5	31	5	6	7	4,155
1906	6	3	0	1	1	75
Totals		104	18	14	22	$27,995

At 3 Years	WON	Kentucky Derby, Hawthorne Handicap, Excelsior Handicap, Endurance Handicap, Oak Park Handicap.
	3RD	Latonia Club Membership Handicap, Flyaway Handicap, Maywood Handicap, Blue Grass Stakes
	UNP	Tennessee Derby, Hotel Gayoso Stakes, Latonia Derby, American Derby
At 4 Years	3RD	Elmridge Handicap, Superior Handicap, August Stakes
At 5 Years	WON	Whirlpool Stakes
	2ND	Speculation Stakes, Park Hotel Stakes
	3RD	Eastman Hotel Stakes
	UNP	Country Club Handicap

At the turn of the century, theater was big in Louisville. The McCauley Theater was the show place for such stage stars as Maurice Barrymore and others. In 1904, the first movie shown in Kentucky was seen in the city. And in April, the first movie house, called the Dreamland, was built at Fifth and Market. It was the third movie house in America.

May 2, 1904

Trainer — C. E. Durnell

Jockey — Frankie Prior

Elwood struck a blow for women's lib when he won the 1904 Derby. He was the first winner owned by a woman; the first starter owned by a woman, and the first winner bred by a woman.

Another first for Elwood: he is the only winner foaled in Missouri.

THIRTIETH RUNNING

ELWOOD

Value $6,000. Net to winner $4,850; second $700; third $300. 140 Nominations.

Horses	Eqt Wt	PP	St	½	¾	1	Str	Fin	Jockeys	Owners	Odds $1 Str't
Elwood ......wb 117	3	4	4¹	4ʰ	4½	5½	1½	Prior	Mrs. C. Durnell	15.00
Ed Tierney ...w 117	5	3	3¹	3¹½	3¹	3²	2³	Dominick	Fay & We'f	1.10
Brancas .....w 117	4	5	5	5	5	2½	3²½	Lyne	Gerst	2.50
P. Silverwings .w 117	1	2	2²	1¹	1¹	1ʰ	4¹	Austin	Talbott Bros.	7.00
Proceeds ....wb 122	2	1	1¹½	2½	2ʰ	4½	5	Helges'n	Brown	1.00

Time: :25, :49½, 1:15¼, 1:42, 2:08½. Track fast.

Winner—B.c. by Free Knight—Petticoat, by Alarm, trained by C. E. Durnell; bred in Missouri by Mrs. J. B. Prather.

Start good. Won driving; second easily. ELWOOD was well ridden. Prior rated him along for the first seven furlongs and never made a more until rounding the turn into the homestretch, where he moved up on the outside and fought it out in turn with BRANCAS, PRINCE SILVERWINGS and ED TIERNEY in the last quarter, and outstayed the latter in the final drive. Dominick nursed ED TIERNEY along for the first half and made a determined effort in the stretch run, tiring in the last fifty yards. BRANCAS stumbled at the start and Lyne kept taking him back in the first half-mile, moved him up fast at the home turn and was in front for a few strides, but tired. PRINCE SILVERWINGS showed much early speed, but tired after a mile. PROCEEDS stumbled at the start but this cut no figure in the result.

THE WINNER'S PEDIGREE AND CAREER HIGHLIGHTS

ELWOOD (Bay Colt)

- Free Knight
  - Ten Broeck
    - *Phaeton
    - Fanny Holton
  - Belle Knight
    - Knighthood
    - Kentucky Belle
- Petticoat
  - Alarm
    - *Eclipse
    - *Maud
  - Lady Scarborough
    - *Leamington
    - *Lady Lumley

Year	Age	Sts	1st	2nd	3rd	Won
1903	2	17	1	2	1	$ 950
1904	3	23	6	4	3	13,580
1905	4	12	1	1	1	1,060
1906	5	3	0	0	0	—
1907	6	3	0	0	0	—
Totals		58	8	7	5	$15,590

At 2 Years	2ND	Youngster Stakes, Competition Stakes
At 3 Years	WON	Kentucky Derby, Latonia Derby
	2ND	California Derby
	3RD	St. Louis Derby
	UNP	American Derby, Clark Stakes

The word "purse" stems from earlier years when money actually was put into a purse for the winning jockey to collect after crossing the finish line. These purses are in the Kentucky Derby Museum.

The last of the mule-drawn street cars were seen on Louisville's streets in 1901, but there were plenty of mules and wagons. This is Main Street, circa 1900.

May 10, 1905

Owner — S. S. Brown

Trainer — Robert Tucker

Jockey — Jack Martin

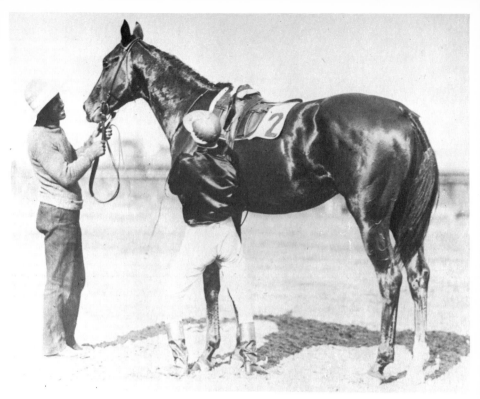

AGILE

Value $6,000. Net to winner $4,850; second $700; third $300. 145 nominations.

Horses	Eqt Wt	PP	St	½	¾	1	Str	Fin	Jockeys	Owners	Odds $1 Str't
Agile	w 122	1	1	1 1½	1 1½	1 1½	1²	1³	Martin	Brown	.33
Ram's Horn..	ws 117	2	2	2⁵	2¹⁰	2¹⁵	2²⁰	2²⁰	Lyne	Williams Co.	2.50
Layson	w 117	3	3	3	3	3	3	3	Austin	Hayes	16.00

Time: :25½, :50, 1:16, 1:42¾, 2:10¾. Track heavy.

Winner—B.c. by Sir Dixon—Apena, by King Alfonso; trained by Robert Tucker; bred in Kentucky by E. F. Clay.

Won easily; second the same. AGILE was full of speed all the way and Martin never let him down at any part of the trip. He drew away under restraint in the last furlong, and was only galloping at the end. Lyne made his move with RAM'S HORN while rounding the turn into the homestretch, but could not get to the winner.

THE WINNER'S PEDIGREE AND CAREER HIGHLIGHTS

AGILE
(Bay Colt)
- Sir Dixon
  - *Billet
    - Voltigeur
    - Calcutta
  - Jaconet
    - *Leamington
    - Maggie B. B.
- Alpena
  - King Alfonso
    - *Phaeton
    - Capitola
  - Penumbra
    - Pat Malloy
    - Penelope

Year	Age	Sts	1st	2nd	3rd	Won
1904	2	21	5	4	2	$ 4,530
1905	3	10	5	5	0	32,835
1906	4	21	2	2	2	1,485
1907	5	14	2	1	5	950
Totals		66	14	12	9	$39,800

At 2 Years	WON	Waldorf Stakes
	2ND	Southhold Handicap
	UNP	Nursery Handicap, Matron Stakes, Hopeful Stakes, Great Trial Stakes, The Daisy Stakes
At 3 Years	WON	Kentucky Derby, Advance Stakes, Phoenix Stakes, Tennessee Derby
	2ND	Brighton Derby, Tidal Stakes, Broadway Stakes
At 4 Years	UNP	Suburban Handicap, Edgemere Handicap, Election Day Handicap
At 5 Years	UNP	Thanksgiving Handicap, Special

Agile led all the way to win the 1905 Kentucky Derby in easy fashion.

Shades of 'Ninety-two, but just in number
For whereas that was quite a hard fought race,
This one was a runaway for AGILE
And the other two could only show and place.
No one likes to lose the race he runs in,
And no one lost — the number saved the day:
When only three, and all three share the money,
It's gonna be, and gotta be, that way.

Thirteen makes a superstitious figure,
But no one needed to worry or to care
For those who didn't put it all on AGILE,
They backed all three and gave each one a share.
No one likes to lose the dough he works for,
And no one lost — the number saved the day;
When only three, and all the figures tally,
It's gonna be, and gotta be, that way.

Save your extra dough for next year's Derby,
There'll probably be more horses on the track;
This one was a runaway for AGILE
But, now, he's out and won't be coming back.
No one likes to lose the race he bets on,
And no one lost — the number saved the day;
When only three, and each one gets a ribbon,
It's gonna be, and gotta be, that way.

P.S. — Head starts often point to speed and courage —
        Today, a head start set the winning pace;
        To coin a word, it favored AGILE'S hurrage,
        And that helped Jockey Martin win the race.

"Kentucky Derby Poems"
by James O. Nall

May 2, 1906

Owner — George J. Long

Trainer — Peter Coyne

Jockey — Roscoe Troxler

SIR HUON

Value $6,000. Net to winner $4,850; second $700; third $300. 110 nominations.

Horses	Eqt Wt	PP	St	½	¾	1	Str	Fin	Jockeys	Owners	Odds $1 Str't
Sir Huon ....w 117		4	2	2²	2²	1nk	1²	1²	Troxler	Long	1.10
Lady Nav'rre..w 117		3	4	4h	3nk	4⁶	2nk	2³	Burns	Ellison	1.80
J's Redd'k..wsb 117		5	5	5²	4³	3h	3¹	3⁵	Dominick	Ellison	1.80
Hyper'n II ..wsb 114		2	1	1³	1²	2½	4h	4¹⁰	Austin	Hawk's Co.	8.00
De Bar.......w 117		1	6	6	5½	5⁶	5¹⁰	5³	Nicol	Shannon Co.	3.50
Velours ....wsb 117		6	3	3nk	6	6	6	6	Walsh	Franklin	40.00

Time: :24⅗, :49⅘, 1:15, 1:41⅖, 2:08⅘. Track fast.

†Coupled in betting as C. R. Ellison entry.

Winner—B.c. by Falsetto—Ignite, by *Woodlands; trained by Peter Coyne; bred in Kentucky by George J. Long.

Start good; won driving; second same. Jockey Troxler rode a well judged race on SIR HUON, saved him from the pace set by HYPERION II, and never made a move until well around the far turn, where the colt came fast, and taking command entering the homestretch, held the race safe all through the last quarter. LADY NAVARRE was interfered with while rounding the turn into the backstretch and made a determined effort on the turn for home, but could never get to the winner. JAMES REDDICK was sore in his warm-up, but ran to his best race. HYPERION II forced a fast pace, but could not stay the route. DE BAR was always outrun. VELOURS cut no figure.

THE WINNER'S PEDIGREE AND CAREER HIGHLIGHTS

SIR HUON (Bay Colt)
- Falsetto
  - Enquirer
    - *Leamington
    - Lida
  - Farfaletta
    - *Australian
    - Elkhorna
- Ignite
  - *Woodlands
    - Nutbourne
    - Whiteface
  - Luminous
    - Alarm
    - *Lady Lumley

Year	Age	Sts	1st	2nd	3rd	Won
1905	2	9	4	2	0	$ 3,775
1906	3	7	5	1	0	34,655
1907	4	1	0	0	0	
1908	5	1	1	0	0	550
Totals		18	10	3	0	$38,980

At 2 Years
- WON Harold Stakes
- 2ND Cincinnati Trophy
- UNP Golden Rod Stakes

At 3 Years
- WON Kentucky Derby, Latonia Derby, Queen City Handicap, Commonwealth Stakes, Seagate Stakes
- 2ND Saratoga Cup
- UNP The Advance Stakes

The Louisville post office looked like this in 1906. It was located at the corner of Fourth and Chestnut. The Renaissance style building was built in the late 1880s on the site of the Industrial Exposition of 1872.

May 6, 1907

Owner — J. H. Woodford

Jockey — Andy Minder

A Kentucky native, Carrie Nation, was making news on the national scene with her crusades against saloons in 1907.

PINK STAR

Value $6,000. Net to winner $4,850; second $700; third $300. 128 nominations.

Horses	Eqt Wt	PP	St	1/2	3/4	1	Str	Fin	Jockeys	Owners	Odds $1 Str't
Pink Star....wb 117		6	6	6	6	4^h	3^4	1^2	Minder	Woodford	15.00
Zal ....w 117		3	1	$1\frac{1}{2}$	1^h	$1\frac{1}{2}$	$1\frac{1}{2}$	$2\frac{1}{2}$	Boland	Gerst	8.00
Ovelando ....w 117		1	2	3^h	2^3	2^1	2^h	3^2	Nicol	Doyle	3.00
Red Gauntlet..w 117		5	5	5^5	4^1	5^4	4^1	4^5	Austin	Hayes	1.50
Wool Sandals.w 117		4	4	$2\frac{1}{2}$	3^h	3^1	5^5	5^6	Koerner	Applegate	3.00
Orlandwick ..w 110		2	3	$4\frac{1}{2}$	5^2	6	6	6	Lee	Steele	10.00

Time: :24, :50, 1:17, 1:45, 2:12-3/5. Track heavy.

Winner—B.c. by Pink Coat—Mary Malloy, by Pat Malloy; trained by W. H. Fizer; bred in Kentucky by J. Hal Woodford.

Start good. Won easily, second driving, third same. PINK STAR, restrained in the early stages, trailed far back for the first three-quarters, moved up gradually until straightened out for the stretch run, where he came with a rush, wore the leaders down and won going away. ZAL showed the most early speed and hung on well for the first mile. OVELANDO was a forward and game contender for a mile. RED GAUNTLET was under a hard drive, but was not good enough. WOOL SANDALS retired after a mile. ORLANDWICK had no mishap.

THE WINNER'S PEDIGREE AND CAREER HIGHLIGHTS

PINK STAR (Bay Colt)
- Pink Coat
  - Leonatus
    - Longfellow
    - Semper Felix
  - Alice Brand
    - Hindoo
    - Lady of the Lake
- Mary Malloy
  - Pat Malloy
    - Lexington
    - Gloriana
  - Favorite
    - *King Ernest
    - Jersey Belle

Year	Age	Sts	1st	2nd	3rd	Won
1906	2	8	2	1	0	$ 825
1907	3	8	1	0	2	4,925
Totals		16	3	1	2	$ 5,750

At 3 Years
- WON Kentucky Derby
- UNP Latonia Derby, Crescent City Derby, City Park Derby

Steeplechase racing was common in the infield at Churchill Downs in the early 1900s.

May 5, 1908

C. E. Hamilton

John Hamilton

Owners

Trainer — J. W. Hall

Jockey — Arthur Pickens

STONE STREET

Value $6,000. Net to winner $4,850; second $700; third $300. 114 nominations.

Horses	Eqt Wt	PP	St	1/2	3/4	1	Str	Fin	Jockeys	Owners	Odds $1 Str't
Stone Street..wb 117		4	6	$2^{1}\frac{1}{2}$	2^h	1^{nk}	1^1	1^3	Pickens	Hamilton	23.72
Sir Cleges ....w 117		2	7	4^1	$3^{1}\frac{1}{2}$	$2\frac{1}{2}$	$3\frac{1}{2}$	2^h	Koerner	Long	1.74
Dunvegan ...wb 114		1	5	3^h	4^2	4^4	2^1	3^h	Warren	Camden, Jr.	†7.37
Synchr'zed ..wsb 112		8	2	5^2	5^3	5^5	4^1	4^h	Burton	Armstrong	68.92
Banbridge ..wsb 110		5	3	$1^{1}\frac{1}{2}$	1^2	3^1	5^5	5^6	Powers	Schreiber	3.24
Milford .....wb 117		3	1	6^1	6^4	6^6	6^1	6^h	Minder	Fizer	3.64
Bill Heron ...wb 114		6	4	7^{10}	7^{20}	7^{15}	7^{20}	7^{20}	Lee	Young	†7.37
Frank Bird...wb 110		7	8	8	8	8	8	8	Williams	Hughes	22.43

Time: :25, :50⅕, 1:17⅖, 1:46, 2:15⅕. Track heavy.

†Dunvegan and Bill Herron coupled as Camden, Jr., and Young entry.

$5 Mutuels Paid—Stone Street, $123.60 straight, $37.90 place, $14.50 show; Sir Cleges, $11.10 place, $8.50 show; Dunvegan, $11.10 show.

Winner—B.c. by Longstreet—Stone Nellie, by *Stonehenge; trained by J. W. Hall; bred in Kentucky by J. B. Haggin.

Start good. Won easily; second and third driving. STONE STREET, favored by the going and in prime condition, ran the best race of his career. He followed BANBRIDGE close up to the three-quarters post, where he went into the lead and easily held the others safe for the rest of the trip. SIR CLEGES disliked the going and sprawled repeatedly, but made a game effort. DUNVEGAN ran fairly well. SYNCHRONIZED closed a big gap in the last half-mile. BANBRIDGE showed the most early speed, but tired after three-quarters. MILFORD was never a factor. The others were always badly outplaced.

THE WINNER'S PEDIGREE AND CAREER HIGHLIGHTS

STONE STREET
(Bay Colt)

Longstreet	Longfellow	{	*Leamington / Nantura
	Semper Idem	{	*Glen Athol / Semper Vive
Stone Nellie	*Stonehenge	{	Blair Athol / Coimbra
	Nell	{	*King Ernest / Miss Nellie

Year	Age	Sts	1st	2nd	3rd	Won
1907	2	17	3	3	1	$ 1,450
1908	3	25	3	1	5	5,828
1909	4	20	3	7	1	1,250
1910	5	10	1	4	0	617
1911	6	20	8	2	2	3,667
Totals		92	18	17	9	$12,812

At 2 Years   **UNP**   Juvenile Stakes

At 3 Years   **WON**   Kentucky Derby

T H I R T Y   F O U R T H   R U N N I N G

Cameramen such as these captured the Kentucky Derby on film for the newsreels which were a big part of the bill at turn-of-the-century movie houses.

The Louisville Free Public Library was completed at 3rd and York. Andrew Carnegie was the principal patron. Readers reportedly checked out 300,000 books the first day.

May 3, 1909

Owner — J. B. Respess

Jockey — Vincent Powers

It is claimed that most horsemen had rather win the Kentucky Derby than any other race. But J. B. "Rome" Respess, owner and breeder of Wintergreen, went a little further: he declared when Wintergreen was but a few weeks old "he will be the winner of the Derby in 1909." He spared no expense to make his prediction — and his wish — come true.

WINTERGREEN

Value $6,000. Net to winner $4,850; second $700; third $300. 117 nominations.

Horses	Eqt Wt	PP	St	½	¾	1	Str	Fin	Jockeys	Owners	Odds $1 Str't
Wintergreen	.wb 117	6	1	1$^{1\frac{1}{2}}$	1^2	1$^{1\frac{1}{2}}$	1^1	1^4	Powers	Respess	1.96
Miami	.w 117	1	8	2$^{1\frac{1}{2}}$	2^2	2$^{1\frac{1}{2}}$	2^h	2^3	Shilling	Camden	2.90
Dr Barkley	...w 117	3	2	4^2	4$^{1\frac{1}{2}}$	5^3	5^2	3^h	Page	Smitha	41.34
Sir Catesby	...w 110	9	9	6$^{1\frac{1}{2}}$	5^2	4^2	3$^{1\frac{1}{2}}$	4^4	Heidel	Hayes	33.58
Fr'nd Harry	.wb 117	7	7	3^h	3^h	3^h	4^2	5^3	Musgrave	Alvey	5.61
Direct	......wsb 117	5	3	7^2	7^6	7^3	6^2	6^3	Walsh	Mackenzie	†10.01
Mich'l Angelo	.w 117	8	4	9^3	8^3	8^{10}	7^2	7^3	Taplin	Hendrie	6.97
Warfield	.....w 117	10	6	5$^{1\frac{1}{2}}$	6$^{1\frac{1}{2}}$	7^4	8^2	8^8	Austin	Lesh	†10.01
Campeon	....w 110	2	5	8^2	9$^{1\frac{1}{2}}$	9^h	9^1	9^2	McGee	Long	51.25
Match Me	..wsb 107	4	10	10	10	10	10	10	Lee	Gorey	56.11

Time: :25, :49⅗, 1:15⅘, 2:08⅕. Track slow.

†Direct and Warfield coupled as Mackenzie and Lesh entry.

$5 Mutuels Paid—Wintergreen, $14.80 straight; $8.75 place, $8.60 show; Miami, $9.15 place, $9.25 show; Dr. Barkley, $20.70 show.

Winner—B.c. by Dick Welles—Winter, by Exile; trained by Chas. Mack; bred in Ohio by J. B. Respess.

Start good. Won easily; second and third driving. WINTERGREEN was bumped into soon after the start by DR. BARKLEY, but recovered quickly and, taking a good lead, held sway throughout and won in a canter. MIAMI, free of interference, followed WINTERGREEN in closest pursuit and finished fast, but was not good enough. DR. BARKLEY ran a cracking good race and outgamed SIR CATESBY in the last few strides. SIR CATESBY closed a gap and finished resolutely. FRIEND HARRY tired badly after three-quarters. DIRECT dropped out after three-quarters. MICHAEL ANGELO began slowly; closed a good gap in the last quarter. The others were never close contenders.

Scratched—T. M. Green, 114; Ada Meade, 112; Woolwinder, 117.

THE WINNER'S PEDIGREE AND CAREER HIGHLIGHTS

WINTERGREEN (Bay Colt)	Dick Welles	King Eric	*King Ernest
			*Cyclone
		Tea's Over	Hanover
			Tea Rose
	Winter	Exile	*Mortemer
			*Second Hand
		Wildflower	*Mr. Pickwick
			Woodflower

Year	Age	Sts	1st	2nd	3rd	Won
1908	2	10	5	1	3	$ 1,660
1909	3	8	1	4	0	5,550
1910	4	5	1	3	1	795
1911	5	5	3	0	1	1,490
1912	6	22	6	4	0	2,940
1913	7	11	0	2	3	385
Totals		61	16	14	8	$12,820

At 2 Years	3RD	Hurricane Stakes
At 3 Years	WON	Kentucky Derby
	2ND	Saranac Handicap, Saratoga Cup
At 4 Years	3RD	Brewers Exchange Stakes
At 5 Years	3RD	Merchants' Stakes
	UNP	Frank Fehr Stakes

Kentucky's new capitol building was completed in 1909 at a cost of $1,820,000. Ground was broken for the project in May, 1905; the cornerstone was laid in June, 1906, and the dedication was held June 1, 1910.

May 10, 1910

Owner — William Gerst

Jockey — Robert Herbert

Donau means Danube in German. William Gerst, the owner, came from Germany as a child and that likely explains the horse's name. Gerst was in the brewery business in Cincinnati and Nashville. He lived in Nashville.

Donau was heavily raced, starting 111 times from age 2 to 5.

THIRTY SIXTH RUNNING

DONAU

Value $6,000. Net to winner $4,850; second $700; third $300. 117 nominations.

Horses	Eqt Wt	PP	St	½	¾	1	Str	Fin	Jockeys	Owners	Odds $1 Str't
Donau	w 117	7	2	$1^{1\frac{1}{2}}$	1^3	1^3	$1^{1\frac{1}{2}}$	$1^{\frac{1}{2}}$	Herbert	Gerst	1.65
Joe Morris...	wb 117	1	1	2^h	2^2	$2^{1\frac{1}{2}}$	2^h	2^h	Powers	Anderson	2.77
Fight'g Bob ..	wb 117	4	5	7	5^1	$3^{1\frac{1}{2}}$	3^4	3^n	Page	Reif	3.49
Boola Boola...	w 117	3	3	6^h	6^{nk}	5^2	4^6	4^{15}	Rice	Camden	17.95
Topland	w 114	5	7	3^h	4^2	4^h	5^1	5^2	Austin	Van Meter	25.10
John Furlong..	w 107	2	6	$5^{\frac{1}{2}}$	3^h	6^4	6^4	6^8	Scoville	Rogers	14.07
Gal't Pirate..	wb 117	6	4	4^1	7	7	7	7	Kennedy	W'wright	37.59

Time: :24, :48⅘, 1:14, 1:39⅘, 2:06⅖. Track fast.

$5 Mutuels Paid—Donau, $13.25 straight, $7.50 place, $7.50 show; Joe Morris, $7.50 place, $7.50 show; Fighting Bob, $8.50 show.

Winner—B.c. by Woolsthorpe—Al Lone, by *Albert; trained by G. Ham; bred in Kentucky by Milton Young.

Start good. Won driving; second and third same. DONAU went into the lead soon after the start, was restrained in front for a mile and when called on, drew away but tired, and just lasted. JOE MORRIS tried to run out on the first turn, moved up with a rush on the stretch turn, tired, only to come again near the end. FIGHTING BOB stood the final drive gamely. BOOLA BOOLA closed a big gap and was going fastest at the end. The others never were serious contenders.
Scratched—Eye White, 114.

THE WINNER'S PEDIGREE AND CAREER HIGHLIGHTS

DONAU (Bay Colt)	*Woolsthorpe	Tibthorpe	Voltigeur
			Little Agnes
		Light of Other Days	Balfe
			Meteor
	Al Lone	*Albert	Albert Victor
			Hawthorn Bloom
		Fronie Louise	*Glengarry
			Rosa Clark

Year	Age	Sts	1st	2nd	3rd	Won
1909	2	41	15	6	14	$ 6,980
1910	3	10	4	0	1	7,186
1911	4	30	6	3	8	2,701
1912	5	30	5	9	7	3,289
Totals		111	30	18	30	$20,156

At 2 Years	WON	Wakefield Stakes
	2ND	San Gabriel Stakes
	3RD	Essex Handicap, Cincinnati Trophy, Bashford Manor Stakes
	UNP	Bell Stakes
At 3 Years	WON	Kentucky Derby, Camden Handicap
	3RD	Latonia Derby
	UNP	Clark Stakes, Brewers' Exchange Stakes, Independence Handicap
At 4 Years	3RD	Brewers Selling Stakes

The first flight of an airplane in the State of Kentucky was made from the infield of Churchill Downs on June 18, 1910. The show was sponsored by the Louisville Times and scenes from the event are pictured.

May 13, 1911

Owner — R. F. Carmen

Jockey — George Archibald

"The Kentucky Derby has been the expression of the character of pioneer American stock compressed in one tremendous emotional gasp of excitement."

Ed Danforth
Atlanta Journal

MERIDIAN

Value $6,000. Net to winner $4,850; second $700; third $300. 117 nominations.

Horses	Eqt Wt	PP	St	½	¾	1	Str	Fin	Jockeys	Owners	Odds $1 Str't
Meridian	w 117	5	1	1⁴	1³	1²	1²	1¾	Archibald	R. F. Carmen	2.90
Gov'n'r Gray	w 119	7	3	6¹	4¹	3¹	2ʰ	2¹⁵	Troxler	R. N. Smith	1.00
Colston	w 110	1	7	3⁴	3½	4²	4⁴	3²	Conley	R. Colston	19.00
Mud Sill	w 107	2	6	4½	6	6	6	4ʰ	Koerner	Woodford-Buckner	17.00
Jack Denm'n	w 117	3	5	5¹	5²	5¹	5¹	5¹	Wilson	F. J. Pons	21.00
R-the-World	w 117	6	2	2²	2³	2ʰ	3²	6¹⁵	McGee	W. G. Yanke	6.50
Col Hogan	w 110	4	4	7	7	7	7	7	McIntyre	Henderson-Hogan	6.00

Time: :23-3/5, :47-4/5, 1:12-4/5, 1:39-1/5, 2:05 (new track record). Track fast.

$2.00 mutuels sold for first time this year.

$2.00 mutuels paid—Meridian, $7.80 straight, $2.70 place, $2.70 show; Governor Gray, $2.70 place, $2.60 show; Colston, $3.80 show.

Winner—B.c. by Broomstick—Sue Smith, by *Masetto; trained by Albert Ewing; bred in Kentucky by C. L. Harrison.

Start good. Won driving; second and third same. MERIDIAN was rushed into a long lead from the start, and after having disposed of ROUND-THE-WORLD and other serious contenders in the first three-quarters, had enough speed in reserve at the end to outstay the fast coming GOVERNOR GRAY. The latter was allowed to drop too far back in the first half, and, coming with a great rush in the last quarter, was going fastest at the end. COLSTON outstayed MUD SILL for third place. ROUND-THE-WORLD tired in the last quarter. MUD SILL finished fast.

Scratched—Ramazan, 110; Jabot, 117; Captain Carmody, 117.

THE WINNER'S PEDIGREE AND CAREER HIGHLIGHTS

MERIDIAN (Bay Colt)			
Broomstick	Ben Brush	Bramble / Roseville
	*Elf	Galliard / *Sylvabelle
Sue Smith	*Masetto	St. Simon / Lady Abbess
	Ethel Lee	*Whistle Jacket / Marmora

Year	Age	Sts	1st	2nd	3rd	Won
1910	2	12	3	3	1	$ 2,395
1911	3	17	6	6	1	11,655
1912	4	23	8	4	2	7,186
1913	5	8	2	0	4	3,780
1914	6	6	1	2	2	1,475
Totals		66	20	15	10	$26,491

At 2 Years	2ND	Double Event
	3RD	Foam Stakes
At 3 Years	WON	Kentucky Derby, National Handicap, Frontier Stakes
	2ND	Blue Grass Stakes, Hamilton Derby, Fourth of July Stakes, Kentucky Stakes
	3RD	Canadian Sportsmen's Handicap
At 4 Years	WON	Washington's Birthday Handicap, Argyle Hotel Handicap, Kentucky Stakes
	2ND	Charleston Hotel Handicap, Latonia Inaugural
	3RD	Criterion Stakes, Juarez Stakes
At 5 Years	WON	Excelsior Handicap
	3RD	Paumonok Handicap, Kings County Handicap
At 6 Years	2ND	Queens County Handicap
	3RD	Brookdale Handicap, Yonkers Handicap

The Majestic Theater was enlarged in 1911 and became one of the first "Palace" movie houses. It was the amusement center for the young people.

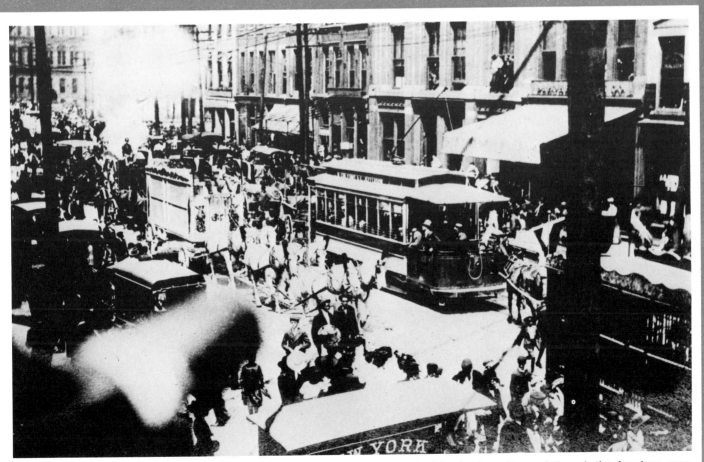

It was a big day when the circus came to town. This parade featured the caged wild animals as it wound through the downtown area.

May 11, 1912

Trainer — F. M. Taylor

Jockey — Carroll Shilling

The year 1912 was a year of tragedy. The Titanic, then the largest ship afloat, was sunk with the loss of 1,513 lives.

And Worth, the 1912 Derby winner, died later that season. He had been the two-year-old champion. He won 15 of 31 starts.

WORTH

Value $6,000. Net to winner $4,850; second $700; third $300. 131 nominations.

Horses	Eqt Wt	PP	St	1/2	3/4	1	Str	Fin	Jockeys	Owners	Odds $1 Str't
Worth ....w 117	5	1	$1^{1\frac{1}{2}}$	$1^{1\frac{1}{2}}$	1^1	1^1	1^{nk}	Shilling	H. C. Hallenbeck	.80
Duval ......wb 117	7	4	4^3	$4^{\frac{1}{2}}$	2^1	2^2	2^5	Fain	Gallaher Bros.	20.00
Flamma ....wb 112	1	7	7	5^1	$3^{1\frac{1}{2}}$	3^1	3^4	Loftus	G. F. Condran	17.00
Free Lance ..wb 117	4	6	$2^{\frac{1}{2}}$	$2^{\frac{1}{2}}$	$5^{\frac{1}{2}}$	$4^{1\frac{1}{2}}$	4^1	Peak	G. J. Long	7.00
Guaranola ..wb 117	3	3	6^2	3^n	4^2	5^4	5^6	Molesworth	Henderson & Hogan	80.00
Sonada .....wb 117	6	5	3^h	7	6^8	6^{10}	6^{20}	Koerner	C. Woolford	12.50
Wheelwright ..w 117	2	2	$5^{\frac{1}{2}}$	$6^{\frac{1}{2}}$	7	7	7	Byrne	J. N. Camden	4.20

Time: :24-3/5, :49-2/5, 1:16-1/5, 1:42-3/5, 2:09-2/5. Track muddy.

$2 Mutuels Paid—Worth, $3.60 straight, $3.90 place, $3.30 show; Duval, $14.00 place, $5.70 show; Flamma, $4.50 show.

Winner—Br.c. by *Knight of the Thistle—Miss Hanover, by Hanover; trained by F. M. Taylor; bred in Kentucky by R. H. Mac. Potter.

Start bad and slow. Won driving; second and third same. WORTH was hustled into the lead and, maintaining an easy advantage under restraint, appeared to be an easy winner to the stretch turn, but tired and had to be hand ridden near the end to shake off DUVAL. The latter was going gamest at the end. FLAMMA acted badly at the post and was away poorly, but closed a big gap into a good third. FREE LANCE tired in the stretch. WHEELWRIGHT and SONADA ran disappointingly.

Scratched—The Manager, 117; Patrouche, 110.

THE WINNER'S PEDIGREE AND CAREER HIGHLIGHTS

WORTH (Brown Colt)			
	*Knight of the Thistle	Rosebery	Speculum / Ladylike
		The Empress Maud	Beauclerc / Stella
	Miss Hanover	Hanover	Hindoo / Bourbon Belle
		Miss Dawn	Strathmore / Dawn of Day

Year	Age	Sts	1st	2nd	3rd	Won
1911	2	13	10	1	0	$16,645
1912	3	18	5	6	3	8,945
Totals		31	15	7	3	$25,590

At 2 Years	WON	Raceland Stakes, Bashford Manor Stakes, Private Sweepstakes of $10,000
At 3 Years	WON	Kentucky Derby, Chesapeake Stakes
	2ND	Washington Handicap
	3RD	Latonia Derby

The Kentucky and Indiana bridge was completed and the first train ran over it in November, 1912.

AMERICAN STANDARD

PLUMBING & HEATING DIVISION

PLUMBING FITTINGS DEPARTMENT

1541 South 7th Street • Louisville, Kentucky

May 10, 1913

Owner — T. P. Hayes

Jockey — Roscoe Goose

Donerail, known to practically everyone as the longest-priced winner of the Derby, set another record in 1913. He broke the track record when he ran the mile and a quarter in 2:04 4/5. It was broken the next year by Old Rosebud.

THIRTY NINTH RUNNING

DONERAIL

$5,000 added. Net to winner $5,475; second $700; third $300. 32 nominations.

Horses	Eqt Wt	PP	St	1/2	3/4	1	Str	Fin	Jockeys	Owners	Odds $1 Str't
Donerail	w 117	5	6	6¹	6¹½	5¹	5²	1½	Goose	T. P. Hayes	91.45
Ten Point	w 117	4	1	1²	1³	1²	1½	2¹½	Buxton	A. L. Aste	1.20
Gowell	w 112	3	5	5²	4ʰ	4¹½	4¹	3ʰ	McCabe	J. T. Weaver	87.00
Foundation ...	w 117	8	2	2¹	2½	2ʰ	3ʰ	4ⁿᵏ	Loftus	C. W. McKenna	2.30
Y Notions ...	wb 117	6	3	3½	3ʰ	3½	2½	5⁵	Glass	H. K. Knapp	4.90
L'd Marsh'll..	wb 117	1	7	7¹	7¹	6²	6¹	6⁸	Steele	J. O. & G. H. Keene	183.00
Jimmie Gill ..	wb 110	2	8	8	8	8	7¹⁰	7¹⁵	Borel	Doerhoefer & West	36.00
Leochares	w 114	7	4	4ʰ	5½	7ʰ	8	8	Peak	J. W. Schorr	14.00

Time: :23-4/5, :47-4/5, 1:12-3/5, 1:39-3/5, 2:04-4/5 (new track record). Track fast.
$2 Mutuels Paid—Donerail, $184.90 straight, $41.20 place, $13.20 show; Ten Point, $3.50 place, $3.30 show; Gowell, $14.10 show.
Winner—B.c. by *McGee—Algie M., by Hanover; trained by T. P. Hayes; bred in Kentucky by T. P. Hayes.

Start good and slow. Won driving; second and third same. DONERAIL, showing startling improvement over his Lexington form, was restrained to the stretch turn, where he moved up with a rush, and, under punishment, drew away in the last sixteenth. TEN POINT showed superior speed for the first mile, tired in the last eighth and was distressed at the finish. GOWELL made a fast and game stretch effort. FOUNDATION raced with TEN POINT to the stretch, then tired. YANKEE NOTIONS ran prominently to the homestretch and tired in the final drive. LEOCHARES was hopelessly beaten.
Scratched—Prince Hermis, 117; Sam Hirsch, 114; Floral Park, 112; Flying Tom, 114.

THE WINNER'S PEDIGREE AND CAREER HIGHLIGHTS

DONERAIL (Bay Colt)			
*McGee	White Knight	Sir Hugo
		Whitelock
	Remorse	Hermit
		Vex
Algie M.	Hanover	Hindoo
		Bourbon Belle
	Johnette	Bramble
		Guildean

Year	Age	Sts	1st	2nd	3rd	Won
1912	2	10	2	0	3	$ 1,025
1913	3	15	3	3	2	8,588
1914	4	28	5	5	5	5,180
1916	6	8	0	3	0	363
1918	8	1	0	0	0	—
Totals		62	10	11	10	$15,166

At 2 Years	3RD	Golden Rod Stakes, Rosedale Stakes
At 3 Years	WON	Kentucky Derby, Canadian Sportsmen's Handicap
	2ND	Windsor Special, Dominion Handicap, Blue Grass Stakes
At 4 Years	WON	Hamilton Cup
	2ND	Latonia Autumn Inaugural, Independence Handicap, George Hendrie Memorial Handicap

The flood which hit Louisville about April 1, 1913 was no April Fool joke. More than seven feet of water surrounded the Ballard Flour Mill. Note the nearly inundated box cars behind the men in the boat.

May 9, 1914

Owner — H. C. Applegate

Trainer — F. D. Weir

Jockey — John McCabe

OLD ROSEBUD

$10,000 added. Net to winner $9,125; second $2,000; third $1,000. 47 nominations.

Horses	Eqt Wt	PP	St	½	¾	1	Str	Fin	Jockeys	Owners	Odds $1 Str't
Old Rosebud	w 114	6	1	1²	1¹½	1²	1⁶	1⁸	McCabe	H. C. Applegate	.85
Hodge	w 114	7	2	2²	2¹½	2⁴	2⁴	2¹½	Taylor	K. Spence	5.40
Bronzewing	wb 117	4	7	7	7	6¹½	3²	3⁴	Hanover	A. P. Humphrey, Jr.	13.50
John Gund	wb 117	3	6	3¹½	3¹½	3¹½	4²	4⁶	Byrne	A. Baker	10.00
Old Ben	wb 114	1	3	6⁵	6³	5¹¹½	5¹	5²	Turner	W. G. Yanke	12.50
Surprising	w 117	5	4	5¹	4¹	4ʰ	6⁵	6³	Peak	R. F. Carman	14.00
Watermelon	wb 112	2	5	4¹¹½	5¹	7	7	7	French	J. E. Madden	15.00

Time: :23-3/5, :47-4/5, 1:13, 1:38-4/5, 2:03-2/5 (new track record). Track fast.
$2 Mutuels Paid—Old Rosebud, $3.70 straight, $3.00 place, $2.80 show; Hodge, $3.60 place, $3.60 show; Bronzewing, $4.00 show.
Winner—B.g. by Uncle—Ivory Bells, by Himyar; trained by F. D. Weir; bred in Kentucky by J. E. Madden.

Start good and slow. Won easily; second and third driving. OLD ROSEBUD set the pace under restraint, although going fast to the stretch turn, where, when called upon, he moved away from the others to win hard held as his rider pleased. HODGE raced in closest pursuit until the last eighth, where he tired, but stood the drive gamely. BRONZEWING closed and came with a rush through the last quarter. JOHN GUND tired racing well up to the stretch. OLD BEN and SURPRISING ran fairly well. WATERMELON quit after three-quarters.
Scratched—Ivan Gardner, 114; Buckley, 110; Belloc, 117; Constant, 117.

THE WINNER'S PEDIGREE AND CAREER HIGHLIGHTS

OLD ROSEBUD (Bay Gelding)

- Uncle
  - *Star Shoot
    - Isinglass
    - Astrology
  - The Niece
    - Alarm
    - Jaconet
- Ivory Bells
  - Himyar
    - Alarm
    - Hira
  - Ida Pickwick
    - *Mr. Pickwick
    - Ida K.

Year	Age	Sts	1st	2nd	3rd	Won
1913	2	14	12	2	0	$19,057
1914	3	3	2	0	0	9,575
1917	6	21	15	1	3	31,720
1919	8	30	9	7	5	12,182
1920	9	8	1	2	0	1,295
1921	10	2	1	0	0	700
1922	11	2	0	0	1	200
Totals		80	40	13	8	$74,729

At 2 Years	**WON**	Yucatan Stakes, Spring Trial Stakes, Harold Stakes, Flash Stakes, U. S. Hotel Stakes, Cincinnati Trophy
	2ND	Idle Hour Stakes, Bashford Manor Stakes
At 3 Years	**WON**	Kentucky Derby
	UNP	Withers Stakes
At 6 Years	**WON**	Clark Handicap, Queen City Handicap, Carter Handicap, Frontier Handicap, Bayview Handicap, Latonia Inaugural Handicap, Delaware Handicap
	3RD	Brooklyn Handicap
	UNP	Kentucky Handicap, Saratoga Handicap
At 8 Years	**2ND**	Paumonok Handicap, Mt. Vernon Handicap
	3RD	Thanksgiving Handicap
	UNP	Yonkers Handicap, Arverne Handicap, Kingsbridge Handicap
At 9 Years	**UNP**	Harford Handicap, Paumonok Handicap, Toboggan Handicap

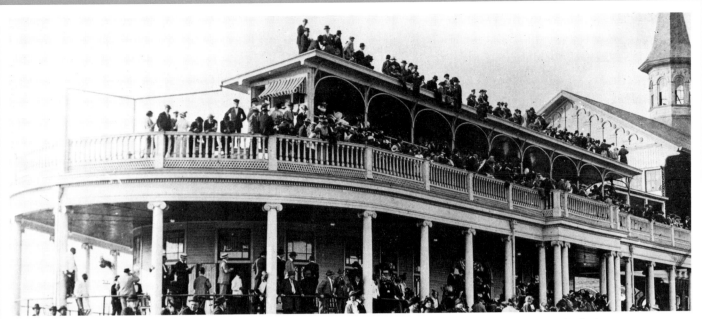

A beautiful veranda was atop the clubhouse in 1914 and the area was filled to watch Old Rosebud win.

The starter got the field underway with a crack of a whip as the web barrier flew up.

May 8, 1915

Owner — H. P. Whitney

Trainer — James Rowe

Jockey — Joe Notter

REGRET

$10,000 added. Net to winner $11,450; second $2,000; third $1,000; fourth $225. 68 nominations.

Horses	Eqt Wt	PP	St	½	¾	1	Str	Fin	Jockeys	Owners	Odds $1 Str't
Regret	w 112	2	1	1½	1½	1½	1¹½	1²	Notter	H. P. Whitney	2.65
Pebbles	wb 117	3	3	2¹	2¹½	2¹½	2²	2²	Borel	J. Butler	6.35
Sharpshooter	wb 114	8	7	3½	3½	3ʰ	3¹	3¹	Butwell	S. L. Parsons	9.60
Royal II	w 117	10	16	12²	9¹	6ⁿᵏ	5ʰ	4³	Neylon	J. Livingston	15.10
E'n Cochran	w 117	5	2	6½	4¹	7½	4½	5½	Taylor	R. L. Baker	16.15
Leo Ray	w 117	11	13	10ʰ	8¹½	8ʰ	7ʰ	6¹½	T McTag't	J. T. Looney	17.90
Double Eagle	wsb 117	13	12	9ʰ	7¹½	9½	6²	7⁴	Burl'game	J. F. Johnson	17.20
Dorch	w 110	1	11	7¹	6½	5¹½	8½	8⁵	Mott	W. W. Darden	†5.40
For Fair	wb 117	4	15	16	15	10½	9½	9½	Warton	G. M. Miller	‡5.40
Ed Crump	wb 117	7	4	4¹½	5½	4½	10½	10ʰ	Goose	J. W. Schorr	‡5.90
Little Strings	w 117	12	10	11¹½	12²	11¹	11¹	11¹½	Pool	M. B. Gruber	†5.40
Goldcrest Boy	w 114	6	8	8½	10½	13¹	12¹	12²	Kederis	J. W. Schorr	‡5.90
Uncle Bryn	wsb 117	16	14	14¹	14¹	12½	13¹	13²	J McTag't	R. W. Walden	†5.40
Tetan	w 117	15	6	13²	13²	14⁶	14⁶	14²	Smyth	Johnson & Crosthwaite	x†5.40
Norse King	wb 117	9	9	5½	11¹	15¹	15²	15⁴	O'Brien	F. B. Le Maire	36.90
Booker Bill	wb 117	14	5	15¹	16	16	16	16	Andress	M. C. Moore	x†5.40

Time: :23-3/5, :48-3/5, 1:13-3/5, 1:39-2/5, 2:05-2/5. Track fast.

Ed Crump and Goldcrest Boy coupled in betting as J. W. Schorr entry; Tetan and Booker Bill coupled as Johnson and Crosthwaite-McMoore entry; Dorch, For Fair, Little Strings, Uncle Bryn, Tetan and Booker Bill coupled in betting as field horses.

$2 Mutuels Paid—Regret, $7.30 straight, $4.00 place, $3.60 show; Pebbles, $7.60 place, $4.80 show; Sharpshooter, $7.10 show.

Winner—Ch.f. by Broomstick—Jersey Lightning, by Hamburg; trained by James Rowe; bred in New Jersey by H. P. Whitney.

Start good and slow. Won easily; second and third driving. REGRET, from a fast start and well ridden, took the lead at once and was rated in front until the last eighth, where she drew away, to win easing up. PEBBLES raced in nearest pursuit and held on gamely in the final drive. SHARPSHOOTER also ran a good race and stood a hard drive resolutely. ROYAL II closed a big gap.

THE WINNER'S PEDIGREE AND CAREER HIGHLIGHTS

REGRET (Chestnut Filly)
- Broomstick
  - Ben Brush
    - Bramble
    - Roseville
  - *Elf
    - Galliard
    - *Sylvabelle
- Jersey Lightning
  - Hamburg
    - Hanover
    - Lady Reel
  - Daisy F.
    - Riley
    - Modesty

Year	Age	Sts	1st	2nd	3rd	Won
1914	2	3	3	0	0	$17,390
1915	3	2	2	0	0	12,500
1916	4	2	1	0	0	560
1917	5	4	3	1	0	4,643
Totals		11	9	1	0	$35,093

At 2 Years	WON	Saratoga Special, Sanford Memorial Handicap, Hopeful Stakes
At 3 Years	WON	Kentucky Derby, Saranac Handicap
At 4 Years	UNP	Saratoga Handicap
At 5 Years	WON	Gazelle Handicap
	2ND	Brooklyn Handicap

94

Col. Matt Winn not only ran Churchill Downs but several other race tracks throughout the country during his career. His travels often brought him into contact with widely known figures. Winn (left) is shown here with the notorious Mexican Chieftian, Pancho Villa (second from left) and two of his associates.

May 13, 1916

Owner — John Sanford

Trainer — Hollie Hughes

Jockey — Johnny Loftus

FORTY SECOND RUNNING

GEORGE SMITH

$10,000 added. Net to winner $9,750; second $2,000; third $1,000; fourth $225. 56 nominations.

Horses	Eqt Wt	PP	St	½	¾	1	Str	Fin	Jockeys	Owners	Odds $1 Str't
George Smith	w 117	8	6	3²	3ʰ	1¹	1²	1ⁿᵏ	Loftus	J. Sanford	4.15
Star Hawk	w 117	3	9	9	7½	5⁴	3²	2³	Lilley	A. K. Macomber	†4.45
Franklin	wb 117	1	2	2²	2¹½	2¹	2ʰ	3½	Rice	Weber & Ward	‡6.45
Dodge	w 117	4	1	5¹	4¹½	4½	4²	4⁶	Murphy	Weber & Ward	‡6.45
Thunderer	w 117	5	7	7¹	5½	6¹	6¹	5¹	T McTag't	H. P. Whitney	§1.05
The Cock	wb 110	7	8	8³	6ʰ	7²	7²	6⁵	Garner	A. K. Macomber	†4.45
Dominant	w 117	2	3	1³	1½	3½	5¹	7⁵	Notter	H. P. Whitney	§1.05
Kinney	wb 117	9	5	6¹½	8⁶	8⁶	8¹⁰	8¹²	Gentry	T. P. Hayes	32.55
Lena Misha	w 117	6	4	4ʰ	9	9	9	9	Dugan	Beverwyck Stable	35.30

Time: 22-2/5, :46-2/5, 1:12-1/5, 1:38-4/5, 2:04. Track fast.

Star Hawk and The Cock coupled in betting as Macomber entry; Franklin and Dodge coupled in betting as Weber and Ward entry; Thunderer and Dominant coupled in betting at H. P. Whitney entry.

$2 Mutuels Paid—George Smith, $10.30 straight, $4.80 place, $2.90 show; Star Hawk, $6.00 place, $4.40 show; Franklin, $3.50 show.

Winner—Blk.c. by *Out of Reach—*Consuelo II, by Bradwardine; trained by Hollie Hughes; bred in Kentucky by Chinn & Forsythe.

Start good and slow. Won driving; second and third same. GEORGE SMITH was well ridden and, after being saved for the first three-quarters, rushed into the lead, but had to be urged at the end to outstay STAR HAWK. The latter, away slowly and trailing for a half-mile, came with a rush through the stretch and almost got up to win. FRANKLIN showed good speed, but tired after racing in the close pursuit. DODGE raced well up throughout. THUNDERER had no mishap. DOMINANT set a fast early pace, but quit badly. LENA MISHA pulled up lame.

Scratched—St. Isidore, 114; Bulse, 117; Huffaker, 117.

THE WINNER'S PEDIGREE AND CAREER HIGHLIGHTS

GEORGE SMITH (Black Colt)

- *Out of Reach
  - Persimmon
    - St. Simon
    - Perdita II
  - *Sandfly
    - Isonomy
    - Sandiway
- *Consuelo II
  - Bradwardine
    - Barcaldine
    - Monte Rosa
  - *Miss Pepper II
    - Pepper and Salt
    - Great Dame

Year	Age	Sts	1st	2nd	3rd	Won
1915	2	12	9	0	0	$10,140
1916	3	4	1	2	0	11,600
1917	4	7	3	1	1	2,594
1918	5	8	4	2	2	18,550
Totals		31	17	5	3	$42,884

At 2 Years
- WON Aberdeen Stakes, Juvenile Stakes, Victoria Stakes, Spring Brewery Stakes, Annapolis Stakes
- UNP Sanford Memorial Handicap, Eastern Shore Handicap, Erdenheim Handicap

At 3 Years
- WON Kentucky Derby
- 2ND Latonia Derby
- UNP Carter Handicap

At 4 Years
- WON Warwick Handicap
- 2ND Long Beach Handicap
- 3RD Belmont Autumn Handicap
- UNP Saratoga Handicap

At 5 Years
- WON Excelsior Handicap, Edgemere Handicap, Yorktown Handicap, Bowie Handicap
- 2ND Bay View Handicap, October Handicap

The start of a race along the backstretch draws a crowd across the infield. Only on Derby Day are spectators allowed into the infield now and more than 75,000 jam the area.

Life was a little slower and less crowded in 1916. These Derby Day fans take life easy under the trees in the paddock area.

May 12, 1917

C. K. G.
Billings

Fred
Johnson

Owners

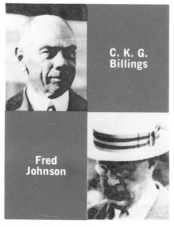

Trainer — C. T. Patterson

Jockey — Charles Borel

*OMAR KHAYYAM

$15,000 added. Net to winner $16,600; second $2,500; third $1,000; fourth $275. 76 nominations.

Horses	Eqt Wt	PP	St	½	¾	1	Str	Fin	Jockeys	Owners	Odds $1 Str't
Omar Khayyam...	wb 117	8	11	10ʰ	10¹	6½	2¹	1²	Borel	Billings & Johnson	12.80
Ticket	wb 117	3	1	3ʰ	3¹½	4½	1½	2¹½	J M'Tag't	A. Miller	1.45
Midway	wb 117	1	12	12¹	9¹	8½	3ʰ	3⁴	Hunt	J. W. Parrish	14.65
Rickety	w 117	11	5	7½	5¹	1ʰ	4½	4¹	Robinson	H. P. Whitney	4.55
War Star	wb 110	9	6	5¹½	6¹	5½	5ʰ	5ʰ	Buxton	A. K. Macomber	†8.65
Manister Toi	wb 117	14	15	13½	11½	10¹	6¹	6ʰ	Keogh	E. Herz	15.45
Skeptic	w 117	4	14	6¹	4ʰ	9¹	7¹	7¹½	Martin	H. H. Hewitt	‡16.45
Guy Fortune	wb 117	2	2	14¹	12¹	12¹	11¹	8½	Connelly	Pastime Stable	‡16.45
Star Master	wb 117	12	9	4½	2ʰ	2ʰ	8¹¹	9ʰ	Loftus	A. K. Macomber	†8.65
Star Gazer	wb 110	13	10	1½	1½	3ʰ	9½	10²	Crump	A. K. Macomber	†8.65
Cudgel	wb 117	5	13	11¹	7¹	13¹	12½	11⁵	Murphy	J. W. Schorr	23.00
Green Jones.......	w 117	7	3	9ʰ	13¹	11½	13¹	12⁸	Goose	W. H. Baker	‡16.45
Top o' the Wave...	wb 117	10	4	15	14²	14¹	14¹	13⁴	Morys	Beverwyck Stable	‡16.45
Berlin	wb 117	6	7	2½	8ʰ	8½	10¹	14¹²	Andress	J. S. Ward	16.20
Acabado	wb 114	15	8	15	15	15	15	15	Schutt'r	Wickliffe Stable	75.45

Time: :23-3/5, :47-3/5, 1:12-4/5, 1:38, 2:04-3/5. Track fast.

War Star, Star Master and Star Gazer coupled in betting as A. K. Macomber entry; Skeptic, Guy Fortune, Green Jones and Top o' the Wave coupled in the field.

$2 Mutuels Paid—Omar Khayyam, $27.60 straight, $10.90 place, $6.20 show; Ticket, $3.70 place, $2.80 show; Midway, $5.10 show.

Winner—Ch.c. by Marco—Lisma, by Persimmon; trained by C. T. Patterson; bred in England by Sir John Robinson.

Start good and slow. Won easily; second and third driving. OMAR KHAYYAM began slowly, gained steadily and, saving much ground when turning into the stretch, outstayed TICKET. The latter, well up from the start, raced into the lead in the stretch, but tired. MIDWAY began slowly, was far back for the first half, but closed an immense gap into a game third. RICKETY tired after taking the lead while rounding into the stretch. WAR STAR raced fairly well. STAR GAZER tired badly in the last quarter.

THE WINNER'S PEDIGREE AND CAREER HIGHLIGHTS

*OMAR KHAYYAM
(Chestnut Colt)

	Marco	Barcaldine	Solon
			Ballyroe
		Novitiate	Hermit
			Retty
	Lisma	Persimmon	St. Simon
			Perdita II
		Luscious	‡Royal Hampton
			Alveole

‡*Harpenden or Royal Hampton.

Year	Age	Sts	1st	2nd	3rd	Won
1916	2	5	1	2	0	$ 3,465
1917	3	13	9	2	0	49,070
1918	4	10	2	1	4	4,475
1919	5	4	1	1	1	1,426
Totals		32	13	6	5	$58,436

At 3 Years	WON	Kentucky Derby, Prospect Handicap, Brooklyn Derby, Kenner Stakes, Travers Stakes, Saratoga Cup, Lawrence Realization, Havre de Grace Handicap, Pimlico Autumn Handicap
At 4 Years	WON	Marines Liberty Bond Handicap
At 5 Years	WON	Rennert Handicap

These pensive folk were attending the 1917 Derby when photographed. The soldier is intent on his Racing Form.

This view from behind the grandstand catches a few vendors in a moment of relaxation, apparently trying to pick a winner.

May 11, 1918

Owner — W. S. Kilmer

Trainer — Henry McDaniel

Jockey — William Knapp

EXTERMINATOR

$15,000 added. Net to winner $14,700; second $2,500; third $1,000; fourth $275. 70 nominations.

Horses	Eqt Wt	PP	St	1/2	3/4	1	Str	Fin	Jockeys	Owners	Odds $1 Str't
Exterminator	.w 114	5	5	5^1	$4\frac{1}{2}$	1^h	2^4	1^1	Knapp	W. S. Kilmer	29.60
Escoba	.....wb 117	1	2	$3^1\frac{1}{2}$	2^h	2^1	1^n	2^8	Notter	K. D. Alexander	4.25
Viva America	.w 113	2	1	$1^1\frac{1}{2}$	$1^1\frac{1}{2}$	3^4	3^2	3^4	War'on	C. T. Worthington	29.00
War Cloud	...w 117	4	7	4^h	5^2	4^4	4^3	4^2	Loftus	A. K. Macomber	1.45
Lucky B	......w 117	6	4	6^h	7^8	$5\frac{1}{2}$	5^6	5^6	McCabe	O. A. Bianchi	6.15
J T Clark	....wb 117	8	8	7^3	6^3	7^6	7^3	6^{12}	Morys	J. W. Schorr	8.90
Sew'l Combs	.wb 117	3	3	2^{nk}	3^1	6^2	$6\frac{1}{2}$	7^1	Gentry	Gallaher Bros.	8.75
Am'n Eagle	.wsb 117	6	6	8	8	8	8	8	Sande	T. C. McDowell	19.25

Time: :24-1/5, :49-1/5, 1:16-1/5, 1:43-3/5, 2:10-4/5. Track muddy.

$2 Mutuels Paid—Exterminator, $61.20 straight, $23.10 place, $12.40 show; Escoba, $4.90 place, $4.60 show; Viva America, $13.20 show.

Winner—Ch.g. by *McGee—Fair Empress, by Jim Gore; trained by Henry McDaniel; bred in Kentucky by F. D. Knight.

Start good and slow. Won handily; second and third driving. EXTERMINATOR moved up fast after going three-quarters and, slipping through on the inner rail, raced into the lead and outstayed ESCOBA. The latter faced forwardly from the start, made a resolute effort in the last eighth, but tired in the last sixteenth. VIVA AMERICA showed the most early speed, but found the distance a trifle too far. WAR CLOUD met with much interference on the first two turns, but remained close up to the last quarter, where he tired.

Overweight—Viva America, 1 pound.

THE WINNER'S PEDIGREE AND CAREER HIGHLIGHTS

EXTERMINATOR (Chestnut Gelding)	*McGee	White Knight	Sir Hugo / Whitelock
		Remorse	Hermit / Vex
	Fair Empress	Jim Gore	Hindoo / Katie
		Merry Thought	*Pirate of Penzance / Raybelle

Year	Age	Sts	1st	2nd	3rd	Won
1917	2	4	2	0	0	$ 1,350
1918	3	15	7	4	3	36,147
1919	4	21	9	6	3	26,402
1920	5	17	10	3	2	52,805
1921	6	16	8	2	5	56,827
1922	7	17	10	1	1	71,075
1923	8	3	1	1	1	4,250
1924	9	7	3	0	2	4,140
Totals		100	50	17	17	$252,996

At 3 Years	WON	Kentucky Derby, Carrollton Handicap, Ellicott City Handicap, Pimlico Autumn Handicap, Latonia Cup, Thanksgiving Handicap
	2ND	Latonia Derby, Kenner Stakes, National Handicap
At 4 Years	WON	Ben Ali Handicap, Camden Handicap, Galt House Handicap, Saratoga Cup, Pimlico Cup Handicap
	2ND	Champlain Handicap, Harford County Handicap, Havre de Grace Handicap, Annapolis Handicap, Latonia Cup
At 5 Years	WON	Long Beach Handicap, Brookdale Handicap, Windsor Jockey Club Handicap, George Hendrie Memorial Handicap, Saratoga Cup, Autumn Gold Cup, Toronto Autumn Cup, Ontario Jockey Club Cup, Pimlico Cup
	2ND	Saratoga Handicap, Champlain Handicap

In his six-, seven-, eight-, and nine-year-old seasons Exterminator won the Long Beach, Independence, Merchants' and Citizens', Harford, Pimlico Spring, Clark, Kentucky, Bayside, Garden City, Brooklyn, Philadelphia Handicaps, Laurel Stakes, Saratoga Cup (twice), Autumn Gold Cup, Toronto Autumn Cup (twice), Pimlico Cup, and Saratoga Cup.

Joseph N. Camden became Churchill Downs' president in 1918.

Exterminator got off to a "clean" start on this muddy track in 1918, and returned a whopping $61.20 to win. He showed his class by winning 50 times in his 100 career starts.

L♥uisville Trust Bank
THE RIGHT BANK IN BLUEGRASS COUNTRY

May 10, 1919

Owner — J. K. L. Ross

Trainer — H. G. Bedwell

Jockey — Johnny Loftus

FORTY FIFTH RUNNING

SIR BARTON

$20,000 added. Net to winner $20,825; second $2,500; third $1,000; fourth $275. 75 nominations.

Horses	Eqt Wt	PP	St	1/2	3/4	1	Str	Fin	Jockeys	Owners	Odds $1 Str't
Sir Barton	wb 112½	1	1	1²	1½	1²	1½	1⁵	Loftus	J. K. L. Ross	‡2.60
Billy Kelly	w 119	11	8	3½	3⁴	2³	2⁴	2¹	Sande	J. K. L. Ross	‡2.60
Under Fire	w 122	7	11	9½	9½	6½	3¹	3¹	Garner	P. Dunne	19.15
Vulcanite	w 110	6	10	10½	5ʰ	4½	4¹	4⁶	Howard	W. F. Polson	70.00
Senn's Park	wb 122	8	9	6²	4½	5½	5¹	5¹	Lunsford	O. A. Bianchi	†14.10
Be Frank	w 119	2	6	7ʰ	7½	7½	6½	6½	Butwell	C. M. Garrison	27.45
Sailor	wb 119	10	12	12	10²	10½	8½	7⁸	McIntyre	J. W. McClelland	§2.10
St Bernard	w 119	4	2	5ʰ	6¹	9¹	7²	8²	Pool	B. J. Brannon	†14.10
Regalo	w 117	9	7	8²	8½	8¹	9²	9⁴	Murphy	Gallaher Bros.	6.05
Eternal	w 122	5	3	2½	2½	3½	10⁵	10¹⁰	Schutter	J. W. McClelland	§2.10
Frogtown	w 119	12	4	11²	11½	11²	11¹⁰	11²⁰	Morys	W. S. Kilmer	22.45
Vindex	w 122	3	5	4ⁿᵏ	12	12	12	12	Knapp	H. P. Whitney	8.15

Time: :24-1/5, :48-2/5, 1:14, 1:41-4/5, 2:09-4/5. Track heavy.

Sir Barton and Billy Kelly coupled in betting as J. K. L. Ross entry; Sailor and Eternal coupled as J. W. McClelland entry; Sennings Park and St. Bernard coupled in betting as field horses.

$2 Mutuels Paid—J. K. L. Ross Entry (Sir Barton and Billy Kelly), $7.20 straight, $6.70 place, $6.00 show; Under Fire, $10.80 show.

Winner—Ch.c. by *Star Shoot—Lady Sterling, by Hanover, trained by H. G. Bedwell; bred in Kentucky by Madden and Gooch.

Start good and slow. Won easily; second and third driving. SIR BARTON raced into the lead at once and, well ridden, led under restraint until reaching the stretch, where he was shaken up and easily held BILLY KELLY safe in the last eighth. BILLY KELLY held to his task well, was under restraint in the early running and finished gamely. UNDER FIRE gained steadily from a slow beginning and finished fast and gamely. VULCANITE ran well and finished close up. ETERNAL was done after going three-quarters. REGALO ran disappointingly.

Scratched—Corson, 122; Clermont, 122. Overweight—Sir Barton, 2½ pounds.

THE WINNER'S PEDIGREE AND CAREER HIGHLIGHTS

SIR BARTON (Chestnut Colt)
- *Star Shoot
  - Isinglass
    - Isonomy
    - Deadlock
  - Astrology
    - Hermit
    - Stella
- Lady Sterling
  - Hanover
    - Hindoo
    - Bourbon Belle
  - *Aquila
    - Sterling
    - Eagle

Year	Age	Sts	1st	2nd	3rd	Won
1918	2	6	0	1	0	$ 4,113
1919	3	13	8	3	2	88,250
1920	4	12	5	2	3	24,494
Totals		31	13	6	5	$116,857

At 2 Years	
2ND	Belmont Futurity
UNP	Tremont Stakes, Flash Stakes, United States Hotel Stakes, Sanford Memorial, Hopeful Stakes

At 3 Years	
WON	Kentucky Derby, Preakness Stakes, Withers Stakes, Belmont Stakes, Potomac Handicap, Maryland Handicap, Pimlico Fall Serial No. 2, Pimlico Fall Serial No. 3
2ND	Dwyer Stakes
3RD	Havre de Grace Handicap, Pimlico Autumn Handicap

At 4 Years	
WON	Climax Handicap, Rennert Handicap, Saratoga Handicap, Dominion Handicap, Merchants' and Citizens' Handicap
2ND	Kenilworth Park Gold Cup (match race with Man o' War), Pimlico Fall Serial No. 3
3RD	Marathon Handicap, Laurel Stakes, Pimlico Fall Serial No. 2

Parking problems and traffic jams are part of Derby Day. This crowd came in their magnificant touring cars and parked in the area near the present bus parking area. It seems that quite a few vehicles are blocked in, but apparently no one was in a hurry to leave.

55 Years Ago, the year of The 45th Kentucky Derby, Reliance Universal, Inc. was founded in Louisville

May 8, 1920

Owner — Ral Parr

Trainer — William Garth

Jockey — Ted Rice

PAUL JONES

$30,000 added. Net to winner $30,375; second $4,000; third $2,000; fourth $275. 107 nominations.

Horses	Eqt	Wt	PP	St	½	¾	1	Str	Fin	Jockeys	Owners	Odds $1 Str't
Paul Jones ...	w	126	2	1	1$\frac{1}{2}$	1$\frac{1}{2}$	1^2	1^h	1^h	Rice	Ral Parr	‡16.20
Upset	w	126	5	4	3^h	3^h	2$\frac{1}{2}$	2^h	2^4	Rodriguez	H. P. Whitney	††1.65
On Watch ..	wb	126	13	16	13$\frac{1}{2}$	7^1	3$\frac{1}{2}$	3^1	3^4	Barrett	G. W. Loft	§4.30
Damask	b	126	8	9	7^h	4^h	4^1	4^1	4^2	Ambrose	H. P. Whitney	††1.65
Donnacona ...	w	126	7	10	6^h	6$\frac{1}{2}$	5$\frac{1}{2}$	5^2	5^4	O'Brien	G. W. Loft	§4.30
Blazes	w	126	15	7	8$\frac{1}{2}$	5^1	6$\frac{1}{2}$	6^1	6$\frac{1}{2}$	Kummer	Ral Parr	‡16.20
By Golly	w	126	4	5	2^h	8^1	8$1\frac{1}{2}$	8^1	7^h	Lyke	E. R. Bradley	†13.20
Wildair	w	126	14	8	4$\frac{1}{2}$	2^h	7^1	7$\frac{1}{2}$	8^h	Fator	H. P. Whitney	††1.65
Bersagliere ..	wb	126	9	3	10$\frac{1}{2}$	11$\frac{1}{2}$	9^1	9^1	9$\frac{1}{2}$	Murray	C. A. Cochran	22.75
Patches	wb	126	6	12	14^1	10^h	10^2	10^h	10^4	Hanover	F. C. Bain	†13.20
Herron	w	126	1	6	9^h	13^2	11$1\frac{1}{2}$	11^2	11$\frac{1}{2}$	Butwell	E. Alvarez	†13.20
Sandy Beal ..	w	126	10	14	15^2	14^2	12^1	12^1	12$\frac{1}{2}$	Williams	W. S. Murray	12.50
Prince Pal ...	w	126	3	2	5^1	12^h	13^2	13^2	13^2	Schut'r	Simms & Oliver	18.90
David Har'm.	wb	126	11	11	11$\frac{1}{2}$	9$\frac{1}{2}$	14^2	14^2	14$1\frac{1}{2}$	Fairb'er	W. R. Coe	‡‡35.20
Cleopatra ..	wb	121	12	13	12^{nk}	15^4	15^5	15^1	15^5	McAtee	W. R. Coe	‡‡35.20
Peace Pen'nt.	wb	126	17	15	16^{10}	16^{20}	16^{20}	16^{20}	16^{20}	Garner	W. F. Polson	6.35
Sterling	wb	126	16	17	17	17	17	17	17	Callahan	C. C. Van Meter	33.00

Time: :23-4/5, :48-1/5, 1:14-4/5, 1:42, 2:09. Track slow.

†Mutuel field. ‡Coupled in betting as R. Parr entry. ††Coupled in betting as H. P. Whitney entry. §Coupled in betting as G. W. Loft entry. ‡‡Coupled in betting as W. R. Coe entry.

$2 Mutuels Paid—Ral Parr entry (Paul Jones and Blazes), $34.40 straight, $12.30 place, $6.60 show; H. P. Whitney entry (Upset and Damask) $3.20 place, $3.00 show; G. W. Loft entry (On Watch and Donnacona) $4.00 show.

Winner—Br.g. by *Sea King—May Florence, by Hamburg, trained by William Garth; bred in Kentucky by J. E. Madden.

Start good and slow. Won driving; second and third same. PAUL JONES was away fast, raced into the lead at once and, holding on in game style, outstayed UPSET in the final drive. The latter moved up menacingly after going a half-mile and, saving ground when coming into the stretch, appeared a winner a sixteenth out, but tired right at the end. ON WATCH came from far back in the last half-mile and finished well. DAMASK raced forwardly, but tired in the stretch. BY GOLLY quit. DONNACONA had no mishap. PEACE PENNANT was always far back. SANDY BEALL retired after going a half-mile and so did BERSAGLIERE.

THE WINNER'S PEDIGREE AND CAREER HIGHLIGHTS

PAUL JONES (Brown Gelding)			
*Sea King	Persimmon	St. Simon
		Perdita II
	Sea Air	Isonomy
		Re-echo
May Florence	Hamburg	Hanover
		Lady Reel
	Fiesole	*Goldfinch
		Firenze

Year	Age	Sts	1st	2nd	3rd	Won
1919	2	12	5	2	2	$ 6,404
1920	3	13	4	2	2	44,636
1921	4	12	1	1	3	2,708
1922	5	13	2	2	2	5,432
1923	6	15	2	5	4	4,991
Totals		65	14	12	13	$64,171

At 2 Years	WON	Aberdeen Stakes, Boquet Selling Stakes, Endurance
At 3 Years	WON	Kentucky Derby, Newark Handicap, Suburban Handicap
At 4 Years	WON	Susquehanna Handicap

104

Construction of some sort seems to be a never-ending part of the Churchill Downs picture. These scenes was photographed in 1920 when the present grandstand area was being added.

The facade of the third floor box area had a little different look in 1920, but the seats in this preferred area were just as hard to come by as they are today.

May 7, 1921

Owner — E. R. Bradley

Trainer — H. J. Thompson

Jockey — Charles Thompson

BEHAVE YOURSELF

$50,000 added. Net to winner $38,450 and $5,000 gold cup; second $10,000; third $5,000; fourth $2,000. 109 nominations.

Horses	Eqt Wt	PP	St	½	¾	1	Str	Fin	Jockeys	Owners	Odds $1 Str't
Behave Yourself....	w 126	1	9	8½	8¹	6½	1½	1h	Thompson	E. R. Bradley	†8.65
Black Servant	w 126	7	2	1¹	1h	1½	2½	2⁶	Lyke	E. R. Bradley	†8.65
Prudery	w 121	2	4	5½	4½	3h	3h	3½	Kummer	H. P. Whitney	‡1.10
Tryster	w 126	10	8	6h	5½	5h	4¹	4⁴	Coltiletti	H. P. Whitney	‡1.10
Careful	w 121	3	7	4h	3h	4h	5²	5⁴	Keogh	W. J. Salmon	13.60
Coyne	w 126	5	3	7²	6h	7²	7¹	6¹	Garner	Harned Bros.	11.20
Leonardo II	w 126	4	5	3½	2³	2½	6½	7½	Schut'r	Xalapa Farm Stable	§4.30
Uncle Velo	ws 126	12	1	11¹	10²	9½	8²	8²	Pool	G. F. Baker	65.30
Bon Homme	wb 126	11	6	10¹	11⁶	11²	10¹	9⁶	Robinson	Xalapa Farm Stable	§4.30
Planet	wb 126	6	12	12	12	12	11½	10⁵	King	H. P. Headley	81.30
Star Voter	w 126	8	11	9¹	7¹	8h	9²	11¹	Ensor	J. K. L. Ross	8.55
Muskall'nge	wb 126	9	10	2¹	9¹	10¹	12	12	Carroll	H. C. Fisher	96.25

Time: :23-1/5, :46-4/5, 1:11-3/5, 1:38-3/5, 2:04-1/5. Track fast.

†Coupled in betting as E. R. Bradley entry. ‡Coupled in betting as H. P. Whitney entry. §Coupled in betting as Xalapa Farm Stable entry.

$2 Mutuels Paid—E. R. Bradley entry (Behave Yourself and Black Servant), $19.30 straight, $13.00 place, $5.60 show; H. P. Whitney entry (Prudery and Tryster), $3.30 show.

Winner—Br.c. by Marathon—Miss Ringlets, by Handball, trained by H. J. Thompson; bred in Kentucky by E. R. Bradley.

Start good and slow. Won driving; second and third same. BEHAVE YOURSELF began slowly, but saved much ground on the last two turns and, going steadily in the stretch, outstayed BLACK SERVANT in a game finish. The latter showed fine speed in pacemaking and disposed of LEONARDO II before going three-quarters, then held on well in the final drive, but tired near the end. PRUDERY made a wide turn into the stretch and finished gamely. TRYSTER was far back in the early running, but finished fast and gaining. LEONARDO II tired after going well for the first mile. CAREFUL was done after going three-quarters. COYNE ran fairly well.

Scratched—Grey Lag, 126; Billy Barton, 126; Firebrand, 126.

THE WINNER'S PEDIGREE AND CAREER HIGHLIGHTS

BEHAVE YOURSELF (Brown Colt)	Marathon	Martagon	Bend Or / Tiger Lily
		*Ondulee	St. Simon / Ornis
	Miss Ringlets	Handball	Hanover / Keepsake
		Bessie	*The Ill-Used / Belle of Nantura

Year	Age	Sts	1st	2nd	3rd	Won
1920	2	7	3	0	1	$17,972
1921	3	11	1	2	0	40,800
Totals		18	4	2	1	$58,772

At 2 Years	WON	Queen City Handicap
	3RD	Kentucky Jockey Club Stakes

At 3 Years	WON	Kentucky Derby
	2ND	Blue Grass Stakes, Latonia Derby
	UNP	Ben Ali Handicap, Kentucky Handicap, Proctor Knott Handicap, Saratoga Handicap, Greenwich Handicap, Latonia Handicap, Latonia Championship Stakes, Twin City Handicap

The field of 12 for the 1921 Derby required no lead ponies as they paraded to the post. That's Behave Yourself No. 1 in line and No. 1 at the finish line.

It takes a sharp eye, but look closely at the 1921 finish and you will see Black Servant just behind Behave Yourself as Col. E. R. Bradley's pair dominated the field.

May 13, 1922

Owner — Ben Block

Trainer — Fred Burlew

Jockey — Albert Johnson

MORVICH

$50,000 added, also $5,000 Gold Cup and $2,000 other gold trophies. Net to winner $46,775; second $6,000; third $3,000; fourth $1,000. 92 nominations.

Horses	Eqt Wt	PP	St	1/2	3/4	1	Str	Fin	Jockeys	Owners	Odds $1 Str't
Morvich	w 126	4	2	$1^{1\frac{1}{2}}$	$1^{1\frac{1}{2}}$	$1^{1\frac{1}{2}}$	$1^{1\frac{1}{2}}$	$1^{1\frac{1}{2}}$	Johnson	Ben Block	1.20
Bet Mosie	w 126	7	8	$8\frac{1}{2}$	6^3	$5\frac{1}{2}$	4^1	2^h	Burke	Idle Hour Stock Farm	†2.90
John Finn	ws 126	1	4	5^1	5^1	6^2	2^h	3^1	Pool	G. F. Baker	22.60
Deadlock	w 126	6	6	4^1	$4\frac{1}{2}$	$4^{1\frac{1}{2}}$	3^h	4^4	Mooney	R. H. Shannon	6.90
My Play	w 126	3	1	2^h	2^h	3^1	5^2	5^4	Robinson	Lexington Stable	19.05
Letterman	w 126	9	9	$7\frac{1}{2}$	$7\frac{1}{2}$	7^1	7^1	6^1	Rice	Greentree Stable	24.80
Surf Rider	wb 126	8	7	6^1	8^1	$8^{1\frac{1}{2}}$	8^1	$7\frac{1}{2}$	Scobie	Montfort Jones	35.75
Startle	w 121	2	3	3^2	3^1	2^h	$6\frac{1}{2}$	8^{nk}	Connelly	H. H. Hewitt	13.90
By Gosh	w 126	10	10	9	9	9	9	9	Barnes	Idle Hour Stock Farm	†2.90
Busy Amer'n	wb 126	5	5	Broke Down					Barrett	Idle Hour Stock Farm	†2.90

Time: :23-4/5, :47-3/5, 1:13, 1:39-1/5, 2:04-3/5. Track fast.
†Coupled in betting as Idle Hour Stock Farm Stable entry.
$2 Mutuels Paid—Morvich, $4.40 straight, $4.30 place, $3.50 show; E. R. Bradley's Idle Hour Stock Farm Stable entry (Bet Mosie, By Gosh and Busy American), $2.90 place, $2.70 show; John Finn, $6.60 show.
Winner—Br.c. by Runnymeade—Hymir, by Dr. Leggo, trained by Fred Burlew; bred in California by A. B. Spreckels.
    Start good and slow. Won easily; second and third driving. MORVICH ran as if he outclassed the others, was kept in the lead under hard restraint for the first mile and drew away in the stretch to win under a pull. BET MOSIE was ridden wide on the turns and lost much ground, but closed a big gap and finished gamely. JOHN FINN raced prominently all the way and finished resolutely. DEADLOCK raced well, but tired in the last quarter. MY PLAY ran well, but finished quite lame. STARTLE was done after going three-quarters. BUSY AMERICAN broke down in the first quarter.
Scratched—Banker Brown, 126.

THE WINNER'S PEDIGREE AND CAREER HIGHLIGHTS

MORVICH (Brown Colt)
- Runnymede
  - *Voter
    - Friar's Balsam
    - *Mavourneen
  - Running Stream
    - Domino
    - Dancing Water
- Hymir
  - Dr. Leggo
    - Puryear D.
    - Sevens
  - Georgia Girl
    - *Solitaire II
    - Georgia VI

Year	Age	Sts	1st	2nd	3rd	Won
1921	2	11	11	0	0	$115,234
1922	3	5	1	2	1	57,675
Totals		16	12	2	1	$172,909

At 2 Years — WON Suffolk Selling Stakes, Greenfield Selling Stakes, U. S. Hotel Stakes, Saratoga Special, Hopeful Stakes, Eastern Shore Handicap, Pimlico Futurity

At 3 Years —
WON Kentucky Derby
2ND Carlton Stakes
3RD Kentucky Special
UNP Latonia Fall Highweight Handicap

The crowds were getting larger and larger and the Derby bigger and bigger under Col. Matt Winn's leadership as this 1922 view of the crowd shows.

Benjamin Block's Morvich and jockey Albert Johnson make their way through the crowd after the Californian's victory.

May 19, 1923

Owner — Harry F. Sinclair

Trainer — D. J. Leary

Jockey — Earl Sande

ZEV

$50,000 added. Net to winner $53,000 and $5,000 Gold Cup; second $6,000; third $3,000; fourth $1,000. 145 nominations.

Horses	Eqt	Wt	PP	St	1/2	3/4	1	Str	Fin	Jockeys	Owners	Odds $1 Str't
Zev	wb	126	10	5	1^2	1^2	$1\frac{1}{2}$	1^2	$1^{1\frac{1}{2}}$	Sande	Rancocas Stable	19.20
Martingale	w	126	19	12	2^2	$2\frac{1}{2}$	2^h	2^1	2^1	Kummer	J. S. Cosden	‡19.75
Vigil	wb	126	5	14	$10\frac{1}{2}$	8^1	$6\frac{1}{2}$	5^1	3^1	Marinelli	W. J. Salmon	15.25
Nassau	w	126	8	4	3^1	3^h	$3^{1\frac{1}{2}}$	3^1	4^n	Garner	F. Johnson	3.25
Chittagong	wb	126	1	2	9^2	7^1	4^1	6^1	$5^{1\frac{1}{2}}$	Heupel	J. Hertz	†5.85
Enchantment	wb	126	11	11	6^h	4^1	$5\frac{1}{2}$	$4\frac{1}{2}$	6^2	McAtee	H. P. Whitney	§2.30
Rialto	w	126	17	15	$12\frac{1}{2}$	10^1	8^h	$7\frac{1}{2}$	7^2	Coltiletti	Greentree Stable	§2.30
Aspiration	wb	126	9	7	7^1	$5\frac{1}{2}$	7^{nk}	9^1	$8^{1\frac{1}{2}}$	Kennedy	B. Block	††29.20
Prince K	w	126	4	1	4^1	$9\frac{1}{2}$	9^h	$11\frac{1}{2}$	$9\frac{1}{2}$	Kelsay	Marshall Bros.	†5.85
Bright Tomorrow	wb	126	7	3	14^h	11^2	10^{nk}	8^1	$10\frac{1}{2}$	Ponce	Idle Hour Stock Farm	28.05
In Memoriam	w	126	21	10	11^h	$12\frac{1}{2}$	$11\frac{1}{2}$	16^1	$11\frac{1}{2}$	Mooney	C. Weidemann	†5.85
Bo McMillan	w	126	20	8	5^1	6^3	12^1	15^h	12^1	Connelly	T. J. Pendergast	11.95
Better Luck	w	126	6	18	8^1	15^1	14^h	$17\frac{1}{2}$	13^1	Johnson	B. Block	††29.20
Wida	w	126	12	9	15^1	$13\frac{1}{2}$	13^h	14^h	14^8	Yerrat	T. E. Mueller	†5.85
Picketer	w	126	18	16	13^1	14^2	15^1	$10\frac{1}{2}$	15^2	Corcoran	H. P. Whitney	§2.30
Gen'l Thatcher	w	126	16	17	16^1	16^2	17^1	13^1	16^2	Robinson	Nevada Stock Farm	12.80
Calcutta	wb	126	14	13	18^1	17^1	$16\frac{1}{2}$	$19\frac{1}{2}$	17^1	Yeargin	G. R. Allen	†5.85
The Clown	w	126	2	21	$17\frac{1}{2}$	19^2	19^1	$18\frac{1}{2}$	18^4	Lunsf'rd	Audley Farm	†5.85
Golden Rule	w	126	15	6	19^1	$18\frac{1}{2}$	18^h	$12\frac{1}{2}$	19^{10}	Lang	J. S. Cosden	‡19.75
Cherry Pie	w	126	3	20	21	21	20^1	20^4	20^2	Penman	Greentree Stable	§2.30
Pravus	wb	126	13	19	20^1	$20\frac{1}{2}$	21	21	21	Owens	F. Wieland	†5.85

Time: :23-2/5, :47-2/5, 1:12-2/5, 1:39, 2:05-2/5. Track fast.

†Mutuel field. ‡Coupled in betting as J. S. Cosden entry. §Coupled in betting as Greentree Stable and H. P. Whitney entry. ††Coupled in betting as B. Block entry.

Winner—Br.c. by The Finn—Miss Kearney, by *Planudes, trained by D. J. Leary; bred in Kentucky by J. E. Madden.

Start good and slow. Won easily; second and third driving. ZEV broke forwardly and, showing high speed, raced into a good lead at once and, withstanding a drive through the stretch, gamely held MARTINGALE safe at the end. MARTINGALE was in closest pursuit nearly throughout and held his position well in the stretch drive. VIGIL began slowly and had to race wide, but closed a big gap and may have been best.

THE WINNER'S PEDIGREE AND CAREER HIGHLIGHTS

ZEV (Brown Colt)	The Finn	*Ogden	Kilwarlin / *Oriole
		Livonia	*Star Shoot / Woodray
	Miss Kearney	*Planudes	St. Simon / Lonely
		Courtplaster	*Sandringham / Set Fast

Year	Age	Sts	1st	2nd	3rd	Won
1922	2	12	5	4	2	$ 24,665
1923	3	14	12	1	0	272,008
1924	4	17	6	3	3	16,966
Totals		43	23	8	5	$313,639

At 2 Years — **WON** Grand Union Hotel Stakes, Albany Handicap

At 3 Years — **WON** Kentucky Derby, Paumonok Handicap, Rainbow Handicap, Withers Stakes, Belmont Stakes, Queens County Handicap, Lawrence Realization, International Special No. 3, Autumn Championship Stakes, Pimlico Fall Serial No. 3, Match Races with In Memoriam ($75,000).

At 4 Years — **WON** Kings County Handicap, Havlin Hotel Handicap, Pimlico Serial No. 1

Zev got away on top (top strip) and led all the way after just a few jumps from the start to post his easy victory.

Kentucky Gov. Edwin Morrow (right) presents the gold trophy to trainer Dave Leary after Zev's victory.

This crowd pondered long and hard but overlooked Zev in the betting and he paid $40.40.

The color and charisma of the Kentucky Derby
is best told in pictures. On the following pages
are scenes from recent Derbies. Opposite is the
1973 Derby winner and the ninth winner of
racing's Triple Crown, Secretariat. Photographer
Tony Leonard captured him as he neared the
Derby finish line. Following Secretariat are photos
of that electric moment of the start; the pageantry
of the centerfield; the crucial first turn with the
famed twin spires as the background; an entire
Derby field framed by excited thousands; the
tulip gardens nodding in the spring sunshine; the
thundering hooves in the stretch; the finish, and
finally the winners' circle where only Derby
winners ever tred.

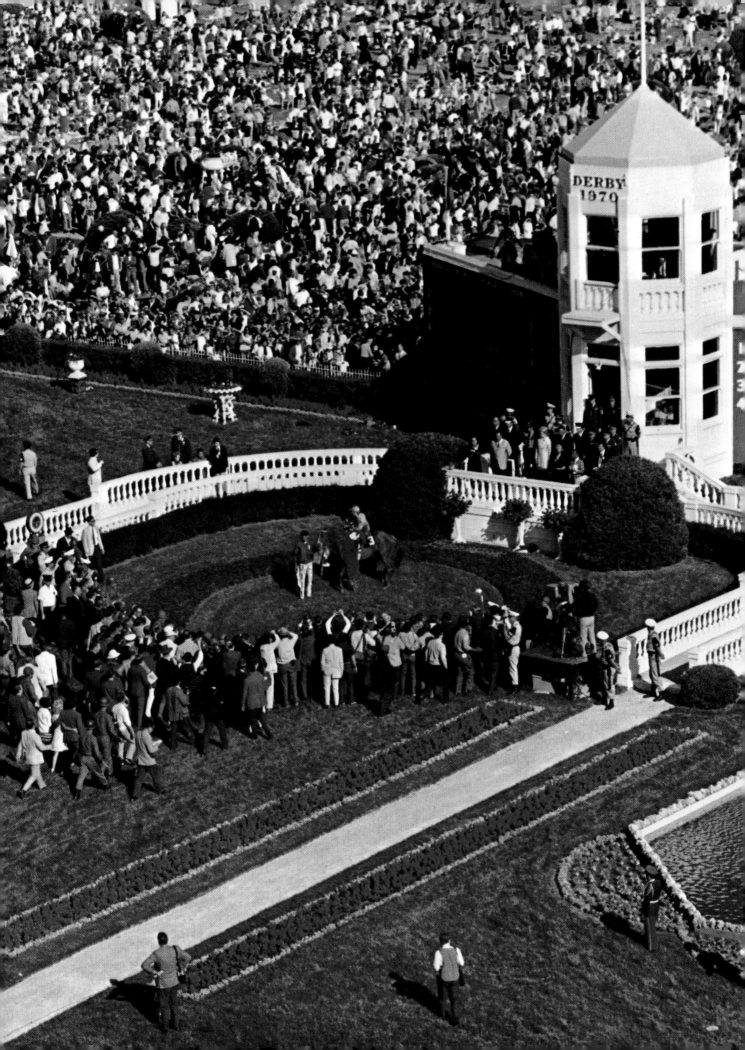

FLOWERS FOR THE WINNER

A wreath, a collar, a blanket, a garland — the flowers for the Kentucky Derby winner have been called all of these since the beginning of the presentation in 1896.

It was in 1896, too, that the Derby distance was shortened to a mile and one-quarter and both features have continued to the present day.

Prior to post time of that 22nd Derby in 1896 "the gorgeous floral wreath to adorn the neck of the winner and a bouquet for the jockey attracted much attention in the grandstand" where they were on exhibit for everyone to see.

This description was written of the presentation:

"Dripping wet, with the whelps of the whip on his side . . . Ben Brush was presented with a very beautiful collar by Charles Reimers. It was of white roses and pink and was tied with white and magenta ribbon. The jockey was also presented with bouquets from Mrs. W. F. Schulte, whose husband is president of the New Louisville Jockey Club, and Charles Reimers. The crowd cheered heartily as the winner was led away adorned with the pretty flowers."

It is indeed possible that these early presentations were sponsored by individuals and not by the Jockey Club. During an interview with the winning jockey the following year, he could not help, as he talked, sticking his nose time and again down in the bouquet of cut flowers, a gift from Secretary [Charles F.] Price.

This was indicated further when Lieber Karl, a 1 to 3 choice in the 1898 Derby, was defeated by a neck. Among his disappointed backers was Mrs. John Schorr, wife of the owner, who had purchased one of the most expensive floral designs in the city. It was to be hung around Lieber Karl's neck, but when the Tennessee favorite walked away to his stable, he was not decorated with flowers.

In 1901, the Derby was run on April 29, the first of only two years that the event has not been held in May. His Eminence with Jimmy Winkfield up was the winner. This description was written about the Derby flowers:

"The jockey was presented with a handsome bouquet and his eyes glistened. As soon as he had dismounted and the saddle had been removed, a blanket made of evergreens and roses of white and red was spread over the victorious colt . . ." and he was paraded up and down in front of the stand while the crowd cheered some more.

1902 brought a different choice of flowers when a blanket of carnations and ferns was thrown over the back of Alan-a-Dale, but two years later, 1904, the first mention of a particular rose, the American Beauty, was made.

Mrs. Charles Elwood Durnell, the first woman to own a Derby winner, watched the 1904 race from a landau that was parked at the end of the grandstand.

"Her gaze was centered far up the track, where her husband and the mite of a boy who was responsible for the victory were hurrying to her side," it was written. "They came with a garland of American Beauties and a pair of arms full of lilies which they tossed at this woman's feet.

Then, womanlike, she embraced both and sat down and cried."

Mrs. Durnell had received the colt, Elwood, as a yearling, a wedding gift from her husband.

The courtesy of presenting the flowers to a lady was repeated in 1907 when jockey A. Minder took his bouquet of roses to the wife of the trainer, Mrs. W. H. Fizer, who was seated in the grandstand. He later sent her the floral wreath.

Roses continued to be the flower to honor the Kentucky Derby winner. It was in 1925 that the late Bill Corum, a New York sports columnist, dubbed the three-year-old classic the "Run for the Roses". Corum later became president of Churchill Down.

Mrs. Kingsley Walker, owner of one of Louisville's oldest florist shops, has designed and made the winner's rose garland since 1931.

In January she orders 500 of the darkest red rose on the market, preferring that they come from local growers. The small, tight buds are delivered on the Wednesday before Derby Day, and Mrs. Walker begins her task about 2:00 p.m. Derby Eve. The garland is completed at 11:30 that night.

After the initial year of working the roses on a table, Mrs. Walker had a wrought iron frame made similar to one used for quilting. On this she laces a foundation of cambric over which she places a protective pad of greenhouse-grown smilax. Each stem is cut to two inches in length, and all thorns are removed. A wire is then inserted and is protectively covered so that the horse will not be irritated. Mrs. Walker starts at each end of the cambric and works toward the middle placing a rose leaf on every other flower. Using green buttonhole thread, she sews each rose three times.

"Never," Mrs. Walker declares, "has a single rose fallen off before being put on the horse!"

When completed, the garland is 2½ yards long and 14 inches wide.

On Derby morning Mrs. Walker sews in the lining of heavy green satin and places similax on the ends to form a graceful oval.

The garland and the jockey's bouquet of five dozen 36-inch stem red roses and 10 yards of red satin ribbon are delivered to the track between 2:30 and 3:00 in the afternoon. At one time cans of dry ice were placed in the corners of the boxes in an effort to preserve the freshness of the flowers, but now a refrigerated truck is used.

Approximately two hours after the roses have been brought to the presentation stand, the garland is placed over the withers of the Derby winner, and the jockey is given his bouquet.

A collar in 1896 or a garland now — the roses are a symbol of the Kentucky Derby, the world's greatest horse race.

May 17, 1924

Owner — Mrs. R. M. Hoots

Trainer — Hedley Webb

Jockey — John Mooney

FIFTIETH RUNNING

BLACK GOLD

$50,000 added and $5,000 Gold Cup. Net to winner $52,775; second, $6,000; third, $3,000; fourth, $1,000. 152 nominations.

Horses	Eqt Wt	PP	St	½	¾	1	Str	Fin	Jockeys	Owners	Odds $1 Str't
Black Gold ....w	126	1	3	5^h	6^h	$3\frac{1}{2}$	3^2	$1\frac{1}{2}$	Mooney	Mrs. R. M. Hoots	1.75
Chilhowee ....w	126	13	6	4^1	3^h	$4\frac{1}{2}$	1^h	2^n	Johnson	Gallagher Bros.	15.25
Beau Butler ..wb	126	10	8	15^h	11^{nk}	10^1	10^h	3^h	Lyke	Idle Hour Stock F'm	‡10.25
Altawood .....w	126	7	19	19	14^1	7^4	5^2	4^h	McDer'tt	C. B. Head	19.10
Bracadale ....wb	126	12	4	$1\frac{1}{2}$	1^3	1^2	$2\frac{1}{2}$	5^8	Sande	Rancocas Stable	§3.40
Transmute ....w	126	2	1	6^1	4^h	2^2	4^3	6^h	McAtee	H. P. Whitney	¶10.25
Revenue Agent .w	126	5	9	$10\frac{1}{2}$	8^1	8^h	7^1	7^h	Hurn	G. A. Cochran	26.75
Thorndale ....wb	126	6	11	7^1	$7\frac{1}{2}$	5^3	$6\frac{1}{2}$	8^2	Marinelli	B. Block	†10.70
Klondyke ....w	126	3	13	8^h	10^h	9^1	9^4	9^4	Parke	H. P. Whitney	¶10.25
Mad Play ....wb	126	9	14	11^h	$9\frac{1}{2}$	$6\frac{1}{2}$	8^h	$10\frac{1}{2}$	Fator	Rancocas Stable	§3.40
King Gorin II...w	126	4	12	12^2	17^2	12^1	13^1	11^2	Garner	P. Coyne	36.60
Cannon Shot..wb	126	8	18	$18\frac{1}{2}$	19	$11\frac{1}{2}$	12^1	$12\frac{1}{2}$	Ellis	C. A. Hartwell	†10.70
Modest ......ws	126	16	15	13^1	18^2	14^h	$11\frac{1}{2}$	13^1	Wallace	E. B. McLean	†10.70
Diogenes ....w	126	15	10	16^h	15^1	13^1	14^1	14^2	Ponce	Mrs. W. M. Jeffords	†10.70
Nautical ......w	126	19	7	9^h	16^h	15^1	15^h	$15\frac{1}{2}$	Lang	J. S. Cosden	†10.70
Mr Mutt ......w	126	17	17	17^1	$13\frac{1}{2}$	17^1	16^1	16^2	Merimee	H. C. Fisher	35.00
Baffling .....wb	126	18	2	$2\frac{1}{2}$	$2\frac{1}{2}$	$16\frac{1}{2}$	17^h	17^1	Carroll	Idle Hour Stock F'm	‡10.25
Wild Aster ....w	126	11	5	3^1	5^1	18^1	18^2	18^4	Coltiletti	Greentree Stable	†10.70
Bob Tail ....w	126	14	16	14^1	$12\frac{1}{2}$	19	19	19	Blind	Idle Hour Stock F'm	‡10.25

Time: :23-2/5, :47-3/5, 1:13, 1:39-1/5, 2:05-1/5. Track fast.

†Mutuel field. ‡Coupled in betting as Idle Hour Stock Farm Stable entry. §Coupled in betting as Rancocas Stable entry. ¶Coupled in betting as H. P. Whitney entry.

$2 Mutuels Paid—Black Gold, $5.50 straight, $5.50 place, $4.40 show; Chilhowee, $12.30 place, $7.30 show; E. R. Bradley's Idle Hour Stock Farm Stable entry (Beau Butler, Baffling and Bob Tail), $4.70 show.

Winner—Blk.c. by Black Toney—Useeit, by Bonnie Joe, trained by Hedley Webb, bred in Kentucky by Mrs. R. M. Hoots.

Start good and slow. Won driving; second and third same. BLACK GOLD, well ridden and prominent in the early racing, moved up resolutely after reaching the stretch and disposed of the others in the last seventy yards. CHILHOWEE ran a good race and headed BRACADALE in the last eighth, but tired slightly near the end. BEAU BUTLER closed a great gap and ran an excellent race. ALTAWOOD closed an immense gap after making a slow beginning. BRACADALE tired after leading to the stretch.

THE WINNER'S PEDIGREE AND CAREER HIGHLIGHTS

BLACK GOLD (Black Colt)	Black Toney	Peter Pan	Commando
			*Cinderella
		Belgravia	Ben Brush
			*Bonnie Gal
	Useeit	Bonnie Joe	Faustus
			Bonnie Rose
		Effie M.	Bowling Green
			Alma Glyn

Year	Age	Sts	1st	2nd	3rd	Won
1923	2	18	9	5	2	$ 19,163
1924	3	13	9	0	2	91,340
1927	6	3	0	0	0	50
1928	7	1	0	0	0	
Totals		35	18	5	4	$111,553

At 2 Years   WON   Bashford Manor Stakes

At 3 Years   WON   Kentucky Derby, Louisiana Derby, Derby Trial, Ohio State Derby, Chicago Derby

These officials operated Churchill Downs for many years. Left to right are Tom Young, track superintendent; Judge Charles F. Price and Judge Bruce Head; Col. Matt Winn, and Daniel E. O'Sullivan, who was resident manager.

This was the Pergola or clubhouse enclosure on Derby Day, 1924.

May 16, 1925

Owner — G. A. Cochran

Trainer — W. B. Duke

Jockey — Earl Sande

FLYING EBONY

$50,000 added and $5,000 Gold Cup. Net to winner $52,775; second, $6,000; third, $3,000; fourth, $1,000. 139 nominations.

Horses	Eqt Wt	PP	St	½	¾	1	Str	Fin	Jockeys	Owners	Odds $1 Str't
Flying Ebony	wb 126	6	4	$1\frac{1}{2}$	$2\frac{1}{2}$	2^3	1^h	$1^{1\frac{1}{2}}$	Sande	G. A. Cochran	†3.15
Captain Hal	w 126	11	5	$2^{1\frac{1}{2}}$	$11\frac{1}{2}$	1^h	$2\frac{1}{2}$	2^n	Heupel	A. A. Kaiser	5.60
Son of John	w 126	12	8	3^h	3^2	3^2	3^2	3^4	Turner	D. W. Scott	‡16.40
Single Foot	w 126	3	1	5^1	$5^{1\frac{1}{2}}$	$4\frac{1}{2}$	$4\frac{1}{2}$	4^1	Johnson	J. E. Griffith	30.15
Step Along	wsb 126	9	7	$6\frac{1}{2}$	6^h	6^h	5^1	5^2	Pool	F. M. Grabner	‡16.40
Swope	wb 126	4	9	8^h	7^2	7^1	6^1	6^n	Legere	H. C. Fisher	†3.15
P of Bourbon	wb 126	14	15	9^2	$10\frac{1}{2}$	8^1	7^1	$7\frac{1}{2}$	Schut'ger	Lexington Stable	§†3.15
Needle Gun	wb 126	2	3	4^h	$4\frac{1}{2}$	$9\frac{1}{2}$	9^1	8^5	Ponce	W. Zeigler, Jr.	†3.15
Ky. Cardinal	w 126	13	10	10^1	11^1	10^1	8^h	9^h	Garner	G. F. Croissant	7.50
Boon Comp'n	w 126	19	16	11^1	14^2	11^1	10^1	10^h	Ambrose	S. A. Cowan	†3.15
Broadway Jones	w 126	8	11	$12\frac{1}{2}$	13^1	12^1	12^h	11^{nk}	Meyer	Idle Hour Stock Farm	50.85
Quatrain	wb 126	17	13	14^1	12^1	14^2	13^1	$12\frac{1}{2}$	Bruening	F. Johnson	1.95
Almadel	wb 126	20	17	19^1	9^1	13^1	14^2	13^4	McD'm't	H. P. Headley	26.45
Backbone	wb 126	18	18	18^1	19^1	16^2	15^2	14^2	McAtee	H. P. Whitney	¶16.20
Sw'p'g Away	wb 126	10	19	13^2	18^1	15^1	17^1	$15^{1\frac{1}{2}}$	Robinson	Xalapa Farm Stable	§†3.15
Elector	wb 126	7	20	20	20	20	$19^{1\frac{1}{2}}$	16^2	Mooney	La Brae Stable	†3.15
The Bat	wb 126	1	6	15^1	15^h	17^1	16^1	$17^{1\frac{1}{2}}$	Parke	H. P. Whitney	¶16.20
Lee O Cotner	wb 126	15	12	7^1	$8\frac{1}{2}$	$5\frac{1}{2}$	11^4	18^6	Fronk	R. W. Collins	†3.15
Voltaic	w 126	16	14	$16\frac{1}{2}$	16^1	18^1	18^2	19^{20}	Coltiletti	R. L. Gerry	160.75
Chief Uncas	w 126	5	2	17^1	17^1	19^1	20	20	McCleary	A. A. Busch	†3.15

Time: :23-2/5, :47-3/5, 1:12-3/5, 1:39-3/5, 2:07-3/5. Track sloppy.

†Mutuel field. ‡D. W. Scott and F. M. Grabner entry; §Lexington Stable and Xalapa Farm Stable entry; ¶H. P. Whitney entry.

$2 Mutuels Paid—Flying Ebony (Field), $8.30 straight, $3.80 place, $2.80 show; Captain Hal, $5.50 place, $4.40 show; Son of John (coupled with Stepalong as D. W. Scott and F. M. Grabner entry), $5.50 show.

Winner—Blk.c. by The Finn—Princess Mary, by Hessian, trained by W. B. Duke; bred in Kentucky by J. E. Madden.

Start good and slow. Won easily; second and third driving. FLYING EBONY, well ridden and away forwardly, set the early pace, then followed CAPTAIN HAL closely and, after a sharp drive through the stretch outstayed the latter and won going away. CAPTAIN HAL showed fine speed and raced into a good lead, but tired slightly and appeared to have suffered from some interference when FLYING EBONY came over in the last eighth.

THE WINNER'S PEDIGREE AND CAREER HIGHLIGHTS

FLYING EBONY (Black Colt)			
The Finn	*Ogden	Kilwarlin
		*Oriole
	Livonia	*Star Shoot
		Woodray
Princess Mary	Hessian	*Watercress
		*Colonial
	Royal Gun	Royal Hampton
		*Spring Gun

Year	Age	Sts	1st	2nd	3rd	Won
1924	2	8	4	1	1	$ 5,320
1925	3	5	2	0	1	57,100
	Totals	13	6	1	2	$62,420

At 2 Years	3RD	Saratoga Sales Stakes
	UNP	Cincinnati Trophy, United States Hotel Stakes
At 3 Years	WON	Kentucky Derby

The paddock area and the racing secretary's office had this look in 1925. This was the year of the first nationwide radio hookup to broadcast the Derby.

On May 16, 1925,
The First Kentucky Derby
To Be Heard On Radio
Was Broadcast By WHAS.

11 whas tv

WHAS RADIO 84

May 15, 1926

Owner — E. R. Bradley

Trainer — H. J. Thompson

Jockey — Albert Johnson

BUBBLING OVER

$50,000 added and $5,000 Gold Cup. Net to winner $50,075; second $6,000; third $3,000; fourth $1,000. 164 nominations.

Horses	Eqt Wt	PP	St	1/2	3/4	1	Str	Fin	Jockeys	Owners	Odds $1 Str't
Bubbling Over	wb 126	11	1	1^1	1^1	1^1	1^2	1^5	Johnson	Idle Hour Stock Farm	‡1.90
Bagenbaggage	wb 126	3	3	7^h	6^2	5^5	2^1	2^3	Blind	Idle Hour Stock Farm	‡1.90
Rock Man	w 126	2	2	3^h	3^3	2^h	3^4	3^n	Coltiletti	Sagamore Stable	42.10
Rhinock	w 126	12	8	8^h	10^h	9^1	5^5	4^4	Garner	Parkview Stable	14.60
Pompey	w 126	9	5	$2\frac{1}{2}$	2^h	3^h	$4\frac{1}{2}$	5^2	Fator	W. R. Coe	2.10
Espino	wb 126	6	6	9^1	5^h	7^2	7^4	6^6	Smith	W. Ziegler, Jr.	39.70
Light Carbine	wb 126	1	4	6^h	11^1	10^h	8^1	7^5	Griffin	I. B. Humpreys	61.00
Canter	w 126	8	11	4^h	4^h	4^h	6^2	8^2	Turner	J. E. Griffith	24.10
Blondin	wsb 126	4	9	10^1	$7\frac{1}{2}$	11^1	9^1	9^h	McAtee	H. P. Whitney	9.30
Display	wb 126	10	13	12^5	12^8	8^2	11^1	10^h	Maiben	W. J. Salmon	16.20
Recollection	wb 126	7	12	13	13	13	12^1	11^h	Callahan	Kohn & Theisen	†11.40
Champ de Mars	w 126	5	7	5^h	8^1	$6\frac{1}{2}$	$10\frac{1}{2}$	12^1	Pool	Keeneland Stud Farm	†11.40
Rovcrofter	w 126	13	10	11^1	9^1	12^4	13	13	Scobie	G. F. Croissant	†11.40

Time: :23, :47, 1:12-1/5, 1:38-1/2, 2:03-4/5. Track fast.

†Mutuel field. ‡Coupled in betting as Idle Hour Stock Farm Stable entry.

$2 Mutuels Paid—E. R. Bradley's Idle Hour Stock Farm Stable entry (Bubbling Over and Bagenbaggage), $5.80 straight, $5.80 place, $4.60 show; Rock Man, $30.00 show.

Winner—Ch.c. by *North Star III—Beaming Beauty, by Sweep, trained by H. J. Thompson; bred in Kentucky by Idle Hour Stock Farm.

Start good and slow. Won easily; second and third driving. BUBBLING OVER raced into the lead at once and setting a great pace under restraint, showed the way until the stretch, where his rider permitted him to sprint away from the others and win away off by himself. BAGENBAGGAGE, began slowly but, making up ground gamely, passed the others and finished a fast-going second. ROCK MAN raced prominently from the start, but was tiring and just lasted to save third place. RHINOCK came with a surprisingly rush near the end. POMPEY was done after racing well for three-quarters and had no mishap. ESPINO raced well. CANTER was close up for most of the way, but quit in the stretch.

THE WINNER'S PEDIGREE AND CAREER HIGHLIGHTS

BUBBLING OVER (Chestnut Colt)	*North Star III	Sunstar	Sundridge / Doris
		Angelic	St. Angelo / Fota
	Beaming Beauty	Sweep	Ben Brush / Pink Domino
		Bellisario	Hippodrome / Biturica

Year	Age	Sts	1st	2nd	3rd	Won
1925	2	10	7	2	1	$24,737
1926	3	3	3	0	0	53,815
Totals		13	10	2	1	$78,552

At 2 Years
- WON Champagne Stakes, Nursery Handicap
- 2ND Breeders' Futurity, Pimlico Futurity
- 3RD Grab Bag Handicap

At 3 Years
- WON Kentucky Derby, Blue Grass Stakes

The area where these fans are standing is now filled with the grandstand terrace seating area — and the tree is gone. This picture was snapped in 1926.

The Derby got full coverage in the newsreels in the 1920s. This cameraman is ready to shoot the 1926 race.

May 14, 1927

Owner — H. P. Whitney

Trainer — Fred Hopkins

Jockey — Linus McAtee

WHISKERY

$50,000 added and $5,000 Gold Cup. Net to winner $51,000; second $6,000; third $3,000; fourth $1,000. 162 nominations.

Horses	Eqt Wt	PP	St	½	¾	1	Str	Fin	Jockeys	Owners	Odds $1 Str't
Whiskery	wb 126	7	6	5^h	3^h	$31\frac{1}{2}$	3^2	1^h	McAtee	H. P. Whitney	‡2.40
Osmand	w 126	10	4	2^1	2^3	$2\frac{1}{2}$	1^h	$21\frac{1}{2}$	Sande	J. E. Widener	§6.90
Jock	w 126	1	3	1^5	1^5	$1\frac{1}{2}$	$2\frac{1}{2}$	3^1	Lang	E. B. McLean	¶37.80
Hydromel	wsb 126	5	8	6^h	7^1	4^{nk}	$4\frac{1}{2}$	4^h	W Garner	J. N. Camden	16.00
Bostonian	w 126	12	11	9^2	$8\frac{1}{2}$	$7\frac{1}{2}$	6^4	5^4	Abel	H. P. Whitney	‡2.40
Buddy Bauer	wb 126	4	10	10^{nk}	$91\frac{1}{2}$	5^3	$51\frac{1}{2}$	6^2	G Johnson	Idle Hour Stock Farm	‖15.40
Royal Julian	w 126	2	1	$71\frac{1}{2}$	5^h	$6\frac{1}{2}$	7^{nk}	7^4	Lilley	W. H. Whitehouse	†14.70
Fred Jr	wb 126	13	15	15	14^2	9^1	9^3	8^6	Burger	S. W. Grant	18.30
Scapa Flow	wb 126	15	7	3^h	$4\frac{1}{2}$	8^2	$8\frac{1}{2}$	9^2	Coltiletti	W. M. Jeffords	7.00
Bl. Panther	wb 126	6	5	8^h	10^1	10^1	10^1	10^8	Schaefer	W. J. Salmon	†14.70
Kiev	wb 126	8	14	11^h	11^2	12^2	12^2	11^2	M Garner	J. E. Widener	§6.90
R. Stocking	wb 126	3	2	$41\frac{1}{2}$	6^h	$11\frac{1}{2}$	11^2	12^3	Pool	J. W. Parrish	4.70
Rip Rap	wb 126	11	13	12^1	12^1	13^4	14^4	13^4	O'Donnell	Sage Stable	11.60
Bewithus	wb 126	9	9	$13\frac{1}{2}$	15	14^2	13^1	14^5	A Johnson	Idle Hour Stock Farm	‖15.40
War Eagle	wb 126	14	12	$141\frac{1}{2}$	13^2	15	15	15	Ambrose	E. B. McLean	¶37.80

Time: :23-1/5, :47-1/5, 1:12-2/5, 1:38-4/5, 2:06. Track slow.
†Mutuel field. ‡H. P. Whitney entry, §J. E. Widener entry, ¶E. B. McLean entry; ‖Idle Hour Stock Farm entry.
Winner—Br.c. by Whisk Broom II—Prudery, by Peter Pan, trained by F. Hopkins; bred in Kentucky by H. P. Whitney.

Start good and slow. Won driving; second and third same. WHISKERY moved up steadily, though racing a trifle wide and, holding on gamely, wore down OSMAND in the last sixteenth. The latter, always well up for the entire distance, held on much gamer than expected in the final drive. JOCK began fast, showed high speed but tired in the last eighth. HYDROMEL showed a fine performance and continued gamely in the stretch. BOSTONIAN was far out of it for a half-mile and closed a big gap. BUDDY BAUER also closed a big gap from a slow beginning.

THE WINNER'S PEDIGREE AND CAREER HIGHLIGHTS

WHISKERY (Brown Colt)

- Whisk Broom II
  - Broomstick
    - Ben Brush
    - *Elf
  - Audience
    - Sir Dixon
    - Sallie McClelland
- Prudery
  - Peter Pan
    - Commando
    - *Cinderella
  - Polly Flinders
    - Burgomaster
    - Slippers

Year	Age	Sts	1st	2nd	3rd	Won
1926	2	18	6	3	7	$ 13,115
1927	3	18	6	4	5	94,950
1928	4	1	0	0	0	500
1929	5	16	0	5	10	1,196
1930	6	15	2	3	9	3,250
1931	7	2	0	1	1	200
Totals		70	14	16	32	$122,211

At 2 Years
- WON Ardsley Handicap
- 2ND Endurance Handicap
- 3RD Pimlico Futurity

At 3 Years
- WON Kentucky Derby, Twin City Handicap, Stanley Produce Stakes, Chesapeake Stakes, Huron Handicap
- 2ND Fairmount Derby, Maryland Handicap, Potomac Handicap
- 3RD Preakness Stakes, Prince Georges Handicap

New York Mayor Jimmy Walker (right) joins owner H. P. Whitney, Sr. and jockey Linus McAtee after Whiskery's victory in 1927. Whitney's Regret won in 1915.

May 19, 1928

Owner — Mrs. John Hertz

Trainer — B. S. Michell

Jockey — Charles Lang

FIFTY FOURTH RUNNING

REIGH COUNT

$50,000 added and $5,000 Gold Cup. Net to winner $55,375; second $6,000; third $3,000; fourth $1,000. 196 nominations.

Horses	Eqt	Wt	PP	St	½	¾	1	Str	Fin	Jockeys	Owners	Odds $1 Str't
Reigh Count	w	126	4	3	5^{h}	5^{h}	$2^{1\frac{1}{2}}$	1^{h}	1^{3}	Lang	Mrs. J. Hertz	‡2.06
Misstep	w	126	1	1	1^{1}	1^{1}	$1^{1\frac{1}{2}}$	2^{4}	2^{2}	Garner	Le Mar Stock Farm	10.20
Toro	w	126	7	6	6^{h}	6^{h}	$3^{\frac{1}{2}}$	$3^{\frac{1}{2}}$	3^{4}	Ambrose	E. B. McLean	4.75
Jack Higgins	w	126	8	7	8^{2}	7^{2}	4^{h}	4^{6}	$4^{1\frac{1}{2}}$	Allen	W. J. Curran	†4.42
Reigh Olga	w	126	5	4	$7^{\frac{1}{2}}$	$8^{\frac{1}{2}}$	$7^{\frac{1}{4}}$	$5^{\frac{3}{8}}$	5^{2}	Pool	O. Lehmann	‡2.06
Lawley	w	126	9	15	16^{1}	$16^{\frac{1}{2}}$	$9^{\frac{1}{2}}$	6^{5}	6^{2}	Thurber	Viking Stable	†4.42
Don Q	w	126	2	20	20^{1}	20^{1}	22	7^{1}	7^{2}	Walls	Sagamore Stable	†4.42
Bobashela	w	126	20	11	11^{1}	11^{1}	5^{h}	11^{1}	8^{2}	Fisher	Audley Farm	§12.08
Blackwood	wb	126	10	2	$2^{1\frac{1}{2}}$	$2^{1\frac{1}{2}}$	$8^{\frac{1}{2}}$	8^{1}	$9^{\frac{1}{2}}$	Chiavetta	Bloomfield Stable	†4.42
Martie Flynn	wb	126	6	5	3^{1}	$3^{1\frac{1}{2}}$	6^{2}	16^{1}	10^{h}	Fronk	S. Peabody	14.18
Sun Beau	wb	126	18	16	18^{1}	18^{1}	14^{1}	10^{1}	11^{h}	Craigmyle	W. S. Kilmer	38.42
Bar None	wb	126	13	19	21^{1}	21^{1}	12^{1}	9^{2}	$12^{\frac{1}{2}}$	Kederis	Longridge Stable	†4.42
Distraction	wb	126	19	21	22	22	19^{1}	$17^{\frac{1}{2}}$	13^{1}	McAuliffe	Wheatley Stable	11.51
Petee-Wrack	wb	126	15	17	14^{1}	14^{1}	10^{1}	18^{1}	14^{3}	Johnson	J. R. Macomber	†4.42
Typhoon	wb	126	17	22	$19^{\frac{1}{2}}$	19^{2}	18^{1}	12^{2}	15^{1}	Barnes	Kenton Farm Stable	41.21
Replevin	wb	126	11	9	12^{h}	12^{h}	16^{1}	13^{1}	16^{1}	Peterson	F. Johnson	†4.42
Cartago	wb	126	3	10	9^{1}	9^{1}	15^{1}	19^{2}	17^{h}	Horvath	R. E. Leichleiter	†4.42
Bonivan		126	21	8	4^{h}	4^{h}	20^{4}	15^{2}	18^{2}	Landolt	A. A. Kaiser	†4.42
Charmarten	wb	126	22	18	$17^{\frac{1}{2}}$	17^{1}	$13^{\frac{1}{2}}$	$14^{\frac{1}{2}}$	19^{2}	Butwell	Wild Rose Farm Stable	†4.42
Vito		126	12	13	$10^{\frac{1}{2}}$	$10^{\frac{1}{2}}$	11^{1}	20^{1}	20^{2}	Kummer	A. H. Cosden	¶39.04
Sortie	wb	126	14	12	15^{1}	15^{1}	$17^{\frac{1}{2}}$	21^{8}	21^{12}	Weiner	A. C. Schwartz	¶39.04
Strolling Player		126	16	14	12^{h}	13^{h}	21^{h}	22	22	Fields	Salubria Stable	§12.08

Time: :24-1/5, :49-3/5, 1:15-4/5, 1:43-2/5, 2:10-2/5. Track Heavy.

†Mutuel field. ‡Coupled in betting as Mrs. J. D. Hertz and O. Lehmann entry. §Coupled in betting as Audley Farm Stable and Salubria Stable entry. ¶Coupled in betting as A. H. Cosden and A. C. Schwartz entry.

Winner—Ch.c. by *Sunreigh—*Contessina, by Count Schomberg, trained by B. S. Michell; bred in Virginia by Willis Sharpe Kilmer.

Start good and slow. Won easily; second and third driving. REIGH COUNT was ridden vigorously in the early running and responded nobly, racing into a forward position in the first half-mile, then forced the pace and, under strong riding in the stretch, took the lead and drew away to win with speed in reserve. MISSTEP began fast next to the inner rail, showed fine speed and, setting a fast pace for the going, finished well.

THE WINNER'S PEDIGREE AND CAREER HIGHLIGHTS

REIGH COUNT (Chestnut Colt)	*Sunreigh	Sundridge	Amphion
			Sierra
		*Sweet Briar II	St. Frusquin
			Presentation
	*Contessina	Count Schomberg	Aughrim
			Clonavarn
		Pitti	St. Frusquin
			Florence

Year	Age	Sts	1st	2nd	3rd	Won	
1927	2	14	4	3	0	$ 56,030	†Includes winnings in England.
1928	3	8	7	0	0	112,640	
1929	4	5	1	1	0	† 12,125	
Totals		27	12	4	0	$180,795	

At 2 Years	**WON**	**Walden Handicap, Kentucky Jockey Club Stakes**
At 3 Years	**WON**	**Kentucky Derby, Miller Stakes, Huron Handicap, Saratoga Cup, Lawrence Realization, Jockey Club Gold Cup**
At 4 Years (In England)	**WON**	**Coronation Cup**

These taxis formed a horseshoe for the photographer but it wasn't long until they were swarmed with fans coming from the Derby.

Samuel A. Culbertson became president of Churchill Downs in 1928.

There is nothing like a little sunshine to help in selecting a winner as these fans at the 1928 Derby indicate. The area is near where the tulip gardens now are located.

May 18, 1929

Owner — H. P. Gardner

Trainer — Clyde Van Dusen

Jockey — Linus McAtee

CLYDE VAN DUSEN

$50,000 added and $5,000 Gold Cup. Net to winner $53,950; second $6,000; third $3,000; fourth $1,000. 159 nominations.

Horses	Eqt Wt	PP	St	½	¾	1	Str	Fin	Jockeys	Owners	Odds $1 Str't
Clyde Van Dusen	wb 126	20	7	1½	1³	1²	1³	1²	McAtee	H. P. Gardner	3.00
Naishapur	wb 126	4	2	12ʰ	12²	8³	5½	2³	Allen	Wilshire Stable	5.57
Panchio	wb 126	13	1	4²	3³	2ʰ	2½	3ⁿ	Coltiletti	Three D's Stock Farm	†§8.44
Blue Larkspar	w 126	21	4	3ʰ	4½	5½	3ʰ	4½	M Garner	E. R. Bradley	‡1.71
Windy City	w 126	19	9	8ʰ	8¹	7³	8½	5ʰ	Pool	F. M. Grabner	22.84
Voltear	wb 126	1	8	5ʰ	5²	6ʰ	7ʰ	6ʰ	O'Donnell	Dixiana	18.42
The Nut	wb 126	18	3	17¹	10¹	4ʰ	6¹	7¹	Robertson	Warm Stable	40.62
Folking	wb 126	14	18	2³	2½	3½	4³	8¹	Pascuma	H. T. Archibald	†8.44
Karl Eitel	wb 126	10	16	7¹	7½	9ʰ	9ʰ	9⁴	Jones	J. J. Coughlin	28.80
Upset Lad	w 126	5	13	10½	17¹	14¹	13¹	10⁶	Chiavetta	Belle Isle Stable	†8.44
Calf Roper	wb 126	9	15	16¹	15¹	10³	10³	11ʰ	Hardy	Three D's Stock Farm	†§8.44
Minotaur	wb 126	7	14	10¹	9²	11²	11½	12ʰ	Halbert	J. R. Thompson	30.80
Bay Beauty	wb 126	15	10	11¹	11½	12ʰ	17¹	13⁴	Horvath	E. R. Bradley	‡1.71
Chicatie	wb 126	3	12	14¹	14ʰ	13¹	13¹	14½	W Garner	Fair Stable	87.09
Paul Bunyan	wb 126	12	17	19²	19¹	18²	15¹	15½	Clelland	L. M. Severson	†8.44
Essare	wb 126	6	5	6½	6¹	15ʰ	14¹	16³	Connelly	Jacques Stable	†8.44
L B'd'lbane	wb 126	8	11	13¹	13¹	16¹	16²	17²	Crump	D. Breckinridge	†8.44
Ben Machree	wb 126	16	21	20³	18ʰ	17¹	18¹	18¹	Abel	C. C. & G. Y. Hieatt	†8.44
Chip	wb 126	11	20	21	20³	19³	19³	19⁶	Heupel	Mrs. E. L. Swikard	†8.44
Prince Pat	wb 126	17	19	18ʰ	21	21	20⁴	20⁴	Laidley	Three D's Stock Farm	†§8.44
Paraphrase	wb 126	2	6	9½	16ʰ	20¹	21	21	Fronk	H. P. Headley	†8.44

Time: :24, :49, 1:15-2/5, 1:42-4/5, 2:10-4/5. Track muddy.

†Mutuel field. ‡Coupled in betting as E. R. Bradley entry. §Coupled in betting as Three D's Stock Farm entry. Winner—Ch.g. by Man o' War—Uncle's Lassie, by Uncle, trained by Clyde Van Dusen; bred in Kentucky by H. P. Gardner.

Start good and slow. Won easily; second and third driving. CLYDE VAN DUSEN took the lead after the first quarter, saved ground while setting the pace and responded to light shaking up to the stretch to hold his opponents safe. NAISHAPUR, slow to start and racing wide, began moving up after going five-eighths and, after being blocked in the stretch, where he swerved, finished with a rush when clear. PANCHIO was prominent for the entire race and, benefited by a strong ride, outfinished BLUE LARKSPUR.

THE WINNER'S PEDIGREE AND CAREER HIGHLIGHTS

CLYDE VAN DUSEN
(Chestnut Gelding)

Man o' War
- Fair Play
  - Hastings
  - *Fairy Gold
- Mahubah
  - *Rock Sand
  - *Merry Token

Uncle's Lassie
- Uncle
  - *Star Shoot
  - The Niece
- Planutess
  - *Planudes
  - Countess Wanda

Year	Age	Sts	1st	2nd	3rd	Won
1928	2	17	8	3	2	$ 55,768
1929	3	10	3	3	2	65,319
1930	4	5	1	0	1	1,025
1933	7	10	0	1	3	290
Totals		42	12	7	8	$122,402

At 2 Years — WON Kentucky Jockey Club Stakes, Orphanage Stakes, Valley Stakes, Idle Hour Stakes

At 3 Years {
WON Kentucky Derby
2ND Latonia Derby
}

These stylishly dressed ladies graced the box area in 1929. Left to right are Mrs. Louise Herrmann, Miss Helen Winn, Mrs. Porter Castleberry, Miss Clare Winn, Mrs. Peter B. Holland and Mrs. Russell Sweeney.

Vice President Charles G. Curtis and his sister saw Clyde Van Dusen win in 1929.

Major Thomas McDowell and Mrs. Thomas LeBus of Lexington also were present.

May 17, 1930

Owner — William Woodward

Trainer — James Fitzsimmons

Jockey — Earl Sande

GALLANT FOX

$50,000 added and $5,000 Gold Cup. Net to winner $50,725; second $6,000; third $3,000; fourth $1,000. 150 nominations.

Horses	Eqt Wt	PP	St	½	¾	1	Str	Fin	Jockeys	Owners	Odds $1 Str't
Gallant Fox	wb 126	7	8	4^1	1^1	1^2	1^2	1^2	Sande	Belair Stud	1.19
Gallant Knight	wb 126	3	7	7^1	$6\frac{1}{2}$	3^3	$2\frac{1}{2}$	2^2	Schutte	Audley Farm	22.73
Ned O	w 126	3	3	$12\frac{1}{2}$	13^h	$9\frac{1}{2}$	4^h	3^1	Mooney	G. W. Foreman	25.79
Gone Away	wb 126	10	14	$14\frac{1}{2}$	$11\frac{1}{2}$	$7\frac{1}{2}$	5^2	4^4	M Garner	W. Ziegler, Jr.	52.92
Crack Brigade	ws 126	6	13	6^1	4^{nk}	2^h	3^h	$5\frac{1}{2}$	Ellis	T. M. Cassidy	16.62
Longus	wb 126	1	15	15	14^4	10^h	7^1	6^2	O'Brien	R. C. Stable	†18.12
Uncle Luther	w 126	2	12	$8\frac{1}{2}$	8^h	$6\frac{1}{2}$	6^1	7^2	Creese	L. Stivers	†18.12
Tannery	w 126	12	2	3^1	3^1	5^h	$8\frac{1}{2}$	8^h	W Garner	E. F. Prichard	3.12
B'y Limited	wb 126	14	11	$10\frac{1}{2}$	$12\frac{1}{2}$	12^2	10^2	$9\frac{1}{2}$	Walls	Three D's Stock Farm	‡50.43
Alcibiades	w 126	4	4	1^2	$2\frac{1}{2}$	4^h	9^h	10^h	Jones	H. P. Headley	†18.12
Kilkerry	w 126	9	9	$11\frac{1}{2}$	10^h	$11\frac{1}{2}$	11^4	11^6	May	Three D's Stock Farm	‡50.43
Breezing Thru	wb 126	13	6	13^1	9^2	14^h	13^1	12^5	Smith	E. R. Bradley	§8.75
Buckeye Poet	wb 126	15	5	2^h	$5\frac{1}{2}$	$8\frac{1}{2}$	12^2	13^1	Legere	E. R. Bradley	§8.75
High Foot	w 126	5	1	5^h	7^1	$13\frac{1}{2}$	14^8	14^8	Meyer	Valley Lake Stable	22.88
Dick O'Hara	w 126	11	10	9^2	15	15	15	15	Barrett	P. H. Joyce	†18.12

Time: :23-3/5, :47-4/5, 1:14, 1:40-4/5, 2:07-3/5. Track good.

†Mutuel field. ‡Coupled as Three D's Stock Farm Stable entry; §E. R. Bradley entry.

$2 Mutuels Paid—Gallant Fox, $4.38 straight, $3.76 place, $3.42 show; Gallant Knight, $14.60 place, $8.78 show; Ned O., $10.14 show.

Winner—B.c. by *Sir Gallahad III—Marguerite, by Celt, trained by James Fitzsimmons; bred in Kentucky by Belair Stud.

Start good out of machine. Won easily; second and third driving. GALLANT FOX, in extremely close quarters for the first three-eighths, raced into the lead on the outside after straightening out in the backstretch, held command under restraint thereafter and won with something in reserve. GALLANT KNIGHT began slowly, worked his way up with a big loss of ground, offered a mild challenge entering the final eighth, but tired badly near the end. NED O. began improving his position after five-eighths, lost ground on the last turn, but finished resolutely. GONE AWAY, on the extreme outside throughout, moved up fast on the stretch turn, but quit in the final eighth.

THE WINNER'S PEDIGREE AND CAREER HIGHLIGHTS

GALLANT FOX (Bay Colt)

- *Sir Gallahad III
  - *Teddy
    - Ajax
    - Rondeau
  - Plucky Liege
    - Spearmint
    - Concertina
- Marguerite
  - Celt
    - Commando
    - Maid of Erin
  - *Fairy Ray
    - Radium
    - Seraph

Year	Age	Sts	1st	2nd	3rd	Won
1929	2	7	2	2	2	$ 19,890
1930	3	10	9	1	0	308,275
Totals		17	11	3	2	$328,165

At 2 Years	WON	Flash Stakes, Junior Champion Stakes
	2ND	United States Hotel Stakes
	3RD	Belmont Futurity
At 3 Years	WON	Kentucky Derby, Wood Memorial Stakes, Preakness Stakes, Belmont Stakes, Dwyer Stakes, Classic Stakes, Saratoga Cup, Lawrence Realization, Jockey Club Gold Cup
	2ND	Travers Stakes

Lord Derby was a heralded visitor in 1930 and participated in the trophy presentation. He is shown with Matt Winn, right.

It was a damp crowd that milled about the winner's circle in 1930. Note that it was on the grandstand side of the track. Also note the policeman on horseback on the track.

May 16, 1931

Owner — Mrs. Payne Whitney

Trainer — James Rowe, Jr.

Jockey — Charles Kurtsinger

FIFTY SEVENTH RUNNING

TWENTY GRAND

$50,000 added and $5,000 Gold Cup. Net to winner $52,350; second $6,000; third $3,000; fourth $1,000. 13 nominations.

Horses	Eqt	Wt	PP	St	½	¾	1	Str	Fin	Jockeys	Owners	Odds $1 Str't
Twenty Grand ...	wb	126	5	9	10$1\frac{1}{2}$	6^1	2^2	1^1	1^4	Kurtsinger	Greentree Stable	‡.88
Sweep All	wb	126	1	10	4^1	3$1\frac{1}{2}$	1$\frac{1}{2}$	2^3	2^3	Coltiletti	Dixiana	26.96
Mate	w	126	10	11	7^h	4^h	3^h	3^4	3^4	Ellis	A. C. Bostwick	2.83
Spanish Play	w	126	6	4	8$1\frac{1}{2}$	8^1	6$1\frac{1}{2}$	5^2	4$1\frac{1}{2}$	Allen	Knebelkamp & Morris	45.09
Boys Howdy	w	126	7	3	2^1	5^1	5^1	4^h	5^6	Riley	H. C. Hatch	23.26
Insco	wb	126	12	6	9^h	11^1	8^3	6^3	6^1	O'Donnell	G. Watkins	†22.91
Pittsburgher	w	126	9	7	11^3	10^1	9$\frac{1}{2}$	8^h	7^h	Corbett	Shady Brook Farm S'ble	8.49
The Mongol	w	126	3	1	5^h	9^h	11^1	9$\frac{1}{2}$	8^1	McCoy	Hamburg Place	†22.91
Ladder	wb	126	4	2	3$\frac{1}{2}$	1$\frac{1}{2}$	4^3	7^1	9^h	Schaefer	W. J. Salmon	26.00
Anchors Aweigh .	wb	126	2	12	12	12	10$1\frac{1}{2}$	10^6	10^2	Steffen	Greentree Stable	‡.88
Surf Board	w	126	8	8	6^h	7^1	7$\frac{1}{2}$	11$1\frac{1}{2}$	11^8	Watters	Greentree Stable	‡.88
Prince d'Amour ..	wb	126	11	5	1^h	2$\frac{1}{2}$	12	12	12	James	J. Leiter	76.23

Time: :23-1/5, :47-2/5, 1:12, 1:37-2/5, 2:01-4/5 (new track record). Track fast.

†Mutuel field. ‡Coupled in betting as Greentree Stable entry.

$2 Mutuels Paid—Twenty Grand (coupled with Anchors Aweigh and Surf Board as Greentree Stable entry), $3.76 straight, $3.00 place, $2.60 show; Sweep All, $15.58 place, $7.16 show; Mate, $3.62 show.

Winner—B.c. by *St. Germans—Bonus, by *All Gold, trained by James Rowe, Jr.; bred in Kentucky by Greentree Stable.

Start good out of machine. Won easily; second and third driving. TWENTY GRAND, slow to begin, was sent up slowly after a half, raced strongly on the outside and, wearing down SWEEP ALL, drew away fast and won with speed in reserve. SWEEP ALL broke away slowly, but saved ground, followed the leaders in the backstretch, raced into a good lead on the stretch turn, but could not withstand the winner's rush. MATE improved his position fast in the first quarter, saved ground on the second turn, but failed to rally under vigorous driving in the stretch. SPANISH PLAY closed with good courage.

THE WINNER'S PEDIGREE AND RACING RECORD

TWENTY GRAND (Bay Colt)	*St. Germans	Swynford	John o' Gaunt / Canterbury Pilgrim
		Hamoaze	Torpoint / Maid of the Mist
	Bonus	*All Gold	Persimmon / Dame d'Or
		Remembrance	Hamburg / Forget

Year	Age	Sts	1st	2nd	3rd	Won
1930	2	8	4	2	1	$ 41,380
1931	3	10	8	1	1	218,545
1932	4	2	1	1	0	915
1935	7	5	1	0	1	950
Totals		25	14	4	3	$261,790

At 2 Years	WON	Kentucky Jockey Club Stakes, Junior Champion Stakes
	2ND	Pimlico Futurity
	3RD	Walden Handicap
At 3 Years	WON	Kentucky Derby, Wood Memorial Stakes, Belmont Stakes, Dwyer Stakes, Travers Mid-Summer Derby, Saratoga Cup, Lawrence Realization, Jockey Club Gold Cup
	2ND	Preakness Stakes
	3RD	Classic Stakes
At 7 Years	UNP	Santa Anita Handicap (U.S.A.), Queen Anne Stakes (England)

The King of Baseball, Babe Ruth, watched the premier race in the Sport of Kings as the guest of Louisville baseball executive Bud Hillerich. Left to right, seated, are Ruth's daughter, Julia; Mrs. Hillerich and Mrs. Ruth; standing are Buck Weaver, Louisville sportswriter; the Babe and Mr. Hillerich.

GREENTREE STABLE

of
MRS. PAYNE WHITNEY
Owner of two Derby Winners — Twenty Grand & Shut Out

Rural Route 3, Paris Pike   Lexington, Kentucky

May 7, 1932

Owner — E. R. Bradley

Trainer — H. J. Thompson

Jockey — Eugene James

BURGOO KING

$50,000 added and $5,000 Gold Cup. Net to winner $52,350; second $6,000; third $3,000; fourth $1,000. 115 nominations.

Horses	Eqt Wt	PP	St	1/2	3/4	1	Str	Fin	Jockeys	Owners	Odds $1 Str't
Burgoo King	w 126	13	4	3^1	3^2	2^3	1^4	1^5	James	E. R. Bradley	‡5.62
Economic	wb 126	10	2	1^2	$1\frac{1}{2}$	1^h	$2\frac{1}{2}$	2^h	Horn	J. H. Loucheim	16.93
Stepenfetchit	wb 126	4	12	$9\frac{1}{2}$	5^1	$4\frac{1}{2}$	4^1	$3\frac{1}{2}$	Ensor	Mrs. J. H. Whitney	§3.28
Brandon Mint	wb 126	11	3	$2\frac{1}{2}$	2^h	3^1	3^h	4^n	Ellis	Brandon Stable	†6.68
Over Time	wb 126	5	13	13^h	8^2	6^3	5^h	5^n	Sande	Mrs. J. H. Whitney	§3.28
Tick On	wb 126	6	14	12^1	10^2	5^2	6^6	6^4	Wall	Loma Stable	1.84
Our Fancy	wb 126	3	1	4^h	$7\frac{1}{2}$	8^2	7^h	7^1	Allen	J. B. Respess	†6.68
Gallant Sir	wb 126	19	18	$11\frac{1}{2}$	6^h	7^3	8^2	8^2	Woolf	Northway Stable	†6.68
Hoops	wb 126	8	9	14^2	11^2	10^4	9^1	$9\frac{1}{2}$	Fischer	W. F. Knebelkamp	28.62
Cold Check	wb 126	12	5	$7\frac{1}{2}$	4^h	9^1	10^2	$10\frac{1}{2}$	Garner W	J. W. Parrish	45.88
Adobe Post	wb 126	7	20	$16\frac{1}{2}$	15^h	16^h	13^1	11^3	Landolt	Knebelkamp & Morris	28.52
Crystal Prince	w 126	1	8	20	14^1	12^h	$12\frac{1}{2}$	12^3	Corbett	P. C. Thompson	†6.68
Oscillation	w 121	2	7	6^1	9^h	11^1	11^h	13^2	Neal	Longridge Stable	†6.68
Prince Hotspur	wb 126	17	16	18^1	16^1	17^2	16^2	$14\frac{1}{2}$	Anderson	J. Leiter Estate	78.37
Cee Tee	w 126	14	11	15^1	18^2	15^h	15^1	15^4	McCros'n	Dixiana	†6.68
Cathop	w 126	20	19	19^1	$17\frac{1}{2}$	18^8	17^2	$16\frac{1}{2}$	Pichon	R. M. Eastman	†6.68
Lucky Tom	wb 126	16	17	8^h	13^2	14^1	14^1	17^8	Pasc'ma	J. J. Robinson	10.64
Thistle Ace	wb 126	9	10	$10\frac{1}{2}$	19	19	19	18^8	Elston	G. Collins	†6.68
Brother Joe	wb 126	18	6	5^h	12^h	13^1	18^h	19	Fator	E. R. Bradley	‡5.62
Lib Limited	wb 126	15	15	17^h	Broke Down				Garner M	Three D's Stock Farm	†6.68

Time: :24-1/5, :48-1/5, 1:13, 1:38-4/5, 2:05-1/5. Track fast.

†Mutuel field. ‡Coupled in betting as E. R. Bradley entry. §Coupled in betting as Mrs. J. H. Whitney entry. $2 Mutuels Paid—Burgoo King (coupled with Brother Joe as E. R. Bradley entry), $13.24 straight, $5.08 place, $4.00 show; Economic, $15.62 place, $8.54 show; Stephenfetchit (coupled with Over Time as Mrs. J. H. Whitney entry), $3.52 show.

Winner—Ch.c. by Bubbling Over—Minawand, by Lonawand, trained by H. J. Thompson; bred in Kentucky by H. N. Davis and Idle Hour Stock Farm.

Start good out of machine. Won easily; second and third driving. BURGOO KING, away fast and well rated, followed the pace closely until reaching the final three-eighths, where he easily wore down ECONOMIC and won easily. ECONOMIC set the pace under good rating, was no match for the winner, but outlasted STEPENFETCHIT. The latter saved ground in the early stages, was under restraint until reaching the closing half-mile and rallied mildly when taken to the outside in the stretch.

THE WINNER'S PEDIGREE AND CAREER HIGHLIGHTS

BURGOO KING (Chestnut Colt)

- Bubbling Over
  - *North Star III
    - Sunstar
    - Angelic
  - Beaming Beauty
    - Sweep
    - Bellisario
- Minawand
  - Lonawand
    - Cupbearer
    - St. Flora
  - *Mintless
    - Minting
    - Gorseberry

Year	Age	Sts	1st	2nd	3rd	Won
1931	2	12	4	0	1	$ 6,000
1932	3	4	2	1	0	102,825
1934	5	5	2	1	2	2,115
Totals		21	8	2	3	$110,940

At 2 Years 3RD Pimlico Futurity

At 3 Years WON Kentucky Derby, Preakness Stakes

This band paraded in the middle of the track as the horses were being brought to the paddock.

On the presentation stand after Burgoo King's victory are, left to right, jockey Eugene James, Col. Matt Winn, owner E. R. Bradley and Gov. Ruby Laffoon.

ANDY FRAIN INCORPORATED

Serving Churchill Downs for the Kentucky Derby Since 1932

May 6, 1933

Owner — E. R. Bradley

Trainer — H. J. Thompson

Jockey — Don Meade

FIFTY NINTH RUNNING

BROKERS TIP

$50,000 added and $5,000 Gold Cup. Net to winner $48,925; second $6,000; third $3,000; fourth $1,000. 118 nominations.

Horses	Eqt Wt	PP	St	1/2	3/4	1	Str	Fin	Jockeys	Owners	Odds $1 Str't
Brokers Tip	wb 126	11	11	11^1	$8\frac{1}{2}$	4^2	$2\frac{1}{2}$	1^n	Meade	E. R. Bradley	8.93
Head Play	w 126	7	5	$3\frac{1}{2}$	$1\frac{1}{2}$	1^1	1^h	2^4	Fisher	Mrs. S. B. Mason	5.64
Charley O	wb 126	1	6	7^h	6^1	$2\frac{1}{2}$	3^4	$3\frac{1}{2}$	Corbett	R. M. Eastman Estate	6.02
Ladysman	wb 126	4	7	$5\frac{1}{2}$	7^3	$5\frac{1}{2}$	$5\frac{1}{2}$	4^n	Workm'n	W. R. Coe	‡1.43
Pomponious	w 126	12	12	$10\frac{1}{2}$	$9\frac{1}{2}$	$6\frac{1}{2}$	6^3	5^3	Bejshak	W. R. Coe	‡1.43
Spicson	wb 126	9	13	13	12^3	$10\frac{1}{2}$	7^1	$6\frac{1}{2}$	Fischer	L. M. Severson	†25.85
Kerry Patch	wb 126	5	1	$6\frac{1}{2}$	$5\frac{1}{2}$	3^h	4^h	7^2	Schaefer	L. Rosenberg	26.89
Mr. Khayyam	w 126	13	9	9^1	11^3	9^h	9^2	$8\frac{1}{2}$	Walls	Catawba Stable	§4.09
Inlander	wb 126	6	8	8^2	10^2	8^1	8^2	$9\frac{1}{2}$	Bellizzi	Brookmeade Stable	44.27
Strideaway	w 126	8	4	$12\frac{1}{2}$	13	12^3	10^3	10^5	Beck	Three D's Stock Farm	†25.85
Dark Winter	wb 126	3	10	4^2	4^h	7^2	11^8	11^{12}	Jones	W. S. Kilmer	†25.85
Isaiah	wb 126	10	2	$2\frac{1}{2}$	$3\frac{1}{2}$	11^2	12^8	12	McCros'n	J. W. Parrish	66.86
Good Advice	wb 126	2	3	1^h	2^h	13	13	P. up.	Legere	Catawba Stable	§4.09

Time: :23-1/5, :47-1/5, 1:12-4/5, 1:40-2/5, 2:06-4/5. Track good.

†Mutuel field. ‡Coupled in betting as W. R. Coe entry. §Coupled in betting as Catawba Stable entry.

$2 Mutuels Paid—Brokers Tip, $19.86 straight, $6.28 place, $4.54 show; Head Play, $5.52 place, $4.08 show; Charley O., $3.84 show.

Winner—Br.c. by Black Toney—*Forteresse, by Sardanaple, trained by H. J. Thompson; bred in Kentucky by Idle Hour Stock Farm.

Start good out of machine. Won driving; second and third same. BROKERS TIP, much the best, began slowly, saved ground when leaving backstretch, but lost some on the stretch turn, then went to the inside and, overcoming interference, was up to win in the final strides after a long and tough drive. HEAD PLAY, rated close to the pace, went to front easily, bore out when increasing his lead on the stretch turn and bumped the winner. CHARLEY O., in hand for three-quarters, challenged gamely, then tired, but held LADYSMAN safe. The latter raced wide most of the way and failed to rally when hard urged.

THE WINNER'S PEDIGREE AND CAREER HIGHLIGHTS

BROKERS TIP (Brown Colt)	Black Toney	Peter Pan	Commando
			*Cinderella
		Belgravia	Ben Brush
			*Bonnie Gal
	*Forteresse	Sardanapale	Prestige
			Gemma
		Guerriere	Ossian
			Amazone III

Year	Age	Sts	1st	2nd	3rd	Won
1932	2	4	0	1	1	$ 600
1933	3	5	1	1	0	49,000
1936	6	5	0	0	0	
	Totals	14	1	2	1	$49,600

At 2 Years   3RD   Cincinnati Trophy

At 3 Years { WON   Kentucky Derby
UNP   Preakness Stakes, Maryland Handicap

This photograph, showing the furious stretch battle between jockeys Don Meade on Brokers Tip (right) and Herb Fisher on Head Play, was almost an accident. Courier-Journal photographer Wallace Lowery lay on the ground, stuck his camera under the rail and shot. This picture is the result. It is probably the most widely circulated picture in the history of the Derby.

May 5, 1934

Owner — Mrs. Dodge Sloane

Trainer — R. A. Smith

Jockey — Willie Garner

S I X T I E T H   R U N N I N G

CAVALCADE

$30,000 added and $5,000 Gold Cup. Net to winner $28,175; second $5,000; third $2,500; fourth $1,000. 124 nominations.

Horses	Eqt Wt	PP	St	½	¾	1	Str	Fin	Jockeys	Owners	Odds $1 Str't
Cavalcade	w 126	8	11	7¹	5½	3¹	2³	1²½	Garner	Brookmeade Stable	‡1.50
Discovery	wb 126	6	4	3²	3¹½	1²	1nk	2⁴	Bejshak	A. G. Vanderbilt	12.10
Agrarian	w 126	9	7	10½	8½	8¹	5ʰ	3ⁿ	Kurtsinger	Mrs. F. J. Heller	14.90
Mata Hari	wb 121	3	1	1ʰ	1ʰ	2ʰ	3⁴	4ⁿ	Gilbert	Dixiana	6.30
Peace Chance	w 126	2	12	12½	10ʰ	9½	6¹	5½	Wright	J. E. Widener	9.70
Spy Hill	w 126	11	10	9¹	7½	7ʰ	7²	6⁴	Coucci	Greentree Stable	33.30
Time Clock	wb 126	1	13	13	11⁶	11⁸	12¹⁰	7ʰ	Bellizzi	Brookmeade Stable	‡1.50
Singing Wood	w 126	7	5	4½	4½	4½	4½	8ʰ	Jones	Mrs. J. H. Whitney	24.10
Bazaar	w 121	12	9	6¹	6½	6½	8²	9⁶	Meade	E. R. Bradley	5.10
Speedmore	w 126	5	2	8ʰ	9½	10½	10½	10½	Horn	J. H. Louchheim	†10.40
Sgt. Byrne	wb 126	10	6	2³	2²	5½	9⁴	11³	Renick	J. Simonetti	†10.40
Sir Thomas	wb 126	4	8	11½	13	12⁴	11²	12¹⁰	Pascuma	A. B. Gordon	36.20
Quasimodo	wb 126	13	3	5¹	12½	13	13	13	Burke	Mrs. B. Franzheim	†10.40

Time: :23, :47-1/5, 1:12-1/5, 1:37-2/5, 2:04. Track fast.

†Mutuel field. ‡Coupled in betting as Brookmeade Stable entry.

$2 Mutuels Paid—Cavalcade (coupled with Time Clock as Brookmeade Stable entry), $5.00 straight, $4.00 place, $3.20 show; Discovery, $9.20 place, $5.80 show; Agrarian, $5.00 show.

Winner—Br.c. by *Lancegaye—*Hastily, by Hurry On, trained by R. A. Smith; bred in New Jersey by F. W. Armstrong.

Start good and slow. Won handily; second and third driving. CAVALCADE, away slowly, was not permitted to make up much ground for a half-mile, then began moving up leaving the backstretch, where he came through between horses, wore down DISCOVERY and drew out for a handy win. DISCOVERY, away fast, drew into an easy lead approaching the stretch, and held on well, but was overmatched. AGRARIAN closed resolutely.

THE WINNER'S PEDIGREE AND CAREER HIGHLIGHTS

CAVALCADE
(Brown Colt)

*Lancegaye
- Swynford
  - John o' Gaunt
  - Canterbury Pilgrim
- Flying Spear
  - Spearmint
  - Gallop-Along

*Hastily
- Hurry On
  - Marcovil
  - Tout Suite
- Henley
  - Junior
  - Helenora

Year	Age	Sts	1st	2nd	3rd	Won
1933	2	11	2	3	3	$ 15,730
1934	3	7	6	1	0	111,235
1935	4	2	0	1	0	200
1936	5	2	0	0	0	200
Totals		22	8	5	3	$127,165

At 2 Years
- WON Hyde Park Stakes
- 2ND Spalding Lowe Jenkins Handicap, Eastern Shore Handicap, Sanford Stakes
- 3RD Saratoga Sales Stakes, Walden Handicap
- UNP Richard Johnson Stakes, United States Hotel Stakes

At 3 Years
- WON Kentucky Derby, Chesapeake Stakes, American Derby, Detroit Derby, Classic Stakes
- 2ND Preakness Stakes

Col. Matt Winn operated Churchill Downs from this office for many years. The large black leather chairs are still part of the decor in the present directors' room.

The crowd spilled onto the track during the running of the 1934 Derby. Knickers were the fashion for boys. Note the old press box on the left portion of the roof.

Always A WINNER on any track
Louisville and Nashville Railroad

May 4, 1935

Owner — William Woodward

Trainer — James Fitzsimmons

Jockey — William Saunders

OMAHA

$40,000 added and $5,000 Gold Cup. Net to winner $39,525; second $6,000; third $3,000; fourth $1,000. 110 nominations.

Horses	Eqt Wt	PP	St	½	¾	1	Str	Fin	Jockeys	Owners	Odds $1 Str't
Omaha	wb 126	10	12	9½	5¹	1²	1¹½	1¹½	Saunders	Belair Stud	4.00
Roman Soldier	wb 126	3	10	11¹	8¹½	4ʰ	2²	2⁴	Balaski	Sachsenmaier & Reu'r	6.20
Whiskolo	w 126	8	15	12½	10¹½	2¹	3²	3¹½	Wright	Milky Way Farms	†8.40
Nellie Flag	w 121	9	1	8¹½	7¹½	5³	4³	4ʰ	Arcaro	Calumet Farm	3.80
Blackbirder	wb 126	13	14	14¹	11¹	11²	5¹	5²	Garner W	Mrs. C. Hainesworth	†8.40
Psychic Bid	wb 126	7	11	4ʰ	4¹	7¹	6³	6⁴	Jones	Brookmeade Stable	49.20
Morpluck	wsb 126	11	16	16¹	13²	12²	7ʰ	7ʰ	Garner M	J. H. Louchheim	†8.40
Plat Eye	wb 126	15	4	1½	1½	3¹	8¹	8¹	Coucci	Greentree Stable	16.40
McCarthy	wb 126	4	18	18	15¹	14⁴	14¹	9³	Finnerty	Morrison & Keating	†8.40
Commonwealth	wb 126	17	17	17⁴	12¹	9ʰ	10²	10²	Woolf	Mrs. W. M. Jeffords	9.50
Sun Fairplay	wb 126	5	3	10¹	9¹½	13³	11¹	11³	Renick	Fairfields Stable	52.30
Today	wb 126	16	6	6¹	6½	8¹	9²	12⁶	Work'an	C. V. Whitney	8.40
Whopper	wsb 126	2	9	5½	3½	6½	12¹	13¹½	Landolt	H. P. Headley	†8.40
Bluebeard	wb 126	6	2	7¹	14¹½	15¹	15¹	14¹½	Schutte	Mrs. R. B. Fairbanks	†8.40
Tutticurio	wb 126	18	13	13ʰ	16⁴	16³	16⁴	15¹	Corbett	Brandon Stable	†8.40
Boxthorn	wb 126	12	8	3¹½	2¹	10ʰ	13¹	16²	Meade	E. R. Bradley	5.00
St Bernard	w 126	1	5	2ʰ	18	18	18	17¹½	Keester	E. G. Shaffer	†8.40
Weston	wb 126	14	7	15ʰ	17¹	17¹	17¹	18	Young	Braedalbane Stable	†8.40

Time: :23, :47-3/5, 1:13-2/5, 1:38-2/5, 2:05. Track good.

†Mutuel field.

$2 Mutuels Paid—Omaha, $10.00 straight, $5.00 place, $3.80 show; Roman Soldier, $6.40 place, $4.20 show; Whiskolo (Field), $3.40 show.

Winner—Ch.c. by Gallant Fox—Flambino, by Wrack, trained by J. Fitzsimmons; bred in Kentucky by Belair Stud.

Start good and slow. Won easily; second and third driving. OMAHA escaped interference in the early crowding, was taken to the outside after the first quarter, raced to the lead gradually after reaching the half-mile post and held sway thereafter, winning easily. ROMAN SOLDIER worked his way to the outside after reaching the backstretch, responded well when called upon, but could not menace the winner. WHISKOLO raced to a contending position with a rush, lost ground on the far turn and tired in the last three-sixteenths. NELLIE FLAG suffered intereference soon after the start, was again impeded on the first turn and could not improve her position when clear in the last five-sixteenths.

THE WINNER'S PEDIGREE AND CAREER HIGHLIGHTS

OMAHA (Chestnut Colt)			
	Gallant Fox	*Sir Gallahad III	*Teddy / Plucky Liege
		Marguerite	Celt / *Fairy Ray
	Flambino	*Wrack	Robert le Diable / Samphire
		*Flambette	*Durbar II / *La Flambee

Year	Age	Sts	1st	2nd	3rd	Won	
1934	2	9	1	4	0	$ 3,850	†Includes
1935	3	9	6	1	2	142,255	winnings in
1936	4	4	2	2	0	†8,650	England.
Totals		22	9	7	2	$154,755	

At 2 Years		2ND	Sanford Stakes
At 3 Years	{	WON	Kentucky Derby, Preakness Stakes, Belmont Stakes, Dwyer Stakes, Classic Stakes
		2ND	Withers Stakes
At 4 Years (In England)	{	WON	Victor Wild Stakes, Queen's Plate

Col. E. R. Bradley and his Idle Hour Stock Farm were household words. He started 27 horses in the Derby between 1920 and 1940 and had four victories. The name of all the Bradley horses began with the letter B.

Churchill Downs for many years had no first-floor boxes all the way to the rail for the Derby as it does today. This workman grooms an area where thousands stood to watch.

145

May 2, 1936

Owner — M. L. Schwartz

Trainer — Max Hirsch

Jockey — Ira Hanford

BOLD VENTURE

$40,000 added and $5,000 Gold Cup. Net to winner $37,725; second $6,000; third $3,000; fourth $1,000. 102 nominations.

Horses	Eqt Wt	PP	St	½	¾	1	Str	Fin	Jockeys	Owners	Odds $1 Str't
Bold Venture	w 126	5	13	8$\frac{1}{2}$	1^1	1$\frac{1}{2}$	1^1	1^h	Hanford	M. L. Schwartz	20.50
Brevity	wb 126	10	10	9$\frac{1}{2}$	6$\frac{1}{2}$	3^1	2^2	2^6	Wright	J. E. Widener	.80
Indian Broom	wb 126	2	7	6^h	3^2	2$^1\frac{1}{2}$	3^5	3^3	Burns	A. C. T. Stock Farm	5.10
Coldstream	w 126	13	6	2^h	4^1	5^3	5^3	4^5	Wall	Coldstream Stud	15.20
Bien Joli	wb 126	6	2	4^h	7^1	6^3	6^2	5^h	Balaski	E. R. Bradley	14.90
Holl Image	wb 126	14	12	12^1	11^1	11$\frac{1}{2}$	7^3	6^4	Fisher	Superior Stable	†43.40
He Did	wsb 126	3	1	1^2	2$\frac{1}{2}$	4^4	4^h	7^h	Kurtsinger	Mrs. S. B. Mason	33.80
Teufel	wb 126	8	9	11$\frac{1}{2}$	10^1	8^h	8^1	8^h	Lit'nb'ger	Wheatley Stable	‡10.60
Gold Seeker	wb 121	12	14	13	12^2	10$\frac{1}{2}$	10^4	9^4	Peters	Foxcatcher Farms	†43.40
Merry Pete	wb 126	1	8	7$\frac{1}{2}$	8^3	7^1	9^h	10^6	Malley	Belair Stud	‡10.60
The Fighter	w 126	7	3	5^h	9^h	12^6	11^4	11^5	Robertson	Milky Way Farms	§16.50
Grand Slam	wb 126	9	5	3^2	5^h	9^2	12^8	12^{10}	Workman	Bomar Stable	19.10
Sangreal	wb 126	11	11	10^2	13	13	13	13	Garner	Milky Way Farms	§16.50
Granville	wb 126	4	4	Lost rider.					Stout	Belair Stud	‡10.60

Time: :23-3/5, :47-4/5, 1:12-3/5, 1:37-4/5, 2:03-3/5. Track fast.

†Mutuel field. ‡Coupled in betting as Wheatley Stable and Belair Stud entry. §Coupled in betting as Milky Way Farms entry.

$2 Mutuels Paid—Bold Venture, $43.00 straight, $11.80 place, $6.60 show; Brevity, $5.00 place, $4.00 show; Indian Broom, $3.80 show.

Winner—Ch.c. by *St. Germans—Possible, by Ultimus, trained by Max Hirsch; bred in Kentucky by M. L. Schwartz.

Start good and slow. Won driving; second and third same. BOLD VENTURE, in close quarters immediately after the start, began to improve his position fast on the outside after about three-eighths, took an easy lead approaching the final half-mile and, holding on with fine courage under strong handling, withstood BREVITY'S bid. The latter, probably best and knocked to his knees within a few strides after the start, had to race wide thereafter, closed resolutely and was wearing down the winner. INDIAN BROOM, blocked in the first quarter, raced to a contending position, made a bid entering the stretch, then weakened.

THE WINNER'S PEDIGREE AND CAREER HIGHLIGHTS

BOLD VENTURE (Chestnut Colt)	{	*St. Germans	{	Swynford	{	John o' Gaunt
						Canterbury Pilgrim
				Hamoaze	{	Torpoint
						Maid of the Mist
	{	Possible	{	Ultimus	{	Commando
						*Running Stream
				Lida Flush	{	*Royal Flush III
						Lida H.

Year	Age	Sts	1st	2nd	3rd	Won
1935	2	8	3	2	0	$ 2,500
1936	3	3	3	0	0	65,800
Totals		11	6	2	0	$68,300

At 2 Years   UNP   Arlington Futurity, Hopeful Stakes

At 3 Years   WON   Kentucky Derby, Preakness Stakes

Few fans saw Granville go to his knees just out of the starting gate. In the mishap, jockey John Stout was thrown off. Notice Granville's head near the ground and Stout, in polka dot shirt, tumbling forward.

Restrictions were fewer and the crowd surged onto the track after Bold Venture won on a fast track.

The temperature reached 78 degrees the day Bold Venture won but raincoats were visible early in the day.

May 8, 1937

Owner — S. D. Riddle

Trainer — George Conway

Jockey — Charles Kurtsinger

WAR ADMIRAL

$50,000 added and $5,000 Gold Cup. Net to winner $52,050; second $6,000; third $3,000; fourth $1,000. 103 nominations.

Horses	Eqt Wt	PP	St	½	¾	1	Str	Fin	Jockeys	Owners	Odds $1 Str't
War Admiral	w 126	1	2	1 1½	1 1	1 1½	1 3	1 1¾	Kurtsinger	Glen Riddle Farms	1.60
Pompoon	w 126	14	6	5 2	4 1	2 2	2 5	2 8	Richards	J. H. Louchheim	8.00
Reaping Reward	wb 126	17	7	8 ½	6 ½	8 3	5 3	3 3	Robertson	Milky Way Farms	‡4.60
Melodist	w 126	3	10	6 h	5 1	5 h	4 h	4 1	Longden	Wheatley Stable	15.10
Sceneshifter	wb 126	12	13	10 ½	12 ½	11 h	7 1½	5 2	Stout	M. Howard	§11.20
Heelfly	w 126	10	1	3 1½	2 2½	3 3	3 ½	6 h	Wright	Three D's Stock Farm	16.20
Dellor	wb 126	2	4	7 1½	9 ½	6 ½	6 ½	7 ½	James	J. W. Parrish	13.70
Burning Star	wb 126	15	15	14 1	13 1	13 1	10 1	8 h	Parke	Shandon Farm	†9.30
Court Scandal	wb 126	6	11	12 ½	8 h	9 3	12 1	9 1	Steffen	T. B. Martin	†9.30
Clodion	wb 126	13	14	13 2	14 ½	12 2	9 h	10 1	Anderson	W. A. Carter	†9.30
Fairy Hill	wb 126	4	3	2 1½	3 3	4 ½	8 1½	11 1½	Peters	Foxcatcher Farms	44.60
Merry Maker	wb 126	7	19	17 2	11 1	10 ½	11 ½	12 ½	Dabson	Miss E. G. Rand	†9.30
No Sir	wb 126	19	17	16 h	17 1	17 ½	13 1½	13 h	Le Blanc	Miss M. Hirsch	†9.30
Grey Gold	wb 126	11	18	19 2	19 1½	19 1	14 ½	14 1	Rosen	E. W. Duffy	†9.30
Military	wsb 126	5	9	15 1½	15 1	15 1	15 1	15 ½	Corbett	Milky Way Farms	‡4.60
Sunset Trail II	wb 126	18	12	20	20	20	16 1½	16 2	Dotter	R. Walsh	†9.30
Fencing	wsb 126	8	12	9 ½	10 ½	16 h	17 2	17 5	Westr'pe	M. Howard	§11.20
Bernard F	w 126	16	16	18 5	18 3	19 ½	18 3	18 1	Hardy	I. J. Collins	†9.30
Sir Damion	wb 126	20	8	11 ½	16 h	14 3	19 4	19 12	Yager	Marshall Field	†9.30
Billionaire	wb 126	9	5	4 h	7 ½	7 2	20	20	Woolf	E. R. Bradley	16.50

Time: :23-1/5, :46-4/5, 1:12-2/5, 1:37-2/5, 2:03-1/5. Track fast.

†Mutuel field. ‡Coupled in betting as Milky Way Farms entry. §Coupled in betting as M. Howard entry.

$2 Mutuels Paid—War Admiral, $5.20 straight, $4.20 place, $3.40 show; Pompoon, $9.40 place, $6.00 show; Reaping Reward (coupled with Military as Milky Way Farms entry), $3.80 show.

Winner—Br.c. by Man o' War—Brushup, by Sweep, trained by George Conway; bred in Kentucky by S. D. Riddle.

Start good and slow. Won easily; second and third driving. WAR ADMIRAL, fractious at post, was away fast, was sent clear of his company, was taken under restraint after racing a quarter-mile, set the pace easily to the final half-mile, increased his advantage gradually on the stretch turn and won in hand. POMPOON, forced wide throughout, was reserved off the pace, offered good response when called upon. REAPING REWARD, in close quarters early, tired.

THE WINNER'S PEDIGREE AND CAREER HIGHLIGHTS

WAR ADMIRAL (Brown Colt)		Man o' War		Fair Play		Hastings
						*Fairy Gold
				Mahubah		*Rock Sand
						*Merry Token
		Brushup		Sweep		Ben Brush
						Pink Domino
				Annette K.		Harry of Hereford
						*Bathing Girl

Year	Age	Sts	1st	2nd	3rd	Won
1936	2	6	3	2	1	$ 14,800
1937	3	8	8	0	0	166,500
1938	4	11	9	1	0	90,840
1939	5	1	1	0	0	1,100
Totals		26	21	3	1	$273,240

At 2 Years	WON	Eastern Shore Handicap
At 3 Years	WON	Kentucky Derby, Chesapeake Stakes, Preakness Stakes, Belmont Stakes, Washington Handicap, Pimlico Special
At 4 Years	WON	Widener Handicap, Queens County Handicap, Wilson Stakes, Saratoga Cup, Whitney Stakes, Saratoga Cup, Jockey Club Gold Cup, Rhode Island Handicap

The 1937 flood inundated Churchill Downs as well as large portions of other Louisville areas. These youngsters were far ahead of other boats racing in front of the plant.

The first tunnel from the grandstand area to the infield was completed in 1937. Construction of this unit is shown here. The second tunnel was completed in 1966 and first used for the Derby in 1967.

149

May 7, 1938

Owner — Herbert M. Woolf

Trainer — B. A. Jones

Jockey — Eddie Arcaro

LAWRIN

$50,000 added and $5,000 Gold Cup. Net to winner $47,050; second $6,000; third $3,000; fourth $1,000. 103 nominations.

Horses	Eqt Wt	PP	St	½	¾	1	Str	Fin	Jockeys	Owners	Odds $1 Str't
Lawrin	w 126	1	5	5^h	$5\frac{1}{2}$	2^h	1^3	1^1	Arcaro	Woolford Farm	8.60
Dauber	wb 126	3	10	$9\frac{1}{2}$	$8\frac{1}{2}$	6^4	3^1	2^5	Peters	Foxcatcher Farms	9.70
Can't Wait	wb 126	7	4	4^1	$3\frac{1}{2}$	3^3	4^4	3^n	Balaski	M. Selznick	24.20
Menow	wb 126	10	7	1^2	$1\frac{1}{2}$	$1\frac{1}{2}$	2^2	4^{nk}	Workm'n	H. P. Headley	8.50
The Chief	w 126	9	8	$6\frac{1}{2}$	6^1	5^h	5^4	5^6	Westrope	M. Howard	12.00
Fighting Fox	w 126	5	6	2^3	2^h	$4\frac{1}{2}$	6^3	6^3	Stout	Belair Stud	1.40
Co-Sport	wb 126	2	9	$8\frac{1}{2}$	9^2	9^5	7^2	7^2	Woolf	B. Friend	89.50
Bull Lea	wb 126	6	1	7^4	$7\frac{1}{2}$	8^3	8^1	8^h	Anderson	Calumet Farm	2.90
Elooto	wb 126	4	2	10	10	10	10	9^2	Faust	Blue Ridge Farm	122.30
Mountain Ridge	w 126	8	3	$3\frac{1}{2}$	4^1	7^2	$9\frac{1}{2}$	10	Robertson	Milky Way Farms	105.20

Time: :23-1/5, :47-2/5, 1:12-2/5, 1:38-1/5, 2:04-4/5. Track fast.

$2 Mutuels Paid—Lawrin, $19.20 straight, $8.80 place, $4.80 show; Dauber, $12.00 place, $6.00 show; Can't Wait, $8.20 show.

Winner—Br.c. by Insco—Margaret Lawrence, by Vulcain, trained by B. A. Jones; bred in Kansas by H. M. Woolf.

Start good and slow. Won driving; second and third same. LAWRIN, saving much ground, responded willingly when called upon, came through on the inside when wearing down MENOW, opened up a commanding advantage approaching the final eighth, then bore out through the last sixteenth, but held DAUBER safe. The latter, badly outrun early, began to improve his position when racing wide on the stretch turn, continued near the middle of the track while closing with fine speed and was getting to the winner. CAN'T WAIT, rated under steady reserve for about three-quarters, outfinished MENOW in the last stride. The latter made a good pace under steady rating, swerved out on the stretch turn and tired under pressure thereafter. THE CHIEF ran an even race. FIGHTING FOX did not respond when urged and gave way badly after a mile.

THE WINNER'S PEDIGREE AND CAREER HIGHLIGHTS

LAWRIN (Brown Colt)
- Insco
  - *Sir Gallahad III
    - *Teddy
    - Plucky Liege
  - *Starflight
    - Sunstar
    - Angelic
- Margaret Lawrence
  - *Vulcain
    - *Rock Sand
    - Lady of the Vale
  - Bohemia
    - *Wagner
    - Mattie T.

Year	Age	Sts	1st	2nd	3rd	Won
1937	2	15	3	6	0	$ 3,060
1938	3	11	6	2	2	123,215
Totals		26	9	8	2	$126,275

At 3 Years
- WON Kentucky Derby, Hialeah Stakes, Flamingo Stakes, Hollywood Trial Stakes
- 2ND Derby Trial
- UNP Bahamas Handicap

Jack Dempsey was a Derby visitor in 1938 . . .

Col. Matt Winn became president of Churchill Downs in 1938, although he had "run" the track since 1902.

. . . as was Elliott Roosevelt, son of President Franklin D. Roosevelt . . .

. . . and Joe E. Brown, that big comedian with the big mouth.

May 6, 1939

Owner — William Woodward

Trainer — James Fitzsimmons

Jockey — James Stout

JOHNSTOWN

$50,000 added and $5,000 Gold Cup. 3-year-olds. Net to winner $46,350; second $6,000; third $3,000; fourth $1,000. 115 nominations.

Horses	Eqt Wt	PP	St	½	¾	1	Str	Fin	Jockeys	Owners	Odds $1 Str't
Johnstown	wb 126	5	2	1²	1⁴	1⁴	1⁵	1⁸	Stout	Belair Stud	.60
Challedon	w 126	7	5	7⁵	5½	4⁶	3¹	2¹	Seabo	W. L. Brann	6.60
Heather Broom	w 126	2	6	4½	6¹	3ʰ	4⁶	3½	James	J. H. Whitney	12.00
Viscounty	wb 126	3	8	6¹	4¹	2¹	2ʰ	4⁶	Bierman	Valdina Farms	52.20
Technician	wb 126	6	4	5¹	7⁸	5½	5⁵	5⁸	Adams	Woolford Farm	5.80
El Chico	w 126	1	1	2½	2½	6⁴	6³	6³	Wall	W. Ziegler, Jr.	8.20
T M Dorsett	wb 126	8	3	3³	3¹	7¹²	7¹⁵	7	Haas	J. W. Brown	64.90
On Location	wb 126	4	7	8	8	8	8	P. up.	Robertson	Milky Way Farms	97.70

Time: :23-2/5, :47-2/5, 1:12-4/5, 1:38, 2:03-2/5. Track fast.

$2 Mutuels Paid—Johnstown, $3.20 straight, $3.00 place, $2.80 show; Challedon, $3.60 place, $3.20 show; Heather Broom, $3.00 show.

Winner—B.c. by Jamestown—La France, by *Sir Gallahad III, trained by James Fitzsimmons; bred in Kentucky by A. B. Hancock.

Start bad and slow. Won easily; second and third driving. JOHNSTOWN swerved to the inside as he took command, made the pace for a mile, was lightly roused in the stretch and quickly increasing his advantage, won with speed in reserve. CHALLEDON was between horses in the early running and began to move up after reaching the last five-eighths. HEATHER BROOM dropped back when racing wide on the first turn, rallied after going seven-eighths and outfinished VISCOUNTY.

THE WINNER'S PEDIGREE AND CAREER HIGHLIGHTS

JOHNSTOWN (Bay Colt)
- Jamestown
  - St. James
    - *Ambassador IV
    - *Bobolink II
  - Mlle. Dazie
    - Fair Play
    - Toggery
- La France
  - *Sir Gallahad III
    - *Teddy
    - Plucky Liege
  - *Flambette
    - *Durbar II
    - *La Flambee

Year	Age	Sts	1st	2nd	3rd	Won
1938	2	12	7	0	2	$ 31,420
1939	3	9	7	0	1	137,895
Totals		21	14	0	3	$169,315

At 2 Years
- WON Babylon Stakes, Richard Johnson Stakes, Remsen Handicap, Breeders' Futurity
- 3RD Hopeful Stakes, Junior Champion Stakes
- UNP Flash Stakes, Belmont Futurity

At 3 Years
- WON Kentucky Derby, Wood Memorial, Paumonok Handicap, Withers Stakes, Belmont Stakes, Dwyer Stakes
- 3RD Classic Stakes
- UNP Preakness Stakes

Ted Husing furnished the "eyes" for millions to enjoy the Derby with his radio calls in the 1930s and 1940s.

One of the great trainers, Sunny Jim Fitzsimmons, is shown with jockey Johnny Stout. Sunny Jim had three Derby winners in the 1930s.

Al Jolson decided the Derby was a good place to get on the other side of a camera and he gags it up for the photographer.

JOHNSTOWN

was one of the more than 220 Stakes Winners bred by the Hancocks at Claiborne.

May 4, 1940

Owner — Mrs. Ethel Mars

Trainer — Roy Waldron

Jockey — Carroll Bierman

GALLAHADION

$75,000 added and Gold Cup. Net to winner $60,150; second $8,000; third $3,000; fourth $1,000. Trainer awards: First $3,000; second $2,000; third $1,000. Breeder's awards: First $2,000; second $1,000; third $500. 127 nominations.

Horses	Eqt Wt	PP	St	1/2	3/4	1	Str	Fin	Jockeys	Owners	Odds $1 Str't
Gallahadion	wb 126	1	4	3^h	2^h	4^1	3^2	$1^{1\frac{1}{2}}$	Bierman	Milky Way Farms	35.20
Bimelech	w 126	2	1	$2\frac{1}{2}$	3^h	1^h	$1\frac{1}{2}$	2^n	F A Smith	E. R. Bradley	.40
Dit	wb 126	6	5	4^1	4^1	3^3	$2\frac{1}{2}$	3^1	Haas	W. A. Hanger	6.70
Mioland	wb 126	3	3	5^2	$5\frac{1}{2}$	5^2	4^1	4^2	Balaski	C. S. Howard	6.40
Sirocco	wb 126	5	6	6^1	6^3	6^5	6^6	5^2	Longden	Dixiana	42.70
Roman	wb 126	4	2	$1\frac{1}{2}$	$1\frac{1}{2}$	2^h	5^h	6^6	McCombs	J. E. Widener	24.20
Royal Man	wb 126	7	7	7^2	7^h	$7\frac{1}{2}$	7^3	7^3	Gilbert	Tower Stable	61.20
Pictor	w 126	8	8	8	8	8	8	8	Woolf	W. L. Brann	18.00

Time: :23-2/5, :48, 1:12-4/5, 1:38-3/5, 2:05. Track fast.

$2 Mutuels Paid—Gallahadion, $74.20 straight, $13.80 place, $4.80 show; Bimelech, $3.20 place, $2.40 show; Dit, $2.80 show.

Winner—B.c. by *Sir Gallahad III—Countless Time, by Reigh Count, trained by Roy Waldron; bred in Kentucky by R. A. Fairbairn.

Start good and slow. Won driving; second and third same. GALLAHADION, away well, moved forward with BIMELECH, responded to strong urging when wearing down BIMELECH, drew out, but won with little left. BIMELECH, first in motion, went wide throughout, moved into command nearing the final quarter-mile, bore out on the stretch turn, held the lead approaching the final furlong, but was unable to hold the winner. DIT, steadied along early, was forced wide entering the stretch.

THE WINNER'S PEDIGREE AND CAREER HIGHLIGHTS

GALLAHADION (Bay Colt)
- *Sir Gallahad III
  - *Teddy
    - Ajax
    - Rondeau
  - Plucky Liege
    - Spearmint
    - Concertina
- Countless Time
  - Reigh Count
    - *Sunreigh
    - *Contessina
  - *Breathing Spell
    - Dark Ronald
    - *Romagne

Year	Age	Sts	1st	2nd	3rd	Won
1939	2	5	0	1	0	$ 180
1940	3	17	5	4	1	89,590
1941	4	14	1	1	3	2,850
Totals		36	6	6	4	$92,620

At 3 Years
- WON: Kentucky Derby, San Vicente Handicap
- 2ND: Derby Trial, Classic Stakes
- 3RD: Preakness Stakes
- UNP: Santa Anita Derby, San Juan Capistrano Handicap, Belmont Stakes, Kent Handicap, American Derby, Lawrence Realization

At 4 Years
- 3RD: Clark Handicap, Stars and Stripes Handicap
- UNP: Ben Ali Handicap, Churchill Downs Handicap, Dixie Handicap, Equipoise Mile

The arrival of celebrities often brought huge crowds to Bowman Field for a glimpse. Arriving on this 1940 Derby special flight were Irene Dunne (note the "plug" for her picture) and Eddie Rickenbacker and his wife.

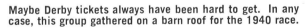

Maybe Derby tickets always have been hard to get. In any case, this group gathered on a barn roof for the 1940 race.

155

May 3, 1941

Owner — Warren Wright

Trainer — B. A. Jones

Jockey — Eddie Arcaro

WHIRLAWAY

$75,000 added and Gold Cup. Net to winner $61,275; second $8,000; third $3,000; fourth $1,000. Trainer awards: First $3,000; second $2,000; third $1,000. Breeder awards: First $2,000; second $1,000; third $500. 112 nominations.

Horses	Eqt Wt	PP	St	1/2	3/4	1	Str	Fin	Jockeys	Owners	Odds $1 Str't
Whirlaway	wb 126	4	6	8^1	$6\frac{1}{2}$	4^1	1^3	1^8	Arcaro	Calumet Farm	2.90
Staretor	w 126	2	1	7^2	$4\frac{1}{2}$	5^3	$2\frac{1}{2}$	2^{nk}	Woolf	H. S. Nesbitt	36.00
Market Wise	wb 126	7	5	6^2	8^4	6^3	5^3	3^2	Anderson	L. Tufano	19.10
Porter's Cap	wb 126	9	4	2^h	3^5	$2\frac{1}{2}$	3^h	4^1	Haas	C. S. Howard	3.30
Little Beans	wb 126	5	10	10^{12}	9^5	8^5	7^2	5^1	Moore	Mrs. L. Palladino	12.10
Dispose	w 126	11	2	1^2	1^2	1^h	4^h	$6^1\frac{1}{2}$	Bierman	King Ranch	7.20
Blue Pair	wb 126	3	3	3^5	2^h	$3\frac{1}{2}$	$6\frac{1}{2}$	$7\frac{1}{2}$	James	Mrs. V. S. Bragg	20.60
Our Boots	w 126	10	9	4^3	$5\frac{1}{2}$	7^2	8^5	8^3	McCreary	Woodvale Farm	3.90
Robert Morris	w 126	8	8	$5^1\frac{1}{2}$	7^1	9^6	9^8	9^{12}	Richards	J. F. Byers	13.90
Valdina Paul	wb 126	6	7	9^3	10^{15}	10^{15}	10^{15}	10^{12}	H Lem'ns	Valdina Farm	†24.30
Swain	wb 126	1	11	11	11	11	11	11	Adams	C. Putnam	†24.30

Time: :23-3/5, :46-3/5, 1:11-3/5, 1:37-2/5, 2:01-2/5 (new track record). Track fast.

†Mutuel field.

$2 Mutuels Paid—Whirlaway, $7.80 straight, $5.00 place, $4.40 show; Staretor, $35.20 place, $17.00 show; Market Wise, $10.80 show.

Winner—Ch.c. by *Blenheim II—Dustwhirl, by Sweep, trained by B. A. Jones; bred in Kentucky by Calumet Farm.

Start good and slow. Won easily; second and third driving. WHIRLAWAY, eased back when blocked in the first eighth and taken to the inside approaching the first turn, started up after reaching the final half-mile, was taken between horses on the final turn, responded with much energy to take command with a rush and, continuing with much power, drew out fast in the final eighth. STARETOR, away slowly, made his move gradually, drifted out slightly before straightening up in the stretch and held on well in the final drive. MARKET WISE, also well back early, rallied after reaching the last five-sixteenths and finished with courage. PORTER'S CAP, a strong factor from the start, tired after reaching the last three-sixteenths.

THE WINNER'S PEDIGREE AND CAREER HIGHLIGHTS

WHIRLAWAY (Chestnut Colt)
- *Blenheim II
  - Blandford
    - Swynford
    - Blanche
  - Malva
    - Charles O'Malley
    - Wild Arum
- Dustwhirl
  - Sweep
    - Ben Brush
    - Pink Domino
  - Ormonda
    - Superman
    - Princess Ormonda

Year	Age	Sts	1st	2nd	3rd	Won
1940	2	16	7	2	4	$ 77,275
1941	3	20	13	5	2	272,386
1942	4	22	12	8	2	211,250
1943	5	2	0	0	1	250
Totals		60	32	15	9	$561,161

At 2 Years
- WON Saratoga Special, Hopeful Stakes, Breeders' Futurity, Walden Stakes
- 2ND United States Hotel Stakes, Grand Union Hotel Stakes
- 3RD Arlington Futurity, Belmont Futurity, Pimlico Futurity

At 3 Years
- WON Kentucky Derby, Preakness Stakes, Belmont Stakes, Saranac Handicap, Travers Stakes, American Derby, Lawrence Realization, Dwyer Stakes
- 2ND Jockey Club Gold Cup, Blue Grass Stakes, Derby Trial, Classic Stakes, Narragansett Special

At 4 Years
- WON Clark Handicap, Dixie Handicap, Brooklyn Handicap, Massachusetts Handicap, Trenton Handicap, Narragansett Special, Jockey Club Gold Cup, Washington Handicap, Pimlico Special, Governor Bowie Handicap, Louisiana Handicap

Kids do it their way — and have a great time — just as these did trying to sneak a peek at the 1941 Derby. The boys take an ice cream break after getting a vantage spot but the young lady has run afoul of the gendarmes.

Calumet Farm

OWNER AND BREEDER OF EIGHT KENTUCKY DERBY WINNERS

WHIRLAWAY 1941	PENSIVE 1944	CITATION 1948	PONDER 1949
HILL GAIL 1952	IRON LIEGE 1957	TIM TAM 1958	FORWARD PASS 1968

Mrs. Gene Markey   •   Versailles Pike   •   Lexington, Kentucky

May 2, 1942

Owner — Mrs. Payne Whitney

Trainer — John M. Gaver

Jockey — Wayne Wright

SIXTY EIGHTH RUNNING

SHUT OUT

$75,000 added and Gold Cup. Net to winner $64,225; second $8,000; third $3,000; fourth $1,000. Trainer awards: First $3,000; second $2,000; third $1,000. Breeder awards: First $2,000; second $1,000; third $500. 150 nominations.

Horses	Eqt Wt	PP	St	½	¾	1	Str	Fin	Jockeys	Owners	Odds $1 Str't
Shut Out	w 126	3	1	4²	3¹½	3h	1½	1²¼	Wright	Greentree Stable	‡1.90
Alsab	wb 126	7	5	10¹	8¹	4½	4²	2h	James	Mrs. A. Sabath	5.10
Valdina Orphan	wb 126	14	10	2h	2¹½	2²	2h	3¹½	Bierman	Valdina Farm	§9.90
With Regards	w 126	15	4	1²	1¹	1½	3²	4½	Longden	Mr. & Mrs. T. D. Grimes	5.40
First Fiddle	wb 126	2	11	11¹½	10h	9h	6³	5³	McCreary	Mrs. E. Mulrenan	†9.20
Devil Diver	wb 126	5	2	5¹½	5¹½	5¹½	5²	6¹½	Arcaro	Greentree Stable	‡1.90
Fair Call	wb 126	1	7	6¹	6¹½	6¹	7¹	7nk	Lingberg	Mill River Stable	†9.20
Dogpatch	wb 126	10	3	3h	4¹½	7h	8¹½	8h	Skelly	Milky Way Farm	59.70
Hollywood	w 126	6	14	14⁵	13¹	12²	10¹	9¹	Woolf	Valdina Farm	§9.90
Sweep Swinger	wb 126	4	15	15	15⁵	13³	11²	10½	Shelhamer	T. D. Buhl	†9.20
Apache	w 126	13	6	7¹	7½	8½	9¹	11¹	Stout	Belair Stud	16.90
Sir War	wb 126	8	8	9¹½	11¹½	11²	12⁴	12⁴	Adams	Circle M Ranch	†9.20
Fairy Manah	wb 126	9	13	12¹	9h	10¹	13²	13⁶	Gilbert	Foxcatcher Farm	39.90
Requested	w 126	12	9	8¹½	12¹½	14⁶	14⁵	14⁵	Haas	B. F. Whitaker	5.10
Boot and Spur	wb 126	11	12	13¹½	15	15	15	15	Craig	E. C. A. Berger	†9.20

Time: :23-3/5, :47-2/5, 1:12-3/5, 1:39, 2:04-2/5. Track fast.

†Mutuel field. ‡Coupled as Greentree Stable entry. §Valding Farm entry.

$2 Mutuels Paid—Greentree Entry (Shut Out and Devil Diver), $5.80 straight, $3.40 place, $3.00 show; Alsab, $6.20 place, $4.80 show; Valdina Farm Entry (Valdina Orphan and Hollywood), $5.20 show.

Winner—Ch.c. by Equipoise—Goose Egg, by *Chicle, trained by J. M. Gaver; bred in Kentucky by Greentree Stable.

Start good from stall gate. Won ridden out; second and third driving. SHUT OUT, taken in hand after being hustled along for three-eighths, went close to the pace under smooth rating, responded when called upon and, wearing down the leaders, continued strongly while drawing out through the last eighth. ALSAB, taken to the outside after a half-mile, started up after three-quarters and closed resolutely to head VALDINA ORPHAN in the final stride. VALDINA ORPHAN forced a fast pace under clever rating.

THE WINNER'S PEDIGREE AND CAREER HIGHLIGHTS

SHUT OUT (Chestnut Colt)
- Equipoise
  - Pennant
    - Peter Pan
    - *Royal Rose
  - Swinging
    - Broomstick
    - *Balancoire II
- Goose Egg
  - *Chicle
    - Spearmint
    - Lady Hamburg II
  - Oval
    - Fair Play
    - Olympia

Year	Age	Sts	1st	2nd	3rd	Won
1941	2	9	3	2	1	$ 17,210
1942	3	12	8	2	0	238,972
1943	4	17	5	2	2	60,925
1944	5	2	0	0	1	400
Totals		40	16	6	4	$317,507

At 2 Years	WON	Grand Union Hotel Stakes
	2ND	Hopeful Stakes, Saratoga Special
At 3 Years	WON	Kentucky Derby, Blue Grass Stakes, Belmont Stakes, Yankee Handicap, Classic Stakes, Travers Stakes
	2ND	Dwyer Stakes
At 4 Years	WON	Wilson Stakes, Laurel Stakes, Pimlico Special
	2ND	Edgemere Handicap, Riggs Handicap

War games were held in the infield of Churchill Downs in 1942 but the races continued in the afternoons.

Race fans downtown jammed the trolley cars to come to see Shut Out win. This shot was taken from the Heyburn Building looking across Fourth and Broadway.

May 1, 1943

Owner — Mrs. John Hertz

Trainer — G. D. Cameron

Jockey — John Longden

COUNT FLEET

$75,000 added and $5,000 Gold Cup. Net to winner $60,725; second $8,000; third $3,000; fourth $1,000. Trainer awards: First $3,000; second $2,000; third $1,000. Breeder awards: First $2,000; second $1,000; third $500. 110 nominations.

Horses	Eqt Wt	PP	St	½	¾	1	Str	Fin	Jockeys	Owners	Odds $1 Str't
Count Fleet .....wb	126	5	1	1h	1²	1²	1²	1³	Longden	Mrs. J. Hertz	.40
Blue Swords .....wb	126	1	2	4½	4¹½	2¹½	2²	2⁶	Adams	A. T. Simmons	9.00
Slide Rule ....wb	126	2	6	6½	3h	4¹½	3³	3⁶	McCreary	W. E. Boeing	10.80
Amber Light .....wb	126	7	5	5¹½	5³	3½	4²	4½	Robertson	Dixiana	17.50
Bankrupt ....w	126	6	9	9³	9¹	7½	6½	5¹½	Zufelt	T. B. Martin	†21.90
No Wrinkles ......w	126	10	7	8³	7½	6¹	7h	6h	Adair	Milky Way Farm	34.60
Dove Pie ....wb	126	4	10	10	10	8²	8¹	7³	Eads	J. W. Rodgers	86.50
Gold Shower .....w	126	9	4	2⁴	2¹	5³	5½	8¹⁰	Atkinson	V. S. Bragg	12.10
Modest Lad .....wb	126	3	8	7h	6h	9⁴	9⁴	9⁸	Swain	Mrs. H. Finch	71.20
Burnt Cork ......wb	126	8	3	3¹	8¹½	10	10	10	Gonzalez	E. Anderson	†21.90

Time: :23-1/5, :48-3/5, 1:12-3/5, 1:37-3/5, 2:04-2/5. Track fast.

†Mutuel field.

$2 Mutuels Paid—Count Fleet, $2.80 straight, $2.40 place, $2.20 show; Blue Swords, $3.40 place, $3.00 show; Slide Rule, $3.20 show.

Winner—Br.c. by Reigh Count—Quickly, by Haste, trained by G. D. Cameron; bred in Kentucky by Mrs. J. Hertz.

Start good from stall gate. Won handily; second and third driving. COUNT FLEET began fast, was hustled along, shook off the bid of GOLD SHOWER and won handily. BLUE SWORDS was in hand until reaching the last half-mile, came determinedly, but was not good enough. SLIDE RULE was blocked when approaching the final turn and, taken out for the drive, could not reach the leaders. AMBER LIGHT made a game bid entering the stretch but tired.

THE WINNER'S PEDIGREE AND CAREER HIGHLIGHTS

COUNT FLEET (Brown Colt)
- Reigh Count
  - *Sunreigh
    - Sundridge
    - *Sweet Briar II
  - *Contessina
    - Count Schomberg
    - Pitti
- Quickly
  - Haste
    - *Maintenant
    - Miss Malaprop
  - Stephanie
    - *Stefan the Great
    - Malachite

Year	Age	Sts	1st	2nd	3rd	Won
1942	2	15	10	4	1	$ 76,245
1943	3	6	6	0	0	174,055
Totals		21	16	4	1	$250,300

At 2 Years
- WON Champagne Stakes, Pimlico Futurity, Walden Stakes, Wakefield Stakes
- 2ND East View Stakes, Washington Park Futurity
- 3RD Belmont Futurity

At 3 Years
- WON Kentucky Derby, Wood Memorial, Preakness Stakes, Withers Stakes, Belmont Stakes

Soldiers were prominent in the 1943 Derby Day Crowd . . . and so were the military police.

The war years brought the nickname "Streetcar Derby" because of the severe limitations on travel. The twin spires hover in the background over these early arrivals in 1943.

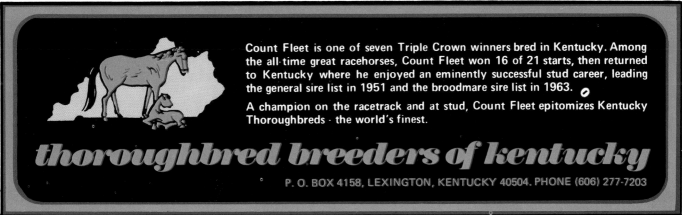

May 6, 1944

Owner — Warren Wright

Trainer — B. A. Jones

Jockey — Conn McCreary

PENSIVE

$75,000 added and $5,000 Gold Cup. Net to winner $64,675; second $8,000; third $3,000; fourth $1,000. Trainer awards: First $3,000; second $2,000; third $1,000. Breeder awards: First $2,000; second $1,000; third $500. 148 nominations.

Horses	Eqt Wt	PP	St	½	¾	1	Str	Fin	Jockeys	Owners	Odds $1 Str't
Pensive	w 126	4	4	13^1	10^h	5$^1\frac{1}{2}$	3$^1\frac{1}{2}$	1$^4\frac{1}{2}$	McCreary	Calumet Farm	7.10
Broadcloth	wb 126	9	7	3$\frac{1}{2}$	3^2	1$\frac{1}{2}$	1^h	2^1	Woolf	Mrs. G. Poulsen	7.40
Stir Up	wb 126	5	5	4$^1\frac{1}{2}$	4^1	2^2	2^h	3^h	Arcaro	Greentree Stable	1.40
Shut Up	wb 126	10	12	14^3	13$^1\frac{1}{2}$	7$^1\frac{1}{2}$	5^2	4^h	Eccard	Erlanger Stable	†7.70
Brief Sigh	wb 126	13	3	9$\frac{1}{2}$	8$^1\frac{1}{2}$	3$^1\frac{1}{2}$	4$^1\frac{1}{2}$	5$^3_4$	Nodarse	River Divide Farm	†7.70
Gay Bit	wb 126	7	16	16	16	16	6$^1\frac{1}{2}$	6^1	Westrope	Bobanet Stable	25.80
Bell Buzzer	wb 126	3	15	15^1	15^3	13^2	9^2	7$^1\frac{1}{2}$	Thompson	D. Ferguson	†7.70
Gr'ps Image	wb 126	14	10	11^1	12$\frac{1}{2}$	9^2	8^h	8^4	Grohs	Mrs. A. J. Abel	20.00
Skytracer	wb 126	2	1	7$\frac{1}{2}$	6^h	6$\frac{1}{2}$	7$\frac{1}{2}$	9^2	Caffarella	M. B. Goff	8.40
Challenge Me	wb 126	1	2	6$^1\frac{1}{2}$	7$\frac{1}{2}$	10^3	10^5	10$\frac{1}{2}$	W Garner	Brolite Farm	8.90
Alorter	wb 126	6	6	5^h	5^h	11^2	11^4	11^5	Adams	A. C. Ernst	19.50
Comenow	wb 126	16	11	2^1	2$^1\frac{1}{2}$	4$\frac{1}{2}$	12$^1\frac{1}{2}$	12^2	Layton	Philip Godfrey	†7.70
Val'y Flares	wb 126	11	14	8$\frac{1}{2}$	11$^1\frac{1}{2}$	12^1	13^2	13^2	Burns	B. R. Patno	†7.70
Diavolaw	wb 126	12	9	1^1	1$\frac{1}{2}$	8$\frac{1}{2}$	14$^1\frac{1}{2}$	14^1	Molbert	W. C. Hobson	†7.70
Rock'd Boy	wb 126	8	8	10^1	9^h	14$^1\frac{1}{2}$	15$^1\frac{1}{2}$	15^5	Bailey	W. C. Davis	†7.70
American Eagle	wb 126	15	13	12^2	14^2	15^4	16	16	Higley	J. V. Maggio	†7.70

Time: :23-3/5, :47-1/5, 1:12-2/5, 1:38-1/5, 2:04-1/5. Track good.

†Mutuel field.

$2 Mutuels Paid—Pensive, $16.20 straight, $7.20 place, $4.60 show; Broadcloth, $6.80 place, $4.60 show; Stir Up, $3.00 show.

Winner—Ch.c. by Hyperion—*Penicuik II, by Buchan, trained by B. A. Jones; bred in Kentucky by Calumet Farm.

Start good from stall gate. Won ridden out; second and third driving. PENSIVE worked his way forward on the outside, was sent to the inside when the leaders swung wide approaching the stretch, came willingly when put to strong pressure, wore down the leaders swiftly and won drawing away. BROADCLOTH took command after three-quarters, was unable to draw clear and failed to withstand the winner. STIR UP moved forward with BROADCLOTH, was forced to lose some ground when challenging for the lead. SHUT UP worked his way forward through the field and closed with a rush. BRIEF SIGH tired in the drive.

THE WINNER'S PEDIGREE AND CAREER HIGHLIGHTS

PENSIVE (Chestnut Colt)

- Hyperion
  - Gainsborough
    - Bayardo
    - *Rosedrop
  - Selene
    - Chaucer
    - Serenissima
- *Penicuik II
  - Buchan
    - Sunstar
    - Hamoaze
  - Pennycomequick
    - Hurry On
    - Plymstock

Year	Age	Sts	1st	2nd	3rd	Won
1943	2	5	2	0	2	$ 5,490
1944	3	17	5	5	2	162,225
Totals		22	7	5	4	$167,715

At 2 Years
- 3RD Champagne Stakes, Oden Bowie Stakes
- UNP Belmont Futurity

At 3 Years
- WON Kentucky Derby, Rowe Memorial Handicap, Preakness Stakes
- 2ND Bowie Handicap, Chesapeake Stakes, Belmont Stakes
- 3RD Classic Stakes

The Kentucky State Fair was held at Churchill Downs in 1902 under the auspices of the Kentucky Livestock Breeders' Association. It also was held here in 1906, 1907, 1944 and 1945. This is a scene from the 1944 Fair, which prohibited children from coming because of the threat of polio.

Calumet Farm

OWNER AND BREEDER OF EIGHT KENTUCKY DERBY WINNERS

WHIRLAWAY	PENSIVE	CITATION	PONDER
1941	1944	1948	1949

	HILL GAIL	IRON LIEGE	TIM TAM	FORWARD PASS
	1952	1957	1958	1968

Mrs. Gene Markey   •   Versailles Pike   •   Lexington, Kentucky

June 9, 1945

Owner — Fred W. Hooper

Trainer — I. H. Parke

Jockey — Eddie Arcaro

HOOP JR.

$75,000 added and $5,000 Gold Cup. Net to winner $64,850; second $8,000; third $3,000; fourth $1.000. Trainer awards: First $3,000; second $2,000; third $1,000. Breeder awards: First $2,000; second $1,000; third $500. 155 nominations.

Horses	Eqt Wt	PP	St	1/4	1/2	3/4	Str	Fin	Jockeys	Owners	Odds $1 Str't
Hoop Jr.	w 126	12	2	1^1	1^1	1^1	1^6	1^6	Arcaro	F. W. Hooper	3.70
Pot O'Luck	w 126	7	15	$14\frac{1}{2}$	$10\frac{1}{2}$	8^2	5^2	$2\frac{3}{4}$	Dodson	Calumet Farm	3.30
Darby Dieppe	wb 126	9	16	12^{hd}	9^1	$6\frac{1}{2}$	$3\frac{1}{2}$	3^{nk}	Calvert	Mrs. W. G. Lewis	5.60
Air Sailor	w 126	5	5	$5\frac{1}{2}$	5^2	3^4	4^2	4^4	Haas	T. D. Buhl	20.90
Jeep	wb 126	3	6	$7\frac{1}{2}$	$7\frac{1}{2}$	5^h	6^4	5^3	Kirkland	C. V. Whitney	6.80
Bymeabond	wb 126	10	1	$2\frac{1}{2}$	2^3	$2\frac{1}{2}$	2^h	6^3	F A Smith	J. K. Houssels	†6.80
Sea Swallow	wb 126	2	3	$6\frac{1}{2}$	$8\frac{1}{2}$	10^3	$7\frac{1}{2}$	$7\frac{1}{2}$	Woolf	Mrs. C. S. Howard	†6.80
Fighting Step	w 126	13	11	4^2	4^1	4^1	8^1	$8\frac{1}{2}$	South	Murlogg Farm	19.80
Burning Dream	w 126	6	7	$10\frac{1}{2}$	$11\frac{1}{2}$	11^4	9^4	9^2	Snider	E. R. Bradley	15.80
Alexis	w 126	11	4	$3\frac{1}{2}$	$3\frac{1}{2}$	$7\frac{1}{2}$	11^6	$10\frac{1}{2}$	Scawth'n	Christiana Stables	12.20
Foreign Agent	wb 126	4	9	9^1	6^{hd}	$9\frac{1}{2}$	$10\frac{1}{2}$	11^5	Knott	Lookout Stock Farm	25.90
Misweet	w 121	1	8	8^h	13^1	13^1	13^4	12^5	Craig	A. Rose	†6.80
Tiger Rebel	w 126	8	10	11^1	12^4	12^5	12^{hd}	$13\frac{1}{2}$	Layton	Brent & Talbot	†6.80
Bert G	wb 126	14	14	15^4	15^{15}	15^{20}	14^1	14^{10}	Summers	T. L. Graham	‡†6.80
Jacobe	wb 126	15	12	$13\frac{1}{2}$	14^4	14^4	15^{20}	15^8	Lindberg	A. R. Wright	†6.80
Kenilworth Lad	wb 126	16	13	16	16	16	16	16	Weid'm'n	T. L. Graham	‡†6.80

Time: :23-1/5, :48, 1:14, 1:41, 2:07. Track muddy.

†Mutuel field. ‡Coupled, Bert G. and Kenilworth Lad.

$2 Mutuels Paid—Hoop Jr., $9.40 straight, $5.20 place, $4.00 show; Pot O' Luck, $4.80 place, $3.60 show; Darby Dieppe, $4.00 show.

Winner—B.c. by *Sir Gallahad III—One Hour, by *Snob II, trained by I. H. Parke; bred in Kentucky by R. A. Fairbairn.

Start good from stall gate. Won easily; second and third driving. HOOP JR., away well, opened up a clear advantage in the first three-sixteenths-mile, was taken in hand to make the pace under a steadying hold to the stretch, responded with much energy when called upon and won with something left. POT O' LUCK, away slowly, started up after reaching the final five furlongs, lost ground on the final turn but cut to the inside while closing fast and overtook AIR SAILOR and DARBY DIEPPE in swift succession near the end. DARBY DIEPPE bettered his position gradually from a sluggish start but weakened suddenly near the end. AIR SAILOR, forwardly placed on the outside from the start, rallied only mildly and faltered in the late stages.

THE WINNER'S PEDIGREE AND CAREER HIGHLIGHTS

HOOP JR. (Bay Colt)
- *Sir Gallahad III
  - *Teddy
    - Ajax
    - Rondeau
  - Plucky Liege
    - Spearmint
    - Concertina
- One Hour
  - *Snob II
    - Prestige
    - May Dora
  - Daylight Saving
    - *Star Shoot
    - Tea Enough

Year	Age	Sts	1st	2nd	3rd	Won
1944	2	5	2	3	0	$ 5,300
1945	3	4	2	1	0	93,990
Totals		9	4	4	0	$99,290

At 2 Years — 2ND Bowie Kindergarten Stakes, Aberdeen Stakes, Pimlico Nursery Stakes

At 3 Years
- WON Kentucky Derby, Wood Memorial Stakes
- 2ND Preakness Stakes

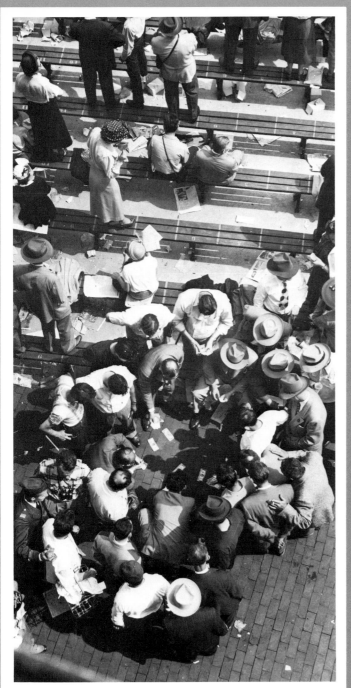

Not all the action was on the track in 1945. The track didn't get a percentage on the bets from this crap game either.

The Women's Ambulance and Defense Corps helped during the 1945 Derby. This group posed while receiving instructions.

May 4, 1946

Owner — Robert Kleberg

Trainer — Max Hirsch

Jockey — Warren Mehrtens

ASSAULT

$100,000 added and $5,000 Gold Cup. Net to winner $96,400; second $10,000; third $5,000; fourth $2,500. Trainer awards: First $3,000; second $2,000; third $1,000. Breeder awards: First $2,000; second $1,000; third $500. 149 nominations.

Horses	Eqt Wt	PP	St	½	¾	1	Str	Fin	Jockeys	Owners	Odds $1 Str't
Assault	wb 126	2	3	5½	4hd	3½	12½	18	Mehrtens	King Ranch	8.20
Spy Song	w 126	6	2	12	1½	1½	22	2hd	Longden	Dixiana	7.80
Hampden	wb 126	17	14	61	5hd	42½	52	31	Jessop	Foxcatcher Farm	5.80
Lord Boswell	w 126	3	1	9½	7½	91½	3½	41½	Arcaro	Maine Chance Farm	‡1.10
Knockdown	w 126	11	4	2½	2½	21½	4½	54	Permane	Maine Chance Farm	‡1.10
Alamond	wb 126	7	8	11½	8½	112	61	61	Kirkland	A. C. Ernst	65.30
Bob Murphy	wb 126	13	16	13½	11½	62	7½	7½	Bodiou	D. Ferguson	†31.80
Pellicle	wb 126	8	11	122	9½	8hd	8hd	8½	Hettinger	H. P. Headley	16.10
Perfect Bahram	w 126	5	12	153	132	10½	11½	9½	Atkinson	Maine Chance Farm	‡1.10
Rippey	w 126	14	7	4hd	61	5hd	91	101	Zufelt	W. Helis	10.20
Jobar	wb 126	16	17	17	17	164	164	111½	Layton	H. W. Fielding	†31.80
Dark Jungle	wb 126	12	6	31½	3hd	7½	10½	122	LoTurco	Lucas B. Combs	60.70
Alworth	wb 126	4	10	101	121	13hd	133	13½	Scurlock	Mrs. R. D. Patterson	†31.80
With Pleasure	wb 126	10	9	7½	101	142	142	141½	Wahler	Brolite Farm	48.30
Marine Victory	wb 126	15	15	141	143	153	15½	151	Padgett	Bobanet Stable	45.00
Wee Admiral	wb 126	9	5	81½	161	12½	122	163	Watson	R. S. McLaughlin	59.40
Kendor	wb 126	1	13	166	151	17	17	17	Johnson	Mrs. D. Hollingsworth	†31.80

Time: :23-2/5, :48, 1:14-1/5, 1:40-4/5, 2:06-3/5. Track slow.

‡Coupled, Lord Boswell, Knockdown and Perfect Bahram. †Mutuel field.

$2 Mutuels Paid—Assault, $18.40 straight, $9.60 place, $6.80 show; Spy Song, $9.00 place, $6.60 show; Hampden, $5.20 show.

Winner—Ch.c. by Bold Venture—Igual, by Equipoise, trained by M. Hirsch; bred in Texas by King Ranch.

Start good from stall gate. Won driving; second and third the same. ASSAULT, forwardly placed and saving ground from the beginning, came through on the inside entering the stretch, quickly disposed of SPY SONG and drew out to win with little left. SPY SONG assumed command early, made the pace until reaching the stretch, then gave way to the winner, but continued resolutely to hold HAMPDEN.

THE WINNER'S PEDIGREE AND CAREER HIGHLIGHTS

ASSAULT (Chestnut Colt)	Bold Venture	*St. Germans	Swynford
			Hamoaze
		Possible	Ultimus
			Lida Flush
	Igual	Equipoise	Pennant
			Swinging
		Incandescent	*Chicle
			Masda

Year	Age	Sts	1st	2nd	3rd	Won
1945	2	9	2	2	1	$ 17,250
1946	3	15	8	2	3	424,195
1947	4	7	5	1	1	181,925
1948	5	2	1	0	0	3,250
1949	6	6	1	1	3	45,900
1950	7	1	1	0	0	2,200
Totals		40	18	6	8	$674,720

At 2 Years	WON	Flash Stakes
At 3 Years	WON	Kentucky Derby, Experimental Free Handicap, Wood Memorial Stakes, Preakness Stakes, Belmont Stakes, Dwyer Stakes, Pimlico Special, Westchester Handicap
At 4 Years	WON	Grey Lag Handicap, Dixie Handicap, Suburban Handicap, Brooklyn Handicap, Butler Handicap
At 6 Years	WON	Brooklyn Handicap

Margaret Truman arrived on a train for the 1946 Derby. Alighting with her are Fred Vinson, then Secretary of the Treasury. Mrs. Vinson is in front.

Heavyweight boxing great Gene Tunney is flanked by Brigadier Generals "Rosie" O'Donnell, left, and Joseph O'Hare. He really didn't need any protection.

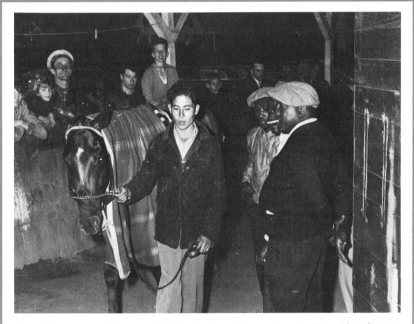

Assault gets a walk around the shedrow to cool out after his victory.

KING RANCH
Kingsville, Texas

King Ranch Kentucky · Old Frankfort Pike Lexington, Kentucky

May 3, 1947

Owner — Mrs. Elizabeth Graham

Trainer — Tom Smith

Jockey — Eric Guerin

JET PILOT

$100,460 added and $5,000 Gold Cup. Net to winner $92,160; second $10,000; third $5,000; fourth $2,500. Trainer awards: First $3,000; second $2,000; third $1,000. Breeder awards: First $2,000; second $1,000; third $500. 135 nominations.

Horses	Eqt Wt	PP	St	½	¾	1	Str	Fin	Jockeys	Owners	Odds $1 Str't
Jet Pilot	w 126	13	1	1 1½	1 1	1 1½	1 1½	1 h	Guerin	Maine Chance Farm	5.40
Phalanx	wb 126	8	13	13	10²	5 1½	5 ½	2 h	Arcaro	C. V. Whitney	2.00
Faultless	w 126	3	2	6 2½	6 1½	4 ½	3 h	3 1	Dodson	Calumet Farm	6.30
On Trust	wb 126	9	5	2 h	2 1	3 1	2 h	4 2¼	Longden	E. O. Stice & Sons	6.70
Cosmic Bomb	wb 126	1	4	3 ½	3 1½	6 2½	6 ½	5 2	Clark	William Helis	31.90
Star Reward	w 126	5	3	5 1	4 h	2 h	4 1	6 1	Brooks	Dixiana	11.20
Bullet Proof	w 126	4	6	9 h	7 1½	7 3	7 5	7 5	Wright	Mrs. M. E. Whitney	13.10
W L Sickle	wb 126	7	11	8 2	8 1½	8 h	8 ½	8 h	Campbell	W-L Ranch	‡16.50
Stepfather	wb 126	6	9	12 1	9 1	9 3	9 2	9 6	Westrope	W-L Ranch	‡16.50
Liberty Road	wb 126	12	10	10 1	11 1	11 5	10 1	10 ½	Jessop	Brookmeade Stable	45.20
Riskolater	wb 126	10	12	11 1	12 1½	10 5	11 6	11 6	Balz'etti	Circle M Farm	15.00
Double Jay	wb 126	2	7	4 3	5 1½	12 6	12 6	12 15	Gilbert	Ridgewood Stable	47.30
Jett-Jett	w 126	11	8	7 h	13	13	13	13	Hanka	W. M. Peavey	†99.40

Time: :24, :49, 1:14-2/5, 1:40-2/5, 2:06-4/5. Track slow.

‡Coupled, W. L. Sickle and Stepfather. †Mutuel field.

$2 Mutuels Paid—Jet Pilot, $12.80 straight, $5.20 place, $4.00 show; Phalanx, $4.00 place, $3.00 show; Faultless, $4.60 show.

Winner—Ch.c. by *Blenheim II—Black Wave, by *Sir Gallahad III, trained by Tom Smith; bred in Kentucky by A. B. Hancock & Mrs. R. A. Van Clief.

Start good from stall gate. Won driving; second and third the same. JET PILOT, alertly handled, assumed command at once, made the pace to the stretch under good rating and, responding readily when hard ridden in the drive, lasted to withstand PHALANX. The latter, away very sluggishly and outrun during the first half mile, worked his way forward steadily thereafter and, taken out for the stretch run, finished fast and was getting to the winner at the end. FAULTLESS, never far back and steadied along to the stretch, responded readily when set down in the drive, then closed strongly in a sharp effort. ON TRUST, forwardly placed from the beginning and in a good effort, failed to rally when roused for the drive and faltered near the finish. COSMIC BOMB a sharp factor early, engaged JET PILOT for five furlongs, then weakened. STAR REWARD made a good bid approaching the stretch, then gave way. BULLET PROOF went evenly and had no mishap. W L SICKLE was never prominent. STEPFATHER, away slowly, was never a serious factor.

THE WINNER'S PEDIGREE AND CAREER HIGHLIGHTS

JET PILOT (Chestnut Colt)
- *Blenheim II
  - Blandford
    - Swynford
    - Blanche
  - Malva
    - Charles O'Malley
    - Wild Arum
- Black Wave
  - *Sir Gallahad III
    - *Teddy
    - Plucky Liege
  - Black Curl
    - Friar Rock
    - *Frizeur

Year	Age	Sts	1st	2nd	3rd	Won
1946	2	12	5	3	2	$ 87,830
1947	3	5	2	0	0	110,910
Totals		17	7	3	2	$198,740

At 2 Years
- WON Pimlico Nursery Stakes, National Stallion Stakes, Tremont Stakes, Pimlico Futurity
- 2ND Arlington Futurity, Commonwealth Stakes
- 3RD Futurity Stakes, Champaigne Stakes

At 3 Years
- WON Kentucky Derby, Jamaica Handicap

Twins? No, that is motion picture star Guy Kibbee at the left and Kentucky Derby impressario Matt Winn. They were look-alikes, as this picture proves. It was taken in Winn's office at Churchill Downs.

Dan Carter has been selling tip sheets at Churchill Downs for more than a quarter of a century.

Bill Corum (center) was a writer with the New York Journal American when this picture was taken. He later became president of Churchill Downs. At the left is Jimmy Cannon of the New York Post and at the right is Blondie Patton.

May 1, 1948

Owner — Warren Wright

Trainer — B. A. Jones

Jockey — Eddie Arcaro

CITATION

$100,000 added and $5,000 Gold Cup. Net to winner $83,400; second $10,000; third $5,000; fourth $2,500. Trainer awards: First $3,000; second $2,000; third $1,000. Breeder awards: First $2,000; second $1,000; third $500. 109 nominations.

Horses	Eqt Wt	PP	St	½	¾	1	Str	Fin	Jockeys	Owners	Odds $1 Str't
Citation	w 126	1	2	2ʰ	2³	2⁵	1²	1³½	Arcaro	Calumet Farm	a-.40
Coaltown	wb 126	2	1	1⁶	1³½	1½	2⁴	2³	Pierson	Calumet Farm	a-.40
My Request	w 126	6	3	4ʰ	4³	3½	3¹	3½	Dodson	B. F. Whitaker	3.80
Billings	w 126	5	6	5½	3½	4⁸	4¹⁵	4²⁰	Peterson	Walmac Stable	14.70
Grandpere	w 126	4	4	3²	6	6	5½	5ⁿᵏ	Gilbert	Mrs. J. P. Adams	17.80
Escadru	wb 126	3	5	6	5⁶	5¹½	6	6	Kirkland	W. L. Brann	7.10

Time: :23-2/5, :46-3/5, 1:11-2/5, 1:38, 2:05-2/5. Track sloppy.

a-Citation and Coaltown coupled as Calumet Farm entry.

$2 Mutuels Paid—Calumet Farm entry (Citation and Coaltown), $2.80 straight. No place or show betting.

Winner—B.c. by Bull Lea—*Hydroplane II, by Hyperion, trained by B. A. Jones; bred in Kentucky by Calumet Farm.

Start good from stall gate. Won handily; second and third driving. CITATION, away forwardly, and losing ground while racing back of COALTOWN to the stretch, responded readily to a steady hand ride after disposing of the latter and drew clear. COALTOWN began fast, established a clear lead before going a quarter and, making the pace on the inside in the stretch, continued willingly, but was not good enough for CITATION, although easily the best of the others. MY REQUEST, bothered slightly after the start, was in hand while improving his position to the stretch, then failed to rally when set down for the drive. BILLINGS suffered interference after the break when GRANDPERE bore to the outside, was in close quarters on the first turn when caught between ESCADRU and CITATION, then could not better his position when clear. GRANDPERE broke into BILLINGS at the start, displayed speed for a half mile, then gave way.

THE WINNER'S PEDIGREE AND CAREER HIGHLIGHTS

CITATION (Bay Colt)	Bull Lea	*Bull Dog	*Teddy / Plucky Liege
		Rose Leaves	Ballot / *Colonial
	*Hydroplane II	Hyperion	Gainsborough / Selene
		Toboggan	Hurry On / Glacier

Year	Age	Sts	1st	2nd	3rd	Won
1947	2	9	8	1	0	$ 155,680
1948	3	20	19	1	0	709,470
1950	5	9	2	7	0	73,480
1951	6	7	3	1	2	147,130
	Totals	45	32	10	2	$1,085,760

At 2 Years	WON	Elementary Stakes, Futurity Stakes, Pimlico Futurity
	2ND	Washington Park Futurity
At 3 Years	WON	Kentucky Derby, Derby Trial, Seminole Handicap, Everglades Handicap, Flamingo Stakes, Chesapeake Stakes, Preakness Stakes, Jersey Stakes, Belmont Stakes, Stars and Stripes Handicap, American Derby, Sysonby Mile, Jockey Club Gold Cup, Pimlico Special, Tanforan Handicap
	2ND	Chesapeake Trial Stakes
At 5 Years	WON	Golden Gate Mile Handicap
	2ND	San Antonio Handicap, Santa Anita Handicap, San Juan Capistrano Handicap, Forty Niners Handicap, Golden Gate Handicap
At 6 Years	WON	American Handicap, Hollywood Gold Cup
	2ND	Argonaut Handicap

Ben Jones was not as good a mudder as Citation and got a "lift" across the sloppy track from assistant starter Tex Johnson.

Warren Wright, the baking powder magnate who started the Calumet dynasty, accepts the Derby trophy from Col. Matt Winn. Watching is Kentucky Sen. Earle Clements (left).

This trio became almost legendary in establishing the Calumet Farm domination of the Derby: at the left is Jimmy Jones, Eddie Arcaro is up on Citation, and Ben Jones leads his winner to get his roses.

Calumet Farm

OWNER AND BREEDER OF EIGHT KENTUCKY DERBY WINNERS

WHIRLAWAY	PENSIVE	CITATION	PONDER
1941	1944	1948	1949

HILL GAIL	IRON LIEGE	TIM TAM	FORWARD PASS
1952	1957	1958	1968

Mrs. Gene Markey   •   Versailles Pike   •   Lexington, Kentucky

May 7, 1949

Owner — Warren Wright

Trainer — B. A. Jones

Jockey — Steve Brooks

PONDER

$100,000 added and $10,000 Gold Cup. Net to winner $91,600; second $10,000; third $5,000; fourth $2,500. Trainer awards: First $3,000; second $2,000; third $1,000. Breeder awards: First $2,000; second $1,000; third $500. 113 nominations.

Horses	Eqt Wt	PP	St	1/2	3/4	1	Str	Fin	Jockeys	Owners	Odds $1 Str't
Ponder	w 126	2	14	14	12^2	6^1	3^1	1^3	Brooks	Calumet Farm	16.00
Capot	wb 126	9	5	2^2	2^1	2^1	1^3	$2^{4\frac{1}{2}}$	Atkinson	Greentree Stable	a13.10
Palestinian	wb 126	13	9	7^1	3^h	3^2	$2\frac{1}{2}$	3^2	W'dhouse	I. Bieber	8.30
Old Rockport	wb 126	15	13	9^1	6^1	4^3	5^5	$4^{4\frac{1}{2}}$	Glisson	C. Mooers	4.90
Halt	wb 126	10	12	11^h	13^{10}	9^3	7^2	5^1	McCreary	Woodvale Farm	14.20
Olympia	w 126	4	1	$11\frac{1}{2}$	1^1	1^1	$4\frac{1}{2}$	$6^{4\frac{1}{2}}$	Arcaro	F. W. Hooper	.80
Model Cadet	w 126	16	8	8^2	$4\frac{1}{2}$	$5^{2\frac{1}{2}}$	$6\frac{1}{2}$	$7\frac{1}{2}$	Scurlock	Mrs. A. L. Rice	66.00
Duplicator	wb 126	14	11	12^3	10^1	$8\frac{1}{2}$	8^4	8^5	James	Mr. & Mrs. J. H. Seley	146.30
Johns Joy	wb 126	7	3	$5^{1\frac{1}{2}}$	5^1	7^h	9^6	9^7	Adams	J. A. Kinard, Jr.	15.50
Ky. Colonel	wb 126	3	4	10^2	11^h	12^1	10^8	10^{nk}	Peterson	J. A. Goodwin	41.60
Lextown	wb 126	11	6	3^h	9^1	$11\frac{1}{2}$	11^1	$11^{1\frac{3}{4}}$	Richard	Lexbrook Stable	f97.30
Jacks Town	wb 126	1	2	$6\frac{1}{2}$	8^h	10^2	12^4	12^5	Taylor	Afton Villa Farm	90.20
Wine List	wb 126	12	7	$4\frac{1}{2}$	7^1	13^8	13	13	Dodson	Greentree Stable	a13.10
Senecas Coin	wb 126	8	10	13^1	14	14	Pulled Up		Duff	Mrs. A. Roth	f97.30

Time: :22-2/5, :46-2/5, 1:12-3/5, 1:38-3/5, 2:04-1/5. Track fast.

f—Mutuel field. a—Capot and Wine List coupled as Greentree Stable entry.

$2 Mutuels Paid—Ponder, $34 straight, $11.60 place, $6.20 show; Greentree entry, $9.60 place, $5.80 show; Palestinian, $4.80 show.

Winner—Dk.b.c. by Pensive—Miss Rushin, by *Blenheim II, trained by B. A. Jones; bred in Kentucky by Calumet Farm.

Start good from stall gate. Won driving; second and third the same. PONDER, away slowly, gradually worked his way forward while racing on the extreme outside, responded to brisk urging entering the stretch and, after wearing down the leaders, won, but had little left. CAPOT, forwardly placed from the start, went to the front when settled in the stretch, held on willingly, but was unable to withstand PONDER, although easily best of the others. PALESTINIAN, well ridden, saved ground to the stretch, then made a bold bid when set down in the drive, but faltered during the last sixteenth. OLD ROCKPORT, on the inside and never far back, could not get to the leaders when hard ridden through the stretch.

THE WINNER'S PEDIGREE AND CAREER HIGHLIGHTS

PONDER
(Dark Bay Colt)
{ Pensive { Hyperion { Gainsborough / Selene
{ { *Penicuik II { Buchan / Pennycomequick
{ Miss Rushin { *Blenheim II { Blandford / Malva
{ { Lady Erne { *Sir Gallahad III / *Erne

Year	Age	Sts	1st	2nd	3rd	Won
1948	2	4	0	1	0	$ 400
1949	3	21	9	5	2	321,825
1950	4	14	5	1	2	218,850
1951	5	1	0	0	0	—
Totals		40	14	7	4	$541,275

At 3 Years	WON	Kentucky Derby, Peter Pan Handicap, Arlington Classic, American Derby, Lawrence Realization, Jockey Club Gold Cup
	2ND	Derby Trial, Belmont Stakes, Whirlaway Stakes
At 4 Years	WON	Santa Anita Maturity, San Antonio Handicap, Marchbank Handicap, Tanforan Handicap, Arlington Handicap
	2ND	Thanksgiving Handicap

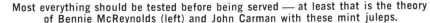

Most everything should be tested before being served — at least that is the theory of Bennie McReynolds (left) and John Carman with these mint juleps.

This two-man clean-up crew browsed through the debris from the 1949 Derby to search for mutuel tickets which might have been discarded through error. The boys are Charles Wise and David Kiesler.

Calumet Farm

OWNER AND BREEDER OF EIGHT KENTUCKY DERBY WINNERS

| WHIRLAWAY 1941 | PENSIVE 1944 | CITATION 1948 | PONDER 1949 |

| HILL GAIL 1952 | IRON LIEGE 1957 | TIM TAM 1958 | FORWARD PASS 1968 |

Mrs. Gene Markey • Versailles Pike • Lexington, Kentucky

May 6, 1950

Owner — Robert J. Kleberg

Trainer — Max Hirsch

Jockey — Bill Boland

MIDDLEGROUND

$100,000 added and $5,000 Gold Cup. Net to winner $92,650; second $10,000; third $5,000; fourth $2,500. Trainer awards: First $3,000; second $2,000; third $1,000. Breeder awards: First $2,000; second $1,000; third $500. 134 nominations.

Horses	Eqt Wt	PP	St	½	¾	1	Str	Fin	Jockeys	Owners	Odds $1 Str't
Middleground	w 126	14	7	5½	3½	2¹	1½	1¹¼	Boland	King Ranch	a-7.90
Hill Prince	wb 126	5	9	8½	6½	5²	3¹½	2½	Arcaro	C. T. Chenery	2.50
Mr. Trouble	wb 126	2	5	3¹	1½	3hd	2¹	3²¾	Dodson	C. V. Whitney	b-6.20
Sunglow	wb 126	8	3	9½	8½	7½	4½	4⁵	Robertson	Brookmeade	27.20
Oil Capitol (dh)	wb 126	6	1	6³	5¹	4¹	6¹	5	Church	T. Gray	8.70
Hawley (dh)	wb 126	13	6	4hd	4hd	9¹	7hd	5¾	Glisson	C. Mooers	82.80
Lotowhite	wb 126	9	4	11³	9¹	10¹	9²	7½	Scurlock	H. P. Headley	37.20
On The Mark	wb 126	11	12	10½	10⁵	8½	8½	8½	Guerin	King Ranch	a-7.90
Your Host	w 126	1	2	1²	2¹½	1½	5½	9⁴	Longden	W. M. Goetz	1.60
Hallieboy	w 126	7	13	12¹	13½	13¹	13¹	10½	Atkins	W. T. Fugate	69.20
Dooly	w 126	3	8	14	12²	12½	11hd	11no	Brooks	C. V. Whitney	b-6.20
Trumpet King	wb 126	4	10	7hd	11½	11hd	10½	12²	Woodhouse	Willorene Farm	106.40
Stranded	wb 126	10	14	13½	14	14	12¹	13¹½	Baird	Am'crombie & Smith	120.90
Black George	wb 126	12	11	2³	7½	6¹	14	14	Nelson	W. H. Veeneman	27.00

Time: :22-4/5, :46-3/5, 1:11-2/5, 1:36-4/5, 2:01-3/5. Track fast.

(dh) Old Capitol and Hawley deadheated for fifth. a—coupled Middleground and On the Mark. b—coupled Mr. Trouble and Dooly.

$2 mutuels paid—Middleground (coupled with On The Mark) $17.80 straight; $5.40 place; $3.80 show. Hill Prince $3.80 place, $3.20 show. Mr. Trouble (coupled with Dooly) $3.60 show.

Winner—Ch.c. by Bold Venture-Verguenza, by Chicaro, trained by Max Hirsch; bred in Texas by King Ranch.

Start good from stall gate. Won driving; second and third the same. MIDDLEGROUND, never far back and saving ground under a steady ride, moved up boldly at the stretch turn and, after taking command, held HILL PRINCE safe. The latter, on the inside from the start, was in close quarters at the upper turn, continued willingly when clear and, after suffering some intereference from the tiring YOUR HOST, closed resolutely, but could not overtake MIDDLEGROUND. MR. TROUBLE, a sharp factor from the start, was much used engaging YOUR HOST until inside the stretch, then failed to rally when set down in the drive. SUNGLOW began fast, dropped back after the start, then recovered and moved up steadily, but could not better his position when hard ridden during the final furlong. OIL CAPITOL began fast, raced well after the break and made a good bid nearing the stretch, then tired, but deadheated with HAWLEY for fifth. HAWLEY tired after showing early speed, but finished on equal terms with OIL CAPITOL.

THE WINNER'S PEDIGREE AND CAREER HIGHLIGHTS

MIDDLEGROUND (Chestnut Colt)			
	Bold Venture	*St. Germains	Swynford / Hamoaze
		Possible	Ultimus / Lida Flush
	Verguenza	Chicaro	*Chicle / Wendy
		Blushing Sister	Bubbling Over / Lace

Year	Age	Sts	1st	2nd	3rd	Won
1949	2	5	4	0	1	$ 54,225
1950	3	10	2	6	1	181,250
Totals		15	6	6	2	235,475

At 2 Years
- WON Hopeful Stakes
- 3RD Arlington Futurity

At 3 Years
- WON Kentucky Derby, Belmont Stakes
- 2ND Derby Trial, Wood Memorial, Withers Stakes, Preakness Stakes
- 3RD Leonard Richards Stakes

Adlai Stevenson, then governor of Illinois, sat with Basil Brooke, president of Northern Ireland, and Mrs. Brooke at the 1950 Derby.

Bob Hope gets a close-up of Kentucky senator Earle Clements while they waited on the presentation stand.

Bill Corum became Churchill Downs' president in 1950.

May 5, 1951

Owner — J. J. Amiel

Trainer — Sol Rutchick

Jockey — Conn McCreary

SEVENTY SEVENTH RUNNING

COUNT TURF

$100,000 added and $5,000 Gold Cup. Net to winner $98,050; second $10,000; third $5,000; fourth $2,500. Trainer awards: First $3,000; second $2,000; third $1,000. Breeder awards: First $2,000; second $1,000; third $500. 122 nominations.

Horses	Eqt	Wt	PP	St	½	¾	1	Str	Fin	Jockeys	Owners	Odds to $1
Count Turf	wb	126	9	18	11^{3}	$6^{1\frac{1}{2}}$	4^{1}	$1^{2\frac{1}{2}}$	1^{4}	McCreary	J. J. Amiel	f-14.60
Royal Mustang	wb	126	16	4	4^{1}	$4\frac{1}{2}$	$6\frac{1}{2}$	5^{2}	2^{h}	Bailey	S. E. Wilson, Jr.	a-53.00
Ruhe	wb	126	10	12	7^{h}	$10\frac{1}{2}$	7^{h}	$6^{1\frac{1}{2}}$	$3^{2\frac{1}{2}}$	Jessop	Mrs. E. Denemark	10.80
Phil D	w	126	18	5	1^{h}	$1\frac{1}{2}$	2^{1}	$3\frac{1}{2}$	4^{h}	York	W. C. Martin	f-14.60
Fanfare	w	126	5	1	$5\frac{1}{2}$	$7\frac{1}{2}$	5^{2}	$4\frac{1}{2}$	$5\frac{3}{4}$	Brooks	Calumet Farm	6.30
Battle Morn	wb	126	11	14	18^{1}	15^{h}	$10\frac{1}{2}$	10^{2}	$6^{1\frac{1}{2}}$	Arcaro	Cain Hoy Stable	2.80
Anyoldtime	w	126	1	2	10^{h}	9^{2}	$9\frac{1}{2}$	$8\frac{1}{2}$	7^{nk}	Baird	W. M. Peavey	b-68.90
Pur Sang	w	126	20	8	$12\frac{1}{2}$	$11^{1\frac{1}{2}}$	$11^{1\frac{1}{2}}$	$9\frac{1}{2}$	$8^{1\frac{1}{2}}$	Adams	Springbrook Farm	f-14.60
Hall of Fame	wb	126	17	6	2^{2}	$2^{1\frac{1}{2}}$	3^{1}	7^{3}	$9\frac{1}{2}$	Atkinson	Greentree Stable	c-8.70
Timely Reward	w	126	3	11	$14\frac{1}{2}$	14^{h}	15^{1}	$13^{1\frac{1}{2}}$	10^{1}	Stout	Mrs. W. Gilroy	8.60
Counterpoint	w	126	2	7	8^{h}	5^{h}	12^{1}	$11\frac{1}{2}$	11^{2}	Gorman	C. V. Whitney	d-5.90
Repetoire	wb	126	19	20	$3^{2\frac{1}{2}}$	3^{h}	1^{1}	2^{1}	12^{nk}	McLean	Mr. & Mrs. S. C. Mikell	8.40
King Clover	wb	126	12	9	$9\frac{1}{2}$	8^{1}	8^{3}	14^{2}	$13\frac{1}{2}$	Bone	C. C. Boshamer	f-14.60
Sonic	w	126	6	3	$6\frac{1}{2}$	$12\frac{1}{2}$	$14\frac{1}{2}$	$15\frac{1}{2}$	$14\frac{1}{2}$	Boland	King Ranch	8.30
Sir Bee Bum	w	126	13	15	17^{6}	18^{4}	17^{2}	16^{3}	15^{n}	Madden	W. M. Peavey	b-68.90
Snuzzle	w	126	14	17	15^{h}	17^{2}	13^{2}	17^{3}	16^{4}	Porch	Brown Hotel Stable	120.70
Fighting Back	wb	126	8	10	13^{1}	$13\frac{1}{2}$	16^{1}	12^{h}	$17^{2\frac{1}{2}}$	Johnson	Murlogg Farm	f-14.90
Big Stretch	wb	126	15	19	$16\frac{1}{2}$	16^{h}	18^{5}	18^{15}	18^{10}	Dodson	Greentree Stable	c-8.70
Golden Birch	wb	126	4	13	19^{3}	19^{10}	19^{4}	19^{5}	19^{5}	Swain	S. E. Wilson, Jr.	a-53.00
Mameluke	wb	126	7	16	20	20	20	20	20	Adair	C. V. Whitney	d-5.90

Time: :23-2/5, :47-2/5, 1:12-2/5, 1:37, 2:02-3/5. Track fast.

f—Mutuel field. a—Coupled, Royal Mustang and Golden Birch; b—Anyoldtime and Sir Bee Bum; c—Hall of Fame and Big Stretch; d—Counterpoint and Mameluke.

$2 mutuels paid—Count Turf (Field), $31.20 straight, $14.00 place, $6.60 show; Royal Mustang (a-Entry), $53.00 place, $24.80 show; Ruhe, $7.80 show.

Winner—B.c., by Count Fleet—Delmarie, by Pompey, trained by Sol Rutchick; bred in Kentucky by Dr. and Mrs. F. P. Miller.

Start good from stall gate. Won driving; second and third the same. COUNT TURF, away well and kept in a forward position from the beginning, raced by REPETOIRE entering the stretch, responded to brisk urging and won going away. ROYAL MUSTANG, never far back, saved ground until the stretch, was forced a bit wide on the turn, then came again under strong handling, but could not get to the winner. RUHE lacked early speed, but steadily improved position after the opening half, was sent around horses entering the stretch and could not overtake ROYAL MUSTANG.

THE WINNER'S PEDIGREE AND CAREER HIGHLIGHTS

COUNT TURF (Bay Colt)	Count Fleet	Reigh Count	*Sunreigh
			*Contessina
		Quickly	Haste
			Stephanie
	Delmarie	Pompey	*Sun Briar
			Cleopatra
		Charming Note	*Polymelian
			*Alburn

Year	Age	Sts	1st	2nd	3rd	Won
1950	2	10	3	2	1	$ 22,200
1951	3	14	3	0	2	107,350
1952	4	10	1	1	0	6,300
1953	5	11	1	1	3	30,525
Totals		45	8	4	6	$164,375

At 2 Years **WON** **Dover Stakes**
At 3 Years **WON** **Kentucky Derby**
At 5 Years **WON** **Questionnaire Handicap**

Screen star Ann Sheridan also attended in 1951. She sat with public relations impressario Steve Hannagan.

Buddy Fogelson and Greer Garson watched Count Turf win. The Fogelsons now are avid horse owners and had Ack Ack, Horse of the Year in 1971.

The Duke and Duchess of Windsor, guests at the 1951 Derby, are escorted to their seats by an Andy Frain usher.

May 3, 1952

Owner — Mrs. Warren Wright

Trainer — B. A. Jones

Jockey — Eddie Arcaro

HILL GAIL

$100,000 added and $10,000 Gold Cup. Net to winner $96,300; second $10,000; third $5,000; fourth $2,500. Trainer awards: First $3,000; second $2,000; third $1,000. Breeder awards: First $2,000; second $1,000; third $500. 167 nominations.

Horses	Eqt Wt	PP	St	$\frac{1}{2}$	$\frac{3}{4}$	1	Str	Fin	Jockeys	Owners	Odds to $1
Hill Gail	w 126	1	1	$2\frac{1}{2}$	$1\frac{1}{2}$	1^5	1^3	1^2	Arcaro	Calumet Farm	1.10
Sub Fleet	w 126	9	8	$6\frac{1}{2}$	$5\frac{1}{2}$	$3\frac{1}{2}$	2^6	$2^{8\frac{3}{4}}$	Brooks	Dixiana	22.90
Blue Man	w 126	14	16	13^2	$12\frac{1}{2}$	6^1	6^2	$3\frac{1}{2}$	McCreary	White Oak Stable	4.40
Master Fiddle	wb 126	13	14	$10\frac{1}{2}$	$9\frac{1}{2}$	5^2	$4\frac{1}{2}$	$4^{1\frac{1}{4}}$	Gorman	Myhelyn Stable	a-9.30
Count Flame	wb 126	4	10	14^4	14^3	13^1	8^3	$5\frac{1}{2}$	Shoemaker	J. J. Amiel	a-9.30
Arroz	w 126	16	13	11^h	10^h	10^2	7^3	$6^{1\frac{1}{4}}$	York	Mrs. G. Guiberson	31.70
Happy Go Lucky	wb 126	12	7	$3\frac{1}{2}$	3^h	4^2	3^h	$7^{2\frac{1}{2}}$	Ferrai'olo	H. G. Bockman	54.60
Hannibal	wb 126	15	3	1^2	2^3	$2\frac{1}{2}$	$5\frac{1}{2}$	8^3	P'more	B. Sharp	76.80
Cold Command	w 126	11	6	15^2	16	11^2	$11\frac{1}{2}$	$9\frac{3}{4}$	Porch	C. V. Whitney	8.50
Smoke Screen	w 126	10	15	16	15^1	12^2	12^4	10^{nk}	Adams	Reverie Knoll	103.70
Gushing Oil	w 126	7	11	$12\frac{1}{2}$	13^2	$8\frac{1}{2}$	$9\frac{1}{2}$	11^{nk}	Atkinson	S. E. Wilson, Jr.	6.70
Pintor	w 126	6	9	$8\frac{1}{2}$	7^2	7^1	10^1	$12^{4\frac{1}{4}}$	Mora	Montpelier Stable	42.50
Shag Tails	wb 126	5	4	4^3	4^2	$9\frac{1}{2}$	13^3	13^2	Nazareth	M. Shagrin	f-18.80
Eternal Moon	wb 126	8	12	9^6	$11\frac{1}{2}$	14^5	14^3	$14^{1\frac{1}{2}}$	Layton	Emerald Hill	f-18.80
Brown Rambler	wb 126	3	2	5^2	6^3	16	15^{10}	15^{18}	Dodson	Mildred F. Underwood	f-18.80
Swoop	w 126	2	5	7^2	$8\frac{1}{2}$	15^2	16	16	Church	High Tide Stable	f-18.80

Time: :23-3/5, :46-4/5, 1:11, 1:35-2/5, 2:01-3/5. Track fast.

f—Mutuel field. a—Coupled, Master Fiddle and Count Flame.

$2 Mutuels Paid—Hill Gail, $4.20 straight, $4.00 place, $3.20 show; Sub Fleet, $14.60 place, $7.80 show; Blue Man, $3.60 show.

Winner—Dk.b.c. by Bull Lea—Jane Gail, by *Blenheim II, trained by B. A. Jones; bred in Kentucky by Calumet.

Start good from stall gate. Won ridden out; second and third driving. HILL GAIL swerved to the outside after the break, crowding SWOOP and BROWN RAMBLER, raced nearest HANNIBAL for five-eighths of a mile, then assumed command and entered the stretch with a clear lead, but was ridden out to withstand SUB FLEET. The latter, on the outside until settled along the backstretch, steadily worked his way forward hereafter, finished willingly under punishment, but could not reach the winner. BLUE MAN, away slowly and on the outside throughout, made up ground steadily, but could not reach the leaders, giving a game effort. MASTER FIDDLE lacked early speed and was in tight quarters approaching the three-quarters mile marker, raced well when clear, but was unable to seriously threaten the top ones. COUNT FLAME lacked early foot, but closed determinedly. ARROZ had a rough trip. HAPPY GO LUCKY was through after the mile. HANNIBAL gave way after racing prominently to the stretch. COLD COMMAND, roughed soon after the start, failed to recover.

THE WINNER'S PEDIGREE AND CAREER HIGHLIGHTS

HILL GAIL
(Dark Bay Colt)

Bull Lea
— *Bull Dog
  — *Teddy
  — Plucky Liege
— Rose Leaves
  — Ballot
  — *Colonial

Jane Gail
— *Blenheim II
  — Blandford
  — Malva
— Lady Higloss
  — Ladkin
  — Hi Gloss

Year	Age	Sts	1st	2nd	3rd	Won
1951	2	7	4	1	0	$ 79,790
1952	3	8	5	1	1	226,725
1953	4	8	2	1	1	21,710
1954	5	9	0	2	1	7,400
Totals		32	11	5	3	$335,625

At 2 Years — WON Arlington Futurity

At 3 Years — WON Kentucky Derby, Derby Trial, San Vicente Stakes, Santa Anita Derby, Phoenix Handicap

Hill Gail crosses the line a handy winner in 1952 and jockey Eddie Arcaro is interviewed afterward by WHAS' Phil Sutterfield. Listening (center) is Gov. Lawrence Wetherby.

Lyndon B. Johnson, then the U.S. Senate majority whip, visited in 1952. He later became the 36th President of the United States.

Calumet Farm

OWNER AND BREEDER OF EIGHT KENTUCKY DERBY WINNERS

WHIRLAWAY	PENSIVE	CITATION	PONDER
1941	1944	1948	1949

HILL GAIL	IRON LIEGE	TIM TAM	FORWARD PASS
1952	1957	1958	1968

Mrs. Gene Markey • Versailles Pike • Lexington, Kentucky

May 2, 1953

Owner — H. F. Guggenheim

Trainer — Eddie Hayward

Jockey — Hank Moreno

DARK STAR

$100,000 added and $5,000 Gold Cup. Net to winner $90,050; second $10,000; third $5,000; fourth $2,500. Trainer awards: First $3,000; second $2,000; third $1,000. Breeder awards: First $2,000; second $1,000; third $500. 137 nominations.

Horses	Eqt Wt	PP	St	½	¾	1	Str	Fin	Jockeys	Owners	Odds to $1
Dark Star	w 126	10	3	$1\frac{1}{2}$	$1\frac{1}{2}$	$1\frac{1}{2}$	$1\frac{1}{2}$	1^h	Moreno	Cain Hoy Stable	24.90
Native Dancer	w 126	6	6	8^3	$4\frac{1}{2}$	4^2	2^1	2^5	Guerin	A. G. Vanderbilt	a-.70
Invigorator	w 126	4	5	$7\frac{1}{2}$	$6\frac{1}{2}$	6^1	4^1	3^2	Shoemaker	Saxon Stable	40.90
Royal Bay Gem	w 126	11	11	11	8^2	$7\frac{1}{2}$	$7\frac{1}{2}$	$4\frac{1}{2}$	Combest	E. Constantin, Jr.	6.80
Correspondent	w 126	2	2	2^2	2^1	$2\frac{1}{2}$	3^1	$5\frac{3}{4}$	Arcaro	Mrs. G. Guiberson	3.00
Straight Face	wb 126	9	7	4^3	3^1	$3\frac{1}{2}$	5^h	6^{nk}	Atkinson	Greentree Stable	10.40
Social Outcast	w 126	8	10	$10\frac{1}{2}$	$10\frac{1}{2}$	8^2	8^2	7^2	Adams	A. G. Vanderbilt	a-.70
Money Broker	wb 126	7	9	$5\frac{1}{2}$	$5\frac{1}{2}$	5^h	6^3	$8^{2\frac{3}{4}}$	Popara	G. & G. Stable	45.80
Ram O' War	wb 126	3	8	$9\frac{1}{2}$	11	10^1	9^1	9^{nk}	Dodson	B. S. Campbell	85.10
Curragh King	wb 126	5	4	6^2	9^1	11	11	10^h	Erb	E. M. Goemans	99.10
Ace Destroyer	wb 126	1	1	$3\frac{1}{2}$	7^2	9^3	10^1	11	Jessop	Mr.-Mrs. T. M. Daniel	91.80

Time: :23-4/5, :47-4/5, 1:12-1/5, 1:36-3/5, 2:02. Track fast.

a—Coupled, Native Dancer and Social Outcast.

$2 Mutuels Paid—Dark Star, $51.80 straight, $13.60 place, $7.00 show; Native Dancer (a-entry), $3.20 place, $2.80 show; Invigorator, $9.40 show.

Winner—Br.c., by *Royal Gem II—Isolde, by *Bull Dog, trained by Eddie Hayward; bred in Kentucky by W. L. Jones.

Start good from stall gate. Won driving; second and third the same. DARK STAR, alertly ridden, took command soon after the start, set the pace to the stretch under steady rating, then responded readily when set down in the drive and lasted to withstand NATIVE DANCER, but won with little left. NATIVE DANCER, roughed at the first turn by MONEY BROKER, was eased back to secure racing room, raced wide during the run to the upper turn, then saved ground entering the stretch and finished strongly, but could not overtake the winner, although probably best. INVIGORATOR, in close quarters entering the backstretch, raced well when clear and closed willingly under urging, but could not threaten the top pair. ROYAL BAY GEM, away sluggishly, was forced to lose ground while working way forward and could not reach the leaders when set down through the stretch. CORRESPONDENT, bumped after the break by ACE DESTROYER, recovered under good handling and raced nearest DARK STAR to the stretch, but had nothing left for the drive. STRAIGHT FACE raced prominently to the mile, then weakened. SOCIAL OUTCAST lacked early speed and was never dangerous.

THE WINNER'S PEDIGREE AND CAREER HIGHLIGHTS

DARK STAR
(Brown Colt)
- *Royal Gem II
  - Dhoti
    - Dastur
    - Tricky Aunt
  - French Gem
    - Beau Fils
    - Fission
- Isolde
  - *Bull Dog
    - *Teddy
    - Plucky Liege
  - Fiji
    - Bostonian
    - O Girl

Year	Age	Sts	1st	2nd	3rd	Won
1952	2	6	3	0	2	$ 24,087
1953	3	7	3	2	0	107,250
Totals		13	6	2	2	$131,337

At 2 Years
- WON Hialeah Juvenile Stakes
- 3RD Belmont Juvenile Stakes, Belmont Futurity
- UNP Champagne Stakes

At 3 Years
- WON Kentucky Derby, Derby Trial Stakes
- UNP Preakness Stakes, Florida Derby

Dark Star seems intent on joining the champagne celebration as he is cooled out after his 1953 victory.

Charles Coburn, a movie star who achieved fame in several pictures about horse racing, relaxes with a mint julep as he studies his program at the 1953 Derby.

DARK STAR

The Only Horse To Defeat The Great Native Dancer

Warner L. Jones, Jr. is the only man to breed and sell a Kentucky Derby winner and a Kentucky Oaks winner. His Hermitage-breds have earned more than $13,000,000.

May 1, 1954

Owner — A. J. Crevolin

Trainer — Willie Molter

Jockey — Ray York

DETERMINE

$100,000 added and $5,000 Gold Cup. Net to winner $102,050; second $10,000; third $5,000; fourth $2,500. 137 nominations.

Horses	Eqt Wt	PP	St	½	¾	1	Str	Fin	Jockeys	Owners	Odds to $1
Determine	wb 126	7	5	3³	3½	2½	1½	1¹½	York	A. J. Crevolin	b-4.30
Hasty Road	wb 126	1	1	11½	1²	1²	2²½	2²½	Adams	Hasty House Farm	a-5.30
Hasseyampa	wb 126	12	12	12¹½	8³	5½	3ʰ	3²½	Kirkland	Walmac Farm	25.60
Goyamo	wb 126	5	16	16⁶	15¹	10¹½	6½	4ⁿᵏ	Arcaro	R. Martin-A. Jones	4.90
Admiral Porter	wb 126	8	3	4¹½	4¹½	4ʰ	4²	5¹	Bailey	Sunny Blue Farm	54.10
Correlation	wb 126	4	15	15¹½	16¹⁰	9¹	5¹	6³¼	Shoemaker	R. S. Lytle	3.00
Fisherman	w 126	16	7	6¹	6½	6½	7²	7²½	Woodhouse	C. V. Whitney	6.30
James Session	w 126	10	8	8ʰ	13½	13¹	13¹	8ⁿ	Risley	Mr.-Mrs. Harry James	71.10
Allied	wb 126	3	10	10¹	7ʰ	8½	9¹	9ʰ	Brooks	A. J. Crevolin	b-4.30
Gov. Browning	wb 126	2	14	14⁶	14²	11½	10½	10¹	Erb	Martin-McKinney	f-16.20
Super Devil	w 126	9	11	11½	9¹	12½	11ʰ	11ⁿᵏ	Baird	Rebel Stable	f-16.20
Red Hannigan	wb 126	13	13	13²	12²	14¹½	14³	12ⁿᵏ	Boland	Woodley Ln. Farm	f-16.20
Black Metal	wb 126	15	6	5½	5ʰ	7½	12ʰ	13²	DeSpirito	Maine Chance Farm	13.20
Timely Tip	w 126	14	2	2³	2³	3¹	8²	14²½	Craig	A. L. Birch	53.70
Sea O Erin	wb 126	6	4	7³	11½	15¹½	15½	15³	McCreary	Hasty House Farm	a-5.30
King Phalanx	w 126	11	17	17	17	16½	16½	16¹	Dodson	S. E. Wilson, Jr.	32.30
Mel Leavitt	wb 126	17	9	9¹	10²	17	17	17	McLaughlin	J. W. Brown	f-16.20

Time: :23-3/5, :47-3/5, 1:12, 1:37, 2:03. Track fast.

f—Mutuel field. b—Coupled, Determine and Allied; a—Hasty Road and Sea O Erin.

$2 Mutuels Paid—Determine (b-entry) $10.60 straight; $5.60 place; $4.80 show; Hasty Road (a-entry) $6.80 place, $5.60 show; Hasseyampa $12.00 show.

Winner—Gr.c., by *Alibhai—Koubis, by *Mahmoud, trained by Willie Molter; bred in Kentucky by Dr. Eslie Asbury.

Start good. Won driving; second and third the same. DETERMINE, roughed immediately after the start in the jam caused by HASTY ROAD and TIMELY TIP, recovered under good handling and raced within striking distance of the leader to the stretch, responded to brisk urging during the drive and, taking command, won going away. HASTY ROAD began fast, bore to the outside in the run to the first turn, retained a clear lead until reaching the stretch, then was unable to withstand the winner. HASSEYAMPA gradually worked way forward while racing in the middle of the track, closed strongly under punishment but was unable to reach the top pair.

THE WINNER'S PEDIGREE AND CAREER HIGHLIGHTS

DETERMINE (Gray Colt)
- *Alibhai
  - Hyperion
    - Gainsborough
    - Selene
  - Teresina
    - Tracery
    - Blue Tie
- Koubis
  - *Mahmoud
    - *Blenheim II
    - Mah Mahal
  - Brown Biscuit
    - Sir Andrew
    - Swing On

Year	Age	Sts	1st	2nd	3rd	Won
1953	2	14	4	1	5	$ 26,435
1954	3	15	10	3	2	328,700
1955	4	15	4	3	2	218,360
	Totals	44	18	7	9	$573,360

At 2 Years	WON	San Francisco Handicap, Robert O'Brien Handicap
At 3 Years	WON	Kentucky Derby, San Gabriel Stakes, San Felipe Handicap, Santa Anita Derby, San Joe Handicap, Peter Clark Handicap, Bay Meadows Derby, Oakland Handicap, Golden Gate Handicap, Debonaire Stakes
At 4 Years	WON	Inglewood Handicap, Golden Gate Mile, Malibu Sequet Stakes, Santa Anita Maturity (through disqualification)

Kentucky senator Alben Barkley (center) is flanked by Ohio Gov. Frank Lausche, and Kentucky Gov. Lawrence Wetherby.

The stands were filled with personalities from all walks, including George Jessel (left), Irene Dunne and Arthur Godfrey.

May 7, 1955

Owner — R. C. Ellsworth

Trainer — M. A. Tenney

Jockey — Bill Shoemaker

SWAPS

$125,000 added and $5,000 Gold Cup. Net to winner $108,400; second $25,000; third $12,500; fourth $5,000. 125 nominations.

Horses	Eqt Wt	PP	St	½	¾	1	Str	Fin	Jockeys	Owners	Odds to $1
Swaps	w 126	8	4	1¹	1¹	1½	1½	1¹½	Shoemaker	R. C. Ellsworth	2.80
Nashua	w 126	5	1	3¹	3¹	2¹	2⁴	2⁶½	Arcaro	Belair Stud	1.30
Summer Tan	wb 126	10	6	4⁶	4⁵	3⁴	3²	3⁴	Guerin	Mrs. J. W. Galbreath	4.90
Racing Fool	w 126	7	5	5¹	5¹	5¹	4³	4½	Moreno	Cain Hoy Stable	a-5.70
Jean's Joe	wb 126	9	9	10	8³	6½	5²	5¹½	Brooks	Murcain Stable	16.20
Flying Fury	w 126	2	10	8³	9¹	9²	6½	6¾	McCreary	Cain Hoy Stable	a-5.70
Honeys Alibi	w 126	4	2	6³	6³	7¹	7½	7³½	Harmatz	W-L Ranch Co.	55.60
Blue Lem	wb 126	1	7	9½	10	10	9⁴	8¹½	Rogers	H. C. Fruehauf	23.30
Nabesna	wb 126	3	8	7³	7¹½	8¹	8¹	9¹⁰	Adams	C. Mooers	52.80
Trim Destiny	w 126	6	3	2²½	2ʰ	4ʰ	10	10	Cook	G. R. White	50.90

Time: :23-3/5, :47-2/5, 1:12-2/5, 1:37, 2:01-4/5. Track fast.
a—Coupled Racing Fool and Flying Fury.
$2 Mutuels Paid—Swaps, $7.60 straight, $3.40 place, $2.60 show; Nashua $3.00 place, $2.40 show; Summer Tan $3.00 show.
Winner—Ch.c. by *Khaled—Iron Reward, by *Beau Pere, trained by M. A. Tenney; bred in California by R. C. Ellsworth.

Start good from stall gate. Won driving; second and third the same. SWAPS, alertly ridden, took command soon after the start, raced TRIM DESTINY into defeat before reaching the upper turn, responded readily when challenged by NASHUA during the stretch run and drew clear in the last sixteenth mile. NASHUA, well placed from the outset, was kept in hand to the last three-eighths mile, moved up boldly on the outside of SWAPS for the stretch run but was not good enough for the latter, although much the best of the others. SUMMER TAN, never far back and reserved to the last half-mile, made a mild bid approaching the stretch, then faltered. RACING FOOL, in hand to the stretch, was unable to threaten the leaders when set down for the drive. JEAN'S JOE lacked early foot and was never dangerous. FLYING FURY was sluggish and was never prominent. HONEYS ALIBI was outrun and had no mishaps. BLUE LEM raced far back the entire trip. NABESNA was through early. TRIM DESTINY raced nearest SWAPS for three-quarters mile, then gave way.

THE WINNER'S PEDIGREE AND CAREER HIGHLIGHTS

SWAPS (Chestnut Colt)
- *Khaled
  - Hyperion
    - Gainsborough
    - Selene
  - Eclair
    - Ethnarch
    - Black Ray
- Iron Reward
  - *Beau Pere
    - Son-in-Law
    - Cinna
  - Iron Maiden
    - War Admiral
    - Betty Derr

Year	Age	Sts	1st	2nd	3rd	Won
1954	2	6	3	0	2	$ 20,950
1955	3	9	8	1	0	418,550
1956	4	10	8	1	0	409,400
Totals		25	19	2	2	$848,900

At 2 Years
- WON June Juvenile Stakes
- 3RD Westchester Stakes, Haggin Stakes

At 3 Years
- WON Kentucky Derby, San Vicente Stakes, Santa Anita Derby, Will Rogers Stakes, Californian Stakes, Westerner Stakes, American Derby
- 2ND Match race with Nashua

At 4 Years
- WON Argonaut, American, Inglewood, Hollywood Gold Cup, Sunset, Washington Handicap

Bill Shoemaker was so swamped with well wishers after the 1955 Derby it took awhile to get dressed. Eddie Arcaro (left) beat him to it and then came by to offer congratulations.

The Schweppes Man, Commander Edward Whitehead, was a visitor to see Swaps beat Nashua in the great 1955 Derby. He is accompanied by Mr. E. E. Beisel of Chicago.

May 5, 1956

Jack Dudley

Bonnie Heath

Owners

Trainer — H. L. Fontaine

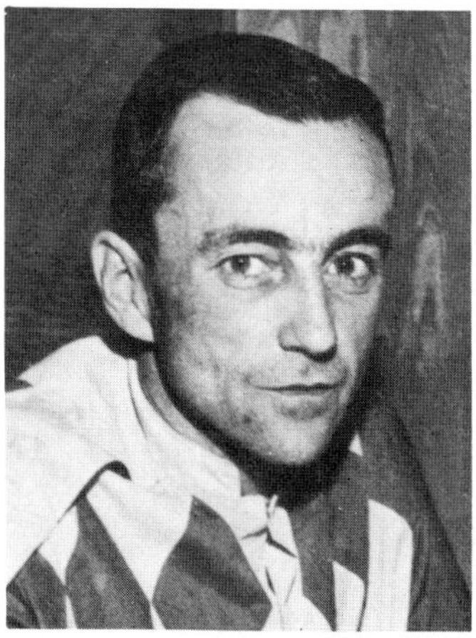

Jockey — Dave Erb

E I G H T Y S E C O N D R U N N I N G

NEEDLES

$125,000 added and $5,000 Gold Cup. Net to winner $123,450; second $25,000; third $12,500; fourth $5,000. 169 nominations.

Horses	Eqt Wt	PP	St	½	¾	1	Str	Fin	Jockeys	Owners	Odds to $1
Needles	w 126	1	12	16^3	16^6	$7\frac{1}{2}$	$2\frac{1}{2}$	$1\frac{3}{4}$	Erb	D & H Stable	1.60
Fabius	wb 126	12	2	3^2	$2^{1\frac{1}{2}}$	$1\frac{1}{2}$	1^h	$2^{1\frac{1}{2}}$	Hartack	Calumet Farm	c-4.00
Come On Red	w 126	10	14	14^1	10^1	$4\frac{1}{2}$	$3^{1\frac{1}{2}}$	$3\frac{3}{4}$	Popara	Helen W. Kellogg	f-29.00
Count Chic	wb 126	5	15	11^2	12^2	9^3	$4\frac{1}{2}$	$4\frac{1}{2}$	Brooks	Mr. & Mrs. D. Lozzi	8.00
Pintor Lea	wb 126	3	11	$12\frac{1}{2}$	$11\frac{1}{2}$	$6^{1\frac{1}{2}}$	5^1	$5^{1\frac{1}{2}}$	Baird	Calumet Farm	c-4.00
Career Boy	wb 126	2	13	15^3	$13\frac{1}{2}$	10^2	$8^{1\frac{1}{2}}$	$6^{2\frac{1}{2}}$	Guerin	C. V. Whitney	a-4.90
No Regrets	wb 126	7	6	5^1	4^h	2^h	$7\frac{1}{2}$	$7^{1\frac{1}{4}}$	Dodson	W. E. Britt	52.80
Head Man	wb 126	4	4	4^h	3^h	5^1	6^1	$8\frac{3}{4}$	Arcaro	C. V. Whitney	a-4.90
King O' Swords ..	wb 126	16	9	$7\frac{1}{2}$	6^1	8^1	9^1	9^1	B'gmnke	Reverie Knoll Farm	f-29.00
High King	w 126	6	17	17	17	17	12^4	10^{nk}	Cook	J. Gavegnano	79.50
Jean Baptiste	wb 126	14	16	$13^{1\frac{1}{2}}$	$15\frac{1}{2}$	$12\frac{1}{2}$	$11\frac{1}{2}$	11no	Nichols	Mrs. L. P. Tate	f-29.00
Terrang	wb 126	11	1	$2^{2\frac{1}{2}}$	$1\frac{1}{2}$	3^1	10^2	12^5	Shoemaker	Rex C. Elsworth	8.30
Black Emperor ...	wb 126	13	10	10^2	14^2	11^3	13^3	13^5	Adams	Hasty House Farm	26.40
Besomer	wb 126	9	8	$8^{1\frac{1}{2}}$	$8^{1\frac{1}{2}}$	14^h	14^2	$14^{1\frac{1}{2}}$	Shuk	Companas Stable	71.20
Invalidate	wb 126	15	3	6^2	7^1	16^3	15^4	15^2	Gilligan	T. A. Grissom	f-29.00
Ben A Jones	wb 126	8	5	1^h	5^3	13^2	17	16^1	Bailey	G & M Stable	53.80
Countermand	wb 126	17	7	9^4	9^h	$15\frac{1}{2}$	16^2	17	Kirkland	Brandywine Stable	12.00

Time: :23-4/5, :47-1/5, 1:11-3/5, 1:36-4/5, 2:03-2/5. Track fast.

a—Coupled, Fabius and Pintor Lea; c—Career Boy and Head Man.

$2 Mutuels Paid—Needles, $5.20 straight, $3.60 place, $3.40 show; Fabius (a-Entry) $3.80 place, $3.60 show; Come On Red (f-Field) $6.60 show.

Winner—B.c., by Ponder—Noodle Soup, by Jack High, trained by H. L. Fontaine; bred in Florida by W. E. Leach.

Start good. Won driving; second and third the same. NEEDLES, well handled, saved ground when outrun to the last three-eighths mile, was sent to the middle of the track for the stretch run and, responding readily to urging, wore down FABIUS and won going away. FABIUS, well placed from the start, took command approaching the stretch, held on gamely when set down in the drive but was unable to withstand NEEDLES. COME ON RED, far back early, moved up boldly entering the stretch, finished willingly under punishment but was not good enough for the top pair. COUNT CHIC, unable to keep up early, made a good bid in the early stretch, then failed to rally when hard urged in the drive. PINTOR LEA gradually worked his way forward to the stretch, remained next to the inner rail for the drive but could not threaten the leaders, pulling up sore.

THE WINNER'S PEDIGREE AND CAREER HIGHLIGHTS

NEEDLES (Bay Colt)	Ponder	Pensive	Hyperion
			*Penicuik II
		Miss Rushin	*Blenheim II
			Lady Erne
	Noodle Soup	Jack High	John P. Grier
			Priscilla
		Supromene	Supremus
			*Melpomene

Year	Age	Sts	1st	2nd	3rd	Won
1955	2	10	6	0	2	$129,805
1956	3	10	4	2	0	440,850
1957	4	3	1	1	1	29,700
Totals		23	11	3	3	$600,355

At 2 Years **WON** **Sapling Stakes, Hopeful Stakes**

At 3 Years **WON** **Kentucky Derby, Flamingo Stakes, Florida Derby, Belmont Stakes**

At 4 Years **WON** **Fort Lauderdale Handicap**

Some high brass looks at some high gold in this picture. Admiring the Triple Crown trophy and the Kentucky Derby trophy, left to right, are Sen. Pat McNamara (Mich.), William Laird (W. Va.), entertainer George Jessel, Sen. Earle Clements (Ky.) and Bobby Baker, then secretary of the majority in the U.S. Senate.

Sen. and Mrs. John Sherman Cooper of Kentucky get a call at their box from Thruston Morton, who later in the year also was elected to the Senate. Morton now is chairman of the board at Churchill Downs.

May 4, 1957

Owner — Mrs. Gene Markey

Trainer — H. A. Jones

Jockey — Bill Hartack

EIGHTY THIRD RUNNING

IRON LIEGE

$125,000 added and $5,000 Gold Cup. Net to winner $107,950; second $25,000; third $12,500; fourth $5,000. 133 nominations.

Horses	Eqt Wt	PP	St	½	¾	1	Str	Fin	Jockeys	Owners	Odds to $1
Iron Liege	w 126	6	4	3³	2¹½	2¹½	1½	1ⁿᵒ	Hartack	Calumet Farm	8.40
Gallant Man	w 126	4	6	7²	7¹	5½	3½	2²¾	Shoemaker	R. Lowe	3.70
Round Table	wb 126	3	5	4³	4³	4²	4h	3³	Neves	Kerr Stable	3.60
Bold Ruler	w 126	7	3	2h	3¹½	3½	5³	4¹¼	Arcaro	Wheatley Stable	1.20
Federal Hill	wb 126	2	1	1¹½	1½	1h	2h	5³¾	Carstens	C. Lussky	7.90
Indian Creek	wb 126	5	7	6²½	6½	7³	7³	6¹	Taniguchi	Mrs. A. L. Rice	73.10
Mister Jive	wb 126	1	2	5³	5²½	6½	6½	7³½	Woodhouse	J. L. Applebaum	55.90
Better Bee	w 126	9	9	9	9	8³	8⁶	8¹⁰	J Adams	W. S. Miller	42.40
Shan Pac	wb 126	8	8	8½	8½	9	9	9	J R Adams	T. A. Grissom	46.50

Time: :23-3/5, :47, 1:11-2/5, 1:36-4/5, 2:02-1/5. Track fast.

$2 Mutuels Paid—Iron Liege, $18.80 straight, $9.40 place, $6.20 show; Gallant Man, $5.00 place, $4.00 show; Round Table, $4.00 show.

Winner—B.c. by Bull Lea—Iron Maiden, by War Admiral, trained by H. A. Jones; bred in Kentucky by Calumet Farm.

Start good. Won driving; second and third the same. IRON LIEGE, away alertly, saved ground while racing nearest FEDERAL HILL to the mile, took command during the drive and, responding to strong handling, held GALLANT MAN safe but won with little left. GALLANT MAN, in hand and saving ground to the last three-eighths mile, moved up determinedly in the early stretch, reached the lead between calls and was going stoutly when his rider misjudged the finish and he could not overtake IRON LIEGE when back on stride. ROUND TABLE, well placed and racing evenly to the stretch, closed willingly under punishment but could not reach the leaders. BOLD RULER, a sharp factor from the outset but racing well out in the track, failed to stay when set down through the stretch. FEDERAL HILL took command at once, set the pace until inside the stretch, then gave way when challenged by IRON LIEGE. INDIAN CREEK was never prominent and had no mishap. MISTER JIVE could not keep up. BETTER BEE was never dangerous. SHAN PAC was over-matched.

THE WINNER'S PEDIGREE AND CAREER HIGHLIGHTS

IRON LIEGE (Bay Colt)
- Bull Lea
  - *Bull Dog
    - *Teddy
    - Plucky Liege
  - Rose Leaves
    - Ballot
    - *Colonial
- Iron Maiden
  - War Admiral
    - Man o' War
    - Brushup
  - Betty Derr
    - *Sir Gallahad III
    - Uncle's Lassie

Year	Age	Sts	1st	2nd	3rd	Won
1956	2	8	2	1	1	$ 10,705
1957	3	17	8	5	3	310,625
1958	4	8	1	3	1	80,840
Totals		33	11	9	5	$402,170

At 2 Years — UNP Belmont Futurity, The Garden State

At 3 Years
- WON Kentucky Derby, Jersey Stakes, Laurance Amour Memorial, Sheridan Handicap
- 2ND Fountain Of Youth, Preakness, Arlington Classic, Clang Handicap, American Derby
- 3RD The Everglades, The Flamingo, Florida Derby

At 4 Years
- WON McLennan Handicap
- 2ND Widener Handicap, Royal Palm Handicap, Royal Poinciana Handicap

This distinguished foursome of writers posed in the press box. Left to right are Arthur Daley of the New York Times; Shirley Povich, Washington Post & Times Herald; Frank Graham, New York Journal American, and Red Smith, New York Herald-Tribune.

Happiness is winning a Kentucky Derby, as this groom from Calumet Farm exemplifies after Iron Liege's victory. That's the winner on the way back to the barn.

Calumet Farm

OWNER AND BREEDER OF EIGHT KENTUCKY DERBY WINNERS

WHIRLAWAY	PENSIVE	CITATION	PONDER
1941	1944	1948	1949

HILL GAIL	IRON LIEGE	TIM TAM	FORWARD PASS
1952	1957	1958	1968

Mrs. Gene Markey • Versailles Pike • Lexington, Kentucky

May 3, 1958

Owner — Mrs. Gene Markey

Trainer — H. A. Jones

Jockey — Ismael Valenzuela

TIM TAM

$125,000 added and $5,000 Gold Cup. Net to winner $116,400; second $25,000; third $12,500; fourth $5,000. 140 nominations.

Horses	Eqt	Wt	PP	St	½	¾	1	Str	Fin	Jockeys	Owners	Odds to $1
Tim Tam	w	126	2	8	8¹	5¹	4ʰᵈ	2³	1½	Valenzuela	Calumet Farm	2.10
Lincoln Road	wb	126	7	1	1²	1²	1¹½	1²	2½	Rogers	Sunny Blue Farm	46.90
Noureddin	wb	126	11	11	12⁴	12³	8½	3²	3⁶	Combest	Crabgrass Stable	15.40
Jewel's Reward	w	126	3	6	6¹½	6ʰᵈ	5¹	4ʰ	4ⁿᵒ	Arcaro	Maine Chance Farm	a2.00
Martin's Rullah	wb	126	5	12	13¹¹	13¹⁰	10³	9³	5³	McCreary	Mr. & Mrs. G. Lewis	43.10
Chance It Tony	w	126	10	13	11¹½	9ʰ	11²	8²	6¹¾	Batchellor	Mrs. A. Cannuli	245.00
A Dragon Killer	w	126	9	9	9²	10ʰ	7²	7½	7ʰ	Hansman	Mrs. S. H. Sadacca	294.40
Gone Fishin'	w	126	4	5	4¹½	2½	2ʰ	5½	8¹	Neves	Llangollen Farm	20.10
Benedicto	w	126	14	10	10²	8½	6ʰ	6³	9²	Dever	Bellardi & Harkins	f59.30
Ebony Pearl	w	126	13	4	3½	3¹½	3⁴	10³	10²½	Ycaza	Maine Chance Farm	a2.00
Red Hot Pistol	w	126	8	3	5³	4ʰ	13	12²	11²½	Dodson	Mrs. S. E. Wilson, Jr.	f59.30
Silky Sullivan	w	126	12	14	14	14	12²	11¹	12¹½	Shoemaker	Ross & Klipsten	2.10
Flamingo	wb	126	6	7	7¹	11³	9³	13	13	Glisson	C. V. Whitney	49.50
Warren G	wb	126	1	2	2	7		Eased		Church	W. G. Reynolds	122.30

Time: :23-1/5, :47-3/5, 1:13-1/5, 1:38-2/5, 2:05. Track muddy.

a—Coupled Jewel's Reward and Ebony Pearl. b—Field.

$2 Mutuels paid—Tim Tam, $6.20 straight, $3.80 place, $3.00 show; Lincoln Road, $26.80 place, $11.40 show; Noureddin, $5.60 show.

Winner—Dk.b.c. by Tom Fool—Two Lea, by Bull Lea. Trained by H. A. Jones, bred in Kentucky by Calumet Farm.

Start good. Won driving. TIM TAM unhurried while being outrun early, commenced to advance along inside after going a half mile, moved through in close quarters on final bend and when brought out between horses for drive he was fully extended to wear down LINCOLN ROAD near the end. LINCOLN ROAD made the pace under a well judged ride, saved ground much of way and held on stubbornly in a long drive. NOUREDDIN far back through first six furlongs, circled his field when commencing his bid on second turn, lost additional ground on entering stretch and finished fastest of all in middle of track to be easily best of others. JEWEL'S REWARD in hand while maintaining a striking position along outside, commenced to advance while continuing slightly wide on final bend but could not gain through final furlong when put to extreme pressure. MARTINS RULLAH closed a big gap in late stages but could not seriously menace top trio. GONE FISHIN' loomed boldly on entering stretch but had little left when real test came. EBONY PEARL stopped badly after making a menacing bid on stretch turn. SILKY SULLIVAN broke well but was allowed to stride while saving ground until final turn where he made only a brief and ineffectual bid of less than a sixteenth mile and refused to extend himself thereafter.

THE WINNER'S PEDIGREE AND CAREER HIGHLIGHTS

TIM TAM (Dark Bay Colt)	Tom Fool	Menow	*Pharamond II / Alcibiades
		Gaga	*Bull Dog / Alpoise
	Two Lea	Bull Lea	Bull Dog / Rose Leaves
		Two Bob	The Porter / Blessings

Year	Age	Sts	1st	2nd	3rd	Won
1957	2	1	0	0	0	$ 275
1958	3	13	10	1	2	467,475
Totals		14	10	1	2	$467,750

At 3 Years
- WON Kentucky Derby, Derby Trial, Preakness Stakes, Everglades Handicap, Flamingo Stakes, Fountain of Youth Stakes, Florida Derby
- 2ND Belmont Stakes
- 3RD Bahamas Handicap

Aly Kahn didn't have a horse in the 1958 Derby but watched as Tim Tam made it two in a row for Calumet.

Gov. Happy Chandler of Kentucky looks entranced as he watches Tim Tam defeat a crack field.

The magic name in the 1958 field was Silky Sullivan. The come-from-behind marvel attracted huge crowds of press and fans every time he left the barn.

Calumet Farm

OWNER AND BREEDER OF EIGHT KENTUCKY DERBY WINNERS

WHIRLAWAY	PENSIVE	CITATION	PONDER
1941	1944	1948	1949

HILL GAIL	IRON LIEGE	TIM TAM	FORWARD PASS
1952	1957	1958	1968

Mrs. Gene Markey   •   Versailles Pike   •   Lexington, Kentucky

May 2, 1959

Owners — Mr.-Mrs. F. Turner, Jr.

Trainer — Frank Childs

Jockey — Bill Shoemaker

*TOMY LEE

$125,000 added and $5,000 Gold Cup. Net to winner $119,650; second $25,000; third $12,500; fourth $5,000. 130 nominations.

Horses	Eqt Wt	PP	1/4	1/2	3/4	1	Str	Fin	Jockeys	Owners	Odds to $1
*Tomy Lee .....wb	126	9	2^2	$2^1{}_2$	1^{hd}	$2^1{}_2$	2^2	1no	Shoemaker	Mr.-Mrs. F. Turner, Jr.	3.70
Sword Dancer ..wb	126	14	4^{hd}	4^{hd}	4^2	$1^1{}_2$	1^{hd}	$2^2{}_4^1$	Boland	Brookmeade Stable	8.80
First Landing ...wb	126	3	7^1	$8^1{}_2$	5^{hd}	$4^1{}_2$	$3^1{}_2$	3^1	Arcaro	Meadow Farm	3.60
Royal Orbit ....wb	126	17	$10^1{}_2$	12^3	11^3	8^2	6^{hd}	4^{hd}	Harmatz	J. Braunstein Est.	46.60
Silver Spoon ....w	121	4	9^1	9^2	$6^1{}_2$	3^2	3^{hd}	$5^2{}_4^1$	York	C. V. Whitney	10.80
Finnegan ......wb	126	8	6^2	6^1	7^{hd}	$5^1{}_2$	7^2	$6^1{}_2$	Longden	Neil McCarthy	10.60
Dunce ....wb	126	7	$14^1{}_2$	13^2	12^3	$11^1{}_2$	8^1	$7^1{}_2$	Brooks	Claiborne Farm	f-7.30
Open View ....wb	126	13	5^2	5^4	$3^1{}_2$	6^2	$5^1{}_2$	8^3	Korte	Elkcam Stable	†17.20
Atoll ....w	126	5	$3^1{}_2$	3^{hd}	$3^1{}_2$	7^1	$9^1{}_2$	9no	Boulmetis	Elkcam & Chesler	†17.20
Rico Tesio ......wb	126	1	17	17	17	13^2	11^1	$10^1{}_2$	Ycaza	Briardale Farm	48.10
Festival King ....w	126	15	$8^1{}_2$	7^{hd}	9^2	9^2	10^{hd}	$11^1{}_2$	Carstens	C. B. Fishbach	f-7.30
John Bruce ......w	126	11	$16^1{}_2$	$16^1{}_2$	$15^1{}_2$	14^3	14^1	12no	Church	K. G. Marshall	34.50
Easy Spur ......w	126	6	13^3	10^{hd}	10^1	$10^1{}_2$	$13^1{}_2$	13^{hd}	Hartack	Spring Hill Farm	7.90
The Chosen One..w	126	16	11^1	14^4	14^4	$12^1{}_2$	$12^1{}_2$	$14^4{}_2^1$	Combest	Mrs. S. H. Sadacca	f-7.30
Our Dad ......wb	126	1	$12^1{}_2$	$11^1{}_2$	13^2	15^2	15^4	15^1	Anderson	Patrice Jacobs	f-8.00
*Die Hard ......w	126	12	15^2	$15^1{}_2$	$16^1{}_2$	16^3	16^8	16^6	Sellers	Jacnot Stable	f-7.30
Troilus ....wb	126	10	$1^1{}_2$	$1^1{}_2$	$2^1{}_2$	17	17	17	Rogers	Bayard Sharp	7.30

Time: :24-1/5, :47-3/5, 1:11-3/5, 1:36, 2:02-1/5. Track fast.

f—Mutuel field. †Coupled.

$2 Mutuels Paid—*Tomy Lee $9.40 straight, $4.80 place, $3.80 show; Sword Dancer $9.00 place, $6.20 show; First Landing $4.00 show.

Winner—B.c. by *Tudor Minstrel—Auld Alliance, by Brantome. Trained by Frank Childs; bred in England by D. H. Wells.

Start good, won driving. *TOMY LEE snugged in off early pace of TROILUS, moved from between horses with SWORD DANCER to assume a slight advantage at half-mile ground, continued slightly wide to be headed on final bend, respond to strong handling and while drifting out, and being carried in, through stretch run he proved narrowly best. *TOMY LEE survived a claim of foul lodged by rider of runner-up for allegedly having carried that one wide from 5/16ths marker to final sixteenth. SWORD DANCER moved to a contending position along outside at once, continued wide to move readily and take command nearing final quarter mile, was carried wide into stretch to continue to show the way and while lugging in he just failed to last. FIRST LANDING loomed up boldly when called upon entering stretch, but could not improve his position.

THE WINNER'S PEDIGREE AND CAREER HIGHLIGHTS

*TOMY LEE (Bay Colt)	*Tudor Minstrel	Owen Tudor	Hyperion / Mary Tudor
		Sansonnet	Sansovino / Lady Juror
	Auld Alliance	Brantome	Blandford / Vitamine
		Iona	Hyperion / Jiffy

Year	Age	Sts	1st	2nd	3rd	Won
1958	2	8	6	1	1	$213,460
1959	3	7	4	2	0	163,657
1960	4	2	0	0	0	5,000
1962	6	1	1	0	0	4,125
1963	7	13	3	1	2	18,722
	Totals	31	14	4	3	$404,964

At 2 Years	WON	Haggin Stakes, C. S. Howard Stakes, Starlet Stakes, Del Mar Futurity
At 3 Years	WON	Kentucky Derby, Blue Grass Stakes

Wathen Knebelkamp became the eighth president of Churchill Downs in 1959.

Visitors in 1959 included actress Jinx Falkenburg and author Alistair Cooke.

CBS newsman Jimmy Dolan (left) joins announcer Fred Capposella in the announcer's booth for a chat on the 1959 field.

May 7, 1960

Owner — Isaac Blumberg

Trainer — V. J. Sovinski

Jockey — Bill Hartack

VENETIAN WAY

$125,000 added and $5,000 Gold Cup. Net to winner $114,850; second $25,000; third $12,500; fourth $5,000. 142 nominations.

Horses	Eqt Wt	PP	St	½	¾	1	Str	Fin	Jockeys	Owners	Odds $1 Str't
Venetian Way	126	9	4^2	$4^2_{\frac12}$	2^2	2^5	1^2	$1^3_{\frac12}$	Hartack	Sunny Blue Farm	6.30
Bally Ache	b 126	3	1^h	$11^1_{\frac12}$	1^2	1^1	2^6	$2^7_{\frac12}$	Ussery	Edgehill Farm	1.70
Victoria Park	b 126	11	9^4	8^3	8^3	5^3	4^3	$3^2_{\frac14}$	Ycaza	Windfields Farm	16.60
Tompion	b 126	13	$3^1_{\frac12}$	3^h	3^2	3^2	3^h	4no	Shoemaker	C. V. Whitney	1.10
Bourbon Prince	b 126	10	$12^1_{\frac12}$	12^5	10^3	8^5	5^1	$5^5_{\frac12}$	Rogers	Mrs. A. L. Rand	77.00
Cuvier Relic	126	4	5^h	5^h	$6^1_{\frac12}$	7^1	6^3	6^5	Sellers	S. I. Crew	22.90
Tony Graff	b 126	6	13	13	13	13	10^5	$7^1_{\frac12}$	Chambers	A. Graffagnini	67.90
Spring Broker	b 126	1	8^h	9^2	9^2	9^6	9^3	$8^1_{\frac12}$	Rotz	M. H. Van Berg	f-40.60
Divine Comedy	b 126	12	6^3	6^2	4^1	4^1	7^h	$9^1_{\frac14}$	I Valenzuela	Llangollen Farm	61.60
Fighting Hodge	126	7	7^h	$7^1_{\frac12}$	7^1	6^h	8^2	10^7	Pierce	Mrs. C. S. Hodge	f-40.60
Yomolka	b 126	2	10^h	10^h	11^h	11^1	11^1	$11^4_{\frac14}$	Grimm	Valley Farm	137.60
Lurullah	b 126	5	11^3	11^3	12^9	12^1	12^6	12^{16}	Brooks	T. A. Grissom	74.20
Henrijan	b 126	8	$2^1_{\frac12}$	2^2	5^h	10^2	13	13	A Valenz'la	Mr.-Mrs. S. H. Elmore	f-40.60

Time: :23-2/5, :46-4/5, 1:11, 1:36-3/5, 2:02-2/5. Track good.

f—Mutuel field.

$2 Mutuels Paid—Venetian Way, $14.60 straight, $4.60 place, $3.40 show; Bally Ache, $3.00 place, $3.00 show; Victoria Park, $5.00 show.

Winner—Ch.c. by Royal Coinage—Firefly, by Papa Redbird, trained by V. J. Sovinski; bred in Kentucky by J. W. Greathouse.

Start good. Won ridden out. VENETIAN WAY, away alertly, remained within striking distance while under snug restraint to the second turn, where he was sent up along the outside, displaced BALLY ACHE for the lead at the top of the front stretch and drew into his commanding advantage while being ridden out. BALLY ACHE displayed his customary speed, shook off HENRIJAN after a quarter mile, was cleverly rated thereafter and, while unable to handle the winner, he was easily best of the others. VICTORIA PARK, allowed to settle in stride, was eased to the outside after six furlongs to commence his bid which fell far short. TOMPION, off in good order, raced in perfect position to the final turn, where he flattened out badly when put to a drive. BOURBON PRINCE made an ineffectual late rally. CUVIER RELIC could not keep pace. TONY GRAFF was void of early speed. DIVINE COMEDY maintained a striking position along the outside for six furlongs and then tired badly. LURULLAH appeared in close quarters shortly following the start. HENRIJAN stopped badly after forcing the issue for nearly five furlongs.

THE WINNER'S PEDIGREE AND CAREER HIGHLIGHTS

VENETIAN WAY (Chestnut Colt)
- Royal Coinage
  - Eight Thirty
    - Pilate
    - Dinner Time
  - Canina
    - *Bull Dog
    - Coronium
- Firefly
  - Papa Redbird
    - Balladier
    - Taj Bibi
  - Minstrelette
    - *Royal Minstrel
    - Bannerette

Year	Age	Sts	1st	2nd	3rd	Won
1959	2	9	4	1	2	$141,902
1960	3	11	3	3	1	217,520
Totals		20	7	4	3	$359,422

At 2 Years — WON Prairie Stakes, Washington Park Futurity

At 3 Years
- WON Kentucky Derby, Warren Wright Memorial Stakes
- 2ND Florida Derby, Belmont Stakes
- 3RD Arlington Classic

Tom Young, for many years the track superintendent at Churchill Downs, chats with Gov. Bert Combs, right, of Kentucky.

Derby Day is fun but it is long and tiring also. Some in this crowd in the terrace area sprawl out on the grass to rest. And if it is cold, what to do? Simply huddle under a blanket, as the couple (upper left) is doing.

May 6, 1961

Owner — Mrs. Katherine Price

Trainer — Jack Price

Jockey — John Sellers

CARRY BACK

$125,000 added and $5,000 Gold Cup. Net to winner $120,500; second $25,000; third $12,500; fourth $5,000. 155 nominations.

Horses	Eqt Wt	PP	1/4	1/2	3/4	1	Str	Fin	Jockeys	Owners	Odds to $1
Carry Back	126	14	11^2	$11\frac{1}{2}$	$11\frac{1}{2}$	$6\frac{1}{2}$	4^3	$1\frac{3}{4}$	Sellers	Mrs. Katherine Price	2.50
Crozier	b 126	11	3^2	2^h	3^6	3^6	$1\frac{1}{2}$	2^2	Baeza	F. W. Hooper	3.50
Bass Clef	126	9	15	15	15	9^1	$5\frac{1}{2}$	$3\frac{1}{2}$	Baldwin	Mrs. V. E. Smith	f16.50
Dr. Miller	b 126	15	$12\frac{1}{2}$	14^3	14^1	14^3	7^3	4^1	Shoemaker	Mrs. E. D. Jacobs	8.60
Sherluck	126	3	9^2	$7\frac{1}{2}$	6^2	4^2	6^2	$5\frac{1}{4}$	Arcaro	Jacob Sher	5.70
Globemaster	126	8	$1\frac{1}{2}$	1^3	$1\frac{1}{2}$	2^3	3^3	$6\frac{3}{4}$	Rotz	L. P. Sasso	8.70
Four-and-Twenty	b 126	4	2^1	3^5	2^2	1^h	2^1	$7\frac{1}{2}$	Longden	Albert Ranches Ltd.	a5.30
Flutterby	b 126	13	$10\frac{1}{2}$	$10\frac{1}{2}$	$10\frac{1}{2}$	10^h	$9\frac{1}{2}$	8^1	Moreno	Albert Ranches Ltd.	a5.30
Loyal Son	b 126	5	13^h	$12\frac{1}{2}$	$12\frac{1}{2}$	$11\frac{1}{2}$	10^3	9^h	Hansman	Eastwood Stable	71.40
On His Metal	126	2	$14\frac{1}{2}$	13^3	13^2	12^1	8^1	10^5	Dodson	J. G. Brown	53.60
Light Talk	126	12	5^2	4^h	5^3	5^2	11^1	$11\frac{1}{2}$	Nono	Jacnot Stable	64.90
Ambiopoise	b 126	10	8^2	8^2	8^2	8^2	12^2	$12\frac{1}{4}$	Ussery	Robert Lehman	16.20
Ronnie's Ace	b 126	6	6^2	9^2	7^1	13^3	13^1	$13\frac{1}{4}$	Maese	Clark-Radkovich	f16.50
Dearborn	b 126	1	4^h	5^2	4^h	7^h	14^3	$14\frac{1}{2}$	Phelps	E. A. Dust	82.40
Jay Fox	b 126	7	7^h	6^h	9^h	15	15	15	Gilligan	Brae Burn Farm	f16.50

Time: :23-4/5, :47-3/5, 1:11-2/5, 1:36-1/5, 2:04. Track good.

f—Mutuel field.　　a—Coupled, Four-and-Twenty and Flutterby.

$2 mutuels paid: Carry Back $7.00 straight, $4.20 place, $3.20 show; Crozier $4.60 place, $4.20 show; Bass Clef (f-Field) $5.60 show.

Winner—Br.c., by Saggy—Joppy, by Star Blen. Trained by J. A. Price. Bred in Florida by J. A. Price.

Start good. Won driving. CARRY BACK, slow to begin as usual, was kept wider than necessary when his rider elected to find the better going, lost additional ground to avoid any possible interference on rounding the second turn, rallied when roused at the top of the stretch to come on strongly and wore down CROZIER even though being carried out slightly by that one in midstretch. CROZIER, restrained off the early pace while placed along the inner rail, was forced to steady momentarily nearing the half-mile ground when blocked, came to the outside when clear to move steadily at the leaders, wore down that pair in the upper stretch while under pressure, commenced drifting out through the closing furlongs but could not withstand the winner. BASS CLEF, badly outrun for the first mile, cut between horses when rallying thereafter, and while running a weaving course through the stretch run he closed a big gap.

THE WINNER'S PEDIGREE AND CAREER HIGHLIGHTS

CARRY BACK (Brown Colt)	Saggy	Swing and Sway		Equipoise
				Nedana
		*Chantress		Hyperion
				Surbine
	Joppy	Star Blen		*Blenheim II
				*Starweed
		Miss Fairfax		Teddy Beau
				Bellicent

Year	Age	Sts	1st	2nd	3rd	Won
1960	2	21	5	4	4	$ 286,299
1961	3	16	9	1	3	565,349
1962	4	18	5	5	2	305,677
1963	5	6	2	1	1	70,340
		61	21	11	10	$1,226,665

At 2 Years	WON	Cowdin Stakes, Garden State Stakes, Remsen Stakes.
At 3 Years	WON	Kentucky Derby, Flamingo Stakes, Everglades Stakes, Florida Derby, Preakness Stakes, Jerome Handicap, Trenton Handicap.
At 4 Years	WON	Metropolitan Handicap, Monmouth Handicap, Whitney Stakes, Palm Beach Handicap.
At 5 Years	WON	Trenton Handicap

Andy Devine, the gravel voiced comedian of stage, screen and television, looks over his program.

Johnny Sellers gets a press escort back to the jockeys' room by (left to right) Tommy Devine of the Miami Daily News; Whitney Tower of Sports Illustrated, and Tom Gray of United Press.

May 5, 1962

Owner — George Pope, Jr.

Trainer — H. A. Luro

Jockey — Bill Hartack

DECIDEDLY

$125,000 added and $5,000 Gold Cup. Net to winner $119,650; second $25,000; third $12,500; fourth $5,000. 139 nominations.

Horses	Eqt Wt	PP	1/4	1/2	3/4	1	Str	Fin	Jockeys	Owners	Odds to $1
Decidedly	b 126	4	10^2	$9\frac{1}{2}$	8^1	$5\frac{1}{1}2$	$3\frac{1}{2}$	$12\frac{1}{4}$	Hartack	El Peco Ranch	8.70
Roman Line	b 126	14	$7\frac{1}{2}$	6^2	6^2	$4\frac{1}{1}2$	1^h	2^{nk}	Combest	T. A. Grissom	26.30
Ridan	126	13	5^1	2^h	2^1	3^2	2^h	3^{nk}	Ycaza	Jolley-Woods-Greer	1.10
Sir Ribot	126	5	2^1	$8\frac{1}{1}2$	7^2	6^2	5^2	$4\frac{1}{1}2$	York	Mr.-Mrs. F. Turner, Jr.	13.00
Sunrise County	b 126	2	4^2	$3\frac{1}{1}2$	1^h	$2\frac{1}{2}$	4^2	5^2	Shoemaker	T. B. Martin	2.80
Crimson Satan	b 126	11	$14\frac{1}{2}$	14^h	12^1	10^3	6^2	$6\frac{1}{1}4$	Phelps	Crimson King Farm	21.50
Green Hornet	126	6	$11\frac{1}{2}$	13^4	13^4	$12\frac{1}{1}2$	9^3	$7\frac{3}{4}$	Longden	Mrs. J. W. Brown	49.50
Good Fight	126	12	$9\frac{1}{1}2$	10^2	10^h	$9\frac{1}{1}2$	$10\frac{1}{1}2$	8^h	Broussard	F and B Farms	f28.70
Admiral's Voyage	126	3	3^1	4^2	3^1	1^h	7^3	$9\frac{1}{1}2$	Baeza	F. W. Hooper	12.10
Royal Attack	b 126	8	$8\frac{1}{1}2$	5^h	$5\frac{1}{2}$	8^2	8^2	10^5	Burns	N. S. McCarthy	81.30
Touch Bar	b 126	10	15	15	15	15	14	$11^2\frac{1}{2}$	Rivera	Estopinal-Arnaud	f28.70
Lee Town	b 126	7	1^2	$1\frac{1}{1}2$	$4\frac{1}{1}2$	$7\frac{1}{1}2$	12^8	12^8	Carstens	J. V. P. Stable	f28.70
Mister Pitt	b 126	9	13^1	11^2	11^2	11^2	11^3	13^7	Harmatz	Golden Tri Stable	123.30
Sharp Count	b 126	1	6^h	$7\frac{1}{1}2$	$9\frac{1}{1}2$	13^1	13^1	14	Curry	Reverie Knoll Farm	f28.70
Prego	126	15	12^3	12^h	14^1	14^2	Pulled up		Adams	Robert Lehman	28.90

Time: :22-3/5, :45-4/5, 1:10-1/5, 1:35-1/5, 2:00-2/5 (new track record). Track fast.

f—Mutuel field.

$2 Mutuels Paid—Decidedly, $19.40, $8.20 place, $4.20 show; Roman Line, $19.20 place, $7.60 show; Ridan, $3.00 show.

Winner—Gr.c. by Determine—Gloire Fille, by War Glory. Trained by H. A. Luro; bred in California by G. A. Pope, Jr.

Start good. DECIDEDLY, taken in hand at the start to be held in reserve for six furlongs, came to the outside thereafter to commence his bid, continued wide to engage the leaders through the upper stretch, moved to the fore leaving the furlong marker and was under pressure to draw off. ROMAN LINE, steadied while maintaining a striking position from the outset, rallied from between horses in the late stages to gain command a furlong out but had little left to contain the belated bid of the winner. RIDAN allowed to settle through the opening quarter mile, moved with a rush along the outside thereafter to prompt the issue in the run down the backstretch, attempted to bear out rather badly on leaving the backstretch but continued gamely to midstretch where he faltered under extreme pressure. SIR RIBOT, away in good order, appeared to run up onto horses' heels entering the first turn, came out thereafter and finished strongly. SUNRISE COUNTY, never far back while going much more kindly than before, dueled vigorously for the lead to the final sixteenth where he gave way suddenly while under pressure.

THE WINNER'S PEDIGREE AND CAREER HIGHLIGHTS

DECIDEDLY (Gray Colt)
- Determine
  - *Alibhai
    - Hyperion
    - Teresina
  - Koubis
    - *Mahmoud
    - Brown Biscuit
- Gloire Fille
  - War Glory
    - Man o' War
    - Annette K.
  - Belle Femme
    - *Beau Pere
    - French Vamp

Year	Age	Sts	1st	2nd	3rd	Won
1961	2	8	2	1	1	$ 7,550
1962	3	12	2	4	1	144,330
1963	4	13	5	1	2	150,309
1964	5	10	2	3	0	16,800
	Totals	43	11	9	4	$318,989

At 3 Years — WON — Kentucky Derby
At 4 Years — WON — Monmouth Handicap, Dominion Day Handicap, Ben Ali Handicap

Walter Cronkite, veteran CBS newsman, enjoys a mint julep and Jonathan Winters, (right) widely known screen and TV personality, looks up from his study of the program at the 1962 Derby.

May 4, 1963

Owner — John W. Galbreath

Trainer — J. P. Conway

Jockey — Braulio Baeza

CHATEAUGAY

$125,000 added and $5,000 Gold Cup. Net to winner $108,900; second $25,000; third $12,500; fourth $5,000. 138 nominations.

Horses	Eqt Wt	PP	1/4	1/2	3/4	1	Str	Fin	Jockeys	Owners	Odds to $1
Chateaugay	126	1	6^1	6^h	6^3	4^2	1^1	$1^{1\frac{1}{4}}$	Baeza	Darby Dan Farm	9.40
Never Bend	126	6	$1\frac{1}{2}$	1^1	1^1	1^1	2^2	2^{nk}	Ycaza	Cain Hoy Stable	3.10
Candy Spots	b 126	9	3^2	$3^{2\frac{1}{2}}$	3^3	3^h	3^2	$3^{4\frac{3}{4}}$	Shoemaker	R. C. Ellsworth	1.50
On My Honor	b 126	8	9	9	9	7^3	6^2	$4^{1\frac{1}{4}}$	Frey	Ambush Stable	30.80
No Robbery	b 126	7	2^3	2^2	2^2	2^2	4^2	$5^{1\frac{1}{4}}$	Rotz	Greentree Stable	2.70
Bonjour	b 126	3	5^2	$4\frac{1}{2}$	4^2	6^7	$5^{1\frac{1}{2}}$	6^3	Valenzuela	Patrice Jacobs	9.30
Gray Pet	b 126	5	4^1	5^4	5^2	5^h	7^6	7^6	Gomez	Walnut Hill Farm	40.00
Investor	b 126	2	8^1	$8\frac{1}{2}$	$8\frac{1}{2}$	9	8^2	$8^{3\frac{1}{2}}$	Callico	J. J. Cherock	37.40
Royal Tower	b 126	4	7^3	7^5	7^3	8^2	9	9	Hernadez	B. J. Ridder	138.70

Time: :23, :46-2/5, 1:10, 1:35-2/5, 2:01-4/5. Track fast.

$2 Mutuels Paid—Chateaugay, $20.80, $7.00 place, $3.60 show; Never Bend, $5.00 place, $3.40 show; Candy Spots, $2.80 show.

Winner—Ch.c., by Swaps—Banquet Bell, by Polynesian. Trained by J. P. Conway; bred in Kentucky by J. W. Galbreath.

CHATEAUGAY, taken well back shortly following the start and held in reserve through the opening six furlongs, was eased to the extreme outside soon after leaving the backstretch, moved with a rush to wear down NEVER BEND through the upper stretch and prevailed in a long drive. NEVER BEND rushed to the lead at once, saved ground under patient handling, drifted out slightly while under pressure in midstretch and held on stubbornly after giving way to the winner. CANDY SPOTS, kept much closer to the pace than before, was forced to check momentarily while racing up onto NO ROBBERY'S heels entering the first turn, remained slightly wide to the second turn where he commenced to advance along the inside, was checked momentarily nearing the three furlongs marker, and once again when blocked along the inside nearing the quarter pole, rallied willingly when clear in the stretch and finished strongly along the outside. ON MY HONOR, badly outrun for a mile, came slightly wide in his belated bid and closed some ground. NO ROBBERY prompted the issue from the start, raced slightly wide while going kindly to the final turn where he attempted to get out a bit. Rotz immediately straightened the colt to bring him back towards the inside, and he continued gamely to the upper stretch where he commenced to falter when put to a drive. BONJOUR maintained a striking position to the final turn and tired. GRAY PET was outrun. INVESTOR and ROYAL TOWER were far back throughout.

THE WINNER'S PEDIGREE AND CAREER HIGHLIGHTS

CHATEAUGAY (Chestnut Colt)

Swaps
- *Khaled
  - Hyperion
  - Eclair
- Iron Reward
  - Beau Pere
  - Iron Maiden

Banquet Bell
- Polynesian
  - Unbreakable
  - Black Polly
- Dinner Horn
  - *Pot au Feu
  - Tophorn

Year	Age	Sts	1st	2nd	3rd	Won
1962	2	5	2	2	0	$ 12,587
1963	3	12	7	1	2	332,585
1964	4	3	1	1	0	11,325
1965	5	4	1	0	0	4,225
Totals		24	11	4	2	$360,722

At 2 Years	UNP	Pimlico Futurity
At 3 Years	WON	Kentucky Derby, Blue Grass Stakes, Jerome Handicap, Belmont Stakes
	2ND	Preakness Stakes
	3RD	Travers Stakes, Dwyer Handicap
At 4 Years	2ND	Roseben Handicap

Kentucky Colonels are all over the world, including Monaco. Prince Rainier gets his commission here. Left to right are John B. Kelly, brother-in-law of the prince; Prince Rainier, Mrs. Ralph Wright and Mr. Wright, making the presentation.

May 2, 1964

Owner — E. P. Taylor

Trainer — H. A. Luro

Jockey — Bill Hartack

NORTHERN DANCER

$125,000 added and $5,000 Gold Cup. Net to winner $114,300; second $25,000; third $12,500; fourth $5,000. 138 nominations.

Horses	Eqt Wt	PP	1/4	1/2	3/4	1	Str	Fin	Jockeys	Owners	Odds to $1
Northern Dancer	.b 126	7	$7^{2\frac{1}{2}}$	6^h	6^2	1^h	1^2	1^{nk}	Hartack	Windfields Farm	3.40
Hill Rise	126	11	$6^{1\frac{1}{2}}$	$7^{2\frac{1}{2}}$	8^h	4^h	$2^{1\frac{1}{2}}$	$2^{3\frac{1}{4}}$	Shoemaker	El Peco Ranch	1.40
The Scoundrel	...b 126	6	$3^{1\frac{1}{2}}$	4^h	3^1	2^1	3^2	3no	Ycaza	R. C. Ellsworth	6.00
Roman Brother	126	12	9^2	$9^{1\frac{1}{2}}$	9^2	6^2	$4^{1\frac{1}{2}}$	4^{nk}	Chambers	Harbor View Farm	30.60
Quadrangle	......b 126	2	5^1	$5^{1\frac{1}{2}}$	4^h	$5^{1\frac{1}{2}}$	5^1	5^3	Ussery	Rokeby Stables	5.30
Mr. Brick	126	1	2^3	$1^{1\frac{1}{2}}$	$1^{1\frac{1}{2}}$	3^1	6^3	$6^{3\frac{1}{4}}$	Valenzuela	Roy Sturgis	15.80
Mr. Moonlight	126	5	8^2	8^1	7^h	7^3	7^4	7^5	Combest	Mrs. M. Dent	54.40
Dandy K.	126	9	12	12	12	8^h	$8^{1\frac{1}{2}}$	$8^{2\frac{1}{4}}$	Solom'ne	Cecil Carmine	17.40
Ishkoodah	......b 126	8	11^2	11^2	11^2	9^2	9^3	9^4	Baldwin	Tumbleweed St.	29.20
Wil Rad	126	3	4^h	$3^{1\frac{1}{2}}$	5^h	$11^{1\frac{1}{2}}$	11^7	10no	Vasquez	Clark-Radkovich	57.70
Extra Swell	.....b 126	4	$10^{1\frac{1}{2}}$	10^h	$10^{1\frac{1}{2}}$	12	10^h	11^{14}	Volzke	Mr.-Mrs. E. Davis	152.20
Royal Shuck	...b 126	10	1^h	2^2	2^h	10^h	12	12	Bolin	E. A. Dust	179.40

Time: :22-2/5, :46, 1:10-3/5, 1:36, 2:00 (new track record). Track fast.

$2 Mutuels Paid—Northern Dancer $8.80, $3.60 place, $3.00 show; Hill Rise $3.00 place, $2.60 show; The Scoundrel $3.20 show.

Winner—B.c., by Nearctic—Natalma, by Native Dancer. Trained by H. A. Luro; bred in Canada by E. P. Taylor.

NORTHERN DANCER, in good order to gain a contending position along the inside, continued to save ground while under restraint, moved up steadily after six furlongs, but was forced to come out midway of the second turn, responded to gain command a quarter out and prevailed under strong left-handed whipping. HILL RISE, unhurried, was bumped twice through the stretch run the first time, continued along the outside thereafter to commence a rally at the half-mile ground, lost additional ground in a wide spread leaving the backstretch, rallied to strong handling on entering the stretch and was slowly getting to the winner. THE SCOUNDREL broke in stride, swerved out to bump with HILL RISE in the run to the initial turn, continued in a forward position to gain command between calls on the second turn and weakened gradually through the closing drive. ROMAN BROTHER, allowed to settle in stride, commenced to advance along the inner railing after seven furlongs and finished strongly even though in slightly close quarters. QUADRANGLE, brushed and squeezed back at the start, wanted for racing room entering the first turn, continued well to the top of the stretch where he lacked a closing rally. MR. BRICK broke alertly but sharply to the outside brushing with QUADRANGLE, continued to make the pace under good rating and gave way suddenly after going a mile. MR. MOONLIGHT swerved to the outside for no apparent reason nearing the half-mile ground and could not threaten thereafter. DANDY K. was outrun, as was ISHKOODAH. WIL RAD was through early. ROYAL SHUCK showed speed for three-quarters and stopped badly.

THE WINNER'S PEDIGREE AND CAREER HIGHLIGHTS

NORTHERN DANCER (Bay Colt)	Nearctic	Nearco	Pharos / Nogara
		*Lady Angela	Hyperion / Sister Sarah
	Natalma	Native Dancer	Polynesian / Geisha
		Almahmoud	*Mahmoud / Arbitrator

Year	Age	Sts	1st	2nd	3rd	Won
1963	2	9	7	2	0	$ 90,635
1964	3	9	7	0	2	490,171
	Totals	18	14	2	2	$580,806

At 2 Years — WON Summer Stakes, Coronation Futurity, Carleton Stakes, Remsen Stakes

At 3 Years — WON Flamingo Stakes, Florida Derby, Blue Grass Stakes, Kentucky Derby, Preakness, Queen's Plate
3RD Belmont Stakes

Bill Hartack isn't being taken to the "hoosegow" — he's just getting an escort back to the jockeys' quarters after accepting his trophy for winning with Northern Dancer in record time.

Louisville's Paul Hornung, the great Notre Dame and Green Bay Packer football star, chats with restaurateur Toots Shor, left.

An enviable record and a tradition of excellence...
Northern Dancer and South Central Bell.

May 1, 1965

Owner — Mrs. Ada L. Rice

Trainer — Frank Catrone

Jockey — Bill Shoemaker

LUCKY DEBONAIR

$125,000 added and $5,000 Gold Cup. Net to winner $112,000; second $25,000; third $12,500; fourth $5,000. 130 nominations.

Horses	Eqt Wt	PP	1/4	1/2	3/4	1	Str	Fin	Jockeys	Owners	Odds to $1
Lucky Debonair	126	8	3^h	2$2\frac{1}{2}$	2$\frac{1}{2}$	2^2	1^3	1^{nk}	Shoemaker	Mrs. Ada L. Rice	4.30
Dapper Dan	b 126	1	11	11	11	7^1	5$\frac{1}{2}$	2^2	Valenzuela	Ogden Phipps	30.00
Tom Rolfe	126	9	7^2	5^1	3$1\frac{1}{2}$	4$1\frac{1}{2}$	3^h	3^1	Turcotte	Powhatan	5.60
Native Charger	..b 126	4	4^3	4$1\frac{1}{2}$	4$\frac{1}{2}$	3$\frac{1}{2}$	4^1	4^{nk}	Rotz	Warner Stable	6.40
Hail to All	126	7	9^2	10^2	9$1\frac{1}{2}$	8^h	6$1\frac{1}{2}$	5$2\frac{1}{4}$	Ycaza	Mrs. Ben Cohen	3.80
Mr. Pak	126	10	8^2	8$2\frac{1}{2}$	7^2	6$\frac{1}{2}$	8^4	6^h	Nichols	Mrs. Mary Keim	53.80
Swift Ruler	126	11	10^h	9$\frac{1}{2}$	8$\frac{1}{2}$	10^2	7$\frac{1}{2}$	7^3	Spraker	Earl Allen	34.90
Flag Raiser	......b 126	5	1^2	1^h	1^h	1^h	2^h	8$2\frac{1}{2}$	Ussery	I. Bieber	17.90
Carpenter's Rule	..b 126	6	6$1\frac{1}{2}$	7^2	10^3	11	9^1	9$\frac{1}{2}$	Harmatz	P. L. Grissom	78.70
Bold Lad	........b 126	3	5^h	6$1\frac{1}{2}$	6$\frac{1}{2}$	5^h	10$\frac{1}{2}$	10^2	Hartack	Wheatley Stable	2.00
Narushua	126	2	2^h	3^h	5^2	9$\frac{1}{2}$	11	11	Dunlavy	J. W. Mecom	92.00

Time: :23-1/5, :47-1/5, 1:11-4/5, 1:37, 2:01-1/5. Track fast.

$2 Mutuels Paid—Lucky Debonair $10.60, $5.40 place, $4.20 show; Dapper Dan—$26.00 place, $12.60 show; Tom Rolfe $4.80 show.

Winner—B.c., by Vertex—Fresh as Fresh, by Count Fleet. Trained by F. Catrone; bred in Kentucky by Danada Farm.

LUCKY DEBONAIR broke alertly to show the way through the opening furlong, dropped back a bit when Shoemaker took a snug hold nearing the sixteenth marker, moved up again to engage FLAG RAISER midway of the first turn, continued to duel with that one while along the outside to the final quarter where he moved to the fore when sharply roused, moved off to a lengthy advantage through the upper stretch but was fully extended to turn back a belated bid from DAPPER DAN. The latter, away slowly and unhurried for six furlongs, moved up along the inside on leaving the backstretch, angled out sharply to launch his closing rally on the final turn and, responding to strong handling, was slowly getting to the winner. TOM ROLFE, in hand for a half mile, moved up boldly along the inside to engage the top flight at the half mile ground, dropped back a bit on rounding the second turn only to come again while under extreme pressure and finished gamely. NATIVE CHARGER, bumped while between horses entering the first turn, quickly recovered to remain in contention while along the outside to loom menacingly on the stretch turn and finished evenly in a good effort. HAIL TO ALL, slow to begin as usual, launched a rally on rounding the second turn and finished boldly while between horses through the closing drive. MR. PAK finished well. SWIFT RULER failed to reach contention. FLAG RAISER came out soon after the start to bump with CARPENTER'S RULE but was quickly straightened away to take a clear lead in the initial run through the stretch, came to the inside thereafter to be well-rated only to weaken badly through the closing drive. CARPENTER'S RULE was bumped soon after the start and failed to reach contention.

THE WINNER'S PEDIGREE AND CAREER HIGHLIGHTS

LUCKY DEBONAIR (Bay Colt)				
	Vertex	The Rhymer	{	*St. Germans / Rhythmic
		Kanace	{	Case Ace / Kanlast
	Fresh as Fresh	Count Fleet	{	Reigh Count / Quickly
		Airy	{	Bull Lea / Proud One

Year	Age	Sts	1st	2nd	3rd	Won
1964	2	1	0	0	0	$ —
1965	3	10	6	3	0	257,210
1966	4	5	3	0	0	113,750
Totals		16	9	3	0	$370,960

At 3 Years { WON Kentucky Derby, San Vicente Handicap, Santa Anita Derby, Blue Grass Stakes
2ND San Felipe Stakes

At 4 Years { WON Santa Anita Handicap

Fire broke out in the clubhouse area in 1965 but there was more smoke than fire. Few spectators left their seats, but those in other areas craned their neck for a view.

May 7, 1966

Owner — Michael J. Ford

Trainer — Henry Forrest

Jockey — Don Brumfield

KAUAI KING

$125,000 added and $5,000 Gold Cup. Net to winner $120,500; second $25,000; third $12,500; fourth $5,000. 150 nominations.

Horses	Eqt Wt	PP	1/4	1/2	3/4	1	Str	Fin	Jockeys	Owners	Odds to $1
Kauai King	b 126	12	1^1	1^3	1^2	1^1	$1^{1\frac{1}{2}}$	$1^{\frac{1}{2}}$	Brumfield	Ford Stable	2.40
Advocator	b 126	5	6^h	5^2	3^2	2^1	3^1	2no	Sellers	Ada L. Rice	16.90
Blue Skyer	b 126	2	11^2	8^1	8^2	3^1	$4^{1\frac{1}{2}}$	$3^{\frac{3}{4}}$	Fires	Padgett-Grant	f-17.00
Stupendous	b 126	3	9^2	6^h	4^h	4^1	$2^{\frac{1}{2}}$	4^{nk}	Baeza	Wheatley Stable	5.40
Abe's Hope	b 126	13	10^h	$12^{1\frac{1}{2}}$	9^h	$5^{\frac{1}{2}}$	5^2	5^1	Shoemaker	Grand Prix Stable	3.20
Rehabilitate	b 126	4	14^3	$11^{\frac{1}{2}}$	13^h	12^3	6^2	$6^{1\frac{1}{4}}$	Turcotte	Robert Lehman	f-17.00
Amberoid	126	1	15	15	12^2	$8^{1\frac{1}{2}}$	7^3	7^8	Boland	R. N. Webster	6.10
Fleet Shoe	b 126	7	$13^{\frac{1}{2}}$	14^2	14^h	11^3	8^3	8^6	Gilligan	George Putnam	33.50
Exhibitionist	b 126	8	5^h	7^2	$7^{\frac{1}{2}}$	9^h	10^2	$9^{1\frac{1}{2}}$	Belmonte	Mrs. E. D. Jacobs	20.10
Sky Guy	126	10	4^2	4^1	5^2	$7^{\frac{1}{2}}$	11^1	10^{nk}	Adams	W. G. Helis, Jr.	68.40
Williamston Kid	126	15	12^1	$13^{1\frac{1}{2}}$	11^1	10^1	12^4	$11^{2\frac{1}{2}}$	Stevenson	Ternes-Bartlett	19.00
Quinta	b 126	14	$2^{1\frac{1}{2}}$	2^4	2^3	$6^{1\frac{1}{2}}$	9^1	$12^{3\frac{1}{2}}$	Kallai	Bokum II-Scott II	63.70
Tragniew	126	11	8^2	10^h	10^1	13^1	13^2	13^3	Pierce	B. J. Richards	11.80
Beau Sub	126	9	$7^{\frac{1}{2}}$	$9^{\frac{1}{2}}$	15	14^5	14^6	14^{14}	Parrott	Clear Springs Stable	f-17.00
Dominar	b 126	6	3^2	3^1	6^h	15	15	15	Harmatz	Flying M Stable	f-17.00

Time: :22-4/5, :46-1/5, 1:10-3/5, 1:35, 2:02. Track fast.

$2 Mutuels Paid—Kauai King $6.80, $4.20 place, $3.60 show. Advocator $13.00 place, $8.60 show. Blue Skyer (In a betting field with Rehabilitate, Beau Sub and Dominar) $5.40 show.

Winner—Dk.b. or Br.c. by Native Dancer—Sweep In, by Blenheim II. Trained by Henry Forrest; bred in Maryland by Pine Brook Farm.

KAUAI KING broke in stride to gain a narrow advantage, continued well out in the track through the initial stretch run, cut to the inside entering the first turn to draw off under patient handling, continued along the inner railing while coasting on the lead, responded when soundly shaken up a quarter out to turn back a bold bid from STUPENDOUS in the upper stretch and was under hard left-handed whipping to hold ADVOCATOR safe. The latter, away in good order, but reserved off the pace for three-quarters, moved up boldly along the outside on the second turn, dropped back a bit in the midstretch, but came again to finish strongly. BLUE SKYER allowed to settle in stride and unhurried for six furlongs, rallied along the extreme outside leaving the backstretch, cut between horses entering the stretch and closed boldly under extreme pressure. STUPENDOUS, in hand for a half-mile, advanced steadily along the inside thereafter to loom boldly through the upper stretch, but appeared to hang through the closing drive. ABE'S HOPE, slow to begin, was forced to come wide when launching his rally on the second turn, remained on the outside entering the stretch and was gaining slowly at the finish. REHABILITATE closed a big gap following a sluggish beginning. AMBEROID stumbled at the start and was far back throughout. SKY GUY broke out at the start into TRAGNIEW.

THE WINNER'S PEDIGREE AND CAREER HIGHLIGHTS

KAUAI KING
(Dk.b. or Br. Colt)

- Native Dancer
  - Polynesian
    - Unbreakable
    - Black Polly
  - Geisha
    - Discovery
    - Miyako
- Sweep In
  - *Blenheim II
    - Blandford
    - Malva
  - Sweepesta
    - Sweep
    - Celesta

Year		Age	Sts	1st	2nd	3rd	Won
1965		2	4	1	1	1	$ 6,120
1966		3	12	8	1	0	375,277
	Totals		16	9	2	1	$381,397

At 2 Years — WON Maiden Race

At 3 Years
- WON Kentucky Derby, Preakness Stakes, Governor's Gold Cup, Prince George's Stakes, Fountain of Youth Stakes
- 2ND Hutcheson Stakes

Churchill Downs president Wathen Knebelkamp takes a turn at the CBS microphone with Jack Whitaker while jockey Don Brumfield and trainer Henry Forrest take a look at the trophies . . .

. . . meanwhile, Kauai King takes a stroll back to the barn in the company of a happy groom.

May 6, 1967

Owners — Mr. and Mrs. John Galbreath

Trainer — Loyd Gentry

Jockey — Bobby Ussery

PROUD CLARION

$125,000 added and $5,000 Gold Cup. Net to winner $119,700; second $25,000; third $12,500; fourth $5,000. 162 nominations.

Horses	Eqt Wt	PP	1/4	1/2	3/4	1	Str	Fin	Jockeys	Owners	Odds to $1
Proud Clarion	b 126	7	9^5	9^3	8^1	5^h	2^2	1^1	Ussery	Darby Dan Farm	30.10
Barbs Delight	b 126	5	1^1	$1^{1\frac{1}{2}}$	1^2	1^1	1^h	2^3	Knapp	Hug'let Jr-Spald'g-St'e Jr	15.70
Damascus	126	2	6^h	4^1	4^1	4^2	3^4	$3^{1\frac{1}{2}}$	Shoemaker	Mrs. E. W. Bancroft	1.70
Reason to Hail	b 126	13	8^2	8^2	$6\frac{1}{2}$	6^2	5^2	$4\frac{1}{2}$	Blum	Patrice Jacobs	20.70
Ask the Fare	b 126	14	5^h	$7\frac{1}{2}$	9^1	8^3	4^h	$5^{2\frac{1}{4}}$	Holmes	Holiday Stable	66.40
Successor	b 126	6	10^2	$10^{1\frac{1}{2}}$	12^1	12^3	6^1	6^1	Baeza	Wheatley Stb.-O M Phipps	4.60
Gen'man James	b 126	10	13^4	12^2	7^2	$7^{1\frac{1}{2}}$	7^1	$7^{1\frac{1}{2}}$	Campbell	M. G. Phipps	37.10
Ruken	b 126	1	12^h	13^6	$10\frac{1}{2}$	9^2	9^2	8^h	Alvarez	Louis Rowan	4.80
Diplomat Way	b 126	4	$3\frac{1}{2}$	3^2	3^4	$2\frac{1}{2}$	8^h	9no	Sellers	Harvey Peltier	7.10
Sec'd Enc'nter	b 126	12	14	14	14	14	13^5	10^2	Phelps	Harris-Pierce, Jr.	f-17.30
Dawn Glory	b 126	8	2^2	$2\frac{1}{2}$	2^h	3^h	10^2	11^1	Fires	Establo Eden	f-17.30
Dr. Isby	126	3	11^2	11^1	11^1	$11\frac{1}{2}$	11^2	12^{nk}	Hartack	P. L. Grissom	11.00
Field Master	126	9	$4^{1\frac{1}{2}}$	5^1	13^{15}	13^{10}	12^6	13^7	Pineda	Mr.-Mrs. J. H. Seley	f-17.30
Lightning Orphan	126	11	7^2	$6^{1\frac{1}{2}}$	$5\frac{1}{2}$	10^1	14	14	Brumfield	Reverie Knoll Farm	78.20

Time: :22-1/5, :46-3/5, 1:10-4/5, 1:36, 2:00-3/5. Track fast.

f—Mutuel field.

$2 Mutuel Prices—Proud Clarion $62.20 straight, $27.80 place, $12.00 show; Barbs Delight $16.00 place, $7.60 show; Damascus $3.40 show.

Winner: B.c., by Hail to Reason—Breath O'Morn, by Djeddah. Trained by Loyd Gentry; bred in Kentucky by J. W. Galbreath.

PROUD CLARION taken in hand at the start and brought to the inside at once, continued to save ground to the half-mile ground, was eased out thereafter to launch his bid, was forced to circle his field when rallying entering the stretch, engaged BARBS DELIGHT a furlong away and proved best in a stiff drive. The latter, sent to the fore at once, raced along the inner railing while being well rated, responded gamely when challenged to turn back DAMASCUS in the upper stretch and held on well in a prolonged drive. DAMASCUS, reserved off the pace for three-quarters, loomed boldly along the outside on the final turn to continue gamely to midstretch where he appeared to hang under extreme pressure. REASON TO HAIL improved his racing position steadily from between horses in the late stages but could not menace the top trio. ASK THE FARE failed to seriously threaten. SUCCESSOR was always outrun and without apparent excuse. RUKEN, void of early speed, appeared in close quarters while along the inside through the run down the backstretch and could not menace. DIPLOMAT WAY raced with the top flight to the top of the stretch and weakened badly. DAWN GLORY tired after prompting the issue for seven furlongs. DR. ISBY was always far back. FIELD MASTER swung wide on the initial turn. LIGHTNING ORPHAN raced wide.

THE WINNER'S PEDIGREE AND CAREER HIGHLIGHTS

PROUD CLARION (Bay Colt)
- Hail To Reason
  - *Turn-To
    - *Royal Charger
    - *Source Sucree
  - Nothirdchance
    - Blue Swords
    - Galla Colors
- Breath O'Morn
  - *Djeddah
    - Djebel
    - Djezima
  - Darby Dunedin
    - *Blenheim II
    - Ethel Dear

Year	Age	Sts	1st	2nd	3rd	Won
1966	2	3	0	0	1	$ 805
1967	3	13	6	2	1	210,525
1968	4	9	0	2	0	7,400
Totals		25	6	4	2	$218,730

At 3 Years
- WON Kentucky Derby, Roamer Handicap
- 2ND Blue Grass Stakes, Queens County Handicap
- 3RD Preakness

Derby Week in 1967 was marked by open-housing demonstrations in the city and on Tuesday, five youths leaped a fence and dashed down the stretch in front of 10 horses in the first race. On Derby Day, the infield was filled with extra National Guardsmen but no trouble developed.

May 4, 1968

Owner — Mrs. Gene Markey

Trainer — Henry Forrest

Jockey — Ismael Valenzuela

FORWARD PASS

$125,000 added and $5,000 Gold Cup. Net to winner $122,600; second $25,000; third $12,500; fourth $5,000. 191 nominations.

Horses	Eqt Wt	PP	½	¾	1	Str	Fin	Jockeys	Owners	Odds to $1
Dancer's Image	w 126	12	14	10½	8hd	11	11½	Ussery	Peter Fuller	3.60
Forward Pass	wb 126	13	44	34	22	2½	2nk	Valenzuela	Calumet Farm	2.20
Francie's Hat	w 126	10	112	72	72	42	32½	Fires	Saddle Rock Farm	23.50
T.V. Commercial	wb 126	2	81	91	6½	5hd	41	Grant	Bwamazon Farm	24.00
Kentucky Sherry	w 126	4	12	12	1hd	32	51	Combest	Mrs. J. W. Brown	f-14.70
Jig Time	wb 126	3	6½	6½	4hd	6hd	6½	Broussard	Cragwood Stable	36.30
Don B.	w 126	7	52	51	51½	74	75	Pierce	D. B. Wood	35.50
Trouble Brewing	w 126	5	91	112	134	124	8nk	Thornburg	Coventry Rock Farm	f-14.70
Proper Proof	w 126	11	121	122	112	8½	94	Sellers	Mrs. M. Fisher	9.90
Te Vega	wb 126	6	13hd	131	122	92	10¾	Manganello	F. C. Sullivan	f-14.70
Captain's Gig	w 126	9	2hd	21	32	102	11½	Ycaza	Cain Hoy Stable	6.10
Iron Ruler	w 126	1	7½	8½	9hd	111	123	Baeza	October House Farm	5.70
Verbatim	wb 126	8	10hd	14	14	14	13no	Cordero	Elmendorf	37.40
Gleaming Sword	wb 126	14	3½	4hd	102	131	14	Belmonte	C. V. Whitney	31.20

Time: :22-1/5, :45-4/5, 1:09-4/5, 1:36-1/5, 2:02-1/5. Track fast.   f—Field.

$2 Mutuels Paid: Dancer's Image, straight $9.20, place $4.40, show $4.00; Forward Pass, place $4.20, show $3.20; Francie's Hat, show $6.40.

f—Field.

DANCER'S IMAGE void of speed through early stages after being bumped at start, commenced a rally after three-quarters to advance between horses on second turn, cut back to inside when clear entering stretch at which point his rider dropped his whip. Responding to a vigorous hand ride the colt continued to save ground to take command nearing furlong marker and was hard pressed to edge FORWARD PASS. The latter broke alertly only to be bumped and knocked into winner, continued gamely while maintaining a forward position along outside, moved boldly to take command between calls in upper stretch and held on stubbornly in a prolonged drive. FRANCIE'S HAT allowed to settle in stride, commenced a rally after three quarters and finished full of run. T. V. COMMERCIAL closed some ground in his late rally but could not seriously menace. KENTUCKY SHERRY broke in stride to make the pace under good rating, saved ground to stretch where he drifted out while tiring. JIG TIME faltered after making a menacing bid on second turn.

The foregoing is an unaltered reprint of a copyrighted record of Triangle Publications. Dancer's Image finished first. Forward Pass second but because of the finding of prohibited medication of Dancer's Image, except for pari-mutuel pay-offs, Forward Pass was held to be the winner and first purse money and gold cup trophy were awarded to its owner, Calumet Farm, by orders of the Kentucky State Racing Commission. See statement on page 224 hereof.

THE WINNER'S PEDIGREE AND CAREER HIGHLIGHTS

FORWARD PASS (Bay Colt)
- On-and-On
  - *Nasrullah
    - Nearco
    - Mumtaz Begum
  - Two Lea
    - Bull Lea
    - Two Bob
- Princess Turia
  - *Helioscope
    - Hyperion
    - Drift
  - Blue Delight
    - Blue Larkspur
    - Chicleight

Year	Age	Sts	1st	2nd	3rd	Won
1967	2	10	2	2	2	$ 33,957
1968	3	13	7	2	0	644,274
Totals		23	10	4	2	$678,231

At 2 Years
- WON Flash Stakes
- 3RD Sanford Stakes

At 3 Years
- WON Hibiscus, Everglades, Florida Derby, Blue Grass Stakes, Kentucky Derby, Preakness, American Derby
- 2ND Belmont Stakes, Travers

A familiar face in the crowd at the 1968 Derby was Richard Nixon, soon to be President. Another widely known political figure in Kentucky at that time was Gov. Louie Nunn (inset) who greets a National Guardsman.

Calumet Farm

OWNER AND BREEDER OF EIGHT KENTUCKY DERBY WINNERS

WHIRLAWAY	PENSIVE	CITATION	PONDER
1941	1944	1948	1949

	HILL GAIL	IRON LIEGE	TIM TAM	FORWARD PASS
	1952	1957	1958	1968

Mrs. Gene Markey • Versailles Pike • Lexington, Kentucky

May 3, 1969

Owner — Frank McMahon

Trainer — Johnny Longden

Jockey — Bill Hartack

MAJESTIC PRINCE

$125,000 added and $5,000 Gold Cup. Net to winner $113,200; second $25,000; third $12,500; fourth $5,000. 187 nominations.

Horses	Wt.	PP.	1/4	1/2	3/4	1	Str.	Fin.	Jockeys	Owners	Odds to $1
Majestic Prince..w	126	8	4h	3½	3½	2³	1½	1nk	Hartack	Frank McMahon	1.40
Arts and Letters.w	126	3	2h	4³	4⁴	1½	2²	2½	Baeza	Rokeby Stable	4.40
Dike ....w	126	7	7⁸	6h	5⁴	3²	3⁷	3¹⁰	Velasquez	Claiborne Farm	4.20
Traffic Mark ....w	126	2	8	8	8	6⁴	4¹½	4¹³⁄₄	Grimm	Mr.-Mrs. R. F. Roberts	45.20
Top Knight ....wb	126	1	3h	2h	1¹	4⁵	5⁸	5¹³	Ycaza	S. B. Wilson Estate	2.30
Ocean Roar ....w	126	6	1⁴	1²	2½	5h	6⁴	6⁹	Stewart	Leo Miller	28.00
Fleet Allied ...wb	126	5	6⁵	7⁷	6²	7⁸	7¹⁰	7⁸	Hall	Mr.-Mrs. V. Kanowsky	57.00
Rae Jet ....wb	126	4	5¹	5¹	7½	8	8	8	Howard	R. E. Harris	70.90

Time: :23-3/5, :48, 1:12-2/5, 1:37-3/5, 2:01-4/5. Track fast.

$2 mutuels paid: Majestic Prince straight $4,80, place $3.40, show $2.60; Arts and Letters place $4.20, show $3; Dike show $2.80.

Winner—Ch.c., by Raise a Native—Gay Hostess. Trainer Johnny Longden; bred in Kentucky by Leslie Combs II.

MAJESTIC PRINCE swerved out a bit through run to the first turn, dropped over while moving at the leaders after three furlongs, continued along the outside to hold his position, rallied when sharply roused on the second turn to wear down ARTS AND LETTERS nearing the furlong marker and was fully extended to prevail. ARTS AND LETTERS in hand early, continued along the inside in a brilliant move to take over the lead on the stretch turn, rallied gamely when headed and gave way grudgingly. DIKE, slow to settle in stride and unhurried for three-quarters, came out to launch his bid on the final turn to loom boldly in midstretch, only to hang slightly through the closing drive. TRAFFIC MARK passed only tiring horses. TOP KNIGHT forwardly placed from the start, moved strongly along the inside to take command midway down the backstretch, drifted out on rounding the second turn and succumbed suddenly. OCEAN ROAR stopped badly after making the pace for five furlongs. FLEET ALLIED dropped back after encountering slightly close quarters entering the first turn and failed to threaten. RAE JET was squeezed back when caught in a speed jam entering the first turn and soon lost contact with the field.

THE WINNER'S PEDIGREE AND CAREER HIGHLIGHTS

MAJESTIC PRINCE (Chestnut Colt)
- Raise a Native
  - Native Dancer
    - Polynesian
    - Geisha
  - Raise You
    - Case Ace
    - Lady Glory
- Gay Hostess
  - Royal Charger
    - Nearco
    - Sun Princess
  - Your Hostess
    - Alibhai
    - Boudoir II

Year	Age	Sts	1st	2nd	3rd	Won
1968	2	2	2	0	0	$ 5,500
1969	3	8	7	1	0	408,700
Totals		10	9	1	0	$414,200

At 2 Years — WON Maiden and Allowance race

At 3 Years — WON Los Feliz Stakes, San Vicente Stakes, San Jacinto Stakes, Santa Anita Derby, Kentucky Derby, Preakness.
2ND Belmont

Richard M. Nixon, the 37th President of the United States, was a visitor at the 1969 Derby. Wathen R. Knebelkamp, (left), President of Churchill Downs, and Gov. Louie B. Nunn of Kentucky entertain the President.

Majestic Prince stays undefeated to win the 1969 Derby in a close finish with Arts and Letters.

Thousands of racing fans jam the infield for a glimpse of the Derby or just to have fun.

May 2, 1970

Owner — R. E. Lehmann

Trainer — Don Combs

Jockey — Mike Manganello

DUST COMMANDER

$125,000 added and $5,000 Gold Cup. Net to winner $127,800; second $25,000; third $12,500; fourth $5,000. 193 nominations.

Horses	Eqt Wt	PP	1/4	1/2	3/4	1	Str	Fin	Jockeys	Owners	Odds to $1
Dust Commander . . wb 126		2	9^2	$6\frac{1}{2}$	5^2	7^1	$1^1\frac{1}{2}$	1^5	Mangan'lo	R. E. Lehmann	15.30
My Dad George . wb 126		12	16^3	14^2	14^1	5^h	3^3	$2\frac{1}{2}$	Broussard	R. M. Curtis	2.80
High Echelon . . . . wb 126		11	17	17	17	15^2	5^2	3^h	Adams	Ethel D. Jacobs	a-4.90
Naskra . . . . wb 126		14	10^2	10^2	$10^2\frac{1}{2}$	8^2	4^h	4^1	Baeza	Her-Jac-Stable	15.90
Silent Screen . . . . w 126		6	6^3	3^h	3^1	1^1	2^1	$5^2\frac{1}{2}$	Rotz	Elberon Farm	5.70
Admiral's Shield . . w 126		15	14^2	16^5	16^2	16	7^3	6^h	Nichols	W. C. Robinson, Jr.	29.70
Corn off the Cob . . w 126		17	5^h	5^2	$6^1\frac{1}{2}$	$3^1\frac{1}{2}$	6^3	7^3	Cordero Jr	Fence Post Farm	13.10
Personality . . . . . wb 126		16	7^h	$9^1\frac{1}{2}$	$11^1\frac{1}{2}$	9^h	8^h	$8^2\frac{1}{2}$	Belmonte	Ethel D. Jacobs	a-4.90
Native Royalty . . . wb 126		8	$8^1\frac{1}{2}$	8^1	8^1	$4^1\frac{1}{2}$	9^2	$9^2\frac{1}{2}$	Valenzuela	Happy Valley Farm	f-10.10
Robin's Bug . . . . wb 126		7	3^h	4^2	4^h	$10^1\frac{1}{2}$	10^3	$10\frac{1}{2}$	Moyers	W. J. Hickey-R. F. Kuhn	f-10.10
Terlago . . . . w 126		13	$4^1\frac{1}{2}$	$7^1\frac{1}{2}$	7^h	11^2	11^2	$11^1\frac{1}{4}$	Shoemaker	S. J. Agnew	7.40
Dr. Behrman . . . . wb 126		3	11^2	11^1	12^1	14^2	12^2	12^2	Baltazar	Lin-Drake Farm	f-10.10
Action Getter . . . . w 126		9	$15^1\frac{1}{2}$	15^h	$15^2\frac{1}{2}$	13^2	13^1	$13^2\frac{1}{2}$	Venezia	E.V. Benjamin-J. Jones Jr.	f-10.10
George Lewis . . . . w 126		1	$2^1\frac{1}{2}$	2^4	$2^1\frac{1}{2}$	$2\frac{1}{2}$	14^1	14^h	Hartack	Mr.-Mrs. A. Magerman	9.40
Fathom . . . . wb 126		10	$12\frac{1}{2}$	13^3	9^1	12^3	15^3	$15^3\frac{1}{2}$	Crump	W. L. L. Brown	f-10.10
Rancho Lejos . . . wb 126		5	1^3	1^3	1^1	6^2	16	16	Campas	S. Carson-I. Apple	f-10.10
Holy Land . . . . . . wb 126		4	13^4	$12\frac{1}{2}$	$13\frac{1}{2}$	Fell			Pilar	Mrs. J. S. Dean, Jr.	15.90

Time: :23-1/5, :46-4/5, 1:12, 1:37-2/5, 2:03-2/5. Track good.

a—Coupled, High Echelon and Personality. f—Mutuel field.

$2 Mutuels Paid: Dust Commander, straight $32.60, place $12.60, show $7; My Dad George, place $5, show $3.20; High Echelon (a-entry), show $4.40.

Winner—Ch.c., by Bold Commander—Dust Storm, by Windy City II. Trained by Don Combs; bred in Illinois by Pullen Bros.

DUST COMMANDER, soundly bumped at the start to be hard held early, commenced to advance along the inside after a half mile, continued to save ground to the final turn where he was forced to come out between horses to launch his rally, remained slightly wide into the stretch and responding to pressure was up leaving the furlong marker and drew well clear under intermittent urging. MY DAD GEORGE, slow to begin and unhurried for three quarters, commenced to advance from between horses upon leaving the backstretch, cut back to the inside on the final turn to loom boldly in the upper stretch but could not sustain his bid. HIGH ECHELON, badly outrun for a mile, came to the extreme outside to circle his field entering the stretch and finished boldly. NASKRA, in hand while being outrun, launched a bid from between horses on the second turn to loom menacingly a furlong away but could not sustain his rally. SILENT SCREEN, soundly bumped and knocked off stride soon after the start, was forced to be sent along to remain in contention, continued along the outside to take command boldly on the final turn, drew off in the upper stretch only to falter.

THE WINNER'S PEDIGREE AND CAREER HIGHLIGHTS

DUST COMMANDER (Chestnut Colt)

Bold Commander	Bold Ruler	*Nasrullah	
		Miss Disco	
	High Voltage	*Ambiorix	
		Dynamo	
Dust Storm	*Windy City II	Wyndham	
		Staunton	
	Challure	Challedon	
		Capitivation	

Year		Age	Sts	1st	2nd	3rd	Won
1969		2	14	4	1	2	$ 25,245
1970		3	23	4	4	2	187,331
	Totals		37	8	5	4	$212,576

At 2 Years   **WON**   City of Miami Beach Handicap

At 3 Years   **WON**   Kentucky Derby, Blue Grass Stakes

Lynn Stone became the ninth president of Churchill Downs in 1970.

A parachutist landed in the infield and another landed just outside the track to provide an added bit of window dressing for the 1970 race.

May 1, 1971

Owner — Edgar Caibett

Trainer — Juan Arias

Jockey — Gustavo Avila

CANONERO II

$125,000 added and $5,000 Gold Cup. Net to winner $145,500; second $25,000; third $12,500; fourth $5,000. 220 nominations.

Horses	Eqt Wt	PP	1/4	1/2	3/4	1	Str	Fin	Jockeys	Owners	Odds to $1
Canonero II	w 126	12	16^1	18^5	15^3	$4\frac{1}{2}$	1^3	$1^{3\frac{1}{4}}$	Avila	Edgar Caibett	f-8.70
Jim French	wb 126	10	10^h	11^2	10^2	7^2	$5\frac{1}{2}$	2^2	C'dero, Jr.	F. J. Caldwell	4.80
Bold Reason	wb 126	14	18^6	$16\frac{1}{2}$	12^2	9^2	6^2	3^{nk}	Cruguet	W. A. Levin	18.30
Eastern Fleet	wb 126	17	6^2	3^h	$2^{1\frac{1}{2}}$	$2^{1\frac{1}{2}}$	2^h	4^h	Maple	Calumet Farm	a-3.80
Unconscious	w 126	8	7^2	6^2	5^1	5^h	$4\frac{1}{2}$	$5^{1\frac{3}{4}}$	Pincay, Jr.	A. A. Seeligson, Jr.	2.80
Vegas Vic	wb 126	7	13^3	13^3	13^1	$13\frac{1}{2}$	7^1	6^{nk}	Grant	Betty Sechrest-C. Fritz	19.30
Tribal Line	wb 126	15	15^2	14^h	17^6	$8^{1\frac{1}{2}}$	8^2	7no	Whited	J. E.-T. A. Grissom	80.80
Bold and Able	wb 126	1	1^h	1^2	$1^{1\frac{1}{2}}$	1^h	3^h	8^3	Velasquez	Calumet Farm	a-3.80
List	wb 126	18	17^h	$17\frac{1}{2}$	14^2	$14^{1\frac{1}{2}}$	9^2	9^3	Nichols	Mrs. J. W. Brown	8.60
Twist the Axe	w 126	11	$9\frac{1}{2}$	10^1	7^1	$6^{1\frac{1}{2}}$	10^2	$10^{1\frac{1}{2}}$	Patterson	Pastorale Stable	c-5.10
Going Straight	w 126	2	11^2	8^h	6^h	10^3	12^2	11^h	Torres	Donamire Farm	45.60
Royal Leverage	w 126	5	19^8	15^2	16^1	18^5	11^h	12^2	Fromin	P. Teinowitz	b-41.60
Impetuosity	w 126	20	$8^{1\frac{1}{2}}$	9^2	8^2	15^1	13^h	$13^{1\frac{1}{2}}$	Guerin	W. P. Rosso	c-5.10
Helio Rise	w 126	16	$12^{1\frac{1}{2}}$	12^1	9^h	11^1	14^1	14^3	Knapp	R.W., V.-R.T. Wilson Jr.	58.20
On the Money	w 126	9	20	20	20	$17^{1\frac{1}{2}}$	$15^{1\frac{1}{2}}$	15^1	Solomone	Teinowitz-Schmidt	b-41.60
Barbizon Streak	w 126	6	2^h	5^1	11^1	12^1	16^6	16^{18}	Brumfield	Mrs. H. J. Udouj	f-8.70
Knight Counter	wb 126	13	4^2	$4^{1\frac{1}{2}}$	3^1	3^1	17^6	17^{11}	Mang'llo	R. Huffman	f-8.70
Jr's Arrowhead	wb 126	4	3^h	2^1	4^1	$16^{1\frac{1}{2}}$	18^2	18^6	Rini	Walnut Hill Farm	f-8.70
Fourulla	w 126	19	5^h	$7\frac{1}{2}$	18^3	19^4	19^4	19^{14}	MacBeth	A. H. Sullivan	f-8.70
Saigon Warrior	w 127	3	14^3	19^9	19^5	20	20	20	Parrott	C. M. Day	f-8.70

Time: :23, :46-4/5, 1:11-3/5, 1:36-1/5, 2:03-1/5. Track fast.

f—Mutuel field. a—Coupled, Eastern Fleet and Bold and Brave; c—Twist the Axe and Impetuosity; b—Royal Leverage and On the Money.

$2 Mutuels Paid: Canonero II (field), straight $19.40, place $8.00; show $4.20; Jim French, place $6.20, show $4.40; Bold Reason, show $12.60.

Winner—B.c., by *Pretendre—Dixieland II, by Nantallah. Trained by Juan Arias; bred in Ky. by E. B. Benjamin.

CANONERO II, void of speed and unhurried for three-quarters, was forced to come to the extreme outside to launch his bid upon leaving the backstretch, continued to circle his field entering the stretch to take command. JIM FRENCH moved up along the inside when launching his bid on the second turn, was forced to come out between horses entering the stretch, but could not reach the winner. BOLD REASON, badly outrun for six furlongs, moved between horses until forced to steady when blocked in the upper stretch, dropped to the inside when clear. EASTERN FLEET, away alertly to gain a forward position along the inside, moved through in slightly close quarters leaving the backstretch, commenced drifting out in the closing drive and gave way willingly. UNCONSCIOUS, never far back along the inner railing, came out for the drive and had little left.

THE WINNER'S PEDIGREE AND CAREER HIGHLIGHTS

CANONERO II (Bay Colt)	*Pretendre	Doutelle	Prince Chevalier / Above Board
		Limicola	Verso II / Uccello
	Dixieland II	Nantallah	Nasrullah / Shimmer
		Ragtime Band	Johnstown / Martial Air

Year	Age	Sts	1st	2nd	3rd	Won
1970	2	4	2	0	1	$ 12,851
1971	3	11	6	0	3	311,983
1972	4	8	1	3	0	35,970
Totals		23	9	3	4	$360,804

At 2 Years   WON Two allowance races in Venezuela

At 3 Years { WON Kentucky Derby, Preakness Stakes (won 4 in Venezuela)
            { 4TH   Belmont Stakes

Trainer Juan Arias leads a happy contingent of Latins away from the presentation stand after his horse's surprise win.

Whether the "language" is with the hands or the feet, the message is the same — happiness is a winner at the race track. The lady is unidentified but the jockey is Gustavo Avila who rode Canonero II.

May 6, 1972

Owner — Mrs. John Tweedy

Trainer — Lucien Laurin

Jockey — Ron Turcotte

RIVA RIDGE

$125,000 added and $5,000 Gold Cup. Net to winner $140,300; second $25,000; third $12,500; fourth $5,000. 258 nominations.

Horses	Eqt Wt	PP	1/4	1/2	3/4	1	Str	Fin	Jockeys	Owners	Odds to $1
Riva Ridge......	wb 126	9	$1\frac{1}{2}$	$1\,1\frac{1}{2}$	$1\,1\frac{1}{2}$	$1\,1\frac{1}{2}$	1^3	$1\,3\frac{3}{4}$	Turcotte	Meadow Stable	1.50
No Le Hace.....	wb 126	16	6^2	6^5	5^3	3^3	3^5	$2\,3\frac{1}{2}$	Rubbicco	J. R. Straus	4.50
Hold Your Peace.	wb 126	3	$3\,1\frac{1}{2}$	$2\frac{1}{2}$	2^5	2^8	2^3	$3\,3\frac{1}{2}$	Marquez	Maribel G. Blum	3.90
Introductivo ...	wb 126	4	8^2	7^2	7^h	8^1	4^3	4^2	Breen	Mr-Mrs CJ Robertson Sr	52.90
Sensitive Music..	wb 126	2	10^2	9^3	9^5	4^1	$5\,1\frac{1}{2}$	$5\,3\frac{3}{4}$	Rotz	F. H. Lindsay	31.00
Freetex	wb 126	1	11^3	11^4	6^h	7^h	6^2	6^1	Baltazar	Middletown Stable	15.90
Big Spruce	w 126	15	$12\frac{1}{2}$	13^2	11^1	13^2	7^2	$7\,1\frac{1}{2}$	Adams	Elmendorf	f-8.90
Head of the River.	w 126	14	9^h	10^h	10^4	9^3	8^6	8^5	Hole	Rokeby Stable	19.00
Big Brown Bear...	w 126	7	14^h	12^1	14^5	12^h	10^2	$9\,1\frac{3}{4}$	Broussard	Mr.-Mrs. A.E. Reinhold	27.80
Kentuckian	wb 126	8	15^4	14^1	12^2	11^5	11^3	$10\,3\frac{3}{4}$	Brumfield	P. W. Madden	16.70
Hassi's Image ..	wb 126	11	5^3	$4\frac{1}{2}$	3^2	6^2	$9\,1\frac{1}{2}$	11^2	Gustines	Hassi Shina	31.00
Majestic Needle.	wb 126	12	$2\frac{1}{2}$	3^2	4^2	5^2	$12\,1\frac{1}{2}$	12no	Mang'llo	R. E. Lehmann	f-8.90
Our Trade Winds .	w 126	6	16	16	16	15^2	$13\frac{1}{2}$	$13\frac{1}{2}$	Nichols	Robert Mitchell	f-8.90
Napoise	wb 126	13	$13\,1\frac{1}{2}$	15^7	15^2	16	14^5	$14\,4\frac{1}{2}$	Kotenko	R. E. Lehmann	f-8.90
Dr. Neale	w 126	5	4^h	5^3	8^1	$10\,1\frac{1}{2}$	16	15^{nk}	Leeling	C. E. Nicholas	f-8.90
Pacallo	wb 126	10	7^1	8^1	13^2	14^3	15^1	16	Avila	Walnut Hill Farm	54.50

Time: :23-4/5, :47-3/5, 1:11-4/5, 1:36, 2:01-4/5. Track fast.

f—Mutuel field.

$2 Mutuels Paid: Riva Ridge straight $5.00; place $3.80; show $3.00; No Le Hace place $4.40; show $3.40; Hold Your Peace, show $3.60.

Winner—B.c. by First Landing—Iberia, by Heliopolis. Trained by Lucien Laurin; bred in Kentucky by Meadow Stud, Inc.

RIVA RIDGE quickly recovered after being bumped at the start to assume command, continued slightly wide while under patient handling, disposed of HOLD YOUR PEACE when ready while drifting out through the upper stretch and encountered little difficulty in holding NO LE HACE safe. The latter, unhurried for a mile, moved up along the outside thereafter, commenced swerving again through the closing drive and was clearly best of the others. HOLD YOUR PEACE away in good order to prompt the pace while in hand, raced slightly wide to maintain a striking position, dropped to the inside in the upper stretch when the winner drifted out but lacked a further response. INTRODUCTIVO improved his racing position steadily in the late stages but could not menace the top trio. SENSITIVE MUSIC passed tiring horses. FREETEX was without speed. BIG SPRUCE was always outrun. HEAD OF THE RIVER failed to enter contention. KENTUCKIAN lacked speed. HASSI'S IMAGE swerved sharply to the inside at the start, bumping with PACALLO, continued in a forward position while saving ground and stopped badly after going seven furlongs. MAJESTIC NEEDLE dropped back steadily.

THE WINNER'S PEDIGREE AND CAREER HIGHLIGHTS

RIVA RIDGE (Bay Colt)	First Landing	*Turn-to	*Royal Charger
			*Source Sucree
		Hildene	Bubbling Over
			Fancy Racket
	Iberia	*Heliopolis	Hyperion
			Drift
		War East	*Easton
			Warrior Lass

Year	Age	Sts	1st	2nd	3rd	Won
1971	2	9	7	0	0	$503,263
1972	3	12	5	1	1	395,632
1973	4	9	5	2	0	212,452
Totals		30	17	3	1	$1,111,347

At 2 Years	WON	Flash Futurity, Champagne, Pimlico-Laurel Futurity, Garden State
At 3 Years	WON	Kentucky Derby, Hibiscus, Blue Grass, Belmont Stakes, Hollywood Derby
At 4 Years	WON	Massachusetts Handicap, Brooklyn Handicap, Stuyvesant.

Perhaps more than any other, this photograph says it all about the Kentucky Derby — the crowd, the horses, the twin spires. It is THE day in racing, the First Saturday in May.

Sen. Edmund Muskie of Maine was a guest of Gov. Wendell Ford at the 1972 Derby. Sen. Muskie then was a candidate for the Democratic presidential nomination.

May 5, 1973

Owner — Mrs. John Tweedy

Trainer — Lucien Laurin

Jockey — Ron Turcotte

SECRETARIAT

$125,000 added and $5,000 Gold Cup. Net to winner $155,050; second $25,000; third $12,500; fourth $6,250. 218 nominations.

Horse	Eqt	Wt	PP	1/4	1/2	3/4	1	Str	Fin	Jockeys	Owners	Odds to $1
Secretariat	wb	126	10	11^h	$6\frac{1}{2}$	5^1	$2^{1\frac{1}{2}}$	$1\frac{1}{2}$	$1^{2\frac{1}{2}}$	Turcotte	Meadow Stable	a-1.50
Sham	wb	126	4	5^1	3^2	2^1	$1\frac{1}{2}$	2^6	2^8	Pincay, Jr.	Sigmund Sommer	2.50
Our Native	wb	126	7	$6\frac{1}{2}$	$8^{1\frac{1}{2}}$	8^1	5^h	3^h	$3\frac{1}{2}$	Brumfield	Pr'ch'd-Thom's-R'g't	10.60
Forego	w	126	9	$9^{1\frac{1}{2}}$	$9\frac{1}{2}$	$6\frac{1}{2}$	6^2	$4\frac{1}{2}$	$4^{2\frac{1}{2}}$	Anderson	Lazy F Ranch	28.60
Restless Jet	w	126	1	$7^{1\frac{1}{2}}$	7^h	$10^{1\frac{1}{2}}$	$7^{1\frac{1}{2}}$	$6^{1\frac{1}{2}}$	$5^{2\frac{1}{4}}$	Hole	Elkwood Farm	28.50
Shecky Greene . .	wb	126	11	$11\frac{1}{2}$	1^3	$11\frac{1}{2}$	3^3	5^1	$6^{1\frac{1}{2}}$	Adams	Joe Kellman	b-5.70
Navajo	w	126	5	$10^{1\frac{1}{2}}$	10^1	11^4	$8\frac{1}{2}$	8^2	7no	Soirez	J. Stevenson-R. Stump	52.30
Royal and Regal . .	w	126	8	3^1	4^3	4^3	4^1	$7\frac{1}{2}$	$8^{3\frac{1}{2}}$	Blum	Aisco Stable	28.30
My Gallant	wb	126	12	8^h	$11^{1\frac{1}{2}}$	12^3	11^2	$10\frac{1}{2}$	9^h	Baeza	A. I. Appleton	b-5.70
Angle Light	w	126	2	4^h	$5^{1\frac{1}{2}}$	7^1	$10^{1\frac{1}{2}}$	$9^{1\frac{1}{2}}$	$10^{1\frac{3}{4}}$	LeBlanc	Edwin Whittaker	a-1.50
Gold Bag	wb	126	13	2^h	2^h	$3\frac{1}{2}$	9^1	11^1	11no	Fires	R. Sechrest-Gottdank	68.30
Twice a Prince . .	wb	126	6	13	13	13	13	12^2	$12^{1\frac{1}{2}}$	Santiago	Elmendorf	62.50
Warbucks	w	126	3	12^1	12^3	9^h	$12^{1\frac{1}{2}}$	13	13	Hartack	E. E. Elzemeyer	7.20

Time: :23-2/5, :47-2/5, 1:11-4/5, 1:36-1/5, 1:59-2/5 (new track record). Track fast.

a—Coupled, Secretariat and Angle Light; b—Shecky Greene and My Gallant.

$2 mutuels paid: Secretariat (coupled with Angle Light) straight, $5.00; place, $3.20; show, $3.00. Sham, place, $3.20; show, $3.00; Our Native, show, $4.20.

Winner—Ch.c. by Bold Ruler—Somethingroyal, by Princequillo. Trainer, Lucien Laurin. Bred in Virginia by Meadow Stud, Inc.

SECRETARIAT relaxed nicely and dropped back last leaving the gate as the field broke in good order, moved between horses to begin improving position entering the first turn, but passed rivals from the outside thereafter. Turcotte roused him smartly with the whip in his right hand leaving the far turn and SECRETARIAT strongly raced to the leaders, lost a little momentum racing into the stretch where Turcotte used the whip again, but then switched it to his left hand and merely flashed it as the winner willingly drew away in record breaking time. SHAM, snugly reserved within striking distance after brushing with NAVAJO at the start, raced around rivals to the front without any need of rousing and drew clear between calls entering the stretch, was under a strong hand ride after being displaced in the last furlong and continued resolutely to dominate the remainder of the field. OUR NATIVE, reserved in the first run through the stretch, dropped back slightly on the turn, came wide in the drive and finished well for his placing. FOREGO, taken to the inside early, veered slightly from a rival and hit the rail entering the far turn, swung wide entering the stretch and vied with OUR NATIVE in the drive. RESTLESS JET saved ground in an even effort. SHECKY GREENE easily set the pace under light rating for nearly seven furlongs and faltered. NAVAJO was outrun. ROYAL AND REGAL raced well for a mile and had nothing left in the drive. MY GALLANT was not a factor. ANGLE LIGHT gave way steadily in a dull effort and was forced to check when crowded by GOLD BAG on the stretch turn.

THE WINNER'S PEDIGREE AND CAREER HIGHLIGHTS

SECRETARIAT (Chestnut Colt)	Bold Ruler	*Nasrullah	Nearco
			Mumtaz Begun
		Miss Disco	Discovery
			Outdone
	Somethingroyal	*Princequillo	Prince Rose
			Cosquilla
		Imperatrice	Caruso
			Cinquepace

Year		Age	Sts	1st	2nd	3rd	Won
1972		2	9	7	1	0	$456,404
1973		3	12	9	2	1	860,404
	Totals		21	16	3	1	$1,316,808

At 2 years {
WON Sanford, Hopeful, Belmont Futurity, Laurel Futurity, Garden State
2ND Champagne (1st, disqualified and placed 2nd)

At 3 years {
WON Kentucky Derby, Preakness, Belmont Stakes, Bay Shore, Gotham, Arlington Invitational, Marlboro Cup, Man o' War, Canadian International.

It's a nice habit, this winning the Derby. Ron Turcotte guides Secretariat under the wire for his second in a row aboard a Meadow Stable entrant trained by Lucien Laurin. Turcotte won aboard Riva Ridge in 1972.

Another nice habit is the toasting of the winner at the post-Derby party. The governor — in this case, Wendell Ford — presents the julep to the winning owner — in this case, Mrs. John Tweedy.

THE MEADOW

Founded in 1936, The Meadow has since bred more than 40 stakes winners. Five of them — Hill Prince, First Landing, Cicada, Riva Ridge, and Secretariat — have been named divisional champions. Two of these, Hill Prince and Secretariat, were named Horse of the Year.

Riva Ridge and Secretariat, winners of the Kentucky Derby in 1972 and 1973, make us one of only two farms ever to individually breed and race back-to-back winners in the "Run for the Roses". Secretariat set the track record in both his Derby and Belmont as he went on to become America's first Triple Crown winner since 1948!

We are proud of these accomplishments, for we think they speak well of the devotion and care which has always been a guideline at The Meadow — and always will!

Howard Gentry, Manager, Doswell, Virginia 23047, (703) 994-2144

RAYMOND JOHNSON

RAYMOND JOHNSON, *Churchill Downs publicity director, is the retired sports editor of The Nashville Tennessean, a paper he served from October 1918 until April 1970. He is past president of the National Turf Writers Association, Football Writers of America, Amateur Softball Association of the Americas, and National Golden Gloves Association and several other organizations such as the Southeastern Amateur Athletic Union and the Southern Association of Baseball Writers. He is a member of Tennessee's Sports Hall of Fame, being inducted in February 1973. Among other honors he has received are the Jake Wade plaque given by the nation's college publicists; the George Barton trophy for amateur boxing, and the Capital City Golf Association's Man of the Year award.*

Records Are Made To Be Broken

What do Secretariat, Decidedly, Whirlaway, Twenty Grand, Donerail and Meridian have in common other than that each shattered the track record the day he won the Kentucky Derby?

All six were beaten in their last start prior to getting their chance in America's most prestigious horse race.

Two of these, Decidedly in 1962, and Whirlaway in 1941, each failed in their last two attempts.

Roman Line beat Decidedly five lengths in an allowance at Keeneland. Then Ridan was four lengths the better in the Blue Grass Stakes.

Those losses didn't worry trainer Horatio A. Luro, who enjoyed the unprecedented honor of having two colts he conditioned better the Derby standard in three years. Northern Dancer, his other champion and one of only two record-breakers to come up to the Derby off wins since the turn of the century, erased Decidedly's mark two years later.

Luro explained his preparation of Decidedly by saying "you do not squeeze ze lemon dry", meaning he didn't feel the El Peco Ranch hopeful was ready to be extended like Bill Hartack had to do in the Run for the Roses.

Whirlaway was the Derby favorite even if he had been beaten six lengths by Our Boots in the Blue Grass and three-quarters of a length by Blue Pair in the Derby Trial.

Although beaten in the Trial, many horsemen said after that race that no horse would be close to Whirlaway in the Derby. "Horses just can't run as fast as Whirlaway did around the final turn," said one veteran. "He was going so fast I thought he was going through the outside fence."

Ben Jones, who saddled a record six Derby winners, did something about Whirlaway going so wide on that turn. He put a full cup blinker on his right eye and removed the cup on the left eye so Mr. Long Tail, as Whirlaway was affectionately known because of his extremely long flowing tail, could see the inside rail but not the crowd in the stands. The result was that he won by eight lengths, covering the last quarter in the sensational time of 23⅗ seconds enroute to a 2:01⅖ mile and a quarter record.

No horse has traveled that last back-breaking quarter as fast before or since until Secretariat did in 1973, although Decidedly cracked Whirlaway's 21-year-old mark and Northern

Dancer in turn established a new one that stood nine years.

Secretariat, beaten four lengths in the Wood Memorial by his stablemate, Angle Light, traveled the last quarter in the amazing time of 23 ⅕ seconds in lowering the Derby record to 1:59⅖.

Twenty Grand erased Old Rosebud's record with a 2:01⅘ clocking in 1931, seven days after he had finished second to Mate in the Preakness. Old Rosebud, like Northern Dancer, had won his last start when he shattered the standard set by Donerail, the longest-priced winner of the 99-year history of the Derby. Donerail had trailed Fountation home in the Blue Grass. Meridian, in 1911, clipped 1⅕ seconds off Lieut. Gibson's 1900 mark. Meridian was beaten by Governor Gray, the Derby favorite, in the Blue Grass.

Secretariat's victory on a day when records fell like tenpins gave Mrs. Helen Tweedy's Meadow Stable, Trainer Lucien Laurin and Jockey Ron Turcotte the distinguished honor of becoming the first to win two Derbys in a row as a team. The Meadow Stud bred Riva Ridge, the 1972 winner which Laurin trained and Turcotte rode in the name of the Meadow Stable.

Saddling back-to-back Derby kings is an immense feat, as underlined by its rarity. Dick Thompson, with Burgoo King (1932) and Brokers Tip (1933); Ben Jones, with Citation (1948) and Ponder (1949); and H. A. (Jimmy) Jones, with Iron Liege (1957) and Tim Tam (1958), are the only others to have done it.

The 1973 Derby established a record American handle of $7,627,965, wiping out the mark set only 12 months earlier. The $3,284,962 bet on the Derby race was also a new high. The preliminary betting on Friday was $279,441 and the combined Friday and Saturday preliminary was $1,771,327, all new marks.

The Derby day attendance of 134,476 also was an American record eclipsing the 1972 figure of 130,564. This marked the fifth straight Derby that the paid attendance soared above 105,000.

Records are made to be broken, as the old saying goes. The 100th anniversary Derby probably will see some of the above smashed.

KENTUCKY DERBY RECORDS

THE WINNERS

Ninety-one colts, seven geldings, and one filly have won the Derby. Regret (1915) was the filly. The geldings were Vagrant (1876), Apollo (1882), Macbeth (1888), Old Rosebud (1914), Exterminator (1918), Paul Jones (1920), Clyde Van Dusen (1929).

BIRTHPLACE

*Tomy Lee (1959), *Omar Khayyam (1917), and Northern Dancer (1964) are the only winners not foaled in the United States. Northern Dancer was foaled in Canada. The other two were foaled in England. *Tomy Lee was brought to this country as a weanling, *Omar Khayyam as a yearling. Cavalcade (1934) and Pensive (1944) are sons of mares bred to stallions in England and brought to America while the mares were carrying the Derby winners.

Seventy-six winners were foaled in *Kentucky*. Lord Murphy, Kingman, and Typhoon II were foaled in *Tennessee;* Assault and Middleground in *Texas;* Spokane in *Montana* (while that state was still part of the *Northwest Territory*); Elwood in *Missouri;* Wintergreen in *Ohio;* Regret and Cavalcade in *New Jersey;* Decidedly, Swaps and Morvich in *California;* Reigh Count and Secretariat in *Virginia;* Lawrin in *Kansas;* Dust Commander in *Illinois;* Needles and Carry Back in *Florida*, and Kauai King in *Maryland*.

COLOR

Determine, 1954 winner, was the first gray to win the Derby. Decidedly was the second. Bay horses have won the Derby 47 times. Chestnuts have won 32 times, browns 14 times, and blacks 4 times.

OWNERS

EIGHT WINNERS: *Calumet Farm* — Whirlaway (1941), Pensive (1944), Citation (1948), Ponder (1949), Hill Gail (1952), Iron Liege (1957), Tim Tam (1958), Forward Pass (1968). The late Warren Wright owned Calumet the first four times the stable won; Mrs. Wright was owner in 1952, later won as Mrs. Gene Markey in 1957, 1958, 1968.

FOUR WINNERS: *E. R. Bradley* — Behave Yourself (1921), Bubbling Over (1926), Burgoo King (1932), Brokers Tip (1933).

TRAINERS

SIX WINNERS: *Ben A. Jones* — Lawrin (1938), Whirlaway (1941), Pensive (1944), Citation (1948), Ponder (1949), Hill Gail (1952).

FOUR WINNERS: *H. J. Thompson* — Behave Yourself (1921), Bubbling Over (1926), Burgoo King (1932), Brokers Tip (1933).

THREE WINNERS: *James Fitzsimmons* — Gallant Fox (1930), Omaha (1935), Johnstown (1939), *Max Hirsch* — Bold Venture (1936), Assault (1946), Middleground (1950).

JOCKEYS

FIVE WINNERS: *Eddie Arcaro* — Lawrin (1938), Whirlaway (1941), Hoop Jr. (1945), Citation (1948), Hill Gail (1952); *Bill Hartack* — Iron Liege (1957), Venetian Way (1960), Decidedly (1962), Northern Dancer (1964), Majestic Prince (1969).

THREE WINNERS: *Isaac Murphy* — Buchanan (1884), Riley (1890), Kingman (1891). *Earl Sande* — Zev (1923), Flying Ebony (1925), Gallant Fox (1930). *Bill Shoemaker* — Swaps (1955), *Tomy Lee (1959), Lucky Debonair (1965).

TWO WINNERS: *Willie Simms* — Ben Brush (1896), Plaudit (1898). *Jimmy Winkfield* — His Eminence (1901), Alan-a-Dale (1902). *Johnny Loftus* — George Smith (1916), Sir Barton (1919). *Albert Johnson* — Morvich (1922), Bubbling Over (1926). *Linus McAtee* — Whiskery (1927), Clyde Van Dusen (1929). *Charles Kurtsinger* — Twenty Grand (1931), War Admiral (1937). *Conn McCreary* — Pensive (1944), Count Turf (1951). *Ron Turcotte* — Riva Ridge (1972), Secretariat (1973).

TWO IN SUCCESSION: *Isaac Murphy, Jimmy Winkfield* and *Ron Turcotte* are the only jockeys to ride successive winners.

NEGRO JOCKEYS: *Isaac Murphy, Willie Simms, Jimmy Winkfield* (see records above). *Oliver Lewis* — Aristides (1875), *Billy Walker* — Baden-Baden (1877). *George Lewis* — Fonso (1880). *Babe Hurd* — Apollo (1882). *Erskine Henderson* — Joe Cotton (1885). *Isaac Lewis* — Montrose (1887). *Alonzo Clayton* — Azra (1892). *James Perkins* — Halma (1895).

APPRENTICE JOCKEYS: *Ira Hanford* on Bold Venture (1936), and *Bill Boland* on Middleground (1950).

FEMALE JOCKEYS: *Diane Crump*, finished 15th aboard Fathom (1970) in 17-horse field.

BREEDERS

EIGHT WINNERS: *Calumet Farm* — Whirlaway (1941), Pensive (1944), Citation (1948), Ponder (1949), Hill Gail (1952), Iron Liege (1957), Tim Tam (1958), Forward Pass (1968).

MOST APPEARANCES: *Eddie Arcaro* rode in the Derby for the 21st time in 1961, a record number of mounts for any rider in the race. *Bill Shoemaker* has ridden in the Derby 17 times.

FIVE WINNERS: *A. J. A. Alexander* — Baden-Baden (1877), Fonso (1880), Joe Cotton (1885), Chant (1894), His Eminence (1901). *John E. Madden* — Old Rosebud (1914), Sir Barton (1919), Paul Jones (1920), Zev (1923), Flying Ebony (1925). Madden bred Sir Barton in partnership with Vivian Gooch of England. All five Madden-bred Derby winners were foaled in the same barn at Hamburg Place near Lexington, Kentucky. It is impossible to determine if the winners bred by Alexander were foaled in the same barn at Wooburn stud.

FOUR WINNERS: *E. R. Bradley* — Behave Yourself (1921), Bubbling Over (1926), Burgoo King (1932), Brokers Tip (1933). Bradley owned Idle Hour Stock Farm in Fayette County, Kentucky and bred Burgoo King in partnership with H. N. Davis.

SIRES

TRIPLE: *Reigh Count* (1928) sired *Count Fleet* (1943) who sired *Count Turf* (1951). *Pensive* (1944) sired *Ponder* (1949) who sired *Needles* (1956).

THREE WINNERS: *Falsetto* — Chant (1894), His Eminence (1901), Sir Huon (1906). *Virgil* — Vagrant (1876), Hindoo (1881), Ben Ali (1886). **Sir Gallahad III* — Gallant Fox (1930), Gallahadion (1940), Hoop Jr. (1945). *Bull Lea* — Citation (1948), Hill Gail (1952), Iron Liege (1957).

TWO WINNERS: *King Alfonso* — Fonso (1880), Joe Cotton (1885). *Longfellow* — Leonatus (1883), Riley (1890). *Broomstick* — Meridian (1911), Regret (1915). **McGee* — Donerail (1913), Exterminator (1918). *The Finn* — Zev (1923), Flying Ebony (1925). *Black Toney* — Black Gold (1924), Brokers Tip (1933). **St. Germans* — Twenty Grand (1931), Bold Venture (1936). *Man o' War* — Clyde Van Dusen (1929), War Admiral (1937). **Blenheim II* — Whirlaway (1941), Jet Pilot (1947). *Bold Venture* (1936) — Assault (1946), Middleground (1950).

DERBY WINNERS: *Halma* (1895) sired Alan-a-Dale (1902). *Bubbling Over* (1926) sired Burgoo King (1932). *Reigh Count* (1928) sired Count Fleet (1943). *Gallant Fox* (1930) sired Omaha (1935). *Bold Venture* (1936) sired Assault (1946) and Middleground (1950). *Pensive* (1944) sired Ponder (1949). *Count Fleet* (1943) sired Count Turf (1951). *Ponder* (1949) sired Needles (1956).

Determine (1954) sired Decidedly (1962). *Swaps* (1955) sired Chateaugay (1963).

SECOND IN DERBY: *Falsetto* (1879) sired three winners, Chant (1894), His Eminence (1901), Sir Huon (1906). *Himyar* (1878) sired Plaudit (1898). *Native Dancer* (1953) sired Kauai King (1966).

THIRD IN DERBY: *Free Knight* (1886) sired Elwood (1904). *First Landing* (1959) sired Riva Ridge (1972).

UNPLACED IN DERBY: *Bob Miles* (1884) sired Manuel (1899). *Insco* (6th, 1931) sired Lawrin (1938). *Bull Lea* (8th, 1938) sired Citation (1948), Hill Gail (1952), and Iron Liege (1957). *Bold Ruler* (4th, 1957) sired Secretariat (1973).

OLDEST: *Falsetto*, 30 years old when Sir Huon won in 1906.

YOUNGEST: *Pensive*, 8 years old when Ponder won in 1949. *Gallant Fox*, 8 years old when Omaha won in 1935. *Royal Coinage*, 8 years old when Venetian Way won in 1960. *Raise a Native*, 8 years old when Majestic Prince won in 1969.

STARTERS

Largest field to start in the Derby was 22 in 1928; the smallest fields were in 1892 and 1905, which had three starters each. The largest number of nominees to the Derby was 258 in 1972; the smallest was 32 in 1913.

FAVORITES

ODDS-ON: In 27 runnings of the Derby there has been an odds-on favorite (a horse, which if he won, would pay less than even money). Of these 15 have won, nine have been second. The others finished worse than third.

POST-TIME: *Himyar* went to post at 1 to 4 in the 1878 Derby. He finished second. *Count Fleet* (1943) and *Citation* (1948, coupled with Coaltown) won at 40 cents to $1. *Bimelech* also was a 40 cents to $1 favorite, finished second in 1940.

PAY-OFF: *Citation* (coupled with Coaltown) and *Count Fleet* each paid $2.80 when they won. These were the smallest winning prices since pari-mutuel betting on the Derby was introduced. Hindoo (1881), Halma (1895), and Agile (1905) each paid 1 to 3 to win the Derby. Donerail (1913) paid $184.90 for each $2 win ticket, record pay-off in the mutuels on the Derby.

TIME

FASTEST: *Spokane* (1889) 2:34 1/2 at mile and one-half. *Secretariat* (1973) 1:59 2/5 at mile and one-quarter.

Venetian Way's 2:02 2/5 was the fastest Derby time for an "off" track. The track was listed as "good" on Derby Day, 1960.

SLOWEST: *Kingman* (1891) 2:52 1/4 at mile and one-half. *Stone Street* (1908) 2:15 1/5 for mile and one-quarter.

FASTEST RUNNINGS OF THE DERBY

1. Secretariat 1:59⅖   (1973)

2. Northern Dancer 2:00   (1964)

3. Decidedly 2:00⅖   (1962)

4. Proud Clarion 2:00⅗   (1967)

5. Lucky Debonair 2:01⅕   (1965)

6. Whirlaway 2:01⅖   (1941)

7. Middleground 2:01⅗   (1950)
   Hill Gail 2:01⅗   (1952)

8. Twenty Grand 2:01⅘   (1931)
   Swaps 2:01⅘   (1955)
   Chateaugay 2:01⅘   (1963)
   Majestic Prince 2:01⅘   (1969)
   Riva Ridge 2:01⅘   (1972)

CHURCHILL DOWNS TRACK RECORDS

DATE	DISTANCE	HORSE	Age	Weight	Time
May 7, 1921	}	Fair Phantom	2	114	:46⅗
May 9, 1921	} 4 Furlongs	Casey	2	111	:46⅗
May 18, 1921	}	Miss Joy	2	110	:46⅗
May 1, 1961	} 4½ Furlongs	Miss Summer Time	2	116	:51⅘
May 6, 1969	}	Vite Flying	2	117	:51⅘
May 18, 1968	5 Furlongs	Santiago Road	2	125	:57⅘
Oct. 8, 1913	5½ Furlongs	Bringhurst	2	92	1:04⅗
May 13, 1961	}	Benedicto	6	117	1:09⅕
Nov. 25, 1970	} 6 Furlongs	Amber Break	6	116	1:09⅕
May 22, 1971	}	Barbizon Streak	3	122	1:09⅕
Nov. 5, 1957	6½ Furlongs	Dogoon	5	121	1:16
April 30, 1964	7 Furlongs	Olden Times	6	124	1:21⅖
Nov. 12, 1957	7½ Furlongs	Aurecolt	3	122	1:29
May 24, 1877	*1 Mile	Ten Broeck	5	109	1:39¾
Nov. 15, 1969	1 Mile	Evasive Action	2	116	1:33⅘
May 13, 1913	1 Mile, 20 Yards	Froglegs	4	107	1:39
Oct. 4, 1916	1 Mile, 50 Yards	Hodge	5	120	1:41⅘
May 30, 1919	1 Mile, 70 Yards	The Porter	4	110	1:41⅗
May 16, 1902	1 Mile, 100 Yards	The Caxton	4	101	1:49½
Nov. 25, 1970	1 1/16 Miles	Yes Sir	5	110	1:41⅗
Nov. 21, 1959	1⅓ Miles	Las Olas	4	111	1:48⅖
Nov. 18, 1961	1⅛ Miles	Aeroflint	3	116	1:48⅖
Nov. 14, 1942	1 3/16 Miles	Bonnie Andrew	5	110	1:58⅗
May 5, 1973	1¼ Miles	Secretariat	3	126	1:59⅖
Oct. 15, 1906	1⅜ Miles	Elliott	6	109	2:20⅗
Oct. 3, 1958	1½ Miles	Perturbed	5	112	2:32⅖
Nov. 10, 1956	1¾ Miles	My Night Out	3	110	3:01⅗
May 29, 1877	*2 Miles	Ten Broeck	5	110	3:27½
Oct. 22, 1921	2 Miles	Bit of White	3	115	3:22⅗
Nov. 11, 1949	2 1/16 Miles	Hi Neighbor	8	117	3:40⅘
Oct. 7, 1915	2¼ Miles	Raincoat	3	90	3:53
Sept. 3, 1876	*3 Miles	Ten Broeck	4	104	5:26½
Sept. 29, 1876	*4 Miles	Ten Broeck	4	107	7:15¾
Oct. 7, 1912	4 Miles	Sotemia	5	119	7:10⅘

*Against time.

STATUS OF PAST DERBY WINNERS

Year	Derby Winner	Present Status	Year	Derby Winner	Present Status
1973	Secretariat	Stud, 1974, Claiborne Farm, Ky.	1951	Court Turf	Died on Oct. 18, 1966, at age 18
1972	Riva Ridge	Stud, 1974, Claiborne Farm, Ky.	1950	Middleground	Died Feb. 16, 1972, at age 25
1971	Canonero II	Stud, Gainesway Farm, Ky.	1949	Ponder	Died on Oct. 10, 1958, at age 12
1970	Dust Commander	Stud, Golden Chance Farm, Ky.	1948	Citation	Died on Oct. 8, 1970, at age 25
1969	Majestic Prince	Stud, Spendthrift Farm, Ky.	1947	Jet Pilot	Died on March 3, 1967, at age 23
1968	Forward Pass	Stud, Calumet Farm, Ky.	1946	Assault	Died on Sept. 1, 1971, at age 28
1967	Proud Clarion	Stud, Spendthrift Farm, Ky.	1945	Hoop Jr.	Died on Nov. 19, 1964, at age 22
1966	Kauai King	Stud, Upend Stud, Newmarket, England	1944	Pensive	Died on May 20, 1949, at age 8
1965	Lucky Debonair	Stud, Danada Farm, Ky.	1943	Count Fleet	Pensioner, Stoner Creek Stud, Ky.
1964	Northern Dancer	Stud, Windfields Farm, Md.	1942	Shut Out	Died on April 23, 1964, at age 25
1963	Chateaugay	Stud, Hokkaido Island, Japan	1941	Whirlaway	Died on April 6, 1953, at age 15
1962	Decidedly	Stud, Spendthrift Farm, Ky.	1940	Galladion	Died in 1958, at age 21
1961	Carry Back	Stud, Dorchester Farm, Fla.	1939	Johnstown	Died on May 14, 1950, at age 14
1960	Venetian Way	Died on Oct. 17, 1964, at age 7	1938	Lawrin	Died on Aug. 31, 1955, at age 20
1959	*Tomy Lee	Died on Oct. 29, 1971, at age 15	1937	War Admiral	Died on Oct. 30, 1959, at age 25
1958	Tim Tam	Stud, Calumet Farm, Ky.	1936	Bold Venture	Died on March 22, 1958, at age 25
1957	Iron Liege	Died in Dec., 1971, at age 17	1935	Omaha	Died on April 24, 1959, at age 27
1956	Needles	Stud, Bonnie Heath Farm, Fla.	1934	Cavalcade	Died on Oct. 21, 1940, at age 9
1955	Swaps	Died Nov. 3, 1972, at age 20	1933	Brokers Tip	Died on July 13, 1953, at age 23
1954	Determine	Died Sept. 27, 1972, at age 21	1932	Burgoo King	Died on May 19, 1946, at age 17
1953	Dark Star	Died Oct. 21, 1972, at age 22	1931	Twenty Grand	Died on March 2, 1948, at age 20
1952	Hill Gail	Died in May, 1968, at age 19	1930	Gallant Fox	Died in Nov., 1954, at age 27

DERBY DAY WAGERING

When Churchill Downs conducted its first race meeting in the Spring of 1875 its patrons were offered two forms of wagering on the outcome of the events — the "new fangled Paris Mutual" system and the auction pool.

Sporting journals of that era gave no space to prices paid those who wagered through the pari-mutuel system, noting only what the different horses sold for in the auction pools. It was not until several years after the opening of the Louisville track that the mutuel pay-off began to appear in race summaries.

No records as to the amount wagered on the early runnings of the Kentucky Derby are available. Although bookmaking also was once the form of wagering used at Churchill Downs, the only method of wagering permitted in Kentucky since 1908 has been the pari-mutuel system.

The $7,627,965 bet on Derby Day 1973 set an American track record.

The tabulation below shows the wagering on the Kentucky Derby and on the entire Derby Day program since 1908:

YEAR	TOTAL	ON DERBY	YEAR	TOTAL	ON DERBY	YEAR	TOTAL	ON DERBY
1909	$ 103,694	$ 31,710	1931	$1,374,822	$ 495,886	1953	$4,306,065	$1,532,731
1910	†146,520	43,465	1932	850,809	277,105	1954	4,234,231	1,543,097
1911	†170,834	†49,380	1933	745,603	229,312	1955	4,280,287	1,677,178
1912	†208,640	†54,945	1934	999,140	382,584	1956	4,360,232	1,666,550
1913	232,771	64,680	1935	1,031,072	412,846	1957	3,800,250	1,401,017
1914	259,561	80,248	1936	1,269,188	472,750	1958	4,227,083	1,635,000
1915	303,675	†88,755	1937	1,535,604	585,606	1959	4,019,824	1,502,151
1916	356,674	†99,468	1938	1,511,689	528,742	1960	4,008,078	1,490,199
1917	409,509	109,395	1939	1,674,599	584,977	1961	3,915,567	1,483,164
1918	525,648	161,565	1940	1,593,983	465,149	1962	4,150,312	1,553,916
1919	833,643	292,244	1941	1,935,651	654,353	1963	4,677,594	1,818,087
1920	1,055,191	375,249	1942	1,983,011	631,198	1964	5,173,018	2,144,079
1921	1,202,342	391,604	1943	1,801,899	537,392	1965	5,285,382	2,227,484
1922	1,195,147	397,848	1944	2,139,982	651,444	1966	5,308,285	2,138,378
1923	1,424,288	408,262	1945	2,380,796	776,408	1967	4,625,222	1,933,028
1924	1,898,566	618,536	1946	3,608,208	1,202,474	1968	5,506,069	2,350,470
1925	1,871,614	661,857	1947	3,636,403	1,253,042	1969	6,106,346	2,625,524
1926	2,096,613	694,870	1948	3,051,779	‡670,833	1970	5,811,127	2,383,972
1927	1,934,232	676,443	1949	3,168,733	1,032,582	1971	6,389,567	2,648,139
1928	1,890,050	620,643	1950	3,559,382	1,248,026	1972	7,164,717	2,885,325
1929	1,790,670	675,106	1951	3,675,542	1,294,474	1973	7,627,965	3,284,962
1930	1,664,409	584,894	1952	4,064,420	1,565,901			

†Indicates these totals were estimated from incomplete figures that are available. All other totals are official.

‡Straight betting only.

FILLIES IN THE DERBY

Twenty-nine fillies have been starters in the Kentucky Derby. Only one, Harry Payne Whitney's Regret in 1915, has won, and six others have finished second or third.

Two fillies were post-time favorites. They were Regret and Calumet Farm's Nellie Flag, which finished fourth in the 1935 Derby. The H. P. Whitney entry of the filly Prudery and the colt Tryster was the favorite in the 1921 Derby. Prudery was third. The twenty-nine fillies which have started in the Kentucky Derby and where they finished follow:

YEAR	FILLY	FINISH	YEAR	FILLY	FINISH	YEAR	FILLY	FINISH
1875	Gold Mine	(unp)	1913	Gowell	(3rd)	1929	Ben Machree	(18th)
1875	Ascension	(unp)	1914	Bronzewing	(3rd)	1930	Alcibiades	(10th)
1876	Marie Michon	(unp)	1914	Watermelon	(7th)	1932	Oscillation	(13th)
1877	Early Light	(unp)	1915	Regret	(1st)	1934	Mata Hari	(4th)
1879	Ada Glen	(unp)	1918	Viva America	(3rd)	1934	Bazaar	(9th)
1879	Wissahicken	(unp)	1919	Regalo	(9th)	1935	Nellie Flag	(4th)
1883	Pike's Pride	(unp)	1920	Cleopatra	(15th)	1936	Gold Seeker	(9th)
1906	Lady Navaree	(2nd)	1921	Prudery	(3rd)	1945	Misweet	(12th)
1911	Round the World	(6th)	1921	Careful	(5th)	1959	Silver Spoon	(5th)
1912	Flamma	(3rd)	1922	Startle	(8th)			

DERBY DAY WEATHER

Louisville Weather Bureau records show the following for Derby Days since 1929:

DERBY DATE	RAINFALL (INCHES)	HIGH TEMP.	DERBY DATE	RAINFALL (INCHES)	HIGH TEMP.	DERBY DATE	RAINFALL (INCHES)	HIGH TEMP.
May 18, 1929	1.19	77	May 7, 1944	—	54	May 2, 1959	—	94
May 17, 1930	.11	69	June 9, 1945	.50	77	May 7, 1960	.20	64
May 16, 1931	—	84	May 4, 1946	.01	68	May 6, 1961	.25	81
May 7, 1932	—	83	May 3, 1947	.02	57	May 5, 1962	—	81
May 6, 1933	.09	59	May 1, 1948	.90	42	May 4, 1963	—	80
May 5, 1934	.04	76	May 7, 1949	—	57	May 2, 1964	—	76
May 4, 1935	.15	47	May 6, 1950	.11	70	May 1, 1965	—	84
May 2, 1936	.34	78	May 5, 1951	.02	67	May 7, 1966	—	67
May 8, 1937	—	71	May 3, 1952	—	79	May 6, 1967	.10	61
May 7, 1938	—	80	May 2, 1953	—	76	May 4, 1968	—	71
May 6, 1939	—	83	May 1, 1954	.15	84	May 3, 1969	—	87
May 4, 1940	—	62	May 7, 1955	.01	85	May 2, 1970	.28	64
May 3, 1941	—	76	May 5, 1956	—	82	May 1, 1971	—	73
May 2, 1942	—	87	May 4, 1957	—	47	May 6, 1972	—	75
May 1, 1943	—	54	May 3, 1958	.11	86	May 5, 1973	—	69

WINNING DERBY POST POSITIONS

YEAR	NAME	BOX NO.	YEAR	NAME	BOX NO.	YEAR	NAME	BOX NO.
1900	Lieut. Gibson	3	1925	Flying Ebony	6	1950	Middleground	14
1901	His Eminence	3	1926	Bubbling Over	11	1951	Count Turf	9
1902	Alan-a-Dale	4	1927	Whiskery	7	1952	Hill Gail	1
1903	Judge Hines	4	1928	Reigh Count	4	1953	Dark Star	10
1904	Elwood	3	1929	Clyde Van Dusen	20	1954	Determine	7
1905	Agile	1	1930	Gallant Fox	7	1955	Swaps	8
1906	Sir Huon	4	1931	Twenty Grand	5	1956	Needles	1
1907	Pink Star	6	1932	Burgoo King	13	1957	Iron Liege	6
1908	Stone Street	4	1933	Brokers Tip	11	1958	Tim Tam	2
1909	Wintergreen	6	1934	Cavalcade	8	1959	*Tomy Lee	9
1910	Donau	7	1935	Omaha	10	1960	Venetian Way	9
1911	Meridian	5	1936	Bold Venture	5	1961	Carry Back	14
1912	Worth	5	1937	War Admiral	1	1962	Decidedly	4
1913	Donerail	5	1938	Lawrin	1	1963	Chateaugay	1
1914	Old Rosebud	6	1939	Johnstown	1	1964	Northern Dancer	7
1915	Regret	2	1940	Gallahadion	1	1965	Lucky Debonair	8
1916	George Smith	8	1941	Whirlaway	4	1966	Kauai King	12
1917	*Omar Khayyam	8	1942	Shut Out	3	1967	Proud Clarion	7
1918	Exterminator	8	1943	Count Fleet	5	1968	Forward Pass	13
1919	Sir Barton	1	1944	Pensive	4	1969	Majestic Prince	8
1920	Paul Jones	2	1945	Hoop Jr.	12	1970	Dust Commander	2
1921	Behave Yourself	1	1946	Assault	2	1971	Canonero II	12
1922	Morvich	4	1947	Jet Pilot	13	1972	Riva Ridge	9
1923	Zev	10	1948	Citation	1	1973	Secretariat	10
1924	Black Gold	1	1949	Ponder	2			

Johnstown (1939) wore saddle-cloth No. 6, but moved into starting box No. 5 by withdrawal of No. 1 horse after programs were printed. Swaps wore saddle cloth No. 7; the entry moved him into No. 8 stall. Needles wore saddle cloth No. 3 because the two entries in this Derby were designated as 1 and 1A, and 2 and 2C. Decidedly carried saddle cloth No. 3. Because several horses were grouped in the mutuel field Kauai King (1966) carried No. 8 saddle cloth. Forward Pass wore saddle Cloth No. 10. Dust Commander wore saddle cloth No. 3. Canonero II wore saddle cloth No. 15. Riva Ridge wore No. 7. Secretariat wore No. 1A.

WINNING HORSES

Agile 1905	Exterminator 1918	Northern Dancer 1964
Alan-a-Dale 1902	Flying Ebony 1925	Old Rosebud 1914
Apollo 1882	Fonso 1880	Omaha 1935
Aristides 1875	Forward Pass 1968	*Omar Khayyam 1917
Assault 1946	Gallahadion 1940	Paul Jones 1920
Azra 1892	Gallant Fox 1930	Pensive 1944
Baden-Baden 1877	George Smith 1916	Pink Star 1907
Behave Yourself 1921	Halma 1895	Plaudit 1898
Ben Ali 1886	Hill Gail 1952	Ponder 1949
Ben Brush 1896	Hindoo 1881	Proud Clarion 1967
Black Gold 1924	His Eminence 1901	Regret 1915
Bold Venture 1936	Hoop Jr. 1945	Reigh Count 1928
Brokers Tip 1933	Iron Liege 1957	Riley 1890
Bubbling Over 1926	Jet Pilot 1947	Riva Ridge 1972
Buchanan 1884	Joe Cotton 1885	Secretariat 1973
Burgoo King 1932	Johnstown 1939	Shut Out 1942
Canonero II 1971	Judge Himes 1903	Sir Barton 1919
Carry Back 1961	Kauai King 1966	Sir Huon 1906
Cavalcade 1934	Kingman 1891	Spokane 1889
Chant 1894	Lawrin 1938	Stone Street 1908
Chateaugay 1963	Leonatus 1883	Swaps 1955
Citation 1948	Lieut. Gibson 1900	Tim Tam 1958
Clyde Van Dusen 1929	Lookout 1893	*Tomy Lee 1959
Count Fleet 1943	Lord Murphy 1879	Twenty Grand 1931
Count Turf 1951	Lucky Debonair 1965	Typhoon II 1897
Dark Star 1953	Macbeth II 1888	Vagrant 1876
Day Star 1878	Majestic Prince 1969	Venetian Way 1960
Decidedly 1962	Manuel 1899	War Admiral 1937
Determine 1954	Meridian 1911	Whirlaway 1941
Donau 1910	Middleground 1950	Whiskery 1927
Donerail 1913	Montrose 1887	Wintergreen 1909
Dust Commander 1970	Morvich 1922	Worth 1912
Elwood 1904	Needles 1956	Zev 1923

OWNERS OF WINNERS

Amiel, J. J. 1951	Darby Dan Farm 1963-1967	Maine Chance Farm 1947
Applegate, H. C. 1914	(John W. Galbreath)	(Mrs. Elizabeth Graham)
Armstrong, Noah 1889	Darden, Geo. W. & Co. 1879	Meadow Stable 1972-1973
Astor, Wm. 1876	Durnell, Mrs. C. E. 1904	Milky Way Farm 1940
Bashford Manor 1892	Dwyer Bros. (M. F. & P. J.) 1881	(Mrs. Ethel V. Mars)
(G. J. Long)	Dwyer, M. F. ("Mike") 1896	McClelland, Byron 1895
Belair Stud 1930-1935-1939	Ellison, C. R. 1903	McDowell, T. C. 1902
(Wm. Woodward)	Ellsworth, R. C. 1955	McGrath, H. P. 1875
Billings & Johnson 1917	El Peco Ranch 1962	McMahon, Frank 1969
Ben Block 1922	(Geo. A. Pope, Jr.)	Morris, A. H. & D. H. 1899
Bradley, E. R. 1921-1932-1933	Ford Stable (Michael Ford) 1966	Morris & Patton 1882
(See Idle Hour Stock Farm)	Gardner, H. P. 1929	Nichols, T. J. 1878
Brookmeade Stable 1934	Gerst, Wm. 1910	Parr, Ral 1920
(Mrs. Isabel Dodge Sloane)	Glen Riddle Farm Stable 1937	Price, Mrs. Katherine 1961
Brown, S. S. 1905	(Samuel D. Riddle)	Rancocas Stable 1923
Cahn, J. C. 1897	Greentree Stable 1931-1942	(H. F. Sinclair)
Caibett, Edgar 1971	(Mrs. Payne Whitney)	Respess, J. B. 1909
Cain Hoy Stables 1953	Haggin, Jas. B. 1886	Rice, Mrs. Ada L. 1965
(H. F. Guggenheim)	Hallenbeck, H. C. 1912	Ross, J. K. L. 1919
Calumet Farm ..1941-1944-1948-1949	Hamilton, C. E. 1908	Sanford, John 1916
(Warren Wright)	Hayes, T. P. 1913	Schwartz, M. L. 1936
Calumet Farm 1952	Hertz, Mrs. John D. 1928-1943	Shawhan, J. S. 1880
(Mrs. Warren Wright)	Hooper, Fred W. 1945	Smith, Chas. H. 1900
Calumet Farm 1957-1958-1968	Hoots, Mrs. R. M. 1924	Sunny Blue Farm 1960
(Mrs. Gene Markey)	Idle Hour Farm 1926	Swigert, Daniel 1877
Carman, R. F. 1911	(E. R. Bradley)	Turner, Mr. and Mrs. Fred Jr. 1959
Chicago Stable 1888	Jacobin Stable 1891	Van Meter, F. B. 1901
(Hankins & Johnson)	Kilmer, W. S. 1918	Whitney, H. P. 1915-1927
Chinn & Morgan 1883	King Ranch 1946-1950	Williams, J. T. 1885
Cochran, G. A. 1925	(Robert J. Kleberg)	Windfields Farm (E. P. Taylor) ...1964
Corrigan, Edward 1890	Labold Bros. 1887	Woodford, J. Hal 1907
Cottrill, William 1884	Lehmann, Robert E. 1970	Woolford Farm 1938
Crevolin, Andrew J. 1954	Leigh & Rose 1894	(Herbert J. Woolf)
Cushing & Orth 1893	Long, George J. 1906	
D & H Stable 1956	(See Bashford Manor)	
(Jack Dudley & Bonnie Heath)	Madden, John E. 1898	

*Imported horse.

TRAINERS OF WINNERS

Allen, Dud	1891
Anderson, Andy	1875
Arias, Juan	1971
Bedwell, H. G.	1919
Bird, Wm.	1884
Brown, Ed.	1877
Burlew, Fred	1922
Cahn, J. C.	1897
Cameron, G. D.	1943
Campbell, John	1888
Campbell, Hardy	1896
Catrone, Frank	1965
Childs, Frank E.	1959
Colston, Raleigh	1883
Combs, Don	1970
Conway, George	1937
Conway, J. P.	1963
Corrigan, Edward	1890
Coyne, Peter	1906
Duke, W. B.	1925
Durnell, C. E. (Boots)	1904
Ewing, Albert	1911
Fitzsimmons, Jas.	1930-1935-1939
Fizer, W. H.	1907
Forrest, Henry	1966-1968
Fontaine, Hugh L.	1956
Garth, Wm.	1920
Gaver, John M.	1942
Gentry, Loyd	1967
Hall, J. W.	1908
Ham, Geo.	1910
Hayes, T. P.	1913
Hayward, Eddie	1953
Hirsch, Max	1936-1946-1950
Hopkins, Fred	1927
Hughes, Chas. H.	1900
Hughes, Hollie	1916
Hutsell, Tice	1880
Jones, Ben A.	1938-1941-1944-1948-1949-1952
Jones, H. A. (Jimmy)	1957-1958
Laurin, Lucien	1972-1973
Leary, David J.	1923
Leigh, Eugene	1894
Longden, John	1969
Luro, Horatio A.	1962-1964
Mack, C.	1909
Madden, John E.	1898
Mayberry, J. P.	1903
McClelland, Byron	1895
McDaniel, Henry	1918
McDaniel, Wm.	1893
McDowell, Thos. Clay	1902
McGinty, John	1887
Michell, Bert S.	1928
Molter, Willie	1954
Morris, Green B.	1882
Morris, John H.	1892
Murphy, Jim	1886
Patterson, C. T.	1917
Paul, Lee	1878
Parke, Ivan H.	1945
Perry, Alex	1885
Price, Jack A.	1961
Rice, Geo.	1879
Rodegap, John	1889
Rowe, James Jr.	1931
Rowe, James Sr.	1881-1915
Rutchick, Sol	1951
Smith, Robt. A.	1934
Smith, Tom	1947
Sovinski, V. J.	1960
Taylor, Frank M.	1912
Tenney, M. A.	1955
Thompson, H. J.	1921-1926-1932-1933
Tucker, Robt.	1905
Van Dusen, Clyde	1929
Van Meter, F. B.	1901
Walden, Robt. J.	1899
Waldron, Roy	1940
Webb, Hedley	1924
Weir, F. D.	1914
Williams, James	1876

WINNING JOCKEYS

Arcaro, Eddie	1938-1941-1945-1948-1952
Archibald, George	1911
Avila, Gustavo	1971
Baeza, Braulio	1963
Bierman, Carroll	1940
Boland, Jimmy	1900
Boland, William	1950
Booker, Hal	1903
Borel, Charles	1917
Brooks, Steve	1949
Brumfield, Don	1966
Carter, J.	1878
Clayton, Alonzo	1892
Covington, G.	1888
Donohue, Billy	1883
Duffy, P.	1886
Erb, Dave	1956
Garner, F. (Buttons)	1897
Garner, Mack	1934
Goodale, Frank	1894
Goose, Roscoe	1913
Guerin, Eric	1947
Hanford, Ira	1936
Hartack, Bill	1957-1960-1962-1964-1969
Henderson, Erskine	1885
Herbert, Robert	1910
Hurd, Babe	1882
James, Eugene	1932
Johnson, Albert	1922-1926
Kiley, Thomas	1889
Knapp, William	1918
Kunze, E.	1893
Kurtsinger, Charles	1931-1937
Lang, Charles	1928
Lewis, George	1880
Lewis, Isaac	1887
Lewis, Oscar	1875
Loftus, Johnny	1916-1919
Longden, Johnny	1943
Manganello, Mike	1970
Martin, Jack	1905
McAtee, Linus (Pony)	1927-1929
McCabe, John	1914
McCreary, Conn	1944-1951
McLaughlin, Jimmy	1881
Meade, Don	1933
Mehrtens, Warren	1946
Minder, Andy	1907
Mooney, John D.	1924
Moreno, Hank	1953
Murphy, Isaac	1884-1890-1891
Notter, Joe	1915
Perkins, James (Soup)	1895
Pickens, Arthur	1908
Powers, Vincent	1909
Prior, Frankie	1904
Rice, Ted	1920
Sande, Earl	1923-1925-1930
Saunders, Wm. (Smoky)	1935
Sellers, John	1961
Shauer, C.	1879
Shilling, Carroll H.	1912
Shoemaker, Willie	1955-1959-1965
Simms, Willie	1896-1898
Stout, James	1939
Swim, Bobby	1876
Taral, Fred	1899
Thompson, Charles	1921
Troxler, Roscoe	1906
Turcotte, Ron	1972-1973
Ussery, Bobby	1967
Valenzuela, Ismael	1958-1968
Walker, William	1877
Winkfield, Jimmy	1901-1902
Wright, Wayne D.	1942
York, Ray	1954

BREEDERS OF WINNERS

Alexander, A. J. 1877-1880-1885
        -1894-1901
Armstrong, F. W. 1934
Armstrong, Noah 1899
Asbury, Dr. Eslie 1954
Baker & Gentry 1900
Belair Stud 1930-1935
  (William Woodward)
Benjamin, E. B. 1971
Bradley, E. R. 1921
  (Idle Hour Stock Farm)
Bradley, E. R., & Davis, H. N. 1932
Calumet Farm 1941-1944-1948-
  (Warren Wright)   1949-1952
Calumet Farm 1957-1958-1968
  (Mrs. Gene Markey)
Camden, J. N. 1903
Carter, J. T. 1879
Chinn & Forsythe 1916
Clay & Woodford 1896
Clay, E. F. 1905
Clay, J. M. 1878
Combs, Leslie II 1969
Cottrill & Guest 1884
Danada Farm 1965
  (Mr. and Mrs. Dan Rice)
Durkee, C. H. 1890
Eastin & Larrabie 1895

Ellsworth, R. C. 1955
Ewing, John B. 1897
Fairbairn, R. A. 1940-1945
Franklin, A. C. 1891
Galbreath, John W. 1963-1967
Gardner, H. P. 1929
Greathouse, John W. 1960
Greentree Stable 1931-1942
  (Mrs. Payne Whitney)
Haggin, J. B. 1908
Hancock, A. B. 1939
Hancock, A. B. &
  Van Clief, Mrs. R. A. 1947
Harrison, C. L. 1911
Hayes, T. P. 1913
Hertz, Mrs. John D. 1943
Hoots, Mrs. R. M. 1924
Idle Hour Stock Farm 1926-1933
  (E. R. Bradley)
Jones, Warner L., Jr. 1953
Kilmer, Willis Sharpe 1928
King Ranch 1946-1950
  (R. J. Kleberg)
Knight, F. D. 1918
Leach, W. E. 1956
Lisle, Rufus 1888
Long, Geo. J. 1892-1899-1906
Madden & Gooch 1919

Madden, John E. 1914-1920-1923-1925
McDowell, T. C. 1902
McGrath, H. P. 1875
Meadow Stud, Inc. 1972-1973
Miller, Dr. and Mrs. F. P. 1951
Miller, John Henry 1883
Neet, Dr. J. D. 1898
Pine Brook Farm 1966
Pope, George A., Jr. 1962
Potter, R. H. McC. 1912
Prather, Mrs. J. B. 1904
Price, Jack A. 1961
Pullen Bros. 1970
Respess, J. B. 1909
Riddle, Samuel D. 1937
  (Glen Riddle Farm Stable)
Robinson, Sir John (of England). . 1917
Sanford, M. H. 1876
Schwartz, M. L. 1936
Scoggan Bros. 1893
Spreckles, A. B. 1922
Swigert, Daniel 1881-1882-1886
Taylor, E. P. 1964
Whitney, H. P. 1915-1927
Wills, D. H. (of England) 1959
Woodford, J. Hal 1907
Woolf, Herbert 1938
Young, Milton 1887-1910

SIRES OF WINNERS

*Alibhai 1954
*Australian 1877
Black Toney 1924-1933
*Blenheim II 1941-1947
Bob Miles 1899
Bold Commander 1970
Bold Ruler 1973
BOLD VENTURE 1946-1950
Bramble 1896
Broomstick 1911-1915
BUBBLING OVER 1932
*Buckden 1884
Bull Lea 1948-1952-1957
COUNT FLEET 1951
DETERMINE 1962
Dick Welles 1909
Duke of Montrose 1887
Equipoise 1942
*Esher 1903
Falsetto 1894-1901-1906
First Landing 1972
Free Knight 1904
GALLANT FOX 1935
*Glengary 1891
G. W. Johnson 1900
Hail to Reason 1967
HALMA 1902

Hanover 1895
Himyar 1898
Hyder Ali 1889
Hyperion (England) 1944
Insco 1938
Jamestown 1939
*Khaled 1955
King Alfonso 1880-1885
*Knight of the Thistle 1912
*Lancegaye 1934
*Leamington 1875
Leaver 1882
Longfellow 1883-1890
Longstreet 1908
Macduff 1888
Man o' War 1929-1937
Marathon 1921
Marco (England) 1917
*McGee 1913-1918
Native Dancer 1966
Nearctic 1964
*North Star III 1926
On-and-On 1968
*Out of Reach 1916
Pat Malloy 1879
PENSIVE 1949
Pink Coat 1907

PONDER 1956
*Pretendre 1971
Raise a Native 1969
Reform 1892
REIGH COUNT 1943
Royal Coinage 1960
*Royal Gem II 1953
Runnymede 1922
Saggy 1961
*Sea King 1920
Sir Dixon 1905
*Sir Gallahad III 1930-1940-1945
*St. Germans 1931-1936
Star Davis 1878
*Star Shoot 1919
*Sunreigh 1928
SWAPS 1963
The Finn 1923-1925
Tom Fool 1958
*Top Gallant 1897
*Troubadour 1893
*Tudor Minstrel 1959
Uncle 1914
Vertex 1965
Virgil 1876-1881-1886
Whisk Broom II 1927
*Woolsthorpe 1910

NOTE: — Runnymede, sire of Morvich, is not the horse of same name which ran in 1882 Derby.
Names in black capital letters denote horses that also won the Kentucky Derby.
*Imported Horse.

POST-TIME FAVORITES

Forty-three post-time favorites in the Kentucky Derby won the race. Of the others, 24 ran second, nine were third, and 23 unplaced.

The shortest priced favorites since installation of pari-mutuel machines in 1908 have been Bimelech in 1940, Count Fleet in 1943, and Citation in 1948 at 40¢ to $1. Bimelech finished second, but Count Fleet and Citation won.

The longest priced winners were in this order: 1913, 1940, 1967, 1918, 1953, 1908, 1936, 1923 and 1920. Donerail, the 1913 winner, paid $91.45 to $1.

Here is a list showing the Derby post-time favorites since 1875, what happened to them, and what was the pay-off on the winner:

YEAR	FAVORITE	PRICE	FINISHED	WINNER AND PRICE
1875	H. P. McGrath Entry (Aristides-Chesapeake)	2-1	Aristides—1st; Chesapeake—8th	Same
1876	Vagrant	9-5	First	Same
1877	Leonard	7-5	Second	Baden-Baden, 8-1
1878	Himyar	1-4	Second	Day Star, 3-1
1879	Lord Murphy	11-10	First	Same
1880	Kimball	3-5	Second	Fonso, 7-1
1881	Hindoo	1-3	First	Same
1882	Runnymede	4-5	Second	Apollo, 10-1
1883	Leonatus	9-5	First	Same
1884	Audrain	2-1	Third	Buchanan, 3-1
1885	Joe Cotton	1-1	First	Same
1886	Ben Ali	1.72-1	First	Same
1887	Banburg	7-5	Fourth	Montrose, 10-1
1888	Gallifet (Gallifet coupled with Alexandria as Melbourne Stable entry)	1-1	Second	Macbeth II, 6-1
1889	Proctor Knott	1-2	Second	Spokane, 10-1
1890	Robespierre	1-1	Third	Riley, 4-1
1891	Kingman	1-2	First	Same
1892	Azra	3-2	First	Same
1893	Cushing-Orth Entry (Lookout-Boundless)	7-10	Lookout—1st; Boundless—3rd	Same
1894	Chant	1-2	First	Same
1895	Halma	1-3	First	Same
1896	Ben Brush	1-2	First	Same
1897	Ornament	1-1	Second	Typhoon II, 3-1
1898	Lieber Karl	1-3	Second	Plaudit, 3-1
1899	Manuel	11-20	First	Same
1900	Lieut. Gibson	7-10	First	Same
1901	Alard Scheck	7-10	Fifth	His Eminence, 3-1
1902	Abe Frank	3-5	Fourth	Alan-a-Dale, 3-2
1903	Early	3-5	Second	Judge Himes, 15-1
1904	Proceeds	1-1	Third	Elwood, 15-1
1905	Agile	1-3	First	Same
1906	Sir Huon	11-10	First	Same
1907	Red Gauntlet	3-2	Fourth	Pink Star, 15-1
1908	Sir Cleges	9-5	Second	Stone Street, 23-72-1
1909	Wintergreen	1.96-1	First	Same
1910	Donau	1.65-1	First	Same
1911	Governor Gray	1-1	Second	Meridian, 2.90-1
1912	Worth	4-5	First	Same
1913	Ten Point	1.20-1	Second	Donerail, 91.45-1
1914	Old Rosebud	85¢-1	First	Same
1915	Regret	2.65-1	First	Same
1916	H. P. Whitney Entry (Thunderer-Dominant)	1.05-1	Thunderer—5th; Dominant—7th	Geo. Smith, 4.15-1
1917	Ticket	1.45-1	Second	*Omar Khayyam, 12.80-1
1918	War Cloud	1.45-1	Fourth	Exterminator, 29.60-1
1919	J. M. McClelland Entry (Sailor-Eternal)	2.10-1	Sailor—7th; Eternal—10th	J. K. L. Ross Entry (Sir Barton) 2.60-1

YEAR	FAVORITE	PRICE	FINISHED	WINNER AND PRICE
1920	H. P. Whitney Entry (Upset-Damask-Wildair)	1.65-1	Upset—2nd; Damask—4th; Wildair—8th	Ral Parr Entry (Paul Jones) 16.20-1
1921	H. P. Whitney Entry (Prudery-Tryster)	1.10-1	Prudery—3rd; Tryster—4th	E. R. Bradley Entry (Behave Yourself) 8.65-1
1922	Morvich	1.20-1	First	Same
1923	H. P. Whitney and Greentree Entry (Enchantment-Whitney); (Picketer-Whitney); (Rialto-Greentree); (Cherry Pie-Greentree)	2.30-1	Enchantment—6th; Rialto—7th; Picketer—15th; Cherry Pie—20th	Zev, 19.20-1
1924	Black Gold	1.75-1	First	Same
1925	Quatrain	1.95-1	Twelfth	Flying Ebony (in field) 3.15-1
1926	E.R. Bradley Entry (Bubbling Over-Bagenbaggage)	1.90-1	Bubbling Over—1st; Bagenbaggage—2nd	Same
1927	H. P. Whitney Entry (Whiskery-Bostonian)	2.40-1	Whiskery—1st; Bostonian—5th	Same
1928	Reigh Count (Mrs. John Hertz); Reigh Olga (O. Lehmann); (Both trained by B. S. Michell, ran as entry)	2.06-1	Reigh Count—1st; Reigh Olga—5th	Same
1929	E. R. Bradley Entry (Blue Larkspur-Bay Beauty)	1.71-1	Blue Larkspur—4th Bay Beauty—13th	Clyde Van Dusen 3-1
1930	Gallant Fox	1.19-1	First	Same
1931	Greentree Stable (Twenty Grand-Anchors Aweigh-Surf Board)	88¢-1	Twenty Grand—1st; Anchors Aweigh—10th; Surf Board—11th	Same
1932	Tick On	1.84-1	Sixth	E. R. Bradley Entry (Burgoo King), 5.61-1
1933	W. R. Coe Entry (Ladysman-Pomponius)	1.43-1	Ladysman—4th; Pomponius—5th	Brokers Tip, 8.93-1
1934	Brookmeade Stable (Cavalcade-Time Clock)	1.50-1	Cavalcade—1st; Time Clock—7th	Same
1935	Nellie Flag	3.80-1	Fourth	Omaha, 4-1
1936	Brevity	80¢-1	Second	Bold Venture, 20.50-1
1937	War Admiral	1.60-1	First	Same
1938	Fighting Fox	1.40-1	Sixth	Lawrin, 8.60-1
1939	Johnstown	60¢-1	First	Same
1940	Bimelech	40c-1	Second	Gallahadion, 35.20-1
1941	Whirlaway	2.90-1	First	Same
1942	Greentree Entry (Shut Out-Devil Diver)	1.90-1	Shut Out—1st; Devil Diver—6th	Same
1943	Count Fleet	40¢-1	First	Same
1944	Stir Up	1.40-1	Third	Pensive, 7.10-1
1945	Pot o'Luck	3.30-1	Second	Hoop, Jr., 3.70-1
1946	Maine Chance Farm Entry (Lord Boswell-Knockdown-Perfect Bahram)	1.10-1	Lord Boswell—4th; Knockdown—5th; Perfect Bahram—9th	Assault, 8.20-1
1947	Phalanx	2.00-1	Second	Jet Pilot, 5.40-1
1948	Calumet Farm Entry (Citation-Coaltown)	40¢-1	Citation—1st; Coaltown—2nd	Same
1949	Olympia	80¢-1	Sixth	Ponder, 16.00-1
1950	Your Host	1.60-1	Ninth	Middleground, 7.90-1
1951	Battle Morn	2.80-1	Sixth	Count Turf, 14.60-1
1952	Hill Gail	1.10-1	First	Same
1953	Native Dancer	70¢-1	Second	Dark Star, 24.90-1
1954	Correlation	3.00-1	Sixth; Allied (9th)	Determine, 4.30-1
1955	Nashua	1.30-1	Second	Swaps, 2.80-1
1956	Needles	1.60-1	First	Same
1957	Bold Ruler	1.20-1	Fourth	Iron Liege, 8.40-1
1958	Maine Chance Entry (Jewel's Reward, Ebony Pearl)	2.00-1	Jewel's Reward—4th; Ebony Pearl—10th	Tim Tam, 2.10-1
1959	First Landing	3.60-1	Third	*Tomy Lee, 3.70-1
1960	Tompion	1.10-1	Fourth	Venetian Way, 6.30-1
1961	Carry Back	2.50-1	First	Same
1962	Ridan	1.10-1	Third	Decidedly, 8.70-1
1963	Candy Spots	1.50-1	Third	Chateaugay, 9.40-1
1964	Hill Rise	1.40-1	Second	Northern Dancer, 3.40-1
1965	Bold Lad	2.00-1	Tenth	Lucky Debonair, 4.30-1
1966	Kauai King	2.40-1	First	Same
1967	Damascus	1.70-1	Third	Proud Clarion, 30.10-1
1968	Forward Pass	2.20-1	Second	Dancer's Image, 3.60-1
1969	Majestic Prince	1.40-1	First	Same
1970	My Dad George	2.80-1	Second	Dust Commander, 15.30-1
1971	Unconscious	2.80-1	Fifth	Canonero II, 8.70-1
1972	Riva Ridge	1.50-1	First	Same
1973	Secretariat	1.50-1	First	Same

Horse	Finished	Year
Abe Frank	4th	1902
Abe's Hope	5th	1966
Acabado	15th	1917
Ace Destroyer	11th	1953
Action Getter	13th	1970
Ada Glenn	unp	1879
Admiral	unp	1884
Admiral Porter	5th	1954
Admiral's Shield	6th	1970
Admiral's Voyage	9th	1962
Adobe Post	11th	1932
Advocator	2nd	1966
A Dragon Killer	7th	1958
Agile	1st	1905
Agrarian	3rd	1934
Air Sailor	4th	1945
Alamond	6th	1946
Alan-a-Dale	1st	1902
Alard Scheck	5th	1901
Al Boyer	4th	1894
Alcibiades	10th	1930
Alexandria	unp	1888
Alexis	10th	1945
Alfambra	3rd	1881
Allied	9th	1954
Almadel	13th	1925
Alorter	11th	1944
Alsab	2nd	1942
Altawood	4th	1924
Alworth	13th	1946
Amber Light	4th	1943
Amberoid	7th	1966
Ambiopoise	12th	1961
American Eagle	8th	1918
American Eagle	16th	1944
Amur	4th	1901
Anchors Aweigh	10th	1931
Angle Light	10th	1973
Anyoldtime	7th	1951
Apache	11th	1942
Apollo	1st	1882
Aristides	1st	1875
Arroz	6th	1952
Arts and Letters	2nd	1969
Ascender	unp	1883
Ascension	10th	1875
Ask the Fare	5th	1967
Aspiration	8th	1923
Assault	1st	1946
Atoll	9th	1959
Audrain	3rd	1884
Autocrat	6th	1888
Azra	1st	1892
Babcock	unp	1882
Backbone	14th	1925
Baden-Baden	1st	1877
Bad News	4th	1903
Baffling	17th	1924
Bagenbaggage	2nd	1926
Balgowan	2nd	1891
Bally Ache	2nd	1960
Banridge	5th	1908
Banburg	4th	1887
Bancroft	3rd	1880
Bankrupt	5th	1943
Ban Yan	6th	1887
Bar None	12th	1928
Barbizon Streak	16th	1971
Barbs Delight	2nd	1967
Bass Clef	3rd	1961
Basso	2nd	1895
Battle Morn	6th	1951
Bay Beauty	13th	1929
Bazaar	9th	1934
Beau Butler	3rd	1924
Beau Sub	14th	1966
Be Frank	6th	1919
Behave Yourself	1st	1921
Bell Buzzer	7th	1944
Ben A. Jones	16th	1956
Ben Ali	1st	1886
Ben Brown	6th	1897
Ben Brush	1st	1896
Ben Eder	2nd	1896
Benedicto	9th	1958
Bengal	3rd	1882
Ben Machree	18th	1929
Berlin	14th	1917
Bernard F.	18th	1937
Bersagliere	9th	1920
Bersan	2nd	1885
Bert G.	14th	1945

Horse	Finished	Year
Besomer	14th	1956
Bet Mosie	2nd	1922
Better Bee	8th	1957
Better Luck	13th	1923
Bewithus	14th	1927
Bien Joli	5th	1936
Big Spruce	7th	1972
Big Brown Bear	9th	1972
Bill Bruce	7th	1875
Big Stretch	18th	1951
Bill Herron	7th	1908
Billings	4th	1948
Billionaire	20th	1937
Bill Letcher	2nd	1890
Billy Kelly	2nd	1919
Bimelech	2nd	1940
Blackbirder	5th	1935
Black Emperor	13th	1956
Black George	14th	1950
Black Gold	1st	1924
Black Metal	13th	1954
Black Panther	10th	1927
Black Servant	2nd	1921
Blackwood	9th	1928
Blazes	6th	1920
Blondin	9th	1926
Bluebeard	14th	1935
Blue Larkspur	4th	1929
Blue Lem	8th	1955
Blue Man	3rd	1952
Blue Pair	7th	1941
Blue Skyer	3rd	1966
Blue Swords	2nd	1943
Blue Wing	2nd	1886
Bobashela	8th	1928
Bob Cook	unp	1884
Bob Miles	unp	1884
Bob Murphy	7th	1946
Bobtail	19th	1924
Bob Wooley	4th	1875
Bold and Able	8th	1971
Bold Lad	10th	1965
Bold Reason	3rd	1971
Bold Ruler	4th	1957
Bold Venture	1st	1936
Bombay	unp	1876
Bo McMillan	12th	1923
Bon Homme	9th	1921
Bonivan	18th	1928
Bonjour	6th	1963
Booker Bill	16th	1915
Boola Boola	4th	1910
Boon Companion	10th	1925
Bootmaker	8th	1889
Boot and Spur	15th	1942
Boreas	unp	1884
Bostonian	5th	1927
Boulevard	unp	1880
Boundless	3rd	1893
Bourbon	3rd	1903
Bourbon Prince	5th	1960
Boxthorn	16th	1935
Boys Howdy	5th	1931
Bracadale	5th	1924
Brancas	3rd	1904
Brandon Mint	4th	1932
Breezing Thru	12th	1930
Brevity	2nd	1936
Brief Sigh	5th	1944
Bright Tomorrow	10th	1923
Broadcloth	2nd	1944
Broadway Jones	11th	1925
Broadway Limited	9th	1930
Brokers Tip	1st	1933
Bronzewing	3rd	1914
Brother Joe	19th	1932
Brown Rambler	15th	1952
Bubbling Over	1st	1926
Buchanan	1st	1884
Buckeye Poet	13th	1930
Buck McCann	unp	1893
Buckner	unp	1879
Buddy Bauer	6th	1927
Bullet Proof	7th	1947
Bullion	unp	1876
Bull Lea	8th	1938
Burgundy	unp	1878
Burning Dream	9th	1945
Burning Star	8th	1937
Burnt Cork	10th	1943
Burgoo King	1st	1932
Busy American	broke down	1922

Horse	Finished	Year
By Golly	7th	1920
By Gosh	9th	1922
Bymeabond	6th	1945
Calcutta	17th	1923
Calf Roper	11th	1929
Calycanthus	unp	1881
Campeon	9th	1909
Candy Spots	3rd	1963
Cannon Shot	12th	1924
Canonero II	1st	1971
Canter	8th	1926
Can't Wait	3rd	1938
Capot	2nd	1949
Captain Hal	2nd	1925
Captain's Gig	11th	1968
Career Boy	6th	1956
Careful	5th	1921
Carpenter's Rule	9th	1965
Carry Back	1st	1961
Cartago	17th	1928
Cathop	16th	1932
Cassius	unp	1889
Cavalcade	1st	1934
Cee Tee	15th	1932
Challedon	2nd	1939
Challenge Me	10th	1944
Champ De Mars	12th	1926
Chance It Tony	6th	1958
Chant	1st	1894
Charley O.	3rd	1933
Charlie Bush	unp	1878
Charmarten	19th	1928
Chateaugay	1st	1963
Chatter	unp	1883
Cherry Pie	20th	1923
Chesapeake	8th	1875
Chicatie	14th	1929
Chief Uncas	20th	1925
Chilhowee	2nd	1924
Chip	19th	1929
Chittagong	5th	1923
Citation	1st	1948
Clarion	unp	1887
Clay Pate	unp	1885
Cleopatra	15th	1920
Clodion	10th	1937
Clyde Van Dusen	1st	1929
Coaltown	2nd	1948
Cold Check	10th	1932
Cold Command	9th	1952
Coldstream	4th	1936
Col. Hogan	7th	1911
Colston	3rd	1911
Col. Zeb Ward	7th	1888
Come Now	12th	1944
Come On Red	3rd	1956
Commonwealth	10th	1935
Corn Off The Cob	7th	1970
Correlation	6th	1954
Correspondent	5th	1953
Corsini	2nd	1899
Cosmic Bomb	5th	1947
Co-Sport	7th	1938
Count Chic	4th	1956
Countermand	17th	1956
Counterpoint	11th	1951
Count Flame	5th	1952
Count Fleet	1st	1943
Count Turf	1st	1951
Court Scandal	9th	1937
Coyne	6th	1921
Crack Brigade	5th	1930
Creedmoor	2nd	1876
Crimson Satan	6th	1962
Crozier	2nd	1961
Crystal Prince	12th	1932
Cudgel	11th	1917
Curator	4th	1895
*Curragh King	10th	1953
Cuvier Relic	6th	1960
Damascus	3rd	1967
Damask	4th	1920
Dancer's Image	1st	1968
Dandy K.	8th	1964
Dan K.	unp	1877
Dapper Dan	2nd	1965
Darby Dieppe	3rd	1945
Dark Jungle	12th	1946
Dark Star	1st	1953
Dark Winter	11th	1933
Dauber	2nd	1938
David Harum	4th	1920

Horse	Finished	Year
Dawn Glory	11th	1967
Day Star	1st	1878
Deadlock	4th	1922
Dearborn	14th	1961
Debar	5th	1906
Decidedly	1st	1962
Dellor	7th	1937
Determine	1st	1954
Devil Diver	6th	1942
Diavolaw	14th	1944
Dick O'Hara	15th	1930
*Die Hard	16th	1959
Dike	3rd	1969
Diogenes	14th	1924
Diplomat Way	9th	1967
Direct	6th	1909
Discovery	2nd	1934
Display	10th	1926
Dispose	6th	1941
Distraction	13th	1928
Dit	3rd	1940
Divine Comedy	9th	1960
Dodge	4th	1916
Dogpatch	8th	1942
Dominant	7th	1916
Dominar	15th	1966
Don B.	7th	1968
Donau	1st	1910
Donerail	1st	1913
Donnacona	5th	1920
Don Q.	7th	1928
Dooly	11th	1950
Dortch	8th	1915
Double Eagle	7th	1915
Double Jay	12th	1947
Dove Pie	7th	1943
Drake Carter	2nd	1883
Dr. Barkley	3rd	1909
Dr. Behrman	12th	1970
Dr. Catlett	3rd	1897
Dr. Isby	12th	1967
Dr. Miller	4th	1961
Dr. Neale	15th	1972
Dr. Shephard	4th	1897
Driscoll	3rd	1901
Dunce	7th	1959
Dunvegan	3rd	1908
Duplicator	8th	1949
Dust Commander	1st	1970
Duval	2nd	1912
Earl of Beaconsfield	unp	1878
Early	2nd	1903
Early Light	unp	1877
Eastern Fleet	4th	1971
Easy Spur	13th	1959
Ebony Pearl	10th	1958
Economic	2nd	1932
Ed Crump	10th	1915
Ed Tierney	2nd	1904
El Chico	6th	1939
Elector	16th	1925
Elooto	9th	1938
Elwood	1st	1904
Emerson Cochran	5th	1915
††Enquirer's Colt	10th	1876
Enchantment	6th	1923
Enlister	11th	1875
Escadru	6th	1948
Escoba	2nd	1918
Espino	6th	1926
Essare	16th	1929
Eternal	10th	1919
Eternal Moon	14th	1952
Exhibitionist	9th	1966
Exploit	unp	1884
Exterminator	1st	1918
Extra Swell	11th	1964
Fabius	2nd	1956
Fair Call	7th	1942
Fairy Hill	11th	1937
Fairy Manah	13th	1942
Falsetto	2nd	1879
Fanfare	5th	1951
Fathom	15th	1970
Faultless	3rd	1947
Favor	4th	1885
Federal Hill	5th	1957
Fencing	17th	1937
Festival King	11th	1959
Field Master	13th	1967
Fighting Back	17th	1951
Fighting Bob	3rd	1910
Fighting Fox	6th	1938
Fighting Hodge	10th	1960
Fighting Step	8th	1945
Finnegan	6th	1959
First Fiddle	5th	1942
First Landing	3rd	1959
First Mate	4th	1896
Fisherman	7th	1954
Flag Raiser	8th	1965
Flamingo	13th	1958
Flamma	3rd	1912
Fleet Allied	7th	1969
Fleet Shoe	8th	1966
Florizar	2nd	1900
Flutterby	8th	1961
Flying Ebony	1st	1925
Flying Fury	6th	1955
Folking	8th	1929
Fonso	1st	1880
Forego	4th	1973
Foreign Agent	11th	1945
Forward Pass	2nd	1968
For Fair	9th	1915
Foundation	4th	1913
Fountainbleu	5th	1899
Four-and-Twenty	7th	1961
Fourulla	19th	1971
Francie's Hat	3rd	1968
Frank Bird	8th	1908
Franklin	3rd	1916
Fred, Jr.	8th	1927
Free Knight	3rd	1886
Free Lance	4th	1912
Freetex	6th	1972
Friend Harry	5th	1909
Frogtown	11th	1919
Gallahadion	1st	1940
Gallant Fox	1st	1930
Gallant Knight	2nd	1930
Gallant Man	2nd	1957
Gallant Pirate	7th	1910
Gallant Sir	8th	1932
Gallifet	2nd	1888
Gay Bit	6th	1944
General Pike	unp	1879
Gen'l Thatcher	16th	1923
Gentleman James	7th	1967
George Lewis	14th	1970
George Smith	1st	1916
Germantown	unp	1876
Getaway	unp	1881
Gleaming Sword	14th	1968
Globemaster	6th	1961
Going Straight	11th	1971
Gold Bag	11th	1973
Gold Mine	15th	1875
Gold Seeker	9th	1936
Gold Shower	8th	1943
Goldcrest Boy	12th	1915
Golden Birch	19th	1951
Golden Rule	19th	1923
Gone Away	4th	1930
Gone Fishin'	8th	1958
Good Advice	pulled up	1933
Good Fight	8th	1962
Goshen	5th	1897
Gov. Browning	10th	1954
Governor Gray	2nd	1911
Gowell	3rd	1913
Goyamo	4th	1954
Gramps Image	8th	1944
Grandpere	5th	1948
Grand Slam	12th	1936
Granville	Lost rider	1936
Gray Pet	7th	1963
Green Hornet	7th	1962
Green Jones	12th	1917
Grey Gold	14th	1937
Grenoble	6th	1875
Grimaldi	6th	1886
Guaranola	5th	1912
Gushing Oil	11th	1952
Guy Fortune	8th	1917
Hail to All	5th	1965
Hall of Fame	9th	1951
Hallieboy	10th	1950
Halma	1st	1895
Halt	5th	1949
Hampden	3rd	1946
Han d'Or	4th	1898
Hannibal	8th	1952
Happy Go Lucky	7th	1952
Harrodsburg	8th	1886
Harry Gilmore	unp	1882
Harry Will	3rd	1876
Hart Wallace	4th	1891
Hasseyampa	3rd	1954
Hassi's Image	11th	1972
Hasty Road	2nd	1954
Hawley	(dh) 5th	1950
Headlight	unp	1877
Head Man	8th	1956
Head of the River	8th	1972
Head Play	2nd	1933
Heather Broom	3rd	1939
He Did	7th	1936
Heelfly	6th	1937
Helio Rise	14th	1971
Henrijan	13th	1960
Herron	11th	1920
High Echelon	3rd	1970
High Foot	14th	1930
Highflyer	unp	1882
High King	10th	1956
Highland Lad	4th	1900
High Tariff	3rd	1891
Hill Gail	1st	1952
Hill Prince	2nd	1950
Hill Rise	2nd	1964
Himyar	2nd	1878
Hindoo	1st	1881
Hindoocraft	unp	1889
Hindus	unp	1900
His Eminence	1st	1901
His Excellency	5th	1900
His Lordship	4th	1899
Hodge	2nd	1914
Hold Your Peace	3rd	1972
Holl Image	6th	1936
Hollywood	9th	1942
Holy Land	fell	1970
Honey's Alibi	7th	1955
Hoop Jr.	1st	1945
Hoops	9th	1932
Huron	2nd	1892
Hydromel	4th	1927
Hyperion II	4th	1906
Impetuosity	13th	1971
Indian Broom	3rd	1936
Indian Creek	6th	1957
Inlander	9th	1933
In Memoriam	11th	1923
Insco	6th	1931
Introductivo	4th	1972
Invalidate	15th	1956
Inventor	2nd	1902
Investor	8th	1963
Invigorator	3rd	1953
Irish Pat	5th	1885
Iron Leige	1st	1957
Iron Ruler	12th	1968
Isabey	3rd	1898
Isaiah	12th	1933
Ishkoodah	9th	1964
Jack Denman	5th	1911
Jack Higgins	4th	1928
Jacks Town	12th	1949
Jacobe	15th	1945
Jacobin	3rd	1887
James Reddick	3rd	1906
James Session	8th	1954
James T. Clark	6th	1918
Jay Fox	15th	1961
Jean Baptiste	11th	1956
Jean's Joe	5th	1955
Jeep	5th	1945
Jet Pilot	1st	1947
Jett-Jett	13th	1947
Jewel's Reward	4th	1958
Jig Time	6th	1968
Jim French	2nd	1971
Jim Gore	2nd	1887
Jim Gray	5th	1886
Jimmie Gill	7th	1913
Jobar	11th	1946
Jock	3rd	1927
Joe Cotton	1st	1885
Joe Morris	2nd	1910
John Bruce	12th	1959
John Finn	3rd	1922
John Furlong	6th	1910
John Gund	4th	1914
Johns Joy	9th	1949
Johnstown	1st	1939
Judge Hines	1st	1903
Jr.'s Arrowhead	18th	1971
Karl Eitel	9th	1929
Kauai King	1st	1966
Kendor	17th	1946
Kenilworth Lad	16th	1945
Kentuckian	10th	1972
Kentucky Cardinal	9th	1925
Kentucky Farmer	6th	1900
Kentucky Sherry	5th	1968
Keokuk	6th	1885
Kerry Patch	7th	1933
Kiev	11th	1927
Kilkerry	11th	1930
Kimball	2nd	1880
King Clover	13th	1951
King Gorin II	11th	1924
Kingman	1st	1891

Horse	Finished	Year
King O' Swords	9th	1956
King Phalanx	16th	1954
King William	3rd	1877
Kinney	8th	1916
Klondyke	9th	1924
Knight Counter	17th	1971
Knockdown	5th	1946
Ky. Colonel	10th	1949
Ladder	9th	1931
Lady Navarre	2nd	1906
Ladysman	4th	1933
Lafitte	9th	1886
Laureate	3rd	1895
Lawley	6th	1928
Lawrin	1st	1938
Layson	3rd	1905
Leamingtonian	unp	1876
Lee O. Cotner	18th	1925
Lee Town	12th	1962
Lelex	2nd	1881
Lena Misha	9th	1916
Leochares	8th	1913
Leonard	2nd	1877
Leonardo II	7th	1921
Leo Ray	6th	1915
Leonatus	1st	1883
Letterman	6th	1922
Leveler	3rd	1878
Lextown	11th	1949
Liberty Limited	broke down	1932
Liberty Road	10th	1947
Lieber Karl	2nd	1898
Lieut. Gibson	1st	1900
Light Carbine	7th	1926
Light Talk	11th	1961
Lightning Orphan	14th	1967
Lijero	4th	1886
Lincoln Road	2nd	1958
Linger	unp	1893
Lisbon	unp	1877
List	9th	1971
Little Beans	5th	1941
Little String	11th	1915
Loftin	2nd	1884
Longus	6th	1930
Lookout	1st	1893
Lord Boswell	4th	1946
Lord Braedalbane	17th	1929
Lord Coleridge	10th	1885
Lord Marshall	6th	1913
Lord Murphy	1st	1879
Lord Raglan	3rd	1883
Lost Cause	unp	1882
Lotowhite	7th	1950
Loyal Son	9th	1961
Lucky B	5th	1918
Lucky Debonair	1st	1965
Lucky Tom	17th	1932
Lurullah	12th	1960
McCarthy	9th	1935
McCreery	12th	1875
McHenry	unp	1878
McWhirter	unp	1877
Mad Play	10th	1924
Macbeth II	1st	1888
Majestic Needle	12th	1972
Majestic Prince	1st	1969
Malvern	unp	1877
Mameluke	20th	1951
Manister Toi	6th	1917
Manuel	1st	1899
Marie Michon	unp	1876
Marine Victory	15th	1946
Market Wise	3rd	1941
Martie Flynn	10th	1928
Martingale	2nd	1923
Martins Rullah	5th	1958
Master Fiddle	4th	1952
Mate	3rd	1931
Mata Hari	4th	1934
Match Me	10th	1909
Masterpiece	10th	1886
Mazo	3rd	1899
Mel Leavitt	17th	1954
Melodist	4th	1937
Menow	4th	1938
Meridian	1st	1911
Merry Maker	12th	1937
Merry Pete	10th	1936
Miami	2nd	1909
Michael Angelo	7th	1909
Middleground	1st	1950
Midway	3rd	1917
Milford	6th	1908
Military	15th	1937

Horse	Finished	Year
Minotaur	12th	1929
Mioland	4th	1940
Mirage	unp	1893
Misstep	2nd	1928
Mister Jive	7th	1957
Mister Pitt	13th	1962
Mistral	unp	1882
Misweet	12th	1945
Model Cadet	7th	1949
Modest	13th	1924
Modest Lad	9th	1943
Money Broker	8th	1953
Monogram	unp	1882
Montrose	1st	1887
Morpluck	7th	1935
Morvich	1st	1922
Mountain Ridge	10th	1938
Mr. Brick	6th	1964
Mr. Khayyam	8th	1933
Mr. Moonlight	7th	1964
Mr. Mutt	16th	1924
Mr. Pak	6th	1965
Mr. Trouble	3rd	1950
Mud Sill	4th	1911
Muskallonge	12th	1921
My Dad George	2nd	1970
My Gallant	9th	1973
My Play	5th	1922
My Request	3rd	1948
Nabesna	9th	1955
Naishapur	2nd	1929
Napoise	14th	1972
Narushua	11th	1965
Nashua	2nd	1955
Naskra	4th	1970
Nassau	4th	1923
Native Charger	4th	1965
Native Dancer	2nd	1953
Native Royalty	9th	1970
Nautical	15th	1924
Navajo	7th	1973
Ned O.	3rd	1930
Neddle Gun	8th	1925
Needles	1st	1956
Nellie Flag	4th	1935
Never Bend	2nd	1963
Newsboy	unp	1882
No Le Hace	2nd	1972
No Regrets	7th	1956
Norse King	15th	1915
Northern Dancer	1st	1964
No Sir	13th	1937
Noureddin	3rd	1958
No Robbery	5th	1963
No Wrinkles	6th	1943
Ocean Roar	6th	1969
Odd Fellow	unp	1877
Oil Capitol	(dh) 5th	1950
Old Ben	5th	1914
Old Rockport	4th	1949
Old Rosebud	1st	1914
Olympia	6th	1949
Omaha	1st	1935
Omar Khayyam	1st	1917
Once Again	3rd	1889
One Dime	3rd	1879
On His Metal	10th	1961
On Location	pulled up	1939
On My Honor	4th	1963
On The Mark	8th	1950
On the Money	15th	1971
On Trust	4th	1947
On Watch	3rd	1920
Open View	8th	1959
Orlandwick	6th	1907
Ornament	2nd	1897
Oscillation	13th	1932
Osmand	2nd	1927
Our Boots	8th	1941
Our Dad	15th	1959
Our Fancy	7th	1932
Our Native	3rd	1973
Our Trade Winds	13th	1972
Outbound	7th	1889
Outlook	5th	1890
Ovelando	3rd	1907
Overtime	5th	1932
Pacallo	16th	1972
Palestinian	3rd	1949
Palisade	4th	1890
Panchio	3rd	1929
Paraphrase	21st	1929
Parole	unp	1876
Parson	6th	1896
Patches	10th	1920

Horse	Finished	Year
††Pat Malloy's Colt	unp	1882
Paul Bunyan	15th	1929
Paul Jones	1st	1920
Peace Chance	5th	1934
Peace Pennant	16th	1920
Pearl Song	2nd	1894
Pebbles	2nd	1915
Pellicle	8th	1946
Pendennis	7th	1887
Pensive	1st	1944
Perfect Bahram	9th	1946
Personality	8th	1970
Petee-Wrack	14th	1928
Phalanx	2nd	1947
Phil D.	4th	1951
Phil Dwyer	3rd	1892
Picketer	15th	1923
Pictor	8th	1940
Pike's Pride	unp	1883
Pink Star	1st	1907
Pintor	12th	1952
Pintor Lea	5th	1956
Pittsburgher	7th	1931
Planet	10th	1921
Plat Eye	8th	1935
Plaudit	1st	1898
Playfair	9th	1885
Plutus	2nd	1893
Pompey	5th	1926
Pomponius	5th	1933
Pompoon	2nd	1937
Ponder	1st	1949
Porter's Cap	4th	1941
Pot o'Luck	2nd	1945
Powhattan III	unp	1884
Pravus	21st	1923
Prego	pulled up	1962
Prince d'Amour	12th	1931
Prince Fonso	6th	1890
Prince Hotspur	14th	1932
Prince K.	9th	1923
Prince of Bourbon	5th	1925
Prince Pal	13th	1920
Prince Pat	20th	1929
Prince Silverwings	4th	1904
Proctor Knott	2nd	1889
Proceeds	5th	1904
Proper Proof	9th	1968
Proud Clarion	1st	1967
Prudery	3rd	1921
Psychic Bid	6th	1935
Pur Sang	8th	1951
Quadrangle	5th	1964
Quasimodo	13th	1934
Quinta	12th	1966
Quito	unp	1880
Quatrain	12th	1925
Racing Fool	4th	1955
Rae Jet	8th	1969
Ram O'War	9th	1953
Ram's Horn	2nd	1905
Rancho Lejos	16th	1970
Reaping Reward	3rd	1937
Reason To Hail	4th	1967
Recollection	11th	1926
Redcoat	unp	1876
Red Gauntlet	4th	1907
Red Hannigan	12th	1954
Red Hot Pistol	11th	1958
Regalo	9th	1919
Regret	1st	1915
Rehabilitate	6th	1966
Reigh Count	1st	1928
Reigh Olga	5th	1928
Repetoire	12th	1951
Replevin	16th	1928
Requested	14th	1942
Respard	unp	1878
Restless Jet	5th	1973
Revenue Agent	7th	1924
Rhinock	4th	1926
Rialto	7th	1923
Rickety	4th	1917
Rico Tesio	10th	1959
Ridan	3rd	1962
Riley	1st	1890
Rippey	10th	1946
Rip Rap	13th	1927
Riskolater	11th	1945
Riva Ridge	1st	1972
Robert Bruce	unp	1882
Robert Morris	9th	1941
Robespierre	3rd	1890
Robin's Bug	10th	1970
Rock Man	3rd	1926

Horse	Finished	Year
Rockwood Boy	15th	1944
Rolled Stocking	12th	1927
Roman	6th	1940
Roman Brother	4th	1964
Roman Line	2nd	1962
Roman Soldier	2nd	1935
Ronnie's Ace	13th	1961
Round Table	3rd	1957
Round the World	6th	1911
Royal II	4th	1915
Royal and Regal	8th	1973
Royal Attack	10th	1962
Royal Bay Gem	4th	1953
Royal Julian	7th	1927
Royal Leverage	12th	1971
Royal Man	7th	1940
Royal Mustang	2nd	1951
Royal Orbit	4th	1959
Royal Shuck	12th	1964
Royal Tower	9th	1963
Roycrofter	13th	1926
Ruhe	3rd	1951
Ruken	8th	1967
Runnymede	2nd	1882
Saigon Warrior	20th	1971
Sailor	7th	1919
Sandy Beal	12th	1920
Sangreal	13th	1936
Sannazarro	2nd	1901
Scapa Flow	9th	1927
Sceneshifter	5th	1937
Sea O Erin	14th	1954
Searcher	9th	1875
Sea Swallow	7th	1945
Second Encounter	10th	1967
Secretariat	1st	1973
Semper Ego	3rd	1896
Senecas Coin	pulled up	1949
Sennings Park	5th	1919
Sensitive Music	5th	1972
Sewell Combs	7th	1918
Sgt. Byrne	11th	1934
Shag Tails	13th	1952
Sham	2nd	1973
Shan Pac	9th	1957
Sharp Count	14th	1962
Sharpshooter	4th	1915
Shecky Greene	6th	1973
Sherluck	5th	1961
Shut Out	1st	1942
Shut Up	4th	1944
Sigurd	3rd	1894
Silent Screen	5th	1970
Silky Sullivan	12th	1958
Silver Spoon	5th	1959
Singing Wood	8th	1934
Single Foot	4th	1925
Sir Barton	1st	1919
Sir Bee Bum	15th	1951
Sir Catesby	4th	1909
Sir Cleges	2nd	1908
Sir Damion	19th	1937
Sir Huon	1st	1906
Sir Joseph	7th	1886
*Sir Ribot	4th	1962
Sirocco	5th	1940
Sir Thomas	12th	1934
Sir War	12th	1942
Skeptic	7th	1917
Skytracer	9th	1944
Sky Guy	10th	1966
Slide Rule	3rd	1943
Sligo	unp	1881
Smoke Screen	10th	1952
Snuzzle	16th	1951
Social Outcast	7th	1953
Solicitor	unp	1878
Sonada	6th	1912
Sonic	14th	1951
Son of John	3rd	1925
Sortie	21st	1928
Spanish Play	4th	1931
Speedmore	10th	1934
Spicson	6th	1933
Spokane	1st	1889
Sportsman	6th	1889
Spring Broken	8th	1960
Spy Hill	6th	1934
Spy Song	2nd	1946
Standiford Keller	unp	1883
Staretor	2nd	1941
Star Hawk	2nd	1916
Star Gazer	10th	1917
Star Master	9th	1917
Star Reward	6th	1947
Startle	8th	1922
Star Voter	11th	1921
St. Bernard	8th	1919
St. Bernard	17th	1935
Sterling	17th	1920
Step Along	5th	1925
Stepenfetchit	3rd	1932
Stepfather	9th	1947
Stir Up	3rd	1944
Stone Street	1st	1908
Straight Face	6th	1953
Stranded	13th	1950
Strathmore	3rd	1879
Strideaway	10th	1933
Strolling Player	22nd	1928
Stupendous	4th	1966
Sub Fleet	2nd	1952
Successor	6th	1967
Summer Tan	3rd	1955
Sun Beau	11th	1928
Sun Fairplay	11th	1935
Sunglow	4th	1950
Sunrise County	5th	1962
Sunset Trial II	16th	1937
Super Devil	11th	1954
Surf Board	11th	1931
Surf Rider	7th	1922
Surprising	6th	1914
Swain	11th	1941
Swaps	1st	1955
Sweep All	2nd	1931
Sweeping Away	15th	1925
Sweep Swinger	10th	1942
Swift Ruler	7th	1965
Swoop	16th	1952
Swope	6th	1925
Sword Dancer	2nd	1959
Synchronized	4th	1908
T.V. Commercial	4th	1968
Tannery	8th	1930
Te Vega	10th	1968
Technician	5th	1939
Ten Booker	3rd	1885
Ten Broeck	5th	1875
Ten Point	2nd	1913
Terlago	11th	1970
Terrang	12th	1956
Tetan	14th	1915
Teufel	8th	1936
The Bat	17th	1925
The Chevalier	5th	1888
The Chief	5th	1938
The Chosen One	14th	1959
The Clown	18th	1923
The Cock	6th	1916
The Dragon	5th	1896
The Fighter	11th	1936
The Mongol	8th	1931
The Nut	7th	1929
The Rival	3rd	1902
The Scoundrel	3rd	1964
The Winner	7th	1896
Thistle	8th	1885
Thistle Ace	18th	1932
Thorndale	8th	1924
Thrive	3rd	1900
Thunderer	5th	1916
Ticket	2nd	1917
Tick On	6th	1932
Tiger Rebel	13th	1945
Time Clock	7th	1934
Timely Reward	10th	1951
Timely Tip	15th	1954
Tim Tam	1st	1958
T. M. Dorsett	7th	1939
Today	12th	1935
Tom Elmore	5th	1894
Tompion	4th	1960
Tom Rolfe	3rd	1965
*Tomy Lee	1st	1959
Tony Graff	7th	1960
Topland	5th	1910
Top Knight	5th	1969
Top O' The Wave	13th	1917
Toro	3rd	1928
Touch Bar	11th	1962
Traffic Mark	4th	1969
Tragniew	13th	1966
Transmute	6th	1924
Treacy	6th	1903
Tribal Line	7th	1971
Trim Destiny	10th	1955
Trinidad	unp	1879
Troilus	17th	1959
Trouble Brewing	8th	1968
Trumpet King	12th	1950
Tryster	4th	1921
Tutticurio	15th	1935
Twenty Grand	1st	1931
Twice A Prince	12th	1973
Twist the Axe	10th	1971
Typhoon	15th	1928
Typhoon II	1st	1897
Ulysses	8th	1896
Uncle Bryn	13th	1915
Uncle Luther	7th	1930
Uncle Velo	8th	1921
Unconscious	5th	1971
Under Fire	3rd	1919
Upset	2nd	1920
Upset Lad	10th	1929
Vagabond	14th	1875
Vagrant	1st	1876
Valdina Orphan	3rd	1942
Valdina Paul	10th	1941
Valley Flares	13th	1944
Vegas Vic	6th	1971
Velours	6th	1906
Venetian Way	1st	1960
Vera Cruz	unp	1877
Verbatim	13th	1968
Verdigris	3rd	1875
Victoria Park	3rd	1960
Vigil	3rd	1923
Vindex	12th	1919
Viscounty	4th	1939
Vito	20th	1928
Viva America	3rd	1918
Volcano	2nd	1875
Voltaic	19th	1925
Voltear	6th	1929
Vulcanite	4th	1919
Wallansee	unp	1882
War Admiral	1st	1937
Warbucks	13th	1973
War Cloud	4th	1918
War Eagle	15th	1927
Warfield	8th	1909
Warren G.	eased	1958
Warsaw	13th	1875
War Star	5th	1917
Watermelon	7th	1914
Wee Admiral	16th	1946
Wendover	unp	1882
Weston	18th	1935
Wheelwright	7th	1912
Whirlaway	1st	1941
Whiskery	1st	1927
Whiskolo	3rd	1935
White	3rd	1888
Whopper	13th	1935
Wida	14th	1923
Wildair	8th	1920
Wild Aster	18th	1924
Wil Rad	10th	1964
Williamston Kid	11th	1966
Windy City	5th	1929
Wine List	13th	1949
Wintergreen	1st	1909
Wissahicken	unp	1879
With Pleasure	14th	1946
With Regards	4th	1942
W. L. Sickle	8th	1947
Woodlake	5th	1903
Wool Sandals	5th	1907
Worth	1st	1912
Yankee Notions	5th	1913
Yomolka	11th	1960
Your Host	9th	1950
Zal	2nd	1907
Zev	1st	1923

678 OWNERS, 1,122 STARTERS

Below are listed the names in which Derby horses have been started, together with the horses started under each name and the year in which each raced in the Kentucky Derby.

—A—

ABEL, MRS. A. J.: Gramp's Image (1944)
A. C. T. STOCK FARM: Indian Broom (1936, third)
ADAMS, MRS. JOHN PAYSON: Grandpere (1948)
AFTON VILLA FARM: Jack Towns (1949)
AGNEW, S. J.; Terlago (1970)
AISCO STABLE (A. I. Savin): Royal and Regal (1973)
ALBERTA RANCHES LTD. (Max Bell and Frank McMahon): Four-and-Twenty and Flutterby (1961)
ALEXANDER, K. S.: Escoba (1918, second)
ALLEN, EARL: Swift Ruler (1965)
ALLEN, G. R.: Calcutta (1923)
ALVAREZ, E.: Herron (1920)
ALVEY, E.: Friend Harry (1909)
AMBERCROMBIE AND SMITH: Stranded (1950)
AMBUSH STABLE (Jack and Michael Stein): On My Honor (1963)
AMIEL, J. J.: Count Turf (1951, won), Count Flame (1952)
ANDERSON, EDDIE: Burnt Cork (1943)
ANDERSON & GOODING: Al Boyer (1894)
ANDERSON, R. H.: Joe Morris (1910, second)
APPLEBAUM, J. L.: Mister Jive (1957)
APPLEGATE, H. C.: Old Rosebud (1914, won)
APPLEGATE, W. E.: Wool Sandals (1907)
APPLETON, A. I.: My Gallant (1973)
ARCHIBALD, H. T.: Folking (1929)
ARMSTRONG, D.: Synchronized (1908)
ARMSTRONG, N.: Lord Raglan (1883, third), Spokane (1889, won)
ASTE, A. L.: Ten Point (1913, second)
ASTOR, WILLIAM: Vagrant (1876, won)
AUDLEY FARM: The Clown (1923), Bobashela (1928), Gallant Knight (1930, second)

—B—

BAIN, F. C.: Patches (1920)
BAKER, A.: John Gund (1914)
BAKER, G. F.: Uncle Velo (1921), John Finn (1922, third)
BAKER, R. L.: Emerson Cochran (1915)
BAKER, W. H.: Green Jones (1917)
BALDWIN, E. J.: Lijero (1886)
BANCROFT, MRS. E. W.: Damascus (1967, third)
BASHFORD MANOR STABLE (see Geo. J. Long also); Hart Wallace (1891), Azra (1892, won), Plutus (1893, second), Sigurd (1894, third), Curator (1895)
BELAIR STUD (William Woodward): Gallant Fox (1930, won), Omaha (1935, won), Merry Pete and Granville (1936), Fighting Fox (1938), Johnstown (1939, won), Apache (1942), Nashua (1955, second)
BELLARDI, MRS. A. and T. I. HAWKINS: Benedicto (1958)
BELLE ISLE STABLE: Upset Lad (1929)
BENJAMIN, E. V., III, and J. MERRICK JONES, JR.: Action Getter (1970)
BENNETT, G. C. & CO.: Abe Frank (1902)
BERGER, E. C. A.: Boot and Spur (1942)
BEVERWYCKE STABLE: Cassius (1889), Lena Misha (1916), Top O The Wave (1917)
BIANCHI, O. A.: Lucky B (1918), Sennings Park (1919)
BIEBER, I.: Palestinian (1949, third), Flag Raiser (1965)
BILLINGS & JOHNSON: Omar Khayyam (1917, won)
BIRCH, DR. A. L.: Timely Tip (1954)
BLOCK, BENJAMIN: Morvich (1922, won), Aspiration and Better Luck (1923), Thorndale (1924)
BLOOMFIELD STABLE: Blackwood (1928)
BLUE RIDGE FARM: Elooto (1938)
BLUM, MARIBEL: Hold Your Peace (1972 third)
BOBANET STABLE: Gay Bit (1944), Marine Victory (1946)
BOCHMAN, H. G.: Happy Go Lucky (1952)
BOEING, W. E.: Slide Rule (1943, third)
BOKUM, RICHARD & DANIEL SCOTT: Quinta (1966)
BOMAR STABLE: Grand Slam (1936)
BOSHAMER, CARY C.: King Clover (1951)
BOSTWICK, A. C.: Mate (1931, third)
BOWEN, G. W. & CO.: One Dime (1879), Alframbra (1881, third), Bengal (1882, third)
BRADLEY, E. R. (See Idle Hour Stock Farm also): By Golly (1920), Behave Yourself and Black Servant (1921, won and second), Blue Larkspur and Bay Beauty (1929), Breezing Thru and Buckeye Poet (1930), Burgoo King and Brother Joe (1932, won and 18th), Brokers Tip (1933, won), Bazaar (1934), Boxthorn (1935), Bien Joli (1936), Billionaire (1937), Bimelech (1940, second), Burning Dream (1945)
BRAE BURN FARM (J. O. McCue): Jay Fox (1961)
BRAEDALBANE STABLE: Weston (1935)
BRAGG, MRS. VERA S.: Blue Pair (1941), Gold Shower (1943)
BRANDON STABLE: Brandon Mint (1932), Tutticurio (1935)
BRANDYWINE STABLE (Donald Ross); Countermand (1956)
BRANN, W. L.: Challedon (1939, second), Pictor (1940), Escadru (1948)

BRANNON, B. J.: St. Bernard (1919)
BRAUNSTEIN, EST. OF J.: Royal Orbit (1959)
BRECKINRIDGE, D.: Lord Braedalbane (1929)
BRENT & TALBOT: Tiger Rebel (1945)
BRIARDALE FARM (J. McCue): Rico Tesio (1959)
BRITT, W. E.: No Regrets (1956)
BROLITE FARM: Challenge Me (1944), With Pleasure (1946)
BROOKMEADE FARM: Inlander (1933), Calvacade and Time Clock (1934, won and seventh), Psychic Bid (1935), Liberty Road (1947), Sunglow (1950), Sword Dancer (1959, second)
BROWN, ED.: Ulysses (1896)
BROWN, J. G.: On His Metal (1961)
BROWN HOTEL STABLE (J. G. Brown): Snuzzle (1951)
BROWN, J. W.: T. M. Dorsett (1939), Mel Leavitt (1954)
BROWN, MRS. JOE W.: Green Hornet (1962), Kentucky Sherry (1968), List (1971)
BROWN, S. S.: Masterpiece (1886), Proceeds (1904), Agile (1905, won)
BROWN, W. L. L.: Fathom (1970)
BUFORD, GEN. ABE: McCreery and Grenoble (1875), McWhirter (1877), McHenry (1878), General Pike (1879)
BUHL, T. D.: Sweep Swinger (1942), Air Sailor (1945)
BUSCH, A. A.: Chief Uncas (1925)
BUTLER, J.: Pebbles (1915, second)
BWAMAZON FARM: T. V. Commercial (1968)
BYERS, J. F.: Robert Morris (1941)

—C—

CADWILLADER, GEORGE: Strathmore (1879, third)
CAHN, J. C.: Typhoon II (1897, won), Thrive (1900, third)
CAIBETT, EDGAR: Canonero II (1971, won)
CAIN HOY STABLE (H. F. Guggenheim): Battle Morn (1951), Dark Star (1953, won), Racing Fool and Flying Fury (1955), Never Bend (1963, second), Captain's Gig (1968)
CALDWELL, FRANK J.: Jim French (1971, second)
CALUMET FARM (Warren Wright): Nellie Flag (1935), Bull Lea (1938), Whirlaway (1941, won), Pensive (1944, won), Pot o' Luck (1945, second), Faultless (1947, third), Citation and Coaltown (1948, won and second), Ponder (1949, won), Fanfare (1951)
CALUMET FARM (Mrs. Warren Wright): Hill Gail (1952, won)
CALUMET FARM (Mrs. Gene Markey): Fabius (1956, second), Pintor Lea (1956), Iron Liege (1957, won), Tim Tam (1958, won), Forward Pass (1968, second), Eastern Fleet and Bold and Able (1971)
CAMDEN, J. N.: Dunvegan (1908, third), Miami (1909, second), Boola Boola (1910), Wheelwright (1912), Hydromel (1927)
CAMPBELL, BRUCE S.: Ram O' War (1953)
CANNULI, MRS. A.: Chance It Tony (1958)
CARMEN, R. F.: Meridian (1911, won), Surprising (1914)
CARMINE, CECIL: Dandy K. (1964)
CARSON, STEVE & IRVING APPLE: Rancho Lejos (1970)
CARTER, W. A.: Clodian (1937)
CASSIDY, T. M.: Crack Brigade (1930)
CATAWBA STABLE: Mr. Khayyam and Good Advice (1933)
CHENERY, C. T. (also see Meadow Farm): Hill Prince (1950, second)
CHEROCK, J. J.: Investor (1963)
CHICAGO STABLE: (Hankins & Johnson): Macbeth II (1888, won)
CHINN & MORGAN: Leonatus (1883, won), Harrodsburg (1886)
CHRISTIANA STABLE: Alexis (1945)
CIRCLE M. FARM (Edward S. Moore): Sir War (1942), Riskolater (1947)
CLAIBORNE FARM (A. B. Hancock): Dunce (1959); Dike (1969, third)
CLARK, WILBUR & WILLIAM RADKOVICH: Ronnie's Ace (1961), Wil Rad (1964)
CLAY, GREEN: Red Coat (1876)
CLAY, T. J.: The Chevalier (1888), Balgowan (1897, 2nd)
CLAY, WOODFORD: Driscoll (1901, third)
CLAY & WOODFORD: Admiral (1884)
CLEAR SPRINGS STABLE (Richard Reynolds): Beau Sub (1966)
COCHRAN, G. A.: Bersagliere (1920), Revenue Agent (1924), Flying Ebony (1925, won)
COE, W. R.: David Harem and Cleopatra (1920), Pompey (1926), Ladysman and Pomponious (1933)
COHEN, MRS. BEN: Hail To All (1965)
COLDSTREAM STUD: Coldstream (1936)
COLLINS, G.: Thistle Ace (1932)
COLLINS, I. J.: Bernard F. (1937)
COLLINS, R. W.: Lee O. Cotner (1925)
COLSTON, R.: Colston (1911, third)
COMBS, LUCAS B.: Dark Jungle (1946)
COMPANAS STABLE (Colin MacLeod, Jr., and Mrs. George Schneider): Besomer (1956)
CONDRAN, G. F.: Flamma (1912, third)
CONSTATIN, E., JR.: Royal Bay Gem (1953)
CORRIGAN, E.: Irish Pat (1885), Riley (1890, won), Huron and Phil Dwyer (1892, second and third), Corsini (1899, second)

CORRIGAN, P.: Free Knight (1886, third)
COSDEN, A. H.: Vito (1928)
COSDEN, J. S.: Martingale and Golden Rule (1923, second and 19th), Nautical (1924)
COTTRILL, W.: Kimball (1880, second), Harry Gilmore (1882), Buchanan (1884, won), Lord Coleridge (1885)
COUGHLIN, J. J.: Karl Eitel (1929)
COVENTRY ROCK FARM: Trouble Brewing (1968)
COWAN, S. A.: Boon Companion (1925)
COYNE, PETE: King Gorin II (1924)
CRABGRASS STABLE: Noureddin (1958, third)
CRAGWOOD STABLE: Jig Time (1968)
CREVOLIN, A. J.: Determine and Allied (1954, won and 9th)
CREW, SIDNEY I.: Cuvier Relic (1960)
CRIMSON KING FARM (Peter W. Salmen Sr.): Crimson Satan (1962)
CROISSANT, G. F.: Kentucky Cardinal (1925), Roycrofter (1926)
CURRAN, W. J.: Jack Higgins (1928)
CURTIS, RAYMOND M.: My Dad George (1970, second)
CUSHING & ORTH: Lookout and Boundless (1893, won and third)

—D—

D. and H. STABLE (Jack Dudley and Bonnie Heath): Needles (1956, won)
DANIEL, MR. and MRS. T. M.: Ace Destroyer (1953)
DARBY DAN FARM (John W. Galbreath): Chateaugay (1963, won), Proud Clarion (1967, won)
DARDEN, GEO. W. & CO.: Lord Murphy (1879, won), Playfair (1885)
DARDEN, W. W.: Dortch (1915)
DAVIS, MR. and MRS. EARLE: Extra Swell (1964)
DAVIS, W. C.: Rockwood Boy (1944)
DAY, C. M.: Saigon Warrior (1971)
DEAN, MRS. J. S., JR.: Holy Land (1970)
DENEMARK, MRS. EMIL: Ruhe (1951, third)
DENT, MRS. MARGRUDER: Mr. Moonlight (1964)
DIXIANA (Charles T. Fisher): Voltear (1929), Sweep All (1931, second), Cee Tee (1932), Mata Hari (1934), Sirocco (1940), Amber Light (1943), Spy Song (1946, second), Star Reward (1947), Sub Fleet (1952, second)
DOERMOEFER & WEST: Jimmie Gill (1913)
DONAMIRE FARM: Going Straight (1971)
DOYLE, M.: Ovelando (1907)
DUFFY, E. W.: Grey Gold (1937)
DUNNE, P.: Under Fire (1919, third)
DURNELL, MRS. C. E.: Elwood (1904, won)
DUST, E. A.: Dearborn (1961), Royal Shuck (1964)
DWYER, M. F.: Ben Brush (1896, won)
DWYER BROTHERS: Quito (1880), Hindoo (1881, won), Runnymede (1882, second)

—E—

EASTIN & LARABIE: High Tariff (1891, third), First Mate (1896)
EASTMAN, R. M.: Cathop (1932)
EASTMAN, R. M. ESTATE: Charley O. (1933, third)
EASTWOOD STABLE (Richard Bittner and James Matia): Loyal Son (1961)
EDGEHILL FARM (Leonard Frutchman): Bally Ache (2nd, 1960)
ELBERON FARM (Mr. and Mrs. David A. Werblin): Silent Screen (1970)
ELKCAM STABLE (Mackle Brothers): Open View (1959)
ELKCAM STABLE and L. CHESLER: Atoll (1959)
ELKWOOD FARM (Margaret Jones, Betty Iselin, Norma Hess and Deana Gross): Restless Jet (1973)
ELLISON, C. R.: Judge Hines (1903, won), Lady Navarre and James Reddick (1906, second and third)
ELLSWORTH, R. C.: Swaps (1955, won), Terrang (1956), Candy Spots (1963, third), The Scoundrel (1964, third)
ELMENDORF: Verbatim (1968), Big Spruce (1972), Twice a Prince (1973)
ELMORE, MR. and MRS. S. H.: Henrijan (1960)
EL PECO RANCH (George A. Pope, Jr.): Decidedly (1962, won), Hill Rise (1964, second)
ELZEMEYER, E. E.: Warbucks (1973)
EMERALD HILL STABLE (M. A. White): Eternal Moon (1952)
ERLANGER STABLE: Shut Up (1944)
ERNST, A. C.: Alorter (1944), Alamond (1946)
ESTABLO, EDEN: Dawn Glory (1967)
ESTOPINAL, H. J. and A. A. ARNAUD: Touch Bar (1962)
EVANS, GEORGE: Pike's Pride (1883)

—F—

F. and B. FARMS (Frank A. and Bernice Bowdon): Good Fight (1962)
FAIR STABLE (Mrs. Graham Fair Vanderbilt): Chicatie (1929)
FAIRBANKS, MRS. R. B.: Bluebeard (1935)
FAIRFIELDS STABLE: Sun Fairplay (1935)
FARRIS, W. H.: Buckner (1879)
FAY & WEHMHOFF: Ed Tierney (1904, second)
FENCE POST FARM (Mr. and Mrs. Theodore Gary): Corn Off The Cob (1970)
FERGUSON, D.: Bell Buzzer (1944), Bob Murphy (1946)
FIELD, L. B.: Headlight (1877)
FIELD, MARSHALL: Sir Damion (1937)
FIELDING, H. W.: Jobar (1946)

FINCH, MRS. H.: Modest Lad (1943)
FISCHBACH, C. B.: Festival King (1959)
FISHER, H. C.: Muskallonge (1921), Mr. Mutt (1924), Swope (1925)
FISHER, MRS. MONTGOMERY: Proper Proof (1968)
FIZER, W. H.: Milford (1908)
FLEETWOOD STABLE: Clarion (1887), Outbound (1889)
FLEISCHMANN, C.: Ben Brown (1897)
FLYING M STABLE: Dominar (1966)
FORD STABLE (Michael Ford): Kauai King (1966, won)
FOREMAN, G. W.: Ned O. (1930, third)
FORSYTHE, J. M.: Fontainbleu (1899)
FOSTER BROTHERS: Dr. Shepherd (1897)
FOX, P. C.: Chestnut Colt by Pat Malloy (1882)
FOXCATCHER FARMS (William du Pont, Jr.): Gold Seeker (1936), Fairy Hill (1937), Dauber (1928, second), Fairy Manah (1942), Hampden (1946, third)
FRANKLIN, H.: Velours (1906)
FRANZHEIM, MRS. B.: Quasimodo (1934)
FRUEHAUF, H. C.: Blue Lem (1955)
FRIEND, B.: Co-Sport (1938)
FUGATE, WALTER T.: Hallieboy (1950)
FULLER, PETER: Dancer's Image (1968, first)
FUNK, JOHN: Harry Hill (1876, third)

—G—

G. & G. STABLE (P. A. Grissom and Edward Grosefield): Money Broker (1953)
G. and M. STABLE (Dr. J. J. Gregory and H. D. Maggio): Ben A. Jones (1956)
GALBREATH, MRS. JOHN W.: Summer Tan (1955, 3rd)
GALLAHER BROTHERS: Duvall (1912, second), Sewell Combs (1918), Regalo (1919), Chilhowee (1924, second)
GARDNER, H. P.: Clyde Van Dusen (1929, won)
GARRISON, C. M.: Be Frank (1919)
GAVEGNANO, J.: High King (1956)
GERRY, R. L.: Voltaic (1925)
GERST, WM.: Brancas (1904, third), Zal (1907, second), Donau (1910, won)
GIBSON, D.: Autocrat (1888)
GILROY, MRS. W.: Timely Reward (1951)
GLEN RIDDLE FARM (S. D. Riddle): War Admiral (1937, won)
GODFREY, PHILIP: Comenow (1944)
GOEMANS, E. M.: °Curragh King (1953)
GOETZ, WILLIAM: Your Host (1950)
GOFF, M. B.: Skytracer (1944)
GOLDEN TRIANGLE STABLE (Thomas A. Eazor): Mister Pitt (1962)
GOODWIN, J. A.: Ky. Colonel (1949)
GORDON, A. B.: Sir Thomas (1934)
GOREY, A. J.: Match Me (1909)
GRABNER, F. M.: Step Along (1925), Windy City (1929)
GRAFFAGNINI, A.: Tony Graff (1960)
GRAHAM, TOM L.: Bert G and Kenilworth Lad (1945)
GRAND PRIX STABLE (Joe Bartell & Robert A. Byfield): Abe's Hope (1966)
GRANT, S. W.: Fred Jr. (1927)
GRAY & CO.: Jim Gray (1886)
GREENER, J. G. & CO.: Lafitte (1886)
GREENTREE STABLE: Letterman (1922), Rialto and Cherry Pie (1923), Wild Aster (1924), Twenty Grand, Anchors Aweigh, and Surf Board (1931, won, tenth, eleventh), Spy Hill (1934), Plat Eye (1935), Shut Out and Devil Diver (1942, won, sixth), Stir Up (1944, third), Capot and Wine List (1949, second, 13th), Hall of Fame and Big Stretch (1951), Straight Face (1953), No Robbery (1963)
GRIFFITH, J. E.: Single Foot (1925), Canter (1926)
GRIMES, MR. & MRS. T. D.: With Regards (1942)
GRINSTEAD, JAMES A.: Gold Mine (1875), Marie Michon (1876)
GRISSOM, J. E.-T. A.: Tribal Line (1971)
GRISSOM, P. L.: Carpenter's Rule (1965), Dr. Isby (1967)
GRISSOM, T. A.: Invalidate (1956), Shan Pac (1957), Lurullah (1960), Roman Line (1962, second)
GRUBER, M. B.: Little Strings (1915)
GUIBERSON, MRS. G.: Arroz (1952), Correspondent (1953)

—H—

HAGGIN, J. B.: Ben Ali (1886, won)
HAINSWORTH, MRS. C.: Blackbirder (1934)
HALLENBACH, H. C.: Worth (1912, won)
HAMBURG PLACE: The Mongol (1931)
HAMILTON, C. E.: Stone Street (1908, won)
HANGER, W. ARNOLD: Dit (1940, third)
HANKINS, G. V.: Robespierre (1890, third)
HAPPY VALLEY FARM (Stephen, Gary and Martin Wolfson): Native Royalty (1970)
HARBOR VIEW FARM (L. E. Wolfson): Roman Brother (1964)
HARNED BROTHERS: Coyne (1921)
HARPER, F. R.: Ten Broeck (1875), Germantown and black colt by

Enquirer (1876), Early Light (1877)
HARRIS, R. E.: Rae Jet (1969)
HARTWELL, C. A.: Cannon Shot (1924)
HASTY HOUSE FARM (Mr. and Mrs. A. E. Reuben), Hasty Road and Sea O Erin (1954, 2nd and 15th), Black Emperor (1956)
HATCH, H. C.: Boys Howdy (1931)
HAWKS, J. S. & CO.: Hyperion II (1906)
HAYES, T. P.: Layson (1905, third), Red Gauntlet (1907), Sir Catesby (1909), Donerail (1913, won), Kinney (1916)
HAYES, WILLIAM: Sannazarro (1901, second)
HEAD, C. BRUCE: Altawood (1924)
HEADLEY, HAL PRICE: Planet (1921), Almadel (1925), Paraphrase (1929), Alcibiades (1930), Whopper (1935), Menow (1938), Pellicle (1946), Lotowhite (1950)
HELIS, WILLIAM: Rippey (1946), Cosmic Bomb (1947)
HELIS, WILLIAM G., JR.: Sky Guy (1966)
HELLER, MRS. F. J.: Agrarian (1934, third)
HENDERSON & HOGAN: Col. Hogan (1911), Guaranola (1912)
HENDRIE, G.: Michael Angelo (1909)
HER-JAC STABLE (Richard Hersch, Peter Jacobs and Harry Gordon): Naskra (1970)
HERTZ, JOHN D.: Chittagong (1923)
HERTZ, MRS. JOHN D.: Reigh Count (1928, won), Count Fleet (1943, won)
HERZ, E.: Mainster Toi (1917)
HEWITT, H. H.: Skeptic (1917), Startle (1922)
HICKEY, WALTER and DR. RICHARD KUHN: Robin's Bug (1970)
HIEATT, C. C. & G. Y.: Ben Machree (1929)
HIGH TIDE STABLE: (Edward G. Burke): Swoop (1952)
HIMYAR STABLE: Parson (1896)
HIRSCH, MARY: No Sir (1937)
HOBSON, W. C.: Diavolaw (1944)
HODGE, MRS. CARL S.: Fighting Hodge (1960)
HOLIDAY STABLE: Ask the Fare (1967)
HOLLINGSWORTH, MRS. D. M.: Kondar (1946)
HOOPER, FRED W.: Hoop Jr. (1945, won), Olympia (1949), Crozier (1961, second), Admiral's Voyage (1962)
HOOTS, MRS. R. M.: Black Gold (1924, won)
HOT SPRINGS STABLE: Ben Eder (1896, second)
HOUSELLS, J. K.: Bymeabond (1945)
HOWARD, C. S.: Mioland (1940), Porter's Cap (1941)
HOWARD, MRS. C. S.: Sea Swallow (1945)
HOWARD, MAXWELL: Sceneshifter and Fencing, (1937), The Chief (1938)
HUFFMAN, ROBERT: Knight Counter (1971)
HUGHES, S. K. & CO.: Tom Elmore (1894)
HUGHES, W. A.: Frank Bird (1908)
HULL, W. C.: Ascension (1875)
HUMPHREY, A. R., JR.: Bronzewing (1914, third)
HUMPHREYS, I. B.: Light Carbine (1926)
HUGUELET, GUY-SPALDING, GENE-HAL STEELE, JR.: Barbs Delight (1967, second)
HUNT, W. P.: Keokuk (1885)

—I—

IDLE HOUR STOCK FARM (see E. R. Bradley also): Bet Mosie, By Gosh, and Busy American (1922, second, ninth and broke down), Bright Tomorrow (1923), Beau Butler, Baffling, Bob Tail (1924, third, 17th and 19th), Broadway Jones (1925), Bubbling Over and Bagenbaggage (1926, won and second), Buddy Bauer and Bewithus (1927)

—J—

JACKSON, A.: Robert Bruce (1882)
JACNOT STABLE (O. T. & J. R. Hogan): *Die Hard (1959), Light Talk (1961)
JACOBS, MRS. ETHEL D.: Dr. Miller (1961), Exhibitionist (1966), High Echelon and Personality (1970, third and eighth)
JACOBIN STABLE: Kingman (1891, won)
JACOBS, PATRICE: Our Dad (1959), Bonjour (1963), Reason to Hail (1967)
JACQUES STABLE: Essare (1929)
JAMES, MR. and MRS. HARRY: James Session (1954)
JEFFORDS, W. M.: Scapa Flow (1927)
JEFFORDS, MRS. W. M.: Diogenes (1924), Commonwealth (1935)
JENNINGS & HUNT: Charlie Bush (1878)
JOHNSON, F.: Nassau (1923), Quatrain (1925), Replevin (1928)
JOHNSON, J. F.: Double Eagle (1915)
JOHNSON, R. A. & CO.: Loftin and Powhattan III (1884, second and unplaced)
JOHNSON & CROSSTHWAITE: Tetan (1915)
JOHNSON & MILLS: Dan K. (1877)
JOLLEY, Mrs. Moody and E. H. Woods and J. L. Greer: Ridan (1962, third)
JONES, MONTFORT: Surf Rider (1922)
JOYCE, P. H.: Dick O'Hara (1930)
J. V. P. STABLE (J. U. Pischier): Lee Town (1962)

—K—

KAISER, A. A.: Captain Hal (1925, second), Bonivan (1928)
KANOWSKY, MR. and MRS. VINCENT: Fleet Allied (1969)

KEENE, J. O. & G. H.: Lord Marshall (1913)
KEENELAND STUD FARM (J. O. Keene): Champ De Mars (1926)
KEIM, MRS. MARY A.: Mr. Pak (1965)
KELLOGG, HELEN W.: Come On Red (1956, third)
KELLMAN, JOSEPH: Shecky Greene (1973)
KENTON FARM STABLE: Typhoon (1928)
KERR STABLE: Round Table (1957, third)
KILMER, W. S.: Exterminator (1918, won), Frogtown (1919), Sun Beau (1928), Dark Winter (1933)
KINARD, J. A., JR.: Johns Joy (1949)
KING RANCH (Robert J. Kleberg): Dispose (1941), Assault (1946, won), Middleground and On The Mark (1950, won and eighth), Sonic (1951)
KNAPP, H. K.: Yankee Notions (1913)
KNEBELKAMP, W. F.: Hoops (1932)
KNEBELKAMP & MORRIS: Spanish Play (1931), Adobe Post (1932)
KOHN & THEISEN: Recollection (1926)
KUHNS, G. & CO.: Highflyer (1882)

—L—

LABOLD BROTHERS: Montrose (1887, won)
LA BRAE STABLE: Elector (1925)
LAKELAND, W.: Babcock (1882)
LAZY F RANCH (Mrs. Libbie Rica Farish and Mrs. Martha Farish Gerry): Forego (1973)
LEHMAN, O.: Reigh Olga (1928)
LEHMAN, ROBERT: Ambiopoise (1961), Prego (1962), Rehabilitate (1966)
LEHMANN, ROBERT E.: Dust Commander (1970, won), Majestic Needle and Napoise (1972)
LEICHLEITER, R. E.: Cartago (1928)
LEITER, J. ESTATE: Prince D'Armour (1931), Prince Hotspur (1932)
LEIGH & ROSE: Chant (1894, won)
LE MAIRE, F. B.: Norse King (1915)
LE MAR STOCK FARM (Leo J. Marks): Misstep (1928, second)
LESH, J. H.: Warfield (1909)
LETCHER, W. R.: Bill Letcher (1890, second)
LEVIN, W. A.: Bold Reason (1971, third)
LEWIS, A. B. & CO.: Vagabond (1875)
LEWIS, C. A.: Verdigris (1875, second)
LEWIS, MR. and MRS. GEO.: Martins Rullah (1958)
LEWIS, MRS. W. G.: Darby Dieppe (1945, third)
LEXBROOK STABLE: Lextown (1949)
LEXINGTON STABLE: My Play (1922), Prince of Bourbon (1925)
LIN-DRAKE FARM (Richard D. Irwin and Mrs. Kathryn U. Schmidt): Dr. Behrman (1970)
LINDSAY, F. H.: Sensitive Music (1972)
LISLE, R.: Jacobin (1887, third)
LIVINGSTON, J.: Royal II (1915)
LLANGOLLEN FARM (Mrs. R. Lunn): Gone Fishin' (1958), Divine Comedy (1960)
LOFT, G. W.: On Watch and Donnacona (1920, third and fifth)
LOMA STABLE: Tick On (1932)
LONG, GEORGE J. (see Bashford Manor also): Hindus (1900), Amur (1901), Sir Huon (1906, won), Sir Cleges (1908, second), Campeon (1909), Free Lance (1912)
LONGRIDGE STABLE (W. V. Thraves): Bar None (1928), Oscillation (1932)
LOOKOUT STOCK FARM (J. Brink): Foreign Agent (1945)
LOONEY, J. T.: Leo Ray (1915)
LORILLARD, P.: Parole (1876)
LOUCHHEIM, J.: Economic (1932, second), Speedmore (1934), Morpluck (1935), Pompoon (1937, second)
LOWE, R.: Gallant Man (1957, second)
LOZZI, MR. and MRS. D.: Count Chic (1956)
LUSSKY, CLIFFORD: Federal Hill (1957)
LYTLE, R. S.: Correlation (1954)

—M—

McCAMPBELL, A. G.: Jim Gore (1887, second)
McCARTHY, NEIL S.: Finnegan (1959), Royal Attack (1962)
McCLELLAND, B.: Halma (1895, won)
McCLELLAND, J. W.: Sailor and Eternal (1919)
McCLELLAND, R. M.: Boreas and Bob Cook (1884)
McCURDY, W. C.: Chatter (1883)
McDOWELL, T. C.: His Excellency (1900), Alan-a-Dale and The Rival (1902, won and third), Bourbon and Woodlake (1903, third and fifth), American Eagle (1918)
McGAVOCK, W. C. & CO.: Boulevard (1880)
McGRATH, H. P.: Aristides and Chesapeake (1875, won and unplaced), Leonard (1877, second), Wissahicken (1879), Sligo and Calycanthus (1881)
McKENNA, C. W.: Foundation (1913)
McLAUGHLIN, R. S.: Wee Admiral (1946)
McLEAN, E. B.: Modest (1924), Jock and War Eagle (1927, third and 15th), Toro (1928, third)
McMAHON, FRANK: Majestic Prince (1969, won)
MACKENZIE, R. J.: Direct (1909)
MACOMBER, A. K.: Star Hawk and The Cock (1916, second and sixth), War Star, Star Master and Star Gazer (1917), War Cloud (1918)
MACOMBER, J. R.: Petee-Wrack (1928)

240

MADDEN, J. E.: Plaudit (1898, won), Mazo (1899, third), Watermelon (1914)
MADDEN, P. W.: Kentuckian (1972)
MAGERMAN, MR. and MRS. ALAN: George Lewis (1970)
MAGGIO, J. V.: American Eagle (1944)
MAINE CHANCE FARM (Mrs. Elizabeth Graham): Lord Boswell, Knockdown and Perfect Bahram (1946), Jet Pilot (1947, won), Black Metal (1954), Jewel's Reward and Ebony Pearl (1958)
MARSHALL, K. G.: John Bruce (1959)
MARSHALL BROTHERS: Prince K. (1923)
MARTIN, T. B.: Court Scandal (1937), Bankrupt (1943), Sunrise County (1962)
MARTIN and McKINNEY: Gov. Browning (1954)
MARTIN, W. C.: Phil D. (1951)
MASON, MRS. SILAS B.: Head Play (1933, second), He Did (1937)
MEADOW STABLE (see C. T. Chenery): First Landing (1959, third), Riva Ridge (1972, won), Secretariat (1973, won)
MECOM, J. W.: Narushua (1965)
MEGIBBEN, J. K. & CO.: Sportsman (1889)
MEGIBBEN, T. J.: Newsboy (1882), Audrain (1884, third)
MELBOURNE STABLE (W. S. Barnes): Blue Wing (1886, second), Callifet and Alexandria (1888, second and unplaced)
MERRILL, J. J.: Odd Fellow (1877)
MIDDLETOWN STABLE: Freetex (1972)
MIKELL, MR. and MRS. S. C.: Repetoire (1951)
MILKY WAY FARM: Whiskolo (1935, third), The Fighter and Sangreal (1936), Reaping Reward and Military (1937, third and 15th), Mountain Ridge (1938), On Location (1939), Gallahadion (1940, won), Dogpatch (1942), No Wrinkles (1943)
MILL RIVER STABLE (Mrs. Barclay Douglas): Fair Call (1942)
MILLER, A.: Ticket (1917, second)
MILLER, G. M.: For Fair (1915)
MILLER, LEO: Ocean Roar (1969)
MILLER, W. S.: Better Bee (1957)
MITCHELL, ROBT.: Our Trade Winds (1972)
MONTPELIER STABLE (Mrs. Marion duPont Scott): Pintor (1952)
MOOERS, CLIFFORD: Old Rockport (1949), Hawley (1950), Nabesna (1955)
MOORE, M. C.: Booker Bill (1915)
MOORE, T. W.: Inventor (1902, second)
MORRIS, A. H. & D. H.: Manuel (1899, won)
MORRIS and PATTON: Apollo (1882, won), Drake Carter (1882, second), Bersan and Favor (1885, second and fourth)
MORRISEY, J. D.: Banburg (1887)
MORRISON & KEATING: McCarthy (1935)
MUELLER, T. E.: Wida (1923)
MULRENAN, MRS. E.: First Fiddle (1942)
MURCAIN STABLE (Mrs. Effie Cain and Mrs. Virginia Murchison): Jean's Joe (1955)
MURLOGG FARM: Fighting Step (1945), Fighting Back (1951)
MURRAY, W. S.: Sandy Beal (1920)
MYHELYN STABLE (Helen Martini): Master Fiddle (1952)

—N—

NESBITT, H. S.: Staretor (1941, second)
NEVADA STOCK FARM: General Thatcher (1923)
NICHOLAS, C. E.: Dr. Neale (1972)
NICHOLS, T. J.: Day Star (1878, won)
NORTHWAY STABLE: Gallant Sire (1932)

—O—

OCTOBER HOUSE FARM: Iron Ruler (1968)
OWENS: R. H.: Leveler (1878, third)

—P—

PADGETT, JIM & HUGH GRANT: Blue Skyer (1966, third)
PALLADINO, MRS. L.: Little Beans (1941)
PARKVIEW STABLE: Rhinock (1926)
PARR, RAL: Paul Jones and Blazes (1920, won and sixth)
PARRISH, J. W.: Midway (1917, third), Rolled Stocking (1927), Cold Check (1932), Isaiah (1932), Dellor (1937)
PARSONS, S. L.: Sharpshooter (1915, third)
PASTIME STABLE: Laureate (1895, third), Guy Fortune (1917)
PASTORALE STABLE: Twist the Axe (1971)
PATE, R. C.: Ascender (1883), Clay Pete (1885)
PATNO, B. R.: Valley Flares (1944)
PATTERSON, C. T. & CO.: Ornament (1897, second)
PATTERSON, MRS. R. D.: Alworth (1946)
PEABODY, S.: Martie Flynn (1928)
PEAVEY, W. M.: Jett Jett (1947), Anyoldtime and Sir Bee Bum (1951)
PELTIER, HARVEY: Diplomat Way (1967)
PENDERGRAST, T. J.: Bo McMillan (1923)
PEPPER, JAMES E.: Mirage (1893), The Dragon (1896)
PHIPPS, OGDEN: Dapper Dan (1965, second)
PHIPPS, M. G.: Gentleman James (1967)
POLSON, W. F.: Vulcanite (1919), Peace Pennant (1920)
PONS, F. J.: Jack Denman (1911)

POULSEN, MRS. G.: Broadcloth (1944, second)
POWHATAN (Raymond Guest): Tom Rolfe, (1965, third)
PRICE, MRS. KATHERINE: Carry Back (1961, won)
PRITCHARD, E. F.: Tannery (1930)
PRITCHARD, MRS. M. J., THOMAS, E. W. and RESSEGUET, W. J., JR.: Our Native (1973, third)
PUTNAM, C.: Swain (1941)
PUTNAM, GEORGE: Fleet Shoe (1966)

—R—

R. C. STABLE: Longus (1930)
RAILEY, C. E.: Linger (1893)
RANCOCAS STABLE (Harry F. Sinclair): Zev (1923, won), Brocadale and Mad Play (1924)
RAND, MRS. ADELE L.: Bourbon Prince (1960)
RAND, MISS E. G.: Merry Maker (1937)
REBEL STABLE (W. Gruber): Super Devil (1954)
REIF, G.: Fighting Bob (1910, third)
REINHOLD, MR. and MRS. A. E.: Big Brown Bear (1972)
RESPESS, J. B.: Wintergreen (1909, won), Our Fancy (1932)
REVERIE KNOLL FARM (Freeman Keyes): Smoke Screen (1952), King O' Swords (1956), Sharp Count (1962), Lightning Orphan (1967)
REYNOLDS, J. W. H.: Falsetto (1879, second)
REYNOLDS, W. G.: Warren G. (1958)
RICE, GEORGE H.: Volcano (1875, second), Malvern (1877)
RICE, MRS. A. L.: Model Cadet (1949), Indian Creek (1957), Lucky Debonair (1965, won), Advocator (1966, second)
RICHARDS, BARRY G.: Tragniew (1966)
RICHARDS, A. KEENE: Bullion (1876)
RIDDER, B. J.: Royal Tower (1963)
RIDGEWOOD STABLE (Boines & Tigani): Double Jay (1947)
RINGGOLD, L. B.: Semper Ego (1896, third)
RIVER DIVIDE FARM: Brief Sigh (1944)
ROBERTS, MR. and MRS. R. F.: Traffic Mark (1969)
ROBERTSON, MR. and MRS. C. J., SR.: Introductivo (1972)
ROBINSON, J. J.: Lucky Tom (1932)
ROBINSON, MORGAN & CO.: Bob Wooley (1875)
ROBINSON, W. C., JR.: Admiral's Shield (1970)
RODES, J. B.: Searcher (1875)
RODEGAP, J.: Goshen (1897)
RODES & CARR: Respond (1878), Wallensee (1882)
RODGERS, J. W.: Dove Pie (1943)
ROGERS, J. C.: John Furlong (1910)
ROKEBY STABLES: Quadrangle (1964), Arts and Letters (1969, second), Head of the River (1972)
ROSE, ARTHUR: Misweet (1945)
ROSENBERG: L.: Kerry Patch (1933)
ROSS, J. K. L.: Sir Barton and Billy Kelly (1919, won and second), Star Voter (1921)
ROSS, TOM AND PHIL KLIPSTEIN: Silky Sullivan (1958)
ROSSO, W. P.: Impetuosity (1971)
ROWAN, LOUIS: Ruken (1967)
ROTH, MRS. A.: Senecas Coin (1949)
RYE, G. M.: Col. Zeb Ward (1888)

—S—

SABATH, MRS. A.: Alsab (1942, second)
SACHSENMAIER & REUTER: Roman Soldier (1935, second)
SADACCA, MRS. S. H.: A Dragon Killer (1958), The Chosen One (1959)
SADDLE ROCK FARM: Francie's Hat (1968, third)
SAGAMORE STABLE: Rock Man (1926, third), Don Q (1928)
SAGE STABLE: Rip Rap (1927)
SALMON, WALTER J.: Careful (1921), Vigil (1923, third), Display (1926), Black Panther (1927), Ladder (1931)
SALUBRIA STABLE: Strolling Player (1928)
SALYERS, S. J.: Bill Bruce (1875)
SANFORD, J.: George Smith (1916, won)
SANTA ANITA STABLE: Pendennis (1887)
SASSO, LEONARD P.: Globemaster (1961)
SAXON STABLE (L. R. Allison & M. R. Prestridge): Invigorator (1953, third)
SCHORR, J. W.: Lieber Karl (1898, second), Alard Scheck (1901), Leochares (1913), Ed Crump and Goldcrest Boy (1915), Cudgel (1917), J. T. Clark (1918)
SCHRIEBER, B.: Banridge (1908)
SCHWARTZ, A. C.: Sortie (1928)
SCHWARTZ, M. L.: Bold Venture (1936, won)
SCOGGAN, H. J.: Florizar and Highland Lad (1900, second and unplaced)
SCOGGAN & BRYANT: Proctor Knott (1889, second)
SCOGGAN BROTHERS: Hindoocraft (1889), Buck McCann (1893)
SCOTT, D. W.: Son of John (1925, third)
SCULLY, W. O.: Ban Yan (1887), White (1888, third)
SECHREST, BETTY-C. FRITZ: Vegas Vic (1971)
SECHREST, RANDY and GOTTDANK, MILTON: Gold Bag (1973)
SELEY. MR. and MRS. J. H.: Duplicator (1949), Field Master (1967)
SELLERS, J. B. & CO.: Wendover (1882)
SELZNICK, MYRON: Can't Wait (1938, third)
SEVERSON, L. M.: Paul Bunyon (1929), Spicson (1933)

SHADY BROOK FARM STABLE: Pittsburgher (1931)
SHAFFER, E. G.: St. Bernard (1935)
SHAGRIN, M.: Shag Tails (1952)
SHANDON FARM: Burning Star (1937)
SHANNON, H. & CO.: De Bar (1906)
SHANNON, R. H.: Deadlock (1922)
SHARP, BAYARD: Hannibal (1952), Troilus (1959)
SHAWHAN, J. S.: Fonso (1880, won)
SEELIGSON, A. A., JR.: Unconscious (1971)
SHER, JACOB: Sherluck (1961)
SHINA, HASSI: Hassi's Image (1972)
SIMMONS, A. T.: Blue Swords (1943, second)
SIMMS & OLIVER: Prince Pal (1920)
SIMONETTI, J.: Sgt. Byrne (1934)
SINGERLY, G. A.: Han d'Or (1898)
SMALLWOOD & CO.: King William (1877, third)
SMITH, C. H.: Pearl Song (1894, second), Basso (1895, second), Lieut.
   Gibson (1900, won)
SMITH, J. D.: His Lordship (1899)
SMITH, R. N.: Governor Gray (1911, second)
SMITH, MRS. V. E.: Bass Clef (1961, third)
SMITHA, L.: Dr. Barkley (1909, third)
SOMMER, SIGMUND: Sham (1973, second)
SPENCE, K.: Hodge (1914, second)
SPETH, P. G.: Thistle (1885)
SPRING BROOK FARM (Reuben Kowal): Pur Sang (1951)
SPRINGFIELD & CLAY: Enlister & Warsaw (1875)
SPRING HILL FARM (J. D. Norris): Easy Spur (1959)
STANTON & TUCKER: Isabey (1898, third)
STEELE, A. S.: Orlandwick (1907)
STEVENS, T. H.: Treacy (1903)
STEVENSON, JOE and STUMP, RAY: Navajo (1973)
STICE, E. O. & SON: On Trust (1947)
STIVERS, L.: Uncle Luther (1930)
STRAUS, A. & CO.: Earl of Beaconfield (1878)
STRAUS, JOE B.: No Le Hace (1972, second)
STURGIS, ROY: Mr. Brick (1964)
SULLIVAN, A. H.: Fourulla (1971)
SULLIVAN, F. C.: Te Vega (1968)
SUNNY BLUE FARM (I. Blumberg): Admiral Porter (1954), Lincoln Road
   (1958, second), Venetian Way (1960, won)
SUPERIOR STABLE: Holl Image (1936)
SWIGERT, D.: Bombay (1876), Baden-Baden and Lisbon (1877, won and
   unplaced), Trinidad (1879)
SWIGERT, J. & J.: Grimaldi (1886)
SWIGERT, R. A.: Sir Joseph (1886)
SWIKARD, MRS. E. L.: Chip (1929)

—T—

TALBOT BROTHERS: Prince Silverwings (1904)
TARLTON, L. P., JR.: Solicitor (1878), Mistral (1882)
TATE, MRS. L. P.: Jean Baptiste (1956)
TEINOWITZ-SCHMIDT: On the Money (1971)
TEINOWITZ, P.: Royal Leverage (1971)
TERNES, PAUL & JAMES BARTLETT: Williamston Kid (1966)
THOMAS, BARAK G.: Himyar (1878, second), Lelex (1881, second)
THOMPSON, J. R.: Minotaur (1929)
THOMPSON, P. C.: Crystal Prince (1932)
THREE D'S STOCK FARM: Panchio, Calf Roper and Prince Pat (1929,
   third, 11th and 20th), Broadway Limited and Kilkerry (1930, ninth and
   11th), Liberty Limited (1932), Strideaway (1933), Heelfly (1937)
TICHENO, M. H. & CO.: Early (1903, second)
TOWER STABLE: Royal Man (1940)
TREACY, B. J.: Outlook (1890)
TUFANO, L.: Market Wise (1941, third)
TUMBLEWOOD STABLE (T. S. Wood, Jr. and Mrs. D. W. Price): Ishkoodah
   (1964)
TURNER, MR. and MRS. FRED, JR.: *Tomy Lee (1959, won), *Sir Ribot
   (1962)
TURNEY BROTHERS: Dr. Catlett (1897, third)
TWYMANN, J. C. & CO.: Prince Fonso (1890)

—U—

UDOUJ, MRS. H. J.: Barbizon Streak (1971)
UNDERWOOD, MILDRED F.: Brown Rambler (1952)

—V—

VALDINA FARMS (Emerson F. Woodward): Viscounty (1939), Valdina Paul
   (1941), Valdina Orphan and Hollywood (1942, third and 9th)
VALLEY FARM (Larry Kratz): Yomolka (1960)
VALLEY LAKE STABLE: High Foot (1930)
VAN BERG, MARION H.: Spring Broker (1960)
VANDERBILT, A. G.: Discovery (1934, second), Native Dancer and Social
   Outcast (1953, second and 7th)
VAN METER, C. C.: Topland (1910), Sterling (1920)
VAN METER, F. B.: His Eminence (1901, won)
VEENEMAN, WILLIAM: Black George (1950)
VIKING STABLE: Lawley (1928)
VISSMAN, H. F.: Leamingtonian (1876)

—W—

WAINWRIGHT, J. R.: Gallant Pirate (1910)
WALDEN, R. W.: Uncle Bryn (1915)
WALLACE, WILLIAM: The Winner (1896)
WALMACS FARM (R. W. McElwain): Billings (1948), Hasseyampa (1954,
   third)
WALNUT HILL FARM (Bruno Ferrari): Gray Pet (1963), Jr.'s Arrowhead
   (1971), Pacallo (1972)
WALSH, R.: Sunset Trail II (1937)
WARD, J. S.: Berlin (1917)
WARM STABLE (Silas B. Mason): The Nut (1929)
WARNER STABLE (Major Albert Warner): Native Charger (1965)
WATKINS, G.: Insco (1931)
WATTS, J. R.: Standiford Keller (1883)
WEAVER, J. T.: Gowell (1913, third)
WEBER & WARD: Franklin & Dodge (1916, third and fourth)
WEBSTER, R. N.: Amberoid (1966)
WEIDEMANN, C.: In Memoriam (1923)
WHEATLEY STABLE: Distraction (1928), Teufel (1936), Melodist (1937),
   Bold Ruler (1957), Bold Lad (1965), Stupendous (1966), Successor
   (1967)
WHITAKER, B. F.: Requested (1942), My Request (1948, third)
WHITE, G. R.: Trim Destiny (1955)
WHITEHOUSE, W. H.: Royal Julian (1927)
WHITE OAK STABLE (A. W. Abbott): Blue Man (1952, third)
WHITNEY, C. V.: Today (1935), Jeep (1945), Phalanx (1947, second),
   Mr. Trouble and Dooly (1950, third and 11th), Counterpoint and
   Mameluke (1951), Cold Command (1952), Fisherman (1954), Career
   Boy and Head Man (1956), Flamingo (1958), Silver Spoon (1959),
   Tompion (1960), Gleaming Sword (1968)
WHITNEY, H. P.: Regret (1915, won), Thunderer and Dominant (1916),
   Rickety (1917), Vindex (1919), Upset, Damask, Wildair (1920, second,
   fourth, eighth), Prudery and Tryster (1921, third and fourth), En-
   chantment and Picketer (1923), Transmute and Klondyke (1924),
   Backbone and The Bat (1925), Bendin (1926), Whiskery and Bostonian
   (1927, won and fifth)
WHITNEY, JOHN HAY: Heather Broom (1939, third)
WHITNEY, MRS. M. E.: Stepenfetchit and Over Time (1932, third and
   fifth), Singing Wood (1934), Bullet Proof (1947)
WHITTAKER, EDWIN: Angle Light (1973)
WICKLIFFE STABLE: Acabado (1917)
WIDENER, J. E.: Osmand and Kiev (1927, second and 12th), Peace
   Chance (1934), Brevity (1936, second), Roman (1940)
WIELAND, F.: Pravus (1923)
WILD ROSE FARM: Charmarten (1928)
WILLIAMS, J. T.: Vera Cruz (1877), Bob Miles (1884), Joe Cotton (1885,
   won)
WILLIAMS, S.: Palisade (1890)
WILLIAMS, W. S. & CO.: Ram's Horn (1905, second)
WILLIAMS & OWINGS: Creedmore (1876, second)
WILLORENE FARM: Trumpet King (1950)
WILSHIRE STABLE: Naishapur (1929, second)
WILSON, G. D.: Ada Glen (1879)
WILSON, R. W. and R. T., JR.: Helio Rise (1971)
WILSON, SAM E., JR.: Royal Mustang and Golden Birch (1951, second
   and 19th), Gushing Oil (1952), King Phalanx (1954)
WILSON, MRS. S. E., JR.: Red Hot Pistol (1958)
WILSON, ESTATE OF STEVEN B.: Top Knight (1969)
WILSON & YOUNG: Bootmaker (1889)
WINDFIELDS FARM (E. P. Taylor): Victoria Park (1960, third), Northern
   Dancer (1964, won)
W-L RANCH (W. L. Sickle): Stepfather (1947), Honeys Alibi (1955)
WOOD, D. B.: Don B. (1968)
WOODFORD, S.: Sonada (1912)
WOODFORD, J. HAL: Pink Star (1907, won)
WOODFORD & BUCKNER: Kentucky Farmer (1900), Bad News (1903),
   Mud Sill (1911)
WOODING, J. M.: Burgundy (1878)
WOODING AND PURYEAR: Exploit (1884)
WOODLEY LANE FARM (J. Straus, L. Ward, S. B. Wilson): Red Hannigan
   (1954)
WOODVALE FARM: Our Boots (1941), Halt (1949), Goyamo (1954)
WOOLFORD FARM (Herbert J. Woolf: Lawrin (1938, won), Technician
   (1939)
WORTHINGTON, C. T.: Viva America (1918, third)
WRIGHT, A. R.: Jacobe (1945)

—X—

XALAPA FARM STABLE (E. Simms): Leonardo II and Bon Homme (1921),
   Sweeping Away (1925)

—Y—

YANKE, W. G.: Round the World (1911), Old Ben (1914)
YOUNG, M.: Bancroft (1880, third), Getaway (1881), Lost Cause (1882),
   Ten Booker (1885, third), Once Again (1889, third)
YOUNG, W. J.: Bill Herron (1908)

—Z—

ZIEGLER, WILLIAM, JR.: Needle Gun (1925), Espino (1926), Gone Away
   (1930), El Chico (1939)

CONDENSED HISTORY — KENTUCKY DERBY

No.	Year	WINNER	SIRE	BREEDER	OWNER	TRAINER	FAVORITE	Odds on Winner
1	1875	Aristides, ch. c.	*Leamington	H. P. McGrath	H. P. McGrath	A. Anderson	Winner (Entry)	2-1
2	1876	Vagrant, br. g.	Virgil	M. H. Sanford	William Astor	James Williams	Winner	9-5
3	1877	Baden-Baden, ch. c.	*Australian	A. J. Alexander	Daniel Swigert	Ed Brown	Leonard (7-5)	8-1
4	1878	Day Star, ch. c.	Star Davis	J. M. Clay	T. J. Nichols	Lee Paul	Himyar (1-4)	3-1
5	1879	Lord Murphy, b. c.	Pat Malloy	J. T. Carter	Geo. W. Darden & Co.	George Rice	Winner	11-10
6	1880	Fonso, ch. c.	King Alfonso	A. J. Alexander	J. S. Shawhan	Tice Hutsell	Kimball (3-5)	7-1
7	1881	Hindoo, b. c.	Virgil	Daniel Swigert	Dwyer Bros.	Jas. Rowe, Sr.	Winner	1-3
8	1882	Apollo, ch. g.	Lever	Daniel Swigert	Morris & Patton	Green B. Morris	Runnymede (4-5)	10-1
9	1883	Leonatus, b. c.	Longfellow	J. Henry Miller	Chinn & Morgan	R. Colston	Winner	9-5
10	1884	Buchanan, ch. c.	*Buckden	Cottrill & Guest	W. Cottrill	Wm. Bird	Audrain (2-1)	3-1
11	1885	Joe Cotton, ch. c.	King Alfonso	A. J. Alexander	J. T. Williams	Alex Perry	Winner	1-1
12	1886	Ben Ali, br. c.	Virgil	Daniel Swigert	J. B. Haggin	Jim Murphy	Winner	1.72-1
13	1887	Montrose, b. c.	Duke of Montrose	Milton Young	Labold Bros.	John McGinty	Banburg (7-5)	10-1
14	1888	Macbeth II, b. g.	Macduff	Rufus Lisle	Chicago Stable	John Campbell	Melbourne Stable Ent. (1-1)	8-1
15	1889	Spokane, ch. c.	Hyder Ali	Noah Armstrong	Noah Armstrong	John Rodegap	Proctor Knott (1-2)	10-1
16	1890	Riley b. c.	Longfellow	C. H. Durkee	Edward Corrigan	Edward Corrigan	Robespierre (1-1)	4-1
17	1891	Kingman, b. c.	*Glengarry	A. C. Franklin	Jacobin Stable	Dud Allen	Winner	1-2
18	1892	Azra, b. c.	Reform	George J. Long	Bashford Manor	John H. Morris	Winner	3-2
19	1893	Lookout, ch. c.	Troubadour	Scoggan Bros.	Cushing & Orth	Will McDaniel	Winner (Entry)	7-10
20	1894	Chant, b. c.	Falsetto	A. J. Alexander	Leigh & Rose	Eugene Leigh	Winner	1-2
21	1895	Halma, blk. c.	Hanover	Easton & Larrabie	Byron McClelland	Byron McClelland	Winner	1-3
22	1896	Ben Brush, b. c.	Bramble	Clay & Woodford	M. F. Dwyer	Hardy Campbell	Winner	1-2
23	1897	Typhoon II, ch. c.	*Top Gallant	John E. Ewing	J. C. Cahn	J. C. Cahn	Ornament (1-1)	3-1
24	1898	Plaudit, br. c.	Himyar	Dr. J. D. Neet	J. E. Madden	J. E. Madden	Lieber Karl (1-3)	3-1
25	1899	Manuel, br. c.	Bob Miles	George J. Long	A. H. & D. H. Morris	Robert J. Walden	Winner	11-20
26	1900	Lieut. Gibson, b. c.	G. W. Johnson	Baker & Gentry	Charles H. Smith	Chas. H. Hughes	Winner	7-10
27	1901	His Eminence, b. c.	Falsetto	A. J. Alexander	F. B. VanMeter	F. B. VanMeter	Alard Scheck (7-10)	3-1
28	1902	Alan-a-Dale, ch. c.	Halma	T. C. McDowell	T. C. McDowell	T. C. McDowell	Abe Frank (3-5)	3-2
29	1903	Judge Himes, b. c.	*Esher	J. N. Camden	C. R. Ellison	J. P. Mayberry	Early (3-5)	10-1
30	1904	Elwood, b. c.	Free Knight	Mrs. J. B. Prather	Mrs. C. E. Durnell	C. E. Durnell	Proceeds (1-1)	15-1
31	1905	Agile, b. c.	Sir Dixon	E. F. Clay	S. S. Brown	Robert Tucker	Winner	1-3
32	1906	Sir Huon, b. c.	Falsetto	George J. Long	George J. Long	Peter Coyne	Winner	11-10
33	1907	Pink Star, b. c.	Pink Coat	J. Hal Woodford	J. Hal Woodford	W. H. Fizer	Red Gauntlet (3-2)	15-1
34	1908	Stone Street, b. c.	Longstreet	J. B. Haggin	C. E. Hamilton	J. Hall	Sir Cleges (9-5)	23.72-1
35	1909	Wintergreen, b. c.	Dick Welles	J. B. Respess	J. B. Respess	C. Mack	Winner	1.96-1
36	1910	Donau, b. c.	*Woolsthorpe	Milton Young	William Gerst	George Ham	Winner	1.65-1
37	1911	Meridian, b. c.	Broomstick	C. L. Harrison	R. F. Carman	A. Ewing	Governor Gray (1-1)	2.90-1
38	1912	Worth, br. c.	*Knight of Thistle	R. H. McC. Potter	H. C. Hallenbeck	Frank M. Taylor	Winner	4-5
39	1913	Donerail, b. c.	*McGee	T. P. Hayes	T. P. Hayes	T. P. Hayes	Ten Point (1.20-1)	91.45-1
40	1914	Old Rosebud, b. g.	Uncle	J. E. Madden	H. C. Applegate	F. D. Weir	Winner	85¢ to 1
41	1915	Regret, ch. f.	Broomstick	H. P. Whitney	H. P. Whitney	Jas. Rowe, Sr.	Winner	2.65-1
42	1916	George Smith, blk. c.	*Out of Reach	Chinn & Forsythe	John Sanford	Hollie Hughes	Whitney Entry (1.05-1)	4.15-1
43	1917	*Omar Khayyam, ch. c.	Marco	Sir John Robinson	Billings & Johnson	C. T. Patterson	Ticket (1.45-1)	12.80-1
44	1918	Exterminator, ch. g.	*McGee	F. D. Knight	W. S. Kilmer	Henry McDaniel	*War Cloud (1.45-1)	29.60-1
45	1919	Sir Barton, ch. c.	*Star Shoot	Madden & Gooch	J. K. L. Ross	H. G. Bedwell	McClelland Entry (2.10-1)	2.60-1
46	1920	Paul Jones, br. g.	*Sea King	J. E. Madden	Ral Parr	Wm. Garth	Whitney Entry (1.65-1)	16.20-1
47	1921	Behave Yourself, b. c.	Marathon	E. R. Bradley	E. R. Bradley	H. J. Thompson	Whitney Entry (1.10-1)	8.65-1
48	1922	Morvich, br. c.	Runnymede	A. B. Spreckles	B. Block	Fred Burlew	Winner	1.20-1
49	1923	Zev, br. c.	The Finn	J. E. Madden	Rancocas Stable	D. J. Leary	Whitney-G'tree Ent. (2.30-1)	19.20-1
50	1924	Black Gold, blk. c.	Black Toney	Mrs. R. M. Hoots	Mrs. R. M. Hoots	Hanly Webb	Winner	1.70-1
51	1925	Flying Ebony, blk. c.	The Finn	J. E. Madden	G. A. Cochran	W. B. Duke	Quatrain (1.95-1) (Field)	3.15-1
52	1926	Bubbling Over, ch. c.	*North Star III	Idle Hour Stock Farm	Idle Hour Stock Farm	H. J. Thompson	Winner (Entry)	1.90-1
53	1927	Whiskery, br. c.	Whisk Broom II	H. P. Whitney	H. P. Whitney	Fred Hopkins	Winner (Entry)	2.40-1
54	1928	Reigh Count, ch. c.	*Sunreigh	Willis Sharpe Kilmer	Mrs. J. D. Hertz	B. S. Michell	Winner (Entry)	2.05-1
55	1929	Clyde Van Dusen, ch. g.	Man o'War	H. P. Gardner	H. P. Gardner	C. Van Dusen	E. R. Bradley Entry (1.71-1)	3-1
56	1930	Gallant Fox, b. c.	*Sir Gallahad III	Belair Stud	Belair Stud	James Fitzsimmons	Winner	1.19-1
57	1931	Twenty Grand, b. c.	*St. Germans	Greentree Stable	Greentree Stable	Jas. Rowe, Jr.	Winner	88¢ to 1
58	1932	Burgoo King, ch. c.	Bubbling Over	E. R. Bradley and	E. R. Bradley	H. J. Thompson	Tick On (1.84-1)	5.62-1
59	1933	Brokers Tip, br. c.	Black Toney	Idle Hour Stock Farm	E. R. Bradley	H. J. Thompson	W. R. Coe Entry (1.43-1)	8.93-1
60	1934	Cavalcade, br. c.	*Lancegaye	F. W. Armstrong	Mrs. Dodge Sloane	R. A. Smith	Winner (Entry)	1.50-1
61	1935	Omaha, ch. c.	Gallant Fox	Belair Stud	Belair Stud	James Fitzsimmons	Nellie Flag (3.80-1)	4-1
62	1936	Bold Venture, ch. c.	*St. Germans	M. L. Schwartz	M. L. Schwartz	Max Hirsch	Brevity (4-5)	20.50-1
63	1937	War Admiral, br. c.	Man o'War	Samuel D. Riddle	Glen Riddle Farm	George Conway	Winner	1.60-1
64	1938	Lawrin, br. c.	Insco	Herbert Woolf	Woolford Farm	B. A. Jones	Fighting Fox (1.40-1)	8.60-1
65	1939	Johnstown, b. c.	Jamestown	A. B. Hancock	Belair Stud	James Fitzsimmons	Winner	60¢ to 1
66	1940	Gallahadion, b. c.	*Sir Gallahad III	R. A. Fairbairn	Milky Way Farm	Roy Waldron	Bimelech (40¢-1)	35.20-1
67	1941	Whirlaway, ch. c.	*Blenheim II	Calumet Farm	Warren Wright	Ben A. Jones	Winner	2.90-1
68	1942	Shut Out, ch. c.	Equipoise	Greentree Stable	Greentree Farm	John M. Gaver	Winner (Entry)	1.90-1
69	1943	Count Fleet, br. c.	Reigh Count	Mrs. John D. Hertz	Mrs. John D. Hertz	G. D. Cameron	Winner	40¢-1
70	1944	Pensive, ch. c.	Hyperion	Calumet Farm	Calumet Farm	Ben A. Jones	Stir Up	7.10-1
71	1945	Hoop Jr., b. c.	*Sir Gallahad III	R. A. Fairbairn	F. W. Hooper	I. H. Parke	Pot o'Luck (3.30-1)	3.70-1
72	1946	Assault, ch. c.	Bold Venture	King Ranch	King Ranch	Max Hirsch	Maine Chance Ent. (1.10-1)	8.20-1
73	1947	Jet Pilot, ch. c.	*Blenheim II	Hancock Van Clief	Maine Chance Farm	Tom Smith	Phalanx (2-1)	5.40-1
74	1948	Citation, b. c.	Bull Lea	Calumet Farm	Calumet Farm	B. A. Jones	Winner (Entry)	40¢-1
75	1949	Ponder, dk. b. c.	Pensive	Calumet Farm	Calumet Farm	B. A. Jones	Olympia (80¢-1)	16.00-1
76	1950	Middleground, ch. c.	Bold Venture	King Ranch	King Ranch	Max Hirsch	Your Host (1.60-1)	7.90-1
77	1951	Count Turf, b. c.	Count Fleet	Dr. & Mrs. F. P. Miller	J. J. Amiel	S. Rutchick	Battle Morn (2.80-1)	f-14.60
78	1952	Hill Gail, dk. b. c.	Bull Lea	Calumet Farm	Calumet Farm	B. A. Jones	Winner	1.10-1
79	1953	Dark Star, br. c.	*Royal Gem II	W. L. Jones, Jr.	Cain Hoy Stable	E. Haywood	Native Dancer (70¢-1)	24.90-1
80	1954	Determine, gr. c.	*Alibhai	Dr. E. Asbury	A. J. Crevolin	W. Molter	Correlation (3.00-1)	4.30-1
81	1955	Swaps, ch. c.	*Khaled	R. C. Ellsworth	R. C. Ellsworth	M. A. Tenney	Nashua (1.30-1)	2.80-1
82	1956	Needles, b. c.	Ponder	W. E. Leach	D & H Stable	H. Fontaine	Winner	1.60-1
83	1957	Iron Liege, b. c.	Bull Lea	Calumet Farm	Calumet Farm	H. A. Jones	Bold Ruler (1.20-1)	8.40-1
84	1958	Tim Tam, dk. bc.	Tom Fool	Calumet Farm	Calumet Farm	H. A. Jones	Maine Chance Ent. (2.00-1)	2.10-1
85	1959	*Tomy Lee, bc.	*Tudor Minstrel	D. H. Willis	Mr. & Mrs. Fred Turner, Jr.	Frank Childs	First Landing (3.60-1)	3.70-1
86	1960	Venetian Way, ch. c.	Royal Coinage	J. W. Greathouse	Sunny Blue Farm	V. J. Sovinski	Tompion (1.10-1)	6.30-1
87	1961	Carry Back, br. c.	Saggy	J. A. Price	Mrs. Katherine Price	J. A. Price	Winner	2.50-1
88	1962	Decidedly, gr. c.	Determine	G. A. Pope, Jr.	El Peco Ranch	H. A. Luro	Ridan (1.10-1)	8.70-1
89	1963	Chateaugay, ch. c.	Swaps	John W. Galbreath	Darby Dan Farm	J. P. Conway	Candy Spots (1.50-1)	9.40-1
90	1964	Northern Dancer, b. c.	Nearctic	E. P. Taylor	Windfields Farm	H. A. Luro	Hill Rise (1.40-1)	3.40-1
91	1965	Lucky Debonair, b. c.	Vertex	Danada Farm	Mrs. Ada L. Rice	Frank Catrone	Bold Lad (2.00-1)	4.30-1
92	1966	Kauai King, dk. b. or br. c.	Native Dancer	Pine Brook Farm	Ford Stable	Henry Forrest	Winner	2.40-1
93	1967	Proud Clarion, b. c.	Hail to Reason	John W. Galbreath	Darby Dan Farm	Loyd Gentry	Damascus (1.70-1)	30.10-1
94	1968	Forward Pass, b. c.	On-and-On	Calumet Farm	Calumet Farm	Henry Forrest	Winner (2.20-1)	3.60-1
95	1969	Majestic Prince, ch. c.	Raise a Native	Leslie Combs II	Frank McMahon	John Longden	Winner	1.40-1
96	1970	Dust Commander, ch. c.	Bold Commander	Pullen Bros.	Robert E. Lehmann	Don Combs	My Dad George (2.80-1)	15.30-1
97	1971	Canonero II	Pretendre	Edward B. Benjamin	Edgar Caibett	Juan Arias	Unconscious (2.80-1)	8.70-1
98	1972	Riva Ridge, b. c.	First Landing	Meadow Stud, Inc.	Meadow Stable	Lucien Laurin	Winner	1.50-1
99	1973	Secretariat, ch. c.	Bold Ruler	Meadow Stud, Inc.	Meadow Stable	Lucien Laurin	Winner	1.50-1

*Imported horse.

Key to owners of stable and farm names above: Chicago Stable (Hankins & Johnson), Bashford Manor (George J. Long), Idle Hour Stock Farm (E. R. Bradley), Rancocas Stable (H. F. Sinclair), Belair Stud (William Woodward), Greentree Stable (Mrs. Payne Whitney), Glen Riddle Farm (Samuel D. Riddle), Woolford Farm (Herbert M. Woolf), Milky Way Farms (Mrs. Ethel V. Mars), Calumet Farm (Warren Wright prior to 1951, Mrs. Warren Wright, 1952, Mrs. Gene Markey, 1953-1973), King Ranch (Robert J. Kleberg), Maine Chance Farm (Mrs. Elizabeth Graham), Cain Hoy Stable (H. F. Guggenheim), D & H Stable (Jack Dudley and Bonnie Heath), Sunny Blue Farm (Isaac Blumberg), El Peco Ranch (George A. Pope, Pr.), Darby Dan Farm (John W. Galbreath), Windfields Farm (E. P. Taylor), Ford Stable (Michael Ford), Pastorale Stable (Mrs. Geo. W. Headley), Meadow Stable (Mrs. John Tweedy).

CONDENSED HISTORY — KENTUCKY DERBY

Date	Winner	Won by	Jockey	Wt.	Second	Third	Nominations	Starters	Winner Net to	Time	Track
May 17, 1875	Aristides	1 lgth.	O. Lewis	100	Volcano	Verdigris	42	15	$ 2,850	2:37¾	Fast
May 15, 1876	Vagrant	2 lgths.	R. Swim	97	Creedmoor	Harry Hill	34	11	2,950	2:38¼	Fast
May 22, 1877	Baden-Baden	2 lgths.	W. Walker	100	Leonard	King William	41	11	3,300	2:38	Fast
May 21, 1878	Day Star	2 lgths.	J. Carter	100	Himyar	Leveler	56	9	4,050	2:37¼	Good
May 20, 1879	Lord Murphy	1 lgth.	C. Shauer	100	Falsetto	Strathmore	46	9	3,550	2:37	Fast
May 18, 1880	Fonso	1 lgth.	G. Lewis	105	Kimball	Bancroft	47	5	3,800	2:37½	Fast
May 17, 1881	Hindoo	4 lgths.	J. McLaughlin	105	Lelex	Alfambra	62	6	4,410	2:40	Fast
May 16, 1882	Apollo	½ lgth.	B. Hurd	102	Runnymede	Bengal	64	14	4,560	2:40¼	Good
May 23, 1883	Leonatus	3 lgths.	W. Donohue	105	Drake Carter	Lord Raglan	50	7	3,760	2:43	Heavy
May 16, 1884	Buchanan	2 lgths.	I. Murphy	110	Loftin	Audrain	51	9	3,990	2:40¼	Good
May 14, 1885	Joe Cotton	Neck	E. Henderson	110	Bersan	Ten Booker	69	10	4,630	2:37¼	Good
May 14, 1886	Ben Ali	½ lgth.	P. Duffy	118	Blue Wing	Free Knight	107	10	4,890	2:36½	Fast
May 11, 1887	Montrose	2 lgths.	I. Lewis	118	Jim Gore	Jacobin	119	7	4,200	2:39¼	Fast
May 14, 1888	Macbeth II	1 lgth.	G. Covington	115	Gallifet	White	95	7	4,740	2:38¼	Fast
May 9, 1889	Spokane	Nose	T. Kiley	118	Proctor Knott	Once Again	94	8	4,880	2:34½	Fast
May 14, 1890	Riley	2 lgths.	I. Murphy	118	Bill Letcher	Robespierre	115	6	5,460	2:45	Heavy
May 13, 1891	Kingman	1 lgth.	I. Murphy	122	Balgowan	High Tariff	83	4	4,550	2:52¼	Good
May 11, 1892	Azra	Nose	A. Clayton	122	Huron	Phil Dwyer	68	3	4,230	2:41½	Heavy
May 10, 1893	Lookout	5 lgths.	E. Kunze	122	Plutus	Boundless	60	6	3,840	2:39¼	Fast
May 15, 1894	Chant	2 lgths.	F. Goodale	122	Pearl Song	Sigurd	55	5	4,020	2:41	Fast
May 6, 1895	Halma	3 lgths.	J. Perkins	122	Basso	Laureate	57	4	2,970	2:37½	Fast
May 6, 1896	Ben Brush	Nose	W. Simms	117	Ben Eder	Semper Ego	171	8	4,850	2:07¾	Slow
May 12, 1897	Typhoon II	Head	F. Garner	117	Ornament	Dr. Catlett	159	6	4,850	2:12½	Heavy
May 4, 1898	Plaudit	Neck	W. Simms	117	Lieber Karl	Isabey	179	4	4,850	2:09	Slow
May 4, 1899	Manuel	2 lgths.	F. Taral	117	Corsini	Mazo	151	5	4,850	2:12	Fast
May 3, 1900	Lieut. Gibson	4 lgths.	J. Boland	117	Florizar	Thrive	131	7	4,850	2:06¼	Fast
Apr. 29, 1901	His Eminence	2 lgths.	J. Winkfield	117	Sannazarro	Driscoll	113	5	4,850	2:07¾	Fast
May 3, 1902	Alan-a-Dale	Nose	J. Winkfield	117	Inventor	The Rival	112	4	4,850	2:08¾	Fast
May 2, 1903	Judge Himes	¾ lgth.	H. Booker	117	Early	Bourbon	140	6	4,850	2:09	Fast
May 2, 1904	Elwood	½ lgth.	F. Pryor	117	Ed. Tierney	Brancas	140	5	4,850	2:08½	Fast
May 10, 1905	Agile	3 lgths.	J. Martin	122	Ram's Horn	Layson	145	3	4,850	2:10¾	Heavy
May 2, 1906	Sir Huon	2 lgths.	R. Troxler	117	Lady Navarre	James Reddick	110	6	4,850	2:08⅘	Fast
May 6, 1907	Pink Star	2 lgths.	A. Minder	117	Zal	Ovelando	128	6	4,850	2:12⅗	Heavy
May 5, 1908	Stone Street	1 lgth.	A. Pickens	117	Sir Cleges	Dunvegan	114	8	4,850	2:15⅕	Heavy
May 3, 1909	Wintergreen	4 lgths.	V. Powers	117	Miami	Dr. Barkley	117	10	4,850	2:08⅕	Slow
May 10, 1910	Donau	½ lgth.	F. Herbert	117	Joe Morris	Fighting Bob	117	7	4,840	2:06⅖	Fast
May 13, 1911	Meridian	¾ lgth.	G. Archibald	117	Governor Gray	Colston	117	7	4,850	2:05	Fast
May 11, 1912	Worth	Neck	C. H. Schilling	117	Duval	Flamma	131	8	4,850	2:09⅖	Muddy
May 10, 1913	Donerail	½ lgth.	R. Goose	117	Ten Point	Gowell	32	8	5,475	2:04⅘	Fast
May 9, 1914	Old Rosebud	8 lgths.	J. McCabe	114	Hodge	Bronzewing	47	7	9,125	2:03⅖	Fast
May 8, 1915	Regret	2 lgths.	J. Notter	112	Pebbles	Sharpshooter	68	16	11,450	2:05⅖	Fast
May 13, 1916	George Smith	Neck	J. Loftus	117	Star Hawk	Franklin	56	9	9,750	2:04	Fast
May 12, 1917	*Omar Khayyam	2 lgths.	C. Borel	117	Ticket	Midway	76	15	16,600	2:04⅗	Fast
May 11, 1918	Exterminator	1 lgth.	W. Knapp	114	Escoba	Viva America	70	8	14,700	2:10⅘	Muddy
May 10, 1919	Sir Barton	5 lgths.	J. Loftus	112½	Billy Kelly	Under Fire	75	12	20,825	2:09⅘	Heavy
May 8, 1920	Paul Jones	Head	T. Rice	126	Upset	On Watch	107	17	30,375	2:09	Slow
May 7, 1921	Behave Yourself	Head	C. Thompson	126	Black Servant	Prudery	109	12	38,450	2:04⅕	Fast
May 13, 1922	Morvich	1½ lgths.	A. Johnson	126	Bet Mosie	John Finn	92	10	48,775	2:04⅗	Fast
May 19, 1923	Zev	1½ lgths.	E. Sande	126	Martingale	Vigil	145	21	53,600	2:05⅖	Fast
May 17, 1924	Black Gold	½ lgth.	J. D. Mooney	126	Chilhowee	Beau Butler	152	19	52,775	2:05⅕	Fast
May 16, 1925	Flying Ebony	1½ lgths.	E. Sande	126	Captain Hal	Son of John	139	20	52,950	2:07⅗	Sloppy
May 15, 1926	Bubbling Over	5 lgths.	A. Johnson	126	Bagenbaggage	Rock Man	164	13	50,075	2:03⅘	Fast
May 14, 1927	Whiskery	Head	L. McAtee	126	Osmond	Jock	162	15	51,000	2:06	Slow
May 19, 1928	Reigh Count	3 lgths.	C. Lang	126	Misstep	Toro	196	22	55,375	2:10⅖	Heavy
May 18, 1929	Clyde Van Dusen	2 lgths.	L. McAtee	126	Naishapur	Panchio	159	21	53,950	2:10⅘	Muddy
May 17, 1930	Gallant Fox	2 lgths.	E. Sande	126	Gallant Knight	Ned O.	150	15	50,725	2:07⅗	Good
May 16, 1931	Twenty Grand	4 lgths.	C. Kurtsinger	126	Sweep All	Mate	130	12	48,725	2:01⅘	Fast
May 7, 1932	Burgoo King	5 lgths.	E. James	126	Economic	Stepenfetchit	115	20	52,350	2:05⅕	Fast
May 6, 1933	Brokers Tip	Nose	D. Meade	126	Head Play	Charley O.	118	13	48,925	2:06⅘	Good
May 5, 1934	Cavalcade	2½ lgths.	M. Garner	126	Discovery	Agrarian	124	13	28,175	2:04	Fast
May 4, 1935	Omaha	1½ lgths.	W. Saunders	126	Roman Soldier	Whiskolo	110	18	39,525	2:05	Good
May 2, 1936	Bold Venture	Head	I. Hanford	126	Brevity	Indian Broom	102	14	37,725	2:03⅗	Fast
May 8, 1937	War Admiral	1¾ lgths.	C. Kurtsinger	126	Pompoon	Reaping Reward	103	20	52,050	2:03⅕	Fast
May 7, 1938	Lawrin	1 lgth.	E. Arcaro	126	Dauber	Can't Wait	103	10	47,050	2:04⅘	Fast
May 6, 1939	Johnstown	8 lgths.	J. Stout	126	Challedon	Heather Broom	115	8	46,350	2:03⅖	Fast
May 4, 1940	Gallahadion	1½ lgths.	C. Bierman	126	Bimelech	Dit	127	8	60,150	2:05	Fast
May 3, 1941	Whirlaway	8 lgths.	E. Arcaro	126	Staretor	Market Wise	112	11	61,275	2:01⅖	Fast
May 2, 1942	Shut Out	2½ lgths.	W. D. Wright	126	Alsab	Valdina Orphan	150	15	64,225	2:04⅖	Fast
May 1, 1943	Count Fleet	3 lgths.	J. Longden	126	Blue Swords	Slide Rule	110	10	60,725	2:04	Fast
May 6, 1944	Pensive	4½ lgths.	C. McCreary	126	Broadcloth	Stir Up	148	16	64,675	2:04⅕	Fast
June 9, 1945	Hoop Jr.	6 lgths.	E. Arcaro	126	Pot o'Luck	Darby Dieppe	155	16	64,850	2:07	Muddy
May 4, 1946	Assault	8 lgths.	W. Mehrtens	126	Spy Song	Hampden	149	17	96,400	2:06⅗	Slow
May 3, 1947	Jet Pilot	Head	E. Guerin	126	Phalanx	Faultless	135	13	92,160	2:06⅘	Slow
May 1, 1948	Citation	3½ lgths.	E. Arcaro	126	Coaltown	My Request	109	6	83,400	2:05⅖	Sloppy
May 7, 1949	Ponder	3 lgths.	S. Brooks	126	Capot	Palestinian	113	14	91,600	2:04⅕	Fast
May 6, 1950	Middleground	1¼ lgths.	W. Boland	126	Hill Prince	Mr. Trouble	134	14	92,650	2:01⅗	Fast
May 5, 1951	Count Turf	4 lgths.	C. McCreary	126	Royal Mustang	Ruhe	122	20	98,050	2:02⅗	Fast
May 3, 1952	Hill Gail	2 lgths.	E. Arcaro	126	Sub Fleet	Blue Man	167	16	96,300	2:01⅗	Fast
May 2, 1953	Dark Star	Head	H. Moreno	126	Native Dancer	Invigorator	137	11	90,050	2:02	Fast
May 1, 1954	Determine	1½ lgths.	R. York	126	Hasty Road	Hasseyampa	137	17	102,050	2:03	Fast
May 7, 1955	Swaps	1½ lgths.	W. Shoemaker	126	Nashua	Summer Tan	125	10	108,400	2:01⅘	Fast
May 5, 1956	Needles	¾ lgth.	D. Erb	126	Fabius	Come On Red	169	17	123,450	2:03⅖	Fast
May 4, 1957	Iron Liege	Nose	B. Hartack	126	Gallant Man	Round Table	133	9	109,550	2:02⅕	Fast
May 3, 1958	Tim Tam	½ lgth.	I. Valenzuela	126	Lincoln Road	Noureddin	140	14	116,400	2:05	Muddy
May 2, 1959	*Tomy Lee	Nose	W. Shoemaker	126	Sword Dancer	First Landing	130	17	119,650	2:02⅕	Fast
May 7, 1960	Venetian Way	3½ lgths.	B. Hartack	126	Bally Ache	Victoria Park	142	13	114,850	2:02⅖	Good
May 6, 1961	Carry Back	¾ lgth.	J. Sellers	126	Crozier	Bass Clef	155	15	120,500	2:04	Good
May 5, 1962	Decidedly	2¼ lgths.	B. Hartack	126	Roman Line	Ridan	139	15	119,650	2:00⅖	Fast
May 4, 1963	Chateaugay	1¼ lgths.	B. Baeza	126	Never Bend	Candy Spots	129	9	108,900	2:01⅘	Fast
May 2, 1964	Northern Dancer	Neck	B. Hartack	126	Hill Rise	The Scoundrel	138	12	114,300	2:00	Fast
May 1, 1965	Lucky Debonair	Neck	W. Shoemaker	126	Dapper Dan	Tom Rolfe	130	11	112,000	2:01⅕	Fast
May 7, 1966	Kauai King	½ lgth.	D. Brumfield	126	Advocator	Blue Skyer	150	15	120,500	2:02	Fast
May 6, 1967	Proud Clarion	1 lgth.	B. Ussery	126	Barbs Delight	Damascus	162	14	119,700	2:00⅗	Fast
May 4, 1968	Forward Pass	—	I. Valenzuela	126	—	—	191	14	122,600	—	Fast
May 3, 1969	Majestic Prince	Neck	B. Hartack	126	Arts and Letters	Dike	187	8	113,200	2:01⅘	Fast
May 2, 1970	Dust Commander	5 lgths.	M. Manganello	126	My Dad George	High Echelon	193	17	127,800	2:03⅖	Good
May 1, 1971	Canonero II	3¾ lgths.	G. Avila	126	Jim French	Bold Reason	220	20	145,500	2:03⅕	Fast
May 6, 1972	Riva Ridge	3¼ lgths.	R. Turcotte	126	No Le Hace	Hold Your Peace	258	16	140,300	2:01⅘	Fast
May 5, 1973	Secretariat	2½ lgths.	R. Turcotte	126	Sham	Our Native	218	13	155,050	1:59⅖	Fast

Acknowledgements

Churchill Downs is indebted to many individuals, firms and organizations who contributed in so many ways to the completion of this official Kentucky Derby book.

Several books have been presented through the years by the track, the last on the 75th anniversary of the Derby in 1949. Each has been different in format.

Two people, Gabe Kaelin and Robert Leaman of Courier-Journal Lithographing Co., merit more than passing mention for their considerable interest and guidance. Mr. Kaelin's encouragement prompted the pursuance of the project and Mr. Leaman's aid in its completion was invaluable.

William Butt was responsible for assembling a multitude of pictures which, it is thought, give a good insight into the growth of Louisville, Jefferson County and the Kentucky Derby in the past 100 years.

Churchill Downs is equally indebted to the following:

Richard Duncan and Ned Tanselle of Caufield & Shook, Inc.; James C. Anderson and the staff at the University of Louisville photo archives; Al Allen of the Louisville Courier-Journal and Times; Martin Schmidt of the Louisville Free Public Library; James Clary of the Filson Club; Mrs. Roberta Ashe of the Churchill Downs staff, and Waters Design, Inc. for the art work.

Finally, considerable thanks should be given to the sponsors who participated. These are proudly enumerated on the next page.

SPONSORS

PHOTO CREDITS

All color photographs, center section, by Caufield & Shook except tulip garden, which is by Kentucky Department of Public Information.
All photographs of owners, trainers, jockeys and Derby winners, Churchill Downs Museum.
Aerial photo of track, page 223, by Billy Davis, Louisville Courier-Journal & Times.